Deaf to the Marrow

Deaf to the Marrow

Deaf Social Organizing and Active Citizenship in Việt Nam

Audrey C. Cooper

Gallaudet University Press
Washington, DC

Gallaudet University Press
Washington, DC 20002
http://gupress.gallaudet.edu

© 2017 by Gallaudet University
All rights reserved.
Published 2017
Printed in the United States of America

Library of Congress Cataloging-in-Publication Data

Names: Cooper, Audrey C., author.
Title: Deaf to the marrow : deaf social organizing and active citizenship in
    Viet Nam/Audrey C. Cooper.
Description: Washington, DC : Gallaudet University Press, [2017] |
    Includes bibliographical references and index.
Identifiers: LCCN 2016057558 |
ISBN 9781563686856 (hardcover : alk. paper) |
ISBN 9781563686863 (e-book)
Subjects: LCSH: Deaf—Vietnam—Political activity. | Social participation—Vietnam.
Classification: LCC HV2380 .C65 2017 | DDC 305.9/08209597—dc23
LC record available at https://lccn.loc.gov/2016057558

∞ This paper meets the requirements of ANSI/NISO Z39.48-1992 (Permanence of Paper).

This book is dedicated to my father, whose passion for understanding and sustaining the planet—water, forests, plants, people, animals, reptiles, and insects—showed me the meaning of love and the importance of advocacy.

Contents

	Foreword	ix
	Acknowledgments	xi
	Abbreviations and Acronyms	xiii
	Research Areas in Việt Nam	xv
	Introduction: Signed Language as Social Participation and National Contribution	xvii
1	Histories and Political Economies of Language and Literacy	1
2	Putting the Study of Signed Language and State Formation in Perspective	36
3	Deaf Education and Deaf Social Organizing: Sites of Social Inclusion and Exclusion	68
4	Being Vietnamese and Điủc Tủy: Negotiating Sociopolitical Visions through Active Linguistic Citizenship	117
5	Postreunification Deaf Marginalization, Deaf-Led Social Change, and Disability-Oriented Development	144
6	HCMSL-Based Citizenship and Market-Socialist Futures: Interactions in the Disability Marketplace	172
7	Conclusion	212
	References	217
	Index	245

Foreword

Nguyễn Trần Thủy Tiên

IN VIỆT NAM, Deaf people strive daily to participate in Vietnamese society and to create those conditions that will support Vietnamese signed languages—in education, employment, and community associations. In the 1980s the Vietnamese government began opening special schools for Deaf students; since that time, parents have enrolled their Deaf children in classes, often paying additional fees for that education, in the hope that their children might learn to speak Vietnamese. Educators and parents have also sought the advice of experts in this endeavor. Meanwhile, Deaf students have labored in classrooms that provide little or no language access. This is still the case today.

There are few government officials that support Vietnamese signed languages. Yet, compared with even five years ago, there has been an noticeable increase in government and public interest in Deaf people. Despite such changes, Deaf people's education, work achievements, and social successes still "make news" in Việt Nam. Our accomplishments are considered unusual and surprising. This is unfair to Deaf people.

Deaf people have already contributed to many activities in Việt Nam: educational programming, language policy and planning, employment training, research projects, and the production of Vietnamese cultural arts, including dance, film, and digital media. In order to contribute more of our knowledge, skills, and creativity, Deaf social leaders ask that hearing people in Việt Nam—and Deaf and hearing supporters around the world—think deeply about the barriers that keep us from taking an equal place in Vietnamese society today. Learn about our experiences and support our leadership—not just in Deaf community activities but in every part of society.

This book contributes to our effort to share our experiences and to increase support for Deaf leadership in Việt Nam. As you read this book you will develop your own understanding of the circumstances of Deaf people's lives in Việt Nam. We hope that you will support sign language–based Deaf education that teaches the full national curriculum up to the 12th grade in a Vietnamese signed language. When Deaf students have access to their natural language early on, and a full education, they can excel academically and become leaders in their chosen professions. Right now we need more Deaf people who have a college or university education. We need Deaf teachers working in primary schools through to the college level. We need Deaf teachers who can teach Vietnamese signed languages and those who can teach

---

Nguyễn Trần Thủy Tiên has a BA in primary level Deaf education from Đồng Nai University in Đồng Nai, Việt Nam, and an MA in sign language education from Gallaudet University in Washington, DC.

VSL(s)-Vietnamese interpretation. We also need administrators who can supervise schools and influence policy.

We look forward to translations of this book into VSLs and Vietnamese. The more that Deaf and hearing people in Việt Nam share our experiences, the more our struggles will be understood as part of a collective national history, one that is already making Vietnamese society stronger.

Acknowledgments

Uống nước nhớ nguồn.
[Drinking water, remember the source.]
—Vietnamese proverb

THE PEOPLE WHO CONTRIBUTED to the research in this book are too numerous to mention individually. Each conversation, each perspective and feeling, taught me so much—as did each instance of direct and incidental instruction in the use of Hồ Chí Minh Sign Language (HCMSL) and Vietnamese Deaf people's descriptions of their social and linguisitic practices and interests. These interactions also taught me about my own assumptions, particularly those regarding the historical forces that shape signed language use in particular places and times, the ways people inhabit and deploy identities such as DEAF and HEARING, and how such identities are often quite distinct from the ways that people socialize and organize their everyday lives. Thus, they also helped me appreciate the diverse ways that language matters and the material importance of language for social relationships and social transformation.

To the Deaf and non-Deaf people in southern Việt Nam, including those who sign and those who do not, I owe all of you—HCMSL teachers, research partners, copresenters, and HCMCSL models—an extraordinary human and intellectual debt. Despite the sociocultural, geographic, and disciplinary boundaries that might separate us, I desire to call each of you "friend." This research would not have been possible without you.

Figure 1. Sculpted mural at Chùa Hộ Quốc, Phú Quốc, Việt Nam (Hộ Quốc Pagoda, Phú Quốc Island, Việt Nam). This section of the mural includes three cities: Hà Nội (National Capital of reunified Việt Nam, 1975 to the present), Huế (Imperial Capital, 1802–1945), and Hồ Chí Minh (capital of French Cochinchina and later the Republic of South Việt Nam, 1955–1975). Underneath the map is the following inscription: *Uống nước nhớ nguồn*. Courtesy of the author.

Các bạn đồng nghiệp—cảm ơn rất nhiều. Tôi mong chúng ta sẽ biết nhau một thời gian dài trong tương lai, và sẽ có nhiều cơ hội để chia sẻ với nhau nữa.

The research that makes up the focus of this book received generous support from American University's College of Arts and Sciences in the form of both a Robyn Rafferty Mathias/Mellon Grant (2007) and a Doctoral Dissertation Fellowship (2008–2009). Later, while on the faculty of the Department of Anthropology at American University, I also received invaluable support in the form of the outstanding Jeanne Hanna, who was my research assistant during the drafting of this manuscript (2014–2016). When I was in a dark mood about ever seeing this work completed, it was Jeanne's enthusiasm for my research topic, coupled with the connections she drew to her own research, which often inspired me to press on. That and her sharp wit, incisive political commentary, and ready laughter.

I am grateful to the American Anthropology Association's Council on Anthropology and Education, which honored me with its Outstanding Dissertation award in 2011. Conferred by none other than Frederick Erickson—whose *Talk and Social Theory: Ecologies of Speaking and Listening in Everyday Life* impressed on me the importance of attending to the microinteractions and the choreography of communication—affirmed for me that I was moving in a fruitful direction. Further research support came in the form of funding from an anonymous donor, whose contributions enabled me to conduct postdoctoral research in 2012 and from 2012 to 2014, following work trips for the Intergenerational Deaf Education Outreach Project—Việt Nam, which was a project of the World Bank implemented by World Concern Development Organization.

I am also extremely grateful to dear friends and colleagues who read multiple iterations of chapter drafts, posed insightful questions, offered trenchant advice, and even provided some much-needed compositional surgery: Zöe Avstreih, Bùi Bích Phượng, Paul G. Dudis, Elijah Adiv Edelman, Erin Moriarty Harrelson, Höching Jiang, Robert E. Johnson, Nikki C. Lane, William L. Leap, Siobhán McGuirk, Nguyễn Hoàng Lâm, Nguyễn Trần Thủy Tiên, Nguyễn Thị Thu, and Khadijat K. Rashid. My gratitude also goes to student-colleagues at American University and Gallaudet University who, through their deep engagement with questions of language-in-context, contributed to my own thinking and also to the book's readability: Tuyết Hoa Adamovich, Toska Broadway, Trisha Clifton, Aaron Graybill, Ikumi Kawamata, Emily Lahaie, Jeana Musacchia, Kate Pashby, Larissa Reed, Hancie Stokes, and Phoebe Tay. Thank you for sharing with me your enthusiasm for multilingual diversity and for your attention to the forms of power and possibility that inhere in language use, representation, and social action.

Abbreviations and Acronyms

APCD	Asia-Pacific Development Center on Disability
ASEAN	Association of Southeast Asian Nations
ASL	American Sign Language
CI	Cochlear Implantation
DC*	The Development Center
DPO	Disabled People's Organizations
EP*	The Education Project
GSO	General Statistics Office [Tổng Cục Thống Kê]
HAD	Hà Nội Association of the Deaf
HCMC	Hả Chí Minh City
HCMSL	Hồ Chí Minh Sign Language [Ngôn Ngữ Ky Hiệu Tp. HCM]
HDC*	HCMC Deaf Club
HIC*	Hearing Impaired Club (associated with the DC*)
HIU*	Hearing Impaired Unit (associated with the DC*)
HNSL	Hà Nội Sign Language [Ngôn Ngữ Ký Hiệu Tp. HN]
HPSL	Hải Phòng Sign Language [Ngôn Ngữ Ký Hiệu Tp. HP]
HTSLI	Hà Nội Team of Sign Language Interpreters
IDEO	Intergenerational Deaf Education Outreach—VN
IE	Inclusive Education [Giáo dục Hoà nhập]
ILO	International Labour Organization
INGO	International Nongovernmental Organization(s)
MDG	United Nations Millennium Development Goals
MOET	Ministry of Education and Training [Bộ Giáo Dục và Đạo Tạo]
MOIC	Ministry of Information and Communication [Bộ Thông Tin và Truyền Thông]
MOLISA	Ministry of Labor, Invalids, and Social Affairs [Bộ Lao Động, Thuếng Binh và Xã Hội]
NCCD	National Coordinating Council on Disability [Điều Phối các Hoạt Động Hỗ Trợ Người Khuyết Tật]
NGO	Nongovernmental Organization(s)
NIES	National Institute of Educational Science [Viện Khoa Học Giáo dục Việt Nam]
PSBI	Pearl S. Buck International
PWD	Persons/People with Disabilities

*denotes pseudonym

SSV	Sign-Supported Vietnamese (speaking Vietnamese while signing in Vietnamese word order)
UNWTO	United Nations World Tourism Organization
USAID	US Agency for International Development
VHLSS	VN Household Living Standards Survey [Mức Sống Hộ Gia Đình của Tỏng Cục Thống Kê]
VSLs	Vietnamese Signed Languages
WCDO	World Concern Development Organization
WFD	World Federation of the Deaf
WHO	World Health Organization
WTO	World Trade Organization

Research Areas in Việt Nam

Introduction
Signed Language as Social Participation and National Contribution

ON A TUESDAY AFTERNOON in late December 2008, the Education Project (EP), located in Đồng Nai, Việt Nam, let classes out early to allow its nearly fifty adult education students watch their classmate's appearance on a provincial television show. Trang, a high school graduate of the EP,[1] had been asked to participate in the show as part of a series of celebrations titled "310 Years of Đồng Nai Province" (1698–2008). At that time, the use of Vietnamese signed languages (VSLs) in government-sponsored special schools for Deaf students was highly contested and rarely seen in any public media. That day, I was observing classroom instruction at the EP as part of my dissertation fieldwork at such sites and in Deaf community organizing. It was therefore with a great sense of excitement that the EP staff, students, and I hurried to take our places on the floor and to arrange ourselves so that everyone could enjoy unobstructed views of the television show.

Hosted by Đồng Nai Television (DN2), "310 Years of Đồng Nai Province" focused on both the history of Đồng Nai province and the contemporary accomplishments of remarkable individuals hailing from or contributing to Đồng Nai's development. Symbolically accentuating the historic contours of the focus of the show, the filming took place outdoors in the courtyard of the Văn Miếu Trấn Biên, or Temple of Literature, on the site of the historic Trấn Biên Temple (see figures 1 and 2).[2] Against this backdrop of revivalist tradition, the show focused on the social achievements of four women: a scholarship recipient entering medical school; a high school chemistry teacher, also known for her accomplishments as a singer; a self-identified person with a disability, well known for earning a graduate degree in the United States but especially for returning to Việt Nam to found a disabled people's organization in Hồ Chí Minh City (HCMC); and Trang, one of the first signing Deaf persons to graduate from high school in Việt Nam.

Trang's imminent appearance on state-run television was intriguing. What forces were now bringing signing Deaf people into the public spotlight? What might this event indicate about official state-institutional orientations toward Deaf people and

---

1. All names are pseudonyms, selected by the research participants themselves, unless otherwise noted. The names of the research sites, which I selected, are also pseudonymous.

2. Trấn Biên Temple was originally constructed in 1715 in honor of Confucius but was destroyed by the French in the mid-1800s. In 2002, the temple was reconstructed and renamed, modeled on the venerated Văn Miếu–Quốc Tử Giám Confucian academy in Hà Nội, which has been preserved since its construction in 1070. Unless otherwise noted, all of the photographs are ones that I took.

signed language?³ And because this program would be broadcast in real time both in Đồng Nai province and nationally, what might Trang, if given the opportunity, say about her experience as a Deaf person in contemporary Việt Nam?

At 24 years of age, Trang appeared the epitome of successful political economic reforms and an outstanding contributor to ongoing market-socialist development and modernization—one of seemingly many potential representatives of Vietnamese Deaf achievement. Such appearances, however, belie the conditions facing Deaf people in the 21st century. At the time of her appearance on television, only about 80 students who had attended the EP since it opened in 2000 had had an opportunity to obtain a secondary-school education and to attend classes taught in a local signed language, Hồ Chí Minh Sign Language (HCMSL).⁴ Although Việt Nam is home to one of the world's first signed language–based schools, the Trường Câm-Điếc Lái Thiêu [Lái Thiêu School for the Mute-Deaf], with the initiation of the political-economic reform period (Đổi Mới; 1986–present), the Vietnamese state began establishing a national system of speech-based special schools founded on instruction in spoken and printed/written Vietnamese. In the mid-1990s, implementation of inclusive education (IE) then promoted the placement of Deaf students into regular education classrooms. Whether attending a school with Deaf peers where signed language was not permitted or where signs might be used in Vietnamese word order (special schools) or attending a school with no Deaf peers and no signed language (IE), both approaches resulted in poor educational outcomes (Reilly & Nguyễn, 2004; Tạc, 2000; cf. Lễ, 2013; NCCD, 2010; Kham, 2014).

At the time Trang appeared on television, Deaf people—specifically, those who either had attended or were then enrolled in school—had little to no access to educational content; those who left school were either unemployed or working as low-wage manual laborers as, prior to 2008, few had formally graduated from high school or college (GSO, 2006; NCCD, 2010).⁵ Therefore, no Deaf person held teaching credentials that would allow them to pursue a career in education, as Trang proposed in her commentary.

---

3. Televised and print media campaigns to raise awareness of people with disabilities were carried out by the project known as "Assisting Vietnamese People with Disabilities between 2006 and 2010" (NCCD, 2010). Such awareness raising may have led to the filming of "310 Years of Đồng Nai"; however, this event, and those that followed, were nevertheless remarkable for being the first instances of signing Deaf people appearing on television and presenting their own perspectives via a HCMSL-Vietnamese interpreter.

4. Note that my use of HCMSL in this book is a departure from my previous individual (Cooper, 2011; 2014) and joint publications (Cooper & Nguyễn, 2015), and from Woodward (2003) and Woodward et al. (2004), and Woodward and Nguyễn (2012). This change reflects ongoing work with Vietnamese Deaf co-researchers who preferentially use the English-language abbreviation HCMSL as this convention resembles the Vietnamese-language abbreviation for Hồ Chí Minh City: Tp. HCM (Thành phố Hồ Chí Minh), and also parallels the convention of representing Hà Nội Sign Language as HNSL and Hải Phòng Sign Language as HPSL (i.e., not adding 'C' for city to the abbreviated form). See Cooper and Nguyễn (2017) for an example of the use of HCMSL.

5. The 2006 Vietnamese Household Living Standards Survey reported that less than 1% of school-age youth with the greatest "hearing difficulty" (about 40,000 persons) attended school or were employed in the work force at any level (GSO, 2006, section 4.25). This survey was more comprehensive than earlier ones and was the first to document disability.

Figure 1. Courtyard of the Temple of Literature (Văn Miếu Trấn Biên; Đồng Nai, Việt Nam).

It is doubtful that many audience members viewing the "310 Years of Đồng Nai" commemoration were aware of the circumstances of the Deaf educational situation, particularly from a Deaf person's perspective. Although special schools for Deaf students were routinely featured in humanitarian and social welfare reportage in 2008, such coverage tended to focus on the problems that school administrators and teachers associated with teaching Deaf students.[6] In such accounts, deafness is characterized as a medical condition involving the absence of certain capacities—no speaking (*không nói chuyện*), no hearing ability (*không có khả năng nghe*), no sound (*không âm thanh*)—and Deaf people are portrayed as a group associated with loss and incapacity and commonly referred to as having a hearing impairment (*khiếm thính*) and a disability (*khuyết tật*). Whereas citizens are expected to fulfill their constitutional duty to "participate in the building of society" (*góp phần xây dựng cho xã hội*) and to "contribute to society" (*đóng góp cho xã hội*), discourses on Deaf people typically describe them as the recipients—rather than the agents—of such action.

Under such circumstances, Trang's presence on television as a representative of signing Deaf persons was quite remarkable, providing an example of the kind of emergent phenomena that Rabinow terms "events": occurrences that "problematize

---

6. Infrastructural conditions are addressed in "Education for the disabled needs more attention" (Bich, 2009). Educational quality is addressed in "In a world without sound: Teachers learn from students" (Nga, 2010).

Figure 2. Poster commemorating "310 Years of Đồng Nai" (Đồng Nai, Việt Nam).

classifications, practices, and things" (2003, p. 67). In the instance of "310 Years of Đồng Nai," the key "event" is the social visibility not simply of a signing Deaf person but also of a Deaf person who possesses capabilities that contribute to national prosperity as a *citizen*.

Conducted in recognizable talk-show format, the program featured the host's interviews with the four participants in spoken Vietnamese. The participants commented on various facets of their lives and on the opportunities that had enabled them to overcome difficulties (*vượt qua khó khan*) in contributing to the nation's growth and prosperity.[7] Trang's remarks focused on the struggle to progress in schools, in which she and her peers were not allowed to use Hồ Chí Minh Sign Language. As one of the EP codirectors interpreted her comments into Vietnamese, Trang charted a rhetorical path much like that of her fellow participants; however, rather than focus on familial or historical circumstances, Trang attributed *difficulty* to the institutionalized disavowal of HCMSL and *overcoming difficulty* to the promise of HCMSL as a formal language of instruction. This perspective is mirrored in contemporary southern Vietnamese

---

7. The notion of overcoming difficulty has roots in Vietnamese morality tales, such as Nguyễn Du's (1766–1820) *Đoạn Trường Tân Thanh* or *Truyện Kiều* [Tale of Kiêu], in which the protagonist, Kiều, overcomes destiny or fate, *mệnh*, the difficulties of which have been brought on by some unusual endowment, *tài*. In the contemporary vernacular, *mệnh* and *tài* are replaced by (số) *phận* and *tài*, as in the expressions *mỗi người có một số phận* [each person has a destiny] and *chúng ta phải vượt lên số phận* [we must overcome fate] (Nguyễn, personal communication). Malarney (2011) also notes that, in the anticolonial revolutionary and early state socialist periods, "overcoming difficulty" referred to the yoke of foreign control, which had resulted in mass illiteracy.

disability advocates' reframing of disability from an individual/family concern to one centered on social-institutional barriers, transforming *vượt qua khó khăn* [overcome difficulties] into *vượt qua rào cản xã hội* [overcome social barriers].⁸ Having had an opportunity to pursue higher education using HCMSL, Trang stated that she hoped to one day become a teacher herself, teaching Deaf students using signed language.

Reporting on her own and her peers' actual lived experiences, Trang framed the nature of Deaf education by implicitly evaluating the conditions they all encountered in striving to fulfill citizenship obligations through education. Trang's evaluation was not directed at a particular special school; rather, she addressed the systematic reproduction of citizenship participation via spoken Vietnamese and normative ideas about what citizens should be able to do and to achieve exclusively in that mode. Trang's remarks are also relevant to citizenship in that she presented a view of Vietnamese society that was not reflected in the wider social, political, or institutional orders. Thus, Trang's commentary advanced a sociopolitical claim: HCMSL should be regarded both as a legitimate language and as the legitimate language of Deaf education in southern Việt Nam. Moreover, Trang's commentary advanced the idea that HCMSL might—and implicitly should—be used by Deaf and non-Deaf teachers in Deaf education schools and other social locations. Emphasizing changes in social attitudes about Deaf people and HCMSL, as well as changes in the distribution of language-related social resources and power, this book shows that such claims emerge through shared signed language practices and contribute to sociopolitical formation (e.g., to legitimate HCMSL practices). Tensions between social participation and contribution, which developed from shared signed language practices and those guided by state-directed language planning, are a major focus of this book. These tensions appear in journalistic reportage that preceded and followed Trang's appearance on television, where references to *bị khiếm thính* [marker of illness/unfortunate status + hearing impairment] dominate social-interest stories about Deaf people. Ostensibly portraying Deaf people's achievements, such negative indexing of the latter's languages and bodies has implications for citizenship, particularly where mass media sources authorize certain forms of information but not others.

Between the time of Trang's appearance in "310 Years of Đồng Nai" and the time of this writing, attention to Deaf people's signed language–based social participation has expanded considerably. A few examples suggest the variety and breadth of these activities: Print and broadcast news outlets now routinely include public-interest stories on Deaf community activities such as signed language classes, Deaf community social voluntarism, and community-based *giao lưu* [cultural or community-building exchanges]. In addition, in 2010, the Law on Persons with Disability acknowledged the right to use sign language in education. In 2012 and 2013, signed language instruction taught by Deaf people was featured in weekly television programming. Furthermore, in February 2015 the state's ratification of the Convention on the Rights of Persons with Disabilities (CRPD) and its acceptance of the CRPD's Optional Protocol

---

8. Disability Research and Capacity Development (formerly named Disability Resource and Development), a HCMC–based organization run by and for people with disabilities, archives news and research related to *vượt qua rào cản xã hội* and other relevant topics. See http://drdvietnam.org

acceded to international standards and compliance measures regarding state-subsidized provision of access to signed languages.[9] Notwithstanding historic changes in Vietnamese policy statements on sign language, their absence or presence in schools and other social locations needs to be clarified, particularly with respect to the linguistic status of VSLs and their perceived human development and social affordances.

This book is a study of the relationships among language practices, ideologies, policies, and programming that exist in sites of Deaf education and Deaf community organizing in and around HCMC. Examining the forces shaping and shaped by such relationships, I focus on ethnographic and language-centered accounts of sociopolitical formation, principally in relation to the modernizing and development-oriented state. My main argument connects three propositions. First, that educational structuring reflects ideologies of sign language (*ngôn ngữ ký hiệu*) and of Deaf people as a subject group, thereby facilitating forms of inclusion and exclusion in the contemporary moment. Second, that Deaf people's responses to educational structuring—and other social and political economic forces—involve HCMSL-centered social action, thus contributing to sociopolitical formation among and between Deaf and non-Deaf people. Third, that such signed language–based social action contributes to broader sociopolitical transformation within Việt Nam. Ultimately I argue that differently positioned evaluations of HCMSL and notions of Deaf social capacity reflect and respond to concerns over the changing limits of citizenship under contemporary market socialism, particularly those connected to increasing demands on the development-oriented state. Moreover, this study shows that differing understandings of, or stances on, "sign language" are strongly influenced by language ideologies connecting language (and language modalities) with idealized forms of national participation.

Describing circumstances of Deaf groups for a postcolonial, market-socialist setting in Southeast Asia, this study examines perspectives not sufficiently represented in Deaf education, Deaf studies, signed language linguistics, or anthropological literatures. With the analysis I develop here, I aim to expand the scope of language-centered anthropological analysis by showing how signed language–based claims contribute to an examination of sociopolitical formation and change. That is, it is not my contention that sociopolitical formation is the exclusive domain of the state. On the contrary, in these chapters I show the ways in which Deaf social action and HCMSL play a role in shaping state-institutional practices. My description of Trang's television appearance that opened this chapter, suggests one potential route: audience appreciation of the performances and perspectives of signing Deaf people, including critiques not accounted for by official rhetoric.

Examining Signed Language-Centered Social Formation: The Salience of the State for Education and Deaf People's Citizenship Participation

There is no Deaf education in a general sense, nor are there (necessarily) shared meanings associated with the linguistic identities, social positions, or contests

---

9. Việt Nam ratified the CRPD on February 5, 2015.

claimed in relation to Deaf education within and across national contexts. Whereas Deaf and signed language–related marginalization is common enough throughout the world to discuss these circumstances in a generalized way, this study shows that Deaf people's marginalization and participation take shape in particular ways in Việt Nam and need to be documented, mapped, and closely considered and clarified—for theoretical and practical purposes. This clarification allows us to address issues related to processes of modernity, intersubjectivity, and linguistic citizenship and sovereignty within and across signed and spoken language groups in Việt Nam. The issues Trang raised during a chance appearance in a televised broadcast she neither organized nor helped to plan demonstrate the importance of ethnographic attention to everyday events and their implications for theorizing social change. How issues of concern are framed and pursued by Deaf and non-Deaf people in Việt Nam expands social scientific understanding of market-socialist forces and the sociocultural dimensions of political-economic change.

Viewed from within anthropology, late-modern systems of education are principal vehicles for the reproduction of state power and the organization of social relations. Schools have been examined as paramount sites for the reproduction of state ideological power (Althusser, 1971) and authority (Bourdieu, 1998). Recently, investigations of sites of everyday practice demonstrate the ways that populations "imagine" (Hanson & Stepputat, 2006) and "culturally constitute" (Sharma & Gupta, 2006) the state and their relationships to one another as state subjects (see also Jaffe, 2009). From the vantage point of culturally specified practices, Sharma and Gupta argue that "anthropological analyses of the state, then, begin with the counter-intuitive notion that states that are structurally similar may nonetheless be profoundly different from each other in terms of the meanings they have for their populations" (ibid., p. 10). Put another way, there is nothing prepolitical or stable about the structure of modern states; rather, as Calhoun argues, it is through "speech, action, and recognition" that nations undergo transformation (2007, p. 153; see also Althusser, 1971; Williams, 1977).

Language-centered anthropological accounts examining relationships between language and inequality provide insight into the state as a chief medium for establishing and transforming political economies of language. For example, Blommaert argues that the state is responsible for organizing the following: "a dynamic between the world system and 'locality'"; "a regime of language perceived as 'national' with particular forms of stratification in value attribution to linguistic varieties and forms of usage"; and "an infrastructure for the reproduction of a particular regime of language: an education system, media, culture production—each time a selective mechanism that includes some forms of language and excludes others" (2005, pp. 396–397). Regimes of language can be observed, for instance, in Deaf education special school requirements to speak Vietnamese. Trang's use of HCMSL during her first opportunity to address the wider Vietnamese society via the televised medium is, significantly, a reflection of her own natural langauge use, as well as a commentary on—or disalignment with—regimes of language connected to spoken Vietnamese and signing in Vietnamese word order. State emphasis given to language modalities in connection to classroom and social conduct, literacy, citizenship education, cultural heritage and obligation, and training for life-after-school, among other areas, indicates the significance of particular notions of language to specific state-directed political and institutional orders.

Where states organize regimes of language to include selected languages and omit others, the excluded languages form a fundamental part of the sociopolitical basis, by which dominant language regimes and dominant language groups claim legitimacy and authority. For example, languages perceived as interfering with certain institutional goals may be characterized as having negative characteristics that differentiate them and their users from ratified languages and their users. Applying this argument to situations of signed language inclusion and exclusion, state approaches to signed languages are one way in which states pursue projects on various scales—locally, nationally, and transnationally. Moreover, signed languages are implicated in state decisions regarding language broadly, as decisions affecting spoken language users also affect signed language users. For example, requiring the use of specific spoken languages to obtain routine government services (e.g., drivers' licenses, passports) disqualifies signed language users from accessing services in many national locations. Current efforts to understand sociopolitical relationships between signed language groups and the dominant spoken language settings in which they are embedded are hampered by a lack of extended ethnographic accounts of Deaf groups tracking relationships between microlevel practices and macrolevel structures and forces. Significantly, this book contributes to such efforts, as well as to collaboration between researchers and research participant groups with respect to best practices for conducting, analyzing, and disseminating such work.

Deaf Education and Deaf Community Organizing in Việt Nam: Sites of Sociopolitical Formation

The formal education of Deaf students in Việt Nam began in 1886 with French colonial establishment of the Trường Câm-Điếc Lái Thiêu [Lái Thiêu School for the Mute-Deaf] in Bình Dương province, just north of present-day Hồ Chí Minh City. Lái Thiêu was the only Deaf education school in the country until after the American-Vietnamese War, when the government established two schools in the north, and parents and parents-turned-educators organized to establish additional schools in the south. It was only with the 1986 initiation of đổi mới [political economic reforms], however, that the state consolidated a national approach to Deaf education that was speech based. Aiming to stimulate economic development and modernization, the state made education the foundation of đổi mới and its top national policy, with a central role given to literacy in spoken and printed/written Vietnamese (Phạm, 2007, pp. 282–283). Passage of the 2010 Law on Persons with Disability officially ended the formal era of speech-based Deaf education by giving students the right to use "sign language" (ngôn ngữ ký hiệu) in school;[10] however, lack of teacher training in the use of the three main varieties of VSLs

---

10. Reference to "sign language" appears one time in the 2010 Law on Persons with Disability. Paragraph 4 of article 27 in the section on education of persons with disability states that người khuyết tật nghe nói được học bằng ngôn ngữ ký hiệu [persons with hearing and speech disabilities can study using sign language].

continues to limit teacher-student engagement and access to educational content.[11] Moreover, there are not enough schools to accommodate the more than 400,000 school-aged youths who are Deaf or hard of hearing, and educational programming in most existing schools ends at the fifth or ninth grade (depending on the school) (GSO, 2009; cf. GSO, 2006, for figures reported at more than double those found in GSO, 2009).

Language Ideology, Special Schools, and Action by Deaf Social Organizers

Emphasizing the importance of the Vietnamese language for Deaf people's human and social development, as well as their role in Việt Nam's future, educational leaders determined that spoken Vietnamese should be the instructional language for the special school system. This approach resulted in increased enrollment but widespread educational failure, with students typically taking two or more years to complete one curricular year of study. Whereas Deaf students could not hear their teachers or visually decipher (i.e., lip-read) the tonal system of Vietnamese, some special school principals and teachers began learning signs from their students; however, believing that students suffered language and intellectual deficits leading them to sign incorrectly, school personnel superimposed Vietnamese word order on the signs they had learned and required students to sign in this manner. As discussed in chapters 3 and 4, student obedience to teachers included efforts to speak Vietnamese and to sign in Vietnamese word order; however, when outside of the direct gaze of school personnel (and often within), students signed in the ways they had developed with one another and the Deaf adults with whom they had contact. Special school language requirements also extended to the family home, with school administrators and teachers encouraging families to exclusively speak with Deaf children and discouraging them from signing.

Trang's early educational career provides an example of these circumstances. When it was time for Trang to enter school, she was given a choice between several HCMC-based schools—an inclusive school (i.e., with no Deaf peers and no signed language) or one of several special schools with Deaf peers but where signed language use was prohibited. Trang and her family chose the latter. In the school she attended (introduced in chapter 1 as Hope C), the school principal required teachers and students to speak Vietnamese and discouraged families from signing with students at home. Trang's educational achievement was limited, and her studies were delayed due to the fact that teachers and students did not share a classroom language. As a result, it took Trang nearly ten years to complete the first through the fifth grade, which she completed at age 16. At home, communication with her family was limited due to the fact that they did not share a home language. Trang's parents and siblings did not sign (and still do not), and she did not speak Vietnamese; moreover, because of her school experiences, she did not feel confident at that time to write to them using the romanized script (*quốc ngữ;* "national language"). Experiences such as Trang's, with language regulation and their effects, are a significant

---

11. One example of sign language training classes cosponsored by MOET is a course organized by MOET's Special Education–Educational Science Institute of Việt Nam and the Association of People with Disabilities, October–December 2014, held in the Thanh Xuân District of Hà Nội. See http://thanhxuan.gov.vn/portal/home/print.aspx?p=1542

focus of Vietnamese Deaf social organizers' critique of special school structuring and of language regulation encountered in other locations (e.g., vocational training, employment).

In the late 1990s, Deaf people began organizing to address their own educational and training interests and to confront the widespread social marginalization related to the use of VSLs. In 2000 these efforts were further facilitated by the establishment of the EP, an internationally funded program that innovated the teaching of the national curriculum in HCMSL.[12] With the support of Deaf networks and associations, the EP drew Deaf students from all over Việt Nam to study at the high-school level and later also at the college and university levels. At the time of this writing the EP is still the only program to offer Deaf people access to higher education up to and beyond high school in HCMSL. The EP is also the only educational program to train students in signed language linguistics and HCMSL instruction, making it the primary (and, until recently, the only) source of training capacity for Deaf people's language-oriented projects.

Since the latter part of the first decade of this century, Deaf community organizing has surged, advanced by general educational and signed language linguistic training through the EP, as well as by collaborative partnerships between Deaf social organizations and both national and international partners supportive of signed language–related research and training. Deaf organizations throughout the country have formed a national network and are poised for official recognition as a national association, much like thousands of other community-based organizations that enjoy official recognition in Việt Nam (Norlund, 2007). However, at the time of this writing the state has yet to grant Deaf community organizations official status. Deaf community organizers address these circumstances by continuing to build the number and capacity of Deaf organizations around the country.[13] They also contribute to social development by hosting events at which Deaf and non-Deaf family and community members socialize using VSLs. In addition, they conduct civic-oriented projects. Settings of educational and community organizing offer Deaf constituencies opportunities to engage in ongoing conversations about the social conditions they encounter and to develop coordinated responses. As explored in chapters 3 through 5, such responses are directed at critical change within Deaf constituencies as well as in the broader society.

Education as Citizenship Participation: Signed Language Literacy and Self-Determination

Around the world, Deaf education projects are fraught with controversy, as is well documented in Deaf studies, Deaf education, and signed language linguistic literatures. Pivoting between oral (or speech-based) and manual (or sign-based) philosophies,

---

12. In 2010 MOET established a sister project to the EP in Hà Nội, offering sixth- through ninth-grade classes in Hà Nội Sign Language. In 2015 MOET extended educational programming to the tertiary level, offering tenth through twelfth-grade classes at the Trường Cao đẳng Sư phạm Trung Ương, Hà Nội [National College for Education, Hà Nội].

13. According to state protocol, Deaf clubs must be established in at least half of the country's 58 provinces and 5 municipalities in order to be eligible for official recognition.

problem-oriented formulations of deafness, language acquisition, and literacy have dominated language planning debates for hundreds of years. See chapter 2 for an in-depth discussion of the historical context and legacies of the oralism vs. manualism debates; briefly, in these debates, expert knowledge typically privileges dominant spoken languages, shaping recommendations for instructional language use in connection to arguments about membership in and productive contributions to societies and nations (Branson & Miller, 2007, 2008; Lane, 1989; Reagan, 2010; see also Tollefson, 2008, for a view from minority spoken languages). Davis (1995) locates the emergence of notions of language ideological and embodied difference in the combined rise of nineteenth-century nationalist discourses and expert rhetoric on deafness (cf. Branson & Miller, 2002).[14] Articulating in the notion that *able-bodies* make an able nation, an able citizen is a normatively speaking citizen, one who calls citizenship into being by producing the national language. Rarely addressed on their own terms, signed languages have been treated largely instrumentally, as methods perceived to support or hinder educational and national goals.

Language practices found in sites of Deaf education and Deaf community organizing in Việt Nam place citizenship in the context of legacies of Confucianism and Marxist-Leninist thought, both of which contribute to the hierarchical nature of state-society relations (Porter, 1993; Tai, 1992). In Việt Nam, anticolonial citizenship education is a core requirement from the sixth through the twelfth grade, while Marxist-Leninist philosophy is a core requirement of all higher education training. As mentioned earlier, in the market-socialist era, citizens are expected to fulfill their constitutional duty to participate in (*góp phần*) and contribute to society (*đóng góp cho xã hội*). In chapter 4 I discuss Reis's (2013) description of *active citizenship* and its expression through hierarchical relations in Việt Nam, and apply that notion to examine the types of citizenship practices carried out by Deaf people at the three major ethnographic sites included in this study.

The data from the three sites suggest that, although the state apparatus provides an efficient delivery system for ideological formations and regulation, state governance cannot determine people's thoughts or the actions they may take with respect to their diverse human experiences and social positions. By sharing language and intersubjective experience, constituent groups may socialize one another to common understandings of their circumstances as subjects within and in relation to the given sociopolitical system and its variable dynamics. Analysis of the current data set shows state governance and Vietnamese Deaf people's social action reflecting *different but interelated* forms of sociopolitical organization, raising the following questions: What forces are promoting speech-based and sign-based regimes in contemporary Deaf

---

14. Growing in popularity throughout the 1800s, this idea reached its apogee at the 1880 Second International Congress on Education for the Deaf, held in Milan, Italy, whereby hearing educators voted to institute a worldwide ban on the use of sign languages in Deaf education. To ensure the vote, Deaf teachers attending the convention were ejected from the proceedings and prohibited from voting. In addition to Davis (1995), a number of scholars have addressed the history and legacy of "Milan" (e.g., Branson & Miller, 2002; Ladd, 2003; Lane, 1984; Van Cleve & Crouch, 1989). See also Haualand and Allen's (2009) "Deaf People and Human Rights," a report for the World Federation of the Deaf.

education? What roles do Deaf citizens and state actors play to connect VSLs to or distance them from institutions of the state? And in what ways does Deaf social action align or disalign with state-authorized forms of citizenship practice?

Meanings of Active Participation and Contribution

The Vietnamese state's platform makes education the primary vehicle for ensuring national economic development, and it sets literacy in the Vietnamese language as the foundation of that education. Minority language claims implicitly complicate these national development goals and established modes of national participation. State approaches to Deaf education and Deaf community–based organizing between 2000 and 2016 nevertheless allowed Deaf people's signed language–centered activities to gain wider circulation—evidencing what some scholars of Việt Nam term "change from within" (Wischermann, 2011; cf. Fforde, 2011, and Thayer, 2009). The Vietnamese state's responsiveness to signed language–centered interests suggests that it is "sensitive to changing definitions of the political" (Faulks, 2006, p. 65). The terms of such sensitivity and related effects are taken up throughout this book.

Discussions of the nature of language in this changing social and political terrain are producing a set of debates about, and distinct agendas related to, language modality and usage. The ways in which normative ideas about both language and bodies interact in the Vietnamese context are discussed throughout this book, especially with regard to the use of HCMSL. Deaf people in Việt Nam broadly encounter notions of their bodies and intellects as "disabled." They also encounter particular gendered and sexual assumptions. Wischermann argues that "categories of gender analysis are central not only to the analysis of states, markets, and families, but also to the analysis of CSA [Citizen Social Action]" (2011, p. 389; see inter alia Howell, 2007, p. 427). In this book, signed language usage is examined as one of the ways that gender and sexuality are attributed, according to particular sites of interaction between Deaf and non-Deaf people and between institutionalized forms of disciplining and regulating bodies.

With respect to language, social expectations of citizenship participation in Việt Nam tend to dichotomize practices of *hearing-speaking* and *seeing-signing*, attaching active roles to the former and passive roles to the latter. Also discussed in depth is the contestation between two forms of signing found in HCMC: One form corresponds to the grammar of HCMSL, and the other to Vietnamese word order. Deaf people's commentaries attach distinct cultural affiliations and social identities and interests to these forms of signing: HCMSL is described as the form of language engaged in by persons who claim cultural Vietnamese and ĐIẾC [Deaf][15] identities and who seek social participation and contribution through the use of HCMSL. By contrast, signing in Vietnamese word order is described (by users of HCMSL) as the form of language engaged in by persons who identify themselves as having a hearing

---

15. Note on the transcription of HCMSL signs: Following signed language linguistic conventions, signs are glossed using small capitalized letters without dashes, and fingerspelled terms are capitalized with dashes between individual letters. Where signers also indicate a particular Vietnamese word or phrase that they connect to a signed concept, I use that word or phrase followed by my English translation. All errors are my own.

impairment or a disability and who seek social participation through Vietnamese language practices. Signing in Vietnamese word order also aligns with efforts by the Ministry of Education and Training (MOET) to standardize the varieties of VSL described for Việt Nam (Woodward, 2003), as well as with MOET's use of *khiếm thính* (hearing impairment) (see chapters 3 through 6 for an in-depth discussion of the historical and social underpinnings of the varieties of signing, signed language ideologies, and identities found in southern Việt Nam).[16] In this book, description of Vietnamese Deaf social action concentrates on the sociolinguistic perspectives of persons who use HCMSL.

The ways in which Deaf social organizers who use HCMSL respond to new signed language–based, market-based niches further illuminate the meanings of citizenship participation and contribution. For example, in 2008 the state enacted the first laws providing tax subsidies to businesses employing or serving persons with disabilities, spurring disability-related business development. "Hearing impaired tourism" was among the first of such businesses, established by a hearing entrepreneur in Hồ Chí Minh City who employed local Deaf tour guides to provide tours in American Sign Language. In the same period, Deaf-owned and -operated tour companies from other countries began appearing. Viewing both forms of tourism as an encroachment on cultural and linguistic sovereignty, Deaf social leaders responded by calling meetings with local and international touring company representatives to encourage the hiring of Vietnamese Deaf people to conduct tours in local VSLs (Cooper, 2015). These practices reflect the hierarchical sociocultural and political-bureaucratic orders in which Deaf community organizing is embedded (Norlund, 2007). Neither criticizing state policy nor making demands on relevant businesses, the Deaf community organizers I observed sought to influence changes in state-institutional and business domains through direct sharing of their perspectives and offering information, encouragement, and support.

Interpreting Signed Language-Centered Social Particpation

My main points of departure for this study are the use of HCMSL and related sociolinguistic practices at sites of Deaf education and Deaf social organizing. According to my analysis, contemporary Deaf social organizing is a response to the institutionalized marginalization of HCMSL (and other VSLs) within the national system of Deaf education special schools. Therefore, they are a significant site of sociopolitical analysis, particularly with respect to the national state, its ideologies and imaginaries, and the material conditions that Deaf individuals and groups draw on to increase their social participation and contribution through the use of HCMSL. During the first phase of *đổi mới* political-economic reform, the state established the goal of educating every Vietnamese citizen for participation in the development, modernization, and defense of a sovereign nation. Very similar to anticolonial approaches to anti-illiteracy, under

---

16. See Woodward (2003) for a description of sign language varieties and standardization in Việt Nam; see also Woodward and Nguyễn (2012) for a discussion of signed language policy and practice.

đổi mới educational leaders made literacy in spoken and written Vietnamese the key driver of national unity, solidarity, and economic progress.

As noted in the foreword to this book, the sociopolitical context in which Deaf education and Deaf community organizing participate is undergoing rapid transformation. This book is coming out at a time when many things or are in the process of changing, including increasing state attention to language recognition, state-subsidized community-based VSL classes, and imminent official recognition of national Deaf associations. Given these circumstances, this book cannot cover the events that will be most immediate to its publication date. Instead it focuses on events that took place between 2008 and 2014 which, I contend, are crucial to our understanding of the circumstances unfolding today. In this book I examine a number of key historical events so that we can better apprehend the way in which Vietnamese Deaf people are now conducting their social organizing work (Rabinow, 2003, p. 67).

The material forming the core of this book is based on a year of ethnographic fieldwork I conducted in 2008 and 2009 in the southern Vietnamese cities of Hồ Chí Minh City and Biên Hoà as part of my doctoral dissertation research. A second data set comes from an additional five months of ethnographic research I conducted between 2012 and 2014 in connection to trips made to Việt Nam for work as an international trainer on a Deaf education–related project.

On a fundamental level, it was *interpreting* that brought me to Việt Nam for the first time in June of 2007 and that provided the critical basis for the study's ethnographic methodology. I initially came to Việt Nam at the invitation of the director of one adult Deaf education project (which I call the Education Project or EP), who asked me to teach EP staff members an introduction to signed/spoken-language interpretation while I was in Việt Nam conducting preliminary fieldwork. In 2007, signed/spoken-language interpretation was almost nonexistent in Việt Nam—a situation that has changed dramatically over the last nine years. Outside of the EP there were no schools, training centers, or organizations that employed skilled bilinguals providing signed/spoken-language translation. Moreover, according to anecdotal reports, such bilingualism was rare in the general population. Within the EP, staff members providing these services had not had an opportunity to study interpreting theory or methods. However, they had had a unique opportunity to interact with Deaf people on a daily basis and to learn HCMSL and related sociolinguistic perspectives from them during those interactions. Such knowledge is a requisite aspect of interpreting practice, in which interpreters co-construct meanings with interactants in two languages based on an appreciation of the respective forms of language, experiences, and values of both groups.[17] For signed/spoken-language interpretation, such appreciation includes a critical understanding of (mis)conceptions about Deaf people and signed language, knowledge of official institutional structuring of Deaf people's opportunities (and often social stratification), Deaf people's diverse preferences for addressing the conditions they encounter, and critical

---

17. I follow Alexandra Jaffe (1999, 2009) in using *interactant* rather than other descriptors such as *interlocutor*. *Interactant* is a broad term that indicates the salience of multiple features of interactions, not simply what is signed or said but also how people use their bodies and the immediate setting to shape sociolinguistic exchanges.

reflection on one's own privileges as a member of the dominant spoken-language group (if one is a hearing interpreter) or as a natively-signing bilingual (if one is a Deaf interpreter).

Prior to coming to Việt Nam I had worked as a community-based American Sign Language–English interpreter for fifteen years and studied anthropology in order to analyze language and power issues emerging in such work. This background informed my approach to the interpreter training I prepared to give EP staff members in 2007 and the questions I wanted to explore ethnographically. At the heart of both of these endeavors was a concern with Deaf people's signed language–based social participation and hearing people's roles in promoting or constraining such involvement—both interpersonally and institutionally. Thinking of participation in the context of signed/spoken–language interpretation raised the following questions:

- In what ways do Deaf and hearing people routinely interact in Việt Nam—in homes, schools, and other sites?
- What kinds of communication practices do Deaf and hearing people enact in these sites, and how are these practices perceived?
- How do Vietnamese Deaf people see their social relationships with one another and with hearing people, and how do such perceptions and relationships inform Deaf people's approaches to particular social projects?

Preliminary findings led me to conduct fieldwork in 2008 and 2009 in three kinds of sites: (1) the classrooms and administrative offices of the EP; (2) the classrooms and administrative offices of five special schools for Deaf students; and (3) one Deaf association in Hồ Chí Minh City. In addition to these main research sites, I also interviewed personnel from various ministries and hearing family members of Deaf people, attended disability-centered events in which Deaf people participated, visited businesses and organizations that provide employment or services to Deaf people, surveyed HCMSL students, and tracked the appearance of Deaf people in televised and print media. Additional insights were developed by presenting at a conference titled "Living with Hearing Loss," hosted by a community-based organization run by and for people with disabilities, continuing to collaborate with the EP to give interpreter training sessions in their offices, and collaborating with the EP and the Deaf Culture Club to host a two-day interpreter-training workshop for special school personnel.

Following completion of the PhD, I joined a team of international education research and training specialists associated with Gallaudet University in Washington, DC, to provide pro bono consultation to the World Concern Development Organization (WCDO), which was then preparing to launch an early childhood education and language-training project in Việt Nam (Intergenerational Deaf Education Outreach–Việt Nam; hereafter, IDEO Project). In 2012 WCDO hired me as an international trainer for that project. My primary responsibility was to train hearing people to facilitate communication between Deaf mentors and family members in early childhood education sessions with Deaf children. The trainees had minimal exposure to a VSL but had expressed, during candidate screening sessions, their dedication to learning and using a VSL to promote family communication and Deaf children's school readiness. Accordingly, the training program (for aspiring interpreters) focused on preinterpreting skills and extralinguistic communication practices that promote involvement by family members in establishing and maintaining joint attention with Deaf mentors and Deaf children. For this work I made four trips to Việt Nam, between December 2012 and August 2014. Each four-to-six-week trip consisted of two to three weeks of training activities, after which I conducted research activities.

WCDO's IDEO Project brought the training team into contact with the highest-ranking educational decision makers in Vietnamese special education administration and research. In addition, the team engaged with approximately 70 Deaf community leaders from four provinces in north, central, and southern Việt Nam; 50 hearing people dedicated to acquiring or expanding the use of VSLs; and approximately 150 hearing families with Deaf children. Although I did not conduct research on these training activities, such interactions nevertheless deepened my appreciation of the perspectives and interests of Deaf community leaders, aspiring VSL(s)-Vietnamese interpreters, family members of Deaf children, national educational leaders, and international development personnel.

As we carried out the various activities that contributed to these two data sets, interpretation and translation played some role in every interaction, often involving explicit discussion of multilingual and multicultural issues. Such interpretive considerations and discussions inform the analysis I pursue throughout the book; however, the responsibility for the conclusions remains my own.

Research Methodology and Ethical Concerns

I conducted extended participant observation in the EP, five special schools, and the HCMC Deaf Club (HDC). I also participated in more than 360 hours of activities related to my work as an international trainer, informing sociolinguistic, state-institutional, and policy insights reflected in my findings. From 2012 to 2014 I also conducted approximately 20 individual and group interviews with Deaf community organizers about their work in southern Việt Nam.

At the EP I participated in numerous activities, including secondary and first-year college-level classes; meetings with the student body conducted by the EP codirector; semester opening and closing ceremonies attended by students' families, college administrators, and Nippon Foundation representatives; and several EP meetings with the college administration to support the EP's preparations to establish a formal interpreter-training program. In July 2008 I taught a six-week course in modern dance for four groups of students, which culminated in a choreographed dance.[18] Occasionally, when the EP director could not be present, I also substituted for English classes.

---

18. The EP students performed the dance in its entirety (approximately 20 minutes) several times for ceremonies at the EP and performed a 5-minute version of the dance on VTV9 television as part of a show honoring the Vietnamese National Day of Care and Protection of Persons with Disabilities (April 18, 2009). An HCMSL-Vietnamese interpreter for these activities was also featured onstage throughout the broadcast. The show, titled "Giới hạn là bầu trời" [The sky's the limit], drew widespread media interest and was reviewed in the *Dân Trí* newspaper (Tùng Nguyên, 2009).

In addition to formal activities, I interacted with EP students and staff before and after the formal schooldays and on weekends.

At the special schools, the extent of my observation was comparatively limited. I focused on upper primary-level classes, conversations between principals and teachers, and interactions with students during lunch periods or as they entered or exited the school. Of all of these activities, the most intensive were those at the HDC. In total I attended more than 20 weekend meetings of the HDC (approximately two hours per meeting) and participated in a range of its activities, including: club activity planning meetings; hosting Deaf guests from other countries; special events, such as Vietnamese New Year (Tết) and International Women's Day; and discussions with the membership about HCMSL and social-change goals. I also collaborated with EP personnel and HDC leaders in the preparation and presentation of an HCMSL interpreting workshop, which was held in the HDC meeting space.[19]

Having conducted preliminary fieldwork at the EP, when I returned to Việt Nam to conduct dissertation fieldwork, my first interviews were drawn from the adult census there (students over 18 years of age).[20] EP students and personnel also introduced me to the HDC, as well as to Deaf residents of HCMC not associated with either the EP or the HDC. A number of EP students and HDC leaders (several of whom were my HCMSL instructors) also invited me to events such as government-sponsored charity functions held annually at the Vietnamese New Year and meetings between HDC leaders and special school or ministry personnel.

All in all, I conducted more than fifty formal interviews, each lasting from one to one and a half hours. Eight of these were group interviews (involving from 2 to 10 people). Forty-eight individuals participated in the interviews (9 participated in more than one interview). Of these interviewees, 32 self-identified as Deaf, 15 as hearing, and 1 as hard of hearing. In addition, I conducted 15–20 informal interviews with special school teachers, families with Deaf children, ministry personnel, owners of businesses that employed Deaf people in HCMC, and one Deaf business owner.

I videotaped all of the interviews with HCMSL users, including those with non-Deaf persons who knew HCMSL (e.g., EP staff members), in order to capture linguistic practices they demonstrated that potentially involved or related to HCMSL, such as code-switching and pointing (deixis). I audiotaped interviews with nonsigners, except when interviewees declined to be audiotaped.

I conducted Interviews with Deaf persons in HCMSL. During the first few of these I noticed that interviewees often used the English-based fingerspelling system. They also indexed concepts they wanted to emphasize and used the English-based fingerspelling system apparently to enhance my sociolinguistic understanding, possibly in the

---

19. One of the EP codirectors presented during this workshop, and the other codirector helped coordinate the event, working throughout the weekend with an interpreter, interpreting between HCMSL, Vietnamese, and English.

20. My participant observation put me in contact with students who were, for the most part, over the age of eighteen. However, in order to ensure that all interviewees met my research criteria and Institutional Review Board protocol, I did not conduct interviews with Deaf education special school students.

belief that I might not be familiar with terms expressed in the Vietnamese-based fingerspelling system. In order to pass the 12th-grade national examination, Vietnamese upper-secondary students must demonstrate proficiency in written English; therefore, EP students also studied English within the EP.[21] After becoming accustomed to interviewees using the English-based fingerspelling system with me, I began responding to their comments that included English words with requests for the same concept expressed as an HCMSL sign and/or in the Vietnamese fingerspelling system. Sometimes Deaf interviewees used the Vietnamese fingerspelling system but omitted the signs representing the diacritics for Vietnamese vowel and tone markers. I then followed these productions with requests for them to "fingerspell the word as you would when communicating with another Deaf person." My aim was also to capture any variation in fingerspelling (e.g., lexicalization, conventionalized dropping of signs representing written tonal diacritics).

During interviews I also kept Vietnamese-English and English-Vietnamese dictionaries handy. Often interviewees and I would look up terms together, which would frequently contribute to a particular thread that developed in the course of the interview. After transcribing the interviews, I shared my transcriptions with the interviewees and edited the interview content for accuracy. These follow-up meetings took place either in person or via Skype.

After discussing informed consent, I typically began interviews with Deaf participants by asking their age. In addition to eliciting crucial demographic data that I could cross-reference with other relevant information, such as the age at which the interviewee had learned sign language and the number of years they had spent at school, this approach provided a cultural frame for the interview, anchoring me, for example, as an older female person (*chị*) and the interviewee as a younger person of either gender (*em*). I would typically follow this with asking questions about the age at which they had first attended school and the name and location of the school. These questions often prompted a less structured discussion about communication at home and school, classroom experiences, individual goals for obtaining education, social experiences with hearing people, and so on. Aside from the initial questions, I followed a semi-structured interview protocol, while at the same time directing the interviews in such a way as to maintain focus on the research focus.

I conducted interviews with non-Deaf persons in Vietnamese or English or both. For interviews conducted exclusively in Vietnamese, Mī (an EP staff member/interpreter) agreed to work with me as a Vietnamese-English interpreter. Her interpretation during these interviews added infinite grace to the quality of the experience and the research data: Not only did I know Mī personally, but so did the interviewees. Mī's presence

---

21. In Việt Nam, instruction in English begins during lower-secondary education (*cấp* 2; U.S. equivalent of grades 6–9). Special schools have only recently begun offering lower-secondary coursework, including English. In 2000, the EP was the first program to offer lower- and upper secondary courses; therefore, EP students have studied English longer than most other Deaf students in Việt Nam. Interaction with American Deaf and hearing scholars gave them opportunities to practice using English via the fingerspelling of terms and by evaluation of their use of written English (e.g., homework).

provided a valuable social introduction, without which the interviewees might have been less likely to share their perspectives and experiences with me. Moreover, Mĩ's own knowledge and experience as an HCMSL/Vietnamese interpreter also meant that she was well versed in terminology related to Deaf people, Deaf education, and related policies and practices.

As an interpreter trained solely through ordinary interactions with Vietnamese Deaf persons, Mĩ told me that her many teachers had taken pains during the prior decade to explain to her the distinctions between HCMSL and signing in Vietnamese word order as well as the sociocultural and linguistic aspects of Deaf people's experiences. Mĩ was also very interested in understanding and conveying intended meanings in her interpretation work. For instance, rather than follow the model of the spoken language interpreters she knew, who created "form-for-form" pairings between words in the source and target languages, Mĩ sought to create conceptual equivalents, as is commonly emphasized in the signed-spoken-language interpretation literatures. She paid close attention to implied meaning. Moreover, in that we were both eager to better understand the circumstances contributing to the marginalization of Deaf people and sign language, after completing an interview Mĩ would often explain to me how certain turns of phrase instantiated Vietnamese speakers' perspectives on a topic, as well as other aspects of the discourse. These conversations with Mĩ are what first drew me to question the differences between terms such as *khiếm thính* [hearing impairment] and *người Điếc* [Deaf person], among other marked and unmarked terms. In chapters 5 and 6 I examine the latter notions and their social implications.

As with Deaf research participants, I began interviews with Vietnamese hearing persons by discussing informed consent. However, unlike interviews with Deaf research participants, when beginning the actual interview I did not ask Vietnamese hearing persons about their age; Mĩ and Vietnamese Deaf people had explained to me that, although Deaf people may inquire about age among themselves, this is not a practice Vietnamese hearing people usually engage in. Rather, hearing people must be circumspect in their attempts to ascertain age or other statuses (marriage, romantic partners). In order to address hearing interactants in an appropriately polite manner, I typically began these interviews by asking about their current employment. This allowed interviewees to establish their area of expertise and status. I then asked questions such as how they came to work with Deaf people, the kinds of activities and programs they administer or teach with Deaf people, communication, difficulties encountered, program outcomes, and their perspective on what would be helpful to fully support their programmatic interests. Before each interview I prepared a series of questions I hoped to cover regarding the interviewees' position relative to the Deaf people they routinely interacted with (e.g., program administrator, teacher) and their particular experience with and perspective relative to deaf people and HCMSL. As with Deaf research participants, once interviews were under way I moved back and forth from pursuing topics raised by interviewees and my prepared questions.

A word about informed consent (IC): 33 out of 48 individuals signed IC documents. All 32 Deaf interviewees agreed to IC: All 32 also agreed to be videotaped; of these, 2 gave permission to publish their image to allow for direct quotation and/or representation of a signed concept. All 15 hearing interviewees read the IC; of these, 9 declined to sign the IC form but agreed to be interviewed. Six of these 9 individuals also declined to be video- or audiotaped but consented to my taking handwritten notes. These individuals told me that they preferred not to appear in audio or video recordings because of the sensitive nature of their job positions. One person in a high position related to education told me that she was concerned about MOET officials learning of her comments. Nonetheless, she decided to participate in the interview because, as she stated, "it is important that people talk about what is really happening in the schools and the better way to teach hearing-impaired students." I provided all interviewees with IC forms in both written Vietnamese and English, whether they chose to sign these documents or not. I also translated the IC into HCMSL, offering interviewees their preferred version(s) of the IC (Vietnamese, English, and/or HCMSL).

In addition to formal and informal interviews, I conducted three surveys with the following groups: (1) HCMSL students (non-Deaf); (2) EP students; and (3) principals of five special schools. Thirty-eight HCMSL students participated in the survey, which posed questions about contact with Deaf people and their reasons for studying HCMSL (see chapter 6). That survey instrument included nine questions, including two closed-end questions regarding length of study and number of teachers, and seven open-ended questions about sociolinguistic attitudes and values. Mī translated this survey into Vietnamese. One of my HCMSL instructors—whom I am calling Nga—collaborated with me to give the survey to one of her classes (six students) and observed my survey protocol. Nga and I then met with two other HCMSL instructors, to whom she explained the survey instrument and protocol. After this we discussed questions about rationale, data analysis, and reporting. Together these three HCMSL instructors then conducted an additional thirty-two surveys (without my participation). The HCMSL students participating in the survey all wrote their responses in Vietnamese.

The second survey I conducted included forty-seven EP students (see chapter 3). This survey contained 12 questions: 4 demographic questions (age, name of primary school, province of family home, and number of other Deaf people [if any] in the family) and 8 descriptive questions (family- and school-based communication, age and manner by which students had learned a signed language, special school teacher responses to their use of signed language, academic and employment experience). Like the HCMSL student survey, I engaged Mī to translate this survey into Vietnamese. Prior to giving this survey to participants I inquired about their preferred format—written Vietnamese or HCMSL. All of the participants chose HCMSL, so I conducted the survey in that language in a group format (8–10 students in each group), asking demographic questions first, then descriptive questions. In response to the latter, students raised their hands to questions such as these: How did your primary school teachers communicate with you—in a signed language? Spoken language? Both? While they signed, I wrote down their responses as quickly as I could in order to avoid interrupting the signers' narratives. Because I was surprised by how eager the survey participants were to share what were, in several cases, extremely painful recollections of being beaten by teachers for their use of a VSL, my handwritten notes have the appearance of a waterfall of words in English and Vietnamese (fingerspelled terms, glosses of signs), angling down the page. In the future, I would videotape surveys conducted in HCMSL, as I believe valuable narrative content was lost as a result of my poor shorthand and my inability to go back later to examine interactions that occurred between the survey participants.

I conducted the third survey by email with four principals and one assistant principal of the five special schools in my research (see chapter 3). During the data-coding process, I realized I did not have consistent demographics for each of the special schools, so I created a survey with eleven questions addressing school demographics and program features, including teacher training, instructional modality, and the year the school initiated inclusive education. To ensure survey clarity, I made an initial translation of the survey into Vietnamese, which Mī then edited. All five respondents completed the surveys, yielding significant details for these schools, both individually and as a representative subset of special schools in the greater Hồ Chí Minh City area.

According to my earlier description of the research methodology, the research process and related analytic findings were clearly shaped by interactions with and input from research participants—particularly Deaf research participants—as well as being influenced by collaborative activities with the latter that were not directly research-related. Such interactions notwithstanding, it would be misleading to suggest that the research described in this book was a joint effort such as that described in recent literature on Deaf community-researcher collaborations, which I discuss further in chapter 2 of the book (Cooper & Nguyễn 2015; Harris, Holmes, & Mertens 2009; Singleton 2014).

Considering the emergence of what I term the "disability marketplace" in Việt Nam, where marking disablement is a way of securing funding nationally and internationally, the circumstances of ASL's encroachment into Deaf Vietnamese enterprises parallel those of geopolitical encroachment confronting the Vietnamese state. Deaf citizens seek a determining role, or active citizenship, in decisions affecting Deaf communities throughout the country—particularly with respect to: official recognition of VSLs; support for VSL(s)-related language policy and planning especially for educational and employment domains as well as for training aspiring VSL teachers and aspiring VSL-Vietnamese interpreters; and, recognition and capacity-building of Deaf clubs and associations throughout Việt Nam.

A description of my first interaction with a southern Vietnamese Deaf person during my first visit to the EP illustrates some of the ways that language, embodied practices, subject statuses, and sociopolitical self-determination are interwoven. This exchange occurred during preliminary fieldwork in June 2007 at the entrance to the main building of the teaching college (now university) from which the EP rents space.

Entering the grounds of the teaching college for the first time—a campus of approximately ten academic buildings, library, recreational facility, faculty and student housing—the codirectors of the EP, who had given me a ride from HCMC that day, had arranged for an EP student to greet me. The student—then approximately 25 years of age—and I approached each other, and he signed CHÀO—a sign I was unfamiliar with. Because this was our first meeting, I expected that it meant something like HELLO (it does). I mirrored his use of the sign, thinking that either our differing signed languages shared a similar form of greeting or, knowing that I used American Sign Language (ASL), the student was accommodating my lack of familiarity with HCMSL. Subsequent interactions confirmed that, at least with this one sign, ASL and HCMSL shared similar linguistic forms. He then signed, with raised eyebrows, what I understood to be ARE YOU DEAF OR HEARING?[22] This construction seemed to be similar to the grammatical form of interrogative yes-no questions in ASL. I reproduced what I thought to be DEAF and HEARING, as if talking to myself. Then I pointed to him with raised eyebrows, mirrored the sign he had just used,[23] and asked "ARE YOU DEAF?" He nodded his head and smiled bemusedly, as if to say "Of course!" He then pointed to himself and again signed DEAF. I followed this confirmation with a return to his original question and, using the sign he had used for HEARING, pointed to myself and nodded in affirmation.

The student then pointed to himself, and fingerspelled his name: M-I-N-H H-A-I. He told me his name sign—produced with the fingerspelled letter *M* on the upper-right eyebrow—and I told him mine—the fingerspelled letter *A* placed in vertical orientation to the right side of my chin.[24] Minh Hai then pointed toward the stairs; I also pointed and, raising my eyebrows, waited to see whether he would understand this as the indicating question I intended (i.e., THIS DIRECTION?). He nodded and continued by signing what I understood to mean WALK TO THE TOP FLOOR (left forearm held vertically, against which the right hand produced a classifier construction for animate motion along a path from elbow to wrist). He followed this by signing TOP (5th) FLOOR," the meaning of which I, again, gleaned contextually, given that the concepts of *floors, stories,* and *top floor* are expressed differently in ASL.

As Minh Hai and I continued walking up the stairs, he used a gesture related to everyday experience in the form of wiping sweat from his forehead and raising his eyebrow, using the nonmanual grammatical forms described earlier. I understood he was inquiring whether the climb was or would be too much of an exertion for me

---

22. Following the Vietnamese Deaf convention of identifying hearing and Deaf statuses, I use DEAF and HEARING to refer to these conceptual devices; however, the sociocultural or linguistic forms and meanings of such devices are not defined here. Rather, I pursue these forms and meanings throughout this book according to the situations in which they are invoked. The Vietnamese language has no popular conception of "hearing person." In the media and everyday forms of conversation, HEARING persons typically refer to those without visible disability as *bình thường* [normal]. People who work with Deaf and hard of hearing persons often use both *bình thường* or *người nghe* [literally "person" + modifier "hear"] to refer to people who hear and speak.

23. Nonmanual (facial) grammar for *wh*-questions (who, what, when, where, and why) are common in many signed languages.

24. As with the names given earlier in this introduction, all of the name signs in this study are pseudonyms. In general, name signs are unique references to persons that are acquired in social interaction with Deaf family members, elders, or peers and do not have written- or spoken-language counterparts. In Việt Nam, name signs may consist of references to features of one's body or personality, as well as familial or social roles. Thus, a name sign might indicate "mole on cheek" or appear in combination with a letter of the fingerspelled alphabet or sign used to describe a particular skill or job. In southern Việt Nam, name signs may also be combined with age-hierarchy references when talking about a Deaf person's age-based location in the family (e.g., THERE ARE FOUR PEOPLE IN MY FAMILY. MY MOTHER AND FATHER, MY OLDER BROTHER, AND ME, EM ÚT (YOUNGEST SIBLING). MY NAME SIGN IS G SIGNED *G ON MOLE ON CHEEK*. MY NAME IS FINGERSPELLED G-I-A-N-G.

(McNeill, 1992). Shaking my head to indicate "no," I smiled and pantomimed lifting weights and, pointing to myself, nodded affirmatively. Nonstandard gesture sets, which are often used by Deaf and hearing interactants that do not share a sign language (e.g., coworkers to communicate with each other), comprise pointing and emblematic gestures such as "thumbs up" in the North American context (Dudis, personal communication). In addition to the exchange of first-language lexical items (signs), when signers meet in language contact settings (e.g., signers using differing varieties of signed languages within a country or in transnational settings), Deaf signers who do not have a language in common often employ a number of strategies to communicate with each other (e.g., the use of gesture, code switching to another signed language, and fingerspelling systems associated with the written or printed forms of the interactants' respective national or subgroup languages (Lane, Hoffmeister, & Bahan, 1996, pp. 207–209; see also Friedner & Kusters, 2015).

By the time we reached the top floor, Minh Hai and I had covered several topics—my flight from the United States, resting the night before, and morning breakfast—as I incorporated the lexical items I understood into my nascent HCMSL lexicon. It is worth noting that, not knowing Vietnamese on this first trip to Việt Nam, I could not have had this level of communication—*or any substantial direct communication*—with people who spoke Vietnamese.

At the top of the stairs a group of 10 or so students was waiting, watching Minh Hai and me as we chatted. I signed CHÀO, and Minh Hai introduced me. He told them I was from the United States ([nước] MỸ). The students then began asking me questions that I could only partially grasp. Minh Hai guided me through these interactions, clarifying the questions and my attempts at answering, both teaching me and interpreting for me in each conversational turn. He both contextualized the new signs I was seeing with those he had already introduced and also utilized the strategies mentioned earlier. Later that morning I learned that Minh Hai was a trained HCMSL teacher, which made sense as he skillfully employed a number of techniques to facilitate my clear communication with the EP junior students. This group of students also asked whether I was "HEARING," prompting me to use my newly acquired sign for this status—about which I had a number of questions.

According to my experience in American Deaf communities, I viewed the question of my hearing status as one that encompassed not only sociocultural affiliation but also experiential, linguistic, and sociopolitical viewpoints (Padden & Humphries, 1990; Lane, Hoffmeister, & Bahan, 1996). Based on the minimal, though closely patterned, exchanges I had participated in during that first hour at the EP, I surmised that I could expect to be asked this question during initial meetings with Deaf people in Việt Nam; however, I wondered what significance the question held for Deaf persons in the southern Vietnamese context: Are HEARING and DEAF forms of categorization used only in the EP, or do these labels refer to socially conventionalized categories? And are such categories conventionalized only among Deaf people, or are they also conventionalized among HEARING people? If conventionalized by both DEAF and HEARING people, what are the attitudes, values, beliefs, and so forth associated with these categories, and how are they deployed beyond everyday description—such as within institutional practices and explanatory systems? When I answered this group of students, "YES, HEARING," they looked surprised and said excitedly, "BUT YOU CAN SIGN!" This response was an initial window into language experiences, attitudes, and practices engaged in by Deaf (and hearing) people in southern Việt Nam, as well as the potential implications for Deaf social access and subjectivity.

By that afternoon, students clustered around the EP office to meet the newcomer who, the first group of students had told them, was a DEAF WOMAN FROM THE UNITED STATES. Over the course of the three weeks of preliminary fieldwork, students to whom I had already been introduced asked me on repeated occasions whether I was DEAF or HEARING. They then asked me to explain how I had come to acquire a sign language and how HEARING and DEAF people communicated in the United States.

These details are salient to understanding the kind of access I ultimately had to Deaf research participants; yet they also highlight the facilitating *route of access,* namely, body practices recognized as meaningful to signers I had not met before and with whom I did not yet share a common language. That is, Minh Hai and I engaged our eyes, faces, hands, and coordinated uses of our whole bodies in ways that are not distinct to either HCMSL (which I did not know) or ASL (which he did not know). This mode of engagement not only made us intelligible to one another on the level of embodiment but also included linguistic features of HCMSL that laid the foundation upon which this whole research project depended. Significantly, these engagements introduced me to the contradictory social conditions confronting Vietnamese Deaf people in their interactions with hearing people—both those that know HCMSL and those that do not. A central feature of those conditions involves what it means to be DEAF; as interview after interview with EP students impressed upon me, to be Deaf is to use VSLs. Deaf sociolinguistic values, sign language-based self-determination, and intersubjective identification are among the topics this study examines and applies in discussions of Deaf social organizers' sociopolitical "transformation-displacement" of hegemonic spoken-language attitudes and related creative practices to advance Deaf sociopolitical power (Pêcheux, 1982).

Research, Language Acquisition and Socialization

On my preliminary research trip to Việt Nam in 2007 the EP codirectors agreed to arrange formal HCMSL lessons for me, which—as my description of meeting Minh Hai demonstrates—began on my first visit to the EP. During that first month in Việt Nam, I participated in HCMSL lessons on a daily basis and socialized with EP students in the evenings and on weekends. These interactions facilitated the growth of my HCMSL lexicon and understanding of HCMSL grammar. During the dissertation research period I continued to take formal lessons, which I eventually phased out as my daily use of HCMSL deepened. However, it was rarely the case that I understood everything that Vietnamese Deaf people signed to me and, rarer still, everything that they signed to one another. Much as Deaf friends and American Sign Language instructors had facilitated my acquisition of ASL by monitoring my responses to their communication and making adjustments in their signed production to match my apparent level of comprehension, Vietnamese Deaf interactants facilitated my sociolinguistic understanding by monitoring my responses to their communication and by confirming my understanding through targeted questions, clarifying statements, repetition, rephrasing, and substitution of alternative fingerspelled words or signs.

Nonsigners and novice signers often characterize signed languages as simple systems. The fact that I was able to use HCMSL to any extent whatsoever within a relatively short period of time makes HCMSL vulnerable to such critique. Such circumstances warrant emphasis on Vietnamese Deaf research participants' communicative labor, the cooperative nature of our communication, and the emergent nature of my HCMSL proficiency throughout the duration of this study. Although there is no doubt that I had substantial, direct communication with Vietnamese Deaf persons via HCMSL, the success of that communication was always contingent upon the patience, analytic and communicative skills, of the Vietnamese Deaf people I interacted with.

Several other factors contributed to the language access I enjoyed at the various research sites, particularly among Deaf research participants and collaborators. A large part of my initial access to HCMSL can be attributed to certain transference effects from ASL that I have used continuously in my personal life and professional work for more than twenty years. Formal lessons in HCMSL then introduced me to an initial vocabulary, with which I began to make lexical substitutions between ASL signs and HCMSL signs. Where concepts in the two languages differed substantially, my teachers and other interactants helped me to develop a uniquely HCMSL lexicon. The grammar of HCMSL took much longer to begin to understand, and I produced it inconsistently—and still do to this day. The same is true for my use of HCMSL fingerspelling. In daily interactions and interviews, I tended to fingerspell the Vietnamese words I knew; when possible, I sought the support of, first, a soft-cover Vietnamese-English dictionary and, later, a Việt-Anh application on my smartphone and on the smartphones of interviewees.

My access to Deaf education special schools was also strongly contingent upon the social relationships shared between the Vietnamese persons who introduced and received me (mostly non-Deaf) and the venue in which the introduction occurred. My initial contact with the special schools, for example, was the outcome of a series of introductions that involved my HCMSL teachers (from the EP), who introduced me to the Development Center in HCMC; the Development Center then invited me to speak at a conference it hosted in 2009, titled "How to Live a Good Life with Hearing Loss." This event was attended by Deaf education special school principals and teachers from the surrounding area. In addition, collaboration with HCMC Deaf Club leaders and EP codirectors to host an HCMSL-Vietnamese interpretation workshop again brought me into contact with special school personnel. As part of the preparation for the seminar, I went with Deaf colleagues and an HCMSL-Vietnamese interpreter to each school to personally invite their staff to attend the workshop. After the event, my contact with special school personnel increased substantially as they welcomed me to make return visits to their schools. My work as an international trainer with the World Concern Development Organization also introduced me to Deaf education colleagues, aspiring VSL instructors and interpreters, and families with Deaf children in four provinces in the northern and southern regions of the country. In addition, I met personnel from the National Institute of Educational Science, special schools in four provinces, MOET deputy ministers and research directors, and INGO leadership and staff.

My introduction to the research sites where I ultimately conducted this study also reflects circumstances of language use, social networks and hierarchy, as well as the nature and degree of state oversight variously acting on the different sites. As noted, language training and socialization in HCMSL were initially facilitated by the EP. My use of HCMSL then facilitated contact with special school personnel through the somewhat circuitous route described earlier. Finally, my HCMSL instructors introduced me to the Development Center and, later, the club which it helped to cofound. Studying Vietnamese—in the United States (weekly classes since November 2008) and in the fall of 2008 at the Trường Đại Học Khoa Học Xã Hội Và Nhân Văn [University of Social Sciences and Humanities, HCMC]—further facilitated exchanges with both Deaf and non-Deaf people.

Although HCMSL was not endorsed by the state until 2010, it had begun to gain attention from the media. At that time, special-school principals commonly remarked that my use of HCMSL was "unusual," given that few non-Deaf people used VSLs at that time.[25] They initially agreed to meet with me because others had given me proper introduction (e.g., indexing my status as a PhD candidate, then later a PhD in anthropology, and/or my national certifications in ASL-English interpretation in the United States). After repeated visits, two principals asked whether I would share educational tools with them or offer other training support. In the early 2010s, social visibility of VSLs had expanded; thus, by 2012, when I began working as an international trainer with the World Concern Development Organization, I did not encounter the kind of profuse commentary about my HCMSL skill that I had in the first few years of my research.

Researcher Access and Privilege

My access to the constituencies and sites described earlier reflects a number of complexly related forms of privilege active in each of the multilingual settings where I conducted my research. Four forms of privilege seemed to have the most bearing for the research reported in this book: (1) my hearing privilege; (2) my knowledge of ASL; (3) my possession of higher-education degrees from several U.S.-based academic institutions; and, (4) my whiteness. First, in conducting research at Deaf education special schools and adult literacy programs, I found that my audiological status—literally, listening to what people said about Deaf people—benefited my research because, as most non-Deaf interactants assumed I did not know Vietnamese, they would say things about Deaf people and/or sign language within hearing distance.

---

25. Out of the estimated 25 special school teachers I met, approximately four teachers used signs with apparent ease. These four teachers used what I'm calling Sign-Supported Vietnamese (speaking and signing in Vietnamese word order). In coordinating the sign language interpreting workshop, HCMSL teachers from the EP screened the signing proficiency of potential registrants. According to their assessment, several special school teachers could communicate by using signs without speaking; however, none of them used HCMSL.

This allowed me to track their beliefs, values, attitudes, and language ideological viewpoints about Deaf people, who were often in the room. Thus, I had certain access to the sites where Deaf people lived and worked that they themselves did not enjoy.[26]

My *supposed* knowledge of ASL prompted several different kinds of attributions that granted me privilege in particular settings. When I used HCMSL in settings with non-Deaf signers, these interactants frequently (and incorrectly) evaluated my signing as demonstrating a high level of proficiency and produced spontaneous comments about the "strength of ASL" in contrast to HCMSL or other VSLs—despite the fact that I did not use ASL in such interactions, or any interactions (except with Deaf visitors from the United States). In the process, they minimized the substantial collective labor expended by my HCMSL instructors in teaching me HCMSL. My possession of higher-education degrees from U.S.-based institutions connects broadly to the high value Vietnamese people and the Vietnamese state place on education; it also indexes a comparative framework that evaluates educational opportunity outside Việt Nam as "superior" to that available within the country, as well as considerable conflation between the United States as a world economic and military power and knowledge supposedly contained in U.S. academic institutions (including ASL).

Whiteness also played a role in my interactions, especially in the peri-urban setting of Đồng Nai province, where, on walks with Deaf colleagues in the evenings, for example, people would approach me and sometimes touch my skin. Whereas the subordinating power of whiteness in Việt Nam goes back several hundred years at least and is most recently connected to French colonial domination and its legacies (cf. Firpo, 2010), attention to the paleness of my skin and attributions involving its "softness" (*mềm*) or "beauty" (*da đẹp*) took place amid a ubiquitous media blitz of white affluence. Skin-care products promised whiter skin, and Vietnamese fashion models' skin tones were routinely photoshopped several tones lighter to satisfy the production interests of the body-whitening economy. Though my friends and colleagues often disputed any special significance to my being a white person, whiteness almost always attracted positive forms of attention and, in the context of research activities, possibly patience as well, which might not ordinarily be given to other Vietnamese (cf. Carruthers, 2002). Together, such features attributed to my person—whiteness, my use of spoken and signed languages, and, indeed, the very luxury of graduate training and funding to conduct research—gave me a prestige status and access to people and sites.

Holding such privileges closely in mind, I attempted to control for the potential effects of these circumstances first of all by collaborating with my research participants and partners to select data elements for analysis. I consulted the latter about both the framing and the timing of research reporting (in order to support and/or to avoid interfering with social organizing activities they might have been pursuing). In addition, I conducted iterative informed consent to confirm the continued interest in research collaborator or participant input. I also carried out iterative consent for the use of photographic images, especially where individuals have worked with me as sign models (as seen throughout this book). Checking for consent on multiple occasions takes into

---

26. For a discussion of hearing privilege see Facundo Element (2012), Fernandes and Myers (2010), Kusters et al.(2017), and Ladd (2003).

consideration that people's lives can change, allowing them to change their mind about the use of their image according to their circumstances or interests. This is particularly important prior to publication, such as with this book, for which I conducted a final round of photograph consent forms for sign models in the summer of 2014; I then contacted the latter again by Skype or email in 2015 and 2016 as the book approached publication.

Translation Conventions and Issues

As I suggest in the earlier description of researcher methods and privilege, issues of translation and their negotiation formed a vital part of everyday and research-related exchanges. In addition to their ethnographic intensity, issues of translation permeated every phase of this study and continue as I write this book. Drawing connections between the global publishing industry, literature, the rise of modern machine translation, and manipulations of the human genome, Apter's discussion of mass and public culture products that "gain international visibility, while others do not" (2001, p. 2) is germane to critical consideration of the following: (1) my own international visibility in the Vietnamese milieu; and (2) production of certain ethnographic materials rather than others, the academic publishing industry's interest in such materials and their circulation among English-language academic and nonacademic audiences, as well as their translation and circulation among Vietnamese and HCMSL language audiences.

One of the issues I encountered in this study was the growing presence of American Sign Language, initially via HCMC-based tourism, and, later, via the entry of foreign tour operators hosting ASL-based tours in Việt Nam (Cooper, 2015). The proliferation of ASL resembles but is also distinct from the widespread proliferation of European language schools in Việt Nam (see figure 3).[27]

In chapter 5, I discuss the proliferation of American Sign Language via educational pathways. Chapter 6 then discusses the forces that facilitate the proliferation of ASL in the disability-market sector. To the extent that VSLs continue to be marginalized within education, employment, and other social and economic domains, forces promoting the ascendancy of ASL compete with the limited power and resources available to HCMSL users (and other VSLs).

With respect to ethical concerns related to this research study and analysis, my selection of HCMSL-based narratives, print-based texts, and other semiotic elements as part of this study (e.g., government posters, slides from PowerPoint presentations, video-screen captures, photographs of sign models) is, as contemporary translation theorists argue, a "domesticating process" (Venuti, 2000, p. 468). Accordingly, all of the "texts" under consideration in this book are "always reconstructed according to a different set of values and always variable according to different languages and cultures" (ibid., p. 470)—namely, my own. Venuti's argument for an "ethics of location"

---

27. Leading in a northeast direction out of the city toward the Hà Nội Highway, the traffic circle depicted in figure 3 forms a nearly complete ring of foreign-language schools (*trường ngoại ngữ*). Other such schools proliferate throughout the city and countryside. The two schools on the left offer Eastern European languages, while the one on the right offers five varieties of English (British, American, Australian, Canadian, and Singaporean).

Figure 3. Foreign-language schools, HCMC.

in translation work connected to "subordinate cultures" is useful to this study in that it recommends an ethnographic as well as a translation-oriented recognition of power differentials permeating both the sites of textual production, the texts, and the translations of texts (Venuti, 1998, p. 186; see also "translational attitude" in Tagore, 2006, p. 81).

An *ethics of location* is also useful in theorizing connections between the state, HCMSL, and perceptions of Deaf people's uses of the body, in that it assumes no singular or fixed state formation but rather a state only partially "visible" according to the ways interactants communicate in specific settings and the embodied circumstances of their production. Accordingly, we may theorize about the ways that particular languages and their related embodiment practices contribute to the creation and the qualitative feeling of sites through linguistic practice, such as the destabilization of spoken languages as normative languages when HCMSL is in use. In this book I "translate" interview narratives, print-based texts, and embodied practices.

Regarding the presentation of language texts, in sign language linguistics there is no conventional way to represent signed utterances and signed languages because they have no written form. To the extent possible, I present both selected narratives and texts in the language in which they were originally produced, as well as translations into English and/or Vietnamese. All translations are my own, unless otherwise indicated. Concepts in HCMSL are provided via HCMSL sign models (appearing throughout the book).

For purposes of scholarship in written languages, concepts may be glossed using terms from an associated written language. For example, the concept "mother," which takes a distinct form as a sign in ASL, might be represented as MOTHER. However, this practice is not unproblematic. If the gloss is given using the words of the target language but the grammar of the source language, it may appear to the naïve reader that the source language is ungrammatical. In context of the worldwide dearth of information about signed languages and sign language linguistics, this practice is vulnerable to reinforcing misconceptions about signed languages. Therefore, I do not gloss HCMSL utterances; rather, I translate them.

There is also no conventional way to select and/or describe embodied practices. However, a number of methods are useful for transcribing body features and body movements, such as Laban notation, which is widely used by dance ethnologists. According to the terms of informed consent and to allow myself to be fully engaged in participant observation activities, I did not videotape many HCMSL-based events. I did, however, videotape interviews and the HCMSL-Vietnamese interpretation workshop (which was a public venue), and examined these extensively for interaction-based practices. Nonetheless, for this study I did not conduct a systematic examination of interactants' body gestures, postures, or movement patterns. Instead, to examine the ways that HCMSL and other uses of the body were approached (e.g., disciplined, regulated, evaluated positively and negatively)—I applied a "wide-angle lens" to instances of signing, speaking, pointing, eye gaze, and other socialization practices involving the body (e.g., tapping a person's shoulder to get that person's attention), as well as the coordination of sociolinguistic repertoires between interactants or those reported by research participants.[28]

Structure of the Book

In chapter 1, I explore connections between state educational initiatives and language ideologies in Việt Nam to show how the historical evaluation of Deaf people's perceived abilities (or lack thereof) (1) conditioned the criteria for participation in state institutions, (2) contributed to discourses on differential abilities to privilege hearing-speaking persons, and (3) facilitated the disciplining of HCMSL-based sociolinguistic practices (and other uses of the body) both in and beyond institutions of the development- and modernization-oriented state. This exploration begins with anticolonial and socialist projects of collective capacity building, in which language claims were elevated alongside claims to national solidarity and sovereignty. I then consider how political and economic decisions initiated in the anticolonial period relate to and were transformed under đổi mới political and economic reform. The historical examination I undertake in this chapter is developed chiefly in relation to institutions of education and discourses on language and the body. While touching on events in Việt Nam's earlier history, the chapter concentrates on events from 1986 to the present, allowing

---

28. Future research would benefit from a close examination of Vietnamese people's linguistic and embodiment practices and of the relationships between such practices and those of non-Deaf people (both nonsigners and signers) in particular settings.

me to trace key ways that state-structured institutions and ideologies contributed to the categorization of Vietnamese citizens as exemplars or problems.

Chapter 2 examines the emergence of the *state idea* and how it has been approached within the social and political science literatures: The state idea was initially taken up but later abandoned for its supposed lack of material substance. In recent decades the state idea has been reinvigorated by new analytic frameworks connected to language, human experience, ideology and power as bases for ethnographic description of states centering on human agents and forms of social, political, and economic action (i.e., as already steeped in ideological universes, embodied preferences, and specific mandates related to social-hierarchical positioning and reproduction in Việt Nam).

Chapter 3 opens with a description of the Vietnamese state system to discuss the contemporary *statification*, or state-led phase of market-socialist transformation, and its effects on educational and social restructuring. I examine stratification in connection to the privatization of education costs (referred to as *xã hội hoá*, or socialization in Việt Nam). I then introduce Blommaert's (2005) framework for characterizing state processes and—drawing on Kleinman's (1988) and Leap's (2011) formulations of *retrospective narratization*—I explore Deaf research participant narratives of signed-language regulation within speech-based special school settings and teacher responses. The rest of the chapter then introduces the three primary research settings: (1) five Deaf education special school sites in or near HCMC; (2) the Education Project, which is the only location in southern Việt Nam where Deaf students can pursue secondary and college/university education; (3) the Hồ Chí Minh City Deaf Club (HDC). Also included are the results from my survey of the five special schools presented in three tables containing student and teacher censuses, as well as language instruction in the five locations. Closing the chapter is a discussion of relationships between geopolitical, economic, and disability-related transformations that facilitate the emergence of new social categories and regulatory mechanisms.

Discussion of *active citizenship* opens chapter 4 to examine southern Deaf students' educational aspirations, barriers to education, and educational marginalization in speech-based educational settings as a foundation for peer-learning strategies in educational settings and for coordination of social organizing strategies. After describing the ideological logics confronting Deaf people in southern Việt Nam in the contemporary period, I present three vignettes that highlight the circumstances of language use, ideology, and social critique in detail for three representative ethnographic moments: a civics lesson at the Hope C Special School; a world history lesson in the Education Project; and two meetings of the Hồ Chí Minh City Deaf Club that focused on promoting Deaf women's social leadership. The chapter closes with a discussion of multilingualism and the role that institutionalization plays in reproducing forms of fluency and dysfluency.

Chapter 5 focuses squarely on international development aid and the international development apparatus, which has, over the last two decades, taken disability as one of its primary development interests. The chapter opens with a discussion of the transition to market-socialism, which, in the early 1980s, the state saw as comprehensive approach for confronting issues of post-reunification poverty, economic underperformance, and an increasingly clear picture of the extent of post-war disabilities.

Examining a 2013 USAID disability assessment report on Việt Nam, I show how the report's methodological and analytic errors influenced a multimillion-dollar bilateral partnership between the United States and Việt Nam. In doing so, these errors not only mischaracterized Deaf social organizing, VSL-Vietnamese interpreting, and disability "needs" but also failed to take into account the actual interests of Deaf social organizing initiatives already under way. Using original ethnographic data, I examine the perceptions of national and INGO disability-oriented development from the perspective of both a journalist assigned to cover disability concerns and fifteen Deaf social organizers. The chapter also examines outputs from national and international development work—sign language vocabulary books—to argue that the latter are not representative of the languages Deaf people actually use in Việt Nam (as they are comprised of single words but no grammatical information on VSLs as complete symbolic systems).

Histories and Political Economies of Language and Literacy   1

THE FOCUS OF THIS BOOK is the ethnographic examination of relationships between language policies, practices, and sociopolitical formation connected to sites of Deaf education and Deaf community organizing in and around Hồ Chí Minh City. As highlighted in the introduction, in order to understand people's actions in the historical present we must first attend to the historical past and people's differing experiences and perceptions of the events that comprise diverse histories. Hồ Chí Minh City and its environs are situated in a particularly rich region for this kind of study. Deaf education has a historically deep presence in the area. A high concentration of Deaf people,[1] Deaf education special school sites, and a growing number of Deaf community organizing groups are found in this region.

French colonial missionaries established formal Deaf education just 10 miles north of HCMC in 1886. In the mid-1980s, after the French and American-Vietnamese wars had ended and the country had reunified, HCMC was one of the first places where Deaf education special schools began sprouting up. The city is also home to one of Việt Nam's two major special education teacher-training departments, as well a number of community-based and international organizations working in the area of disability-related development. Representing differing sociolinguistic viewpoints and methodologies of social change, these diverse actors participate in community and institutional networks, prompting and responding to national debates on the educational, sociocultural, economic, and national benefits and disadvantages perceived to be associated with signed and spoken languages.

Whereas Deaf education language debates had been dominated for decades by proponents of spoken Vietnamese, since the early 2010s, public and official forms of support for Vietnamese signed languages have swelled.[2] Superficially resembling other

---

1. Hồ Chí Minh City is the largest municipality in Việt Nam (more than 7 million; 92 million total population for the country in 2014). National population figures for hearing disability range between 1 million (GSO, 2009) and 2.5 million persons (GSO, 2006) for the whole country. Although these figures are not broken down by city, 3% of Deaf and hard of hearing persons live in the southern region (approximately 75,000 persons) (GSO, 2006). This would be approximately 30,000 Deaf or hard of hearing persons (GSO, 2009).

2. Woodward's (2003) analysis argues that three distinct signed language varieties are in use in Việt Nam. They correspond to the areas in and around the northern cities of Hà Nội and Hải Phòng and the southern city of Hồ Chí Minh. As this research was based on interviews with persons participating in Deaf clubs in urban centers, it does not represent the full scope of signed language variety in the country. Therefore, further descriptive and corpus-based research on signed language varieties in Việt Nam is warranted.

global Deaf[3] sociopolitical contexts (Branson & Miller, 2002; Jankowski, 1997; Reagan, 2007, 2010; Reilly & Reilly, 2005), in Việt Nam, signed language debates emerged and continue to evolve under unique historical, social, and geopolitical circumstances.

China's millennium-long colonization of Việt Nam—and repeated incursions by the Chinese, French, Japanese, and other groups—coalesced in the early 20th century in mass movements for national independence and cultural survival that shaped, and continue to shape, demands for citizenship participation involving language and other uses of the body. After decades of war and state socialist-led rebuilding, political economic reforms initiated in the 1980s and 1990s established a market-socialist approach that showed early and steady movement toward economic rebound, particularly via development and modernization projects. In the more politically relaxed environment of the early 2000s, community membership groups and NGOs appeared in greater numbers to address social concerns not sufficiently addressed by the state. Among these, advocacy efforts placed the devastating human and environmental effects of unexploded ordnance and dioxin contamination resulting from U.S. military intervention into the national and international spotlight to bring attention to disability, often discursively representing it as a misfortune and a geopolitical effect.

Forms of Deaf social action examined in this study are connected to forces of signed language inclusion and exclusion, as well as formation and enlistment of subjectivities related to such forces (hearing impairment, Deaf). Confronting (negative) notions of HCMSL and disability, as well as notions of Deaf people's susceptibility to foreign encroachment, Deaf community organizers (re)frame VSLs as national assets and as rich expressions of Vietnamese heritage. These are exemplified in Deaf narratives of their own national and ethnocultural minority subjectivity as Việt Nam's "55th cultural group."[4] Such sociopolitical and cultural framings of VSLs and Vietnamese Deaf culture reflect and respond to historically deep struggles for national independence and sovereignty that facilitated the promotion of ideal languages and ideal forms of physical fortitude by social institutions. Sociopolitical and cultural framings of VSLs and Vietnamese Deaf culture also influence contemporary encounters with state agents, as well as national and international experts, particularly those connected to Deaf education and disability initiatives.

---

3. Note on terminology: In U.S.-based Deaf Studies and sign language linguistic circles D/d has been used to distinguish between cultural-linguistic and audiological identifications. Recently, social contestation over the D/d device has spurred research into the ways everyday people and expert discourses invoke D/d (and d/D) (Brueggemann, 2009; Kermit, 2009; Kusters et al., 2017; Senghas & Monaghan, 2002; Willard, 2007). In this study I do not distinguish Deaf persons according to D/d or d/D regimes because the latter were not ethnographically attested in the 2007–2014 period. Rather, research participants stated emphatically that they preferred uppercase "Deaf" in a marker of both signed language usage and Vietnamese Deaf cultural group membership.

4. One example of this narrative of the 55th ethnocultural group is instantiated in the 2015 video project *Nghe Bằng Mắt* [Listening by eye]. This narrative appears at two minutes and eight seconds into the video (2:08) and closes at the 2:30 mark. See the video at https://www.youtube.com/watch?v=8vaJz8zEvYg

In this chapter I place Deaf educational continuity and change in the context of broader Vietnamese language and literacy movements and state reform of mass education. Intertwined with ongoing state formation and political-economic agendas, language and literacy have long been paramount national concerns and key mechanisms in national development and modernization. Describing major historical forces involved in shaping relationships between language policy and education structuring in Việt Nam, I focus on events that propel the (trans)formation of language ideologies primarily affecting the structuring and conduct of Deaf education. It is not my intention to present a definitive history of language and literacy in Việt Nam. Rather, I relate the ways in which histories of language management for mass education and for Deaf education special schools plausibly relate to one another and to wider national and geopolitical goals.

Introduction to the Ethnographic Sites, Languages, and Language Politics

This book's concern with language policies, ideologies, and practices stems from my observation of the ways in which Deaf and hearing people interacted at sites of Deaf education and Deaf community organizing. It also derives from the affordances of signers and speakers associated with the two language codes (cultural, educational, economic, social, national).

During my fieldwork I engaged seven sites: six formal educational institutions (five special schools and the Education Project) and one community-based membership organization, the Hồ Chí Minh City Deaf Club. Two of these sites, the EP and one special school, are located in Biên Hòa, the largest provincial city in Việt Nam (1 million population circa 2012), which is surrounded by Đồng Nai province's extensive industrial production and export-processing zones. Of the five remaining sites, three special schools and the HDC are located in HCMC, and one special school is located just outside the city limits. Hồ Chí Minh City is the largest city in Việt Nam (12 million/92 million total population circa 2014) and Việt Nam's center of trade and commerce. Biên Hòa and HCMC are located about 20 miles apart, or around one hour and fifteen minutes by motorbike in light traffic.

Throughout the book I sometimes describe the special schools as an aggregate. My rationale for doing so follows from: (1) correspondences between teacher training (and lack thereof); (2) correspondences in classroom communication practices; (3) significant differences in the communication practices documented for special schools in comparison to the EP and the HDC; and, most remarkably, (4) Deaf research participants' comments about features they contended were typical of the Deaf education schools generally—schools that they had attended or visited and/or that other Deaf community members and social organizing colleagues had described. The special schools are also connected by a shared set of state mandates and international instruments.[5] All of the special schools sites at which I conducted research are housed in stand-alone buildings and marked with signage indicating that they are schools for

---

5. State mandates include the following: the 1998 Law on Disabled Persons (no. 06/1998/PL-UBTVQH10); the 2004 Law on Child Protection, Care, and Education (no. 25/2004/QH11); the 2005 Law on Education (no. 38/2005/QH11); and the 2010 Law on Persons with Disability (no. 51/2010/QH12). International instruments include a number of UN conventions (particularly those related to Education for All and special needs education) and, prominently, Việt Nam's 2015 ratification of the UN Convention on the Rights of Persons with Disabilities.

"children with hearing impairment" (trẻ khiếm thính) or "children with disability" (trẻ khuyết tật). Nevertheless, these schools have several distinctions that I encourage readers to keep in mind.

Four of the five schools offered both primary-level programming (cấp 1, grades 1–5) and lower-secondary education (cấp 2, grades 6–9), and one school offered preschool and primary education. The students I interacted with in grades 5 through 9 were between 18 and 25 years of age; these students often shared classrooms with younger classmates, who were sometimes 12 years of age and older. All five sites operated according to a monolingual norm, using spoken and written/printed Vietnamese for instruction, although I also observed signing in Vietnamese word order in these schools (typically used by school personnel), as well as HCMSL (typically used by older students); however, the ways these norms were socially organized and enforced differed from school to school and indeed from classroom to classroom. For example, the principals of two schools spoke and signed in Vietnamese word order, and endorsed this way of communicating for instruction in the upper-grade levels but not the lower.

Other features are also significant: two schools are located in a peri-urban setting, while the other three are located in major districts of Hồ Chí Minh City; the tuition of two schools was fully "socialized" (with families paying the cost of education; see chapters 2 and 3 for further discussion of this term), while the other three were state subsidized. All five schools provided primary-level instruction, while four offered lower-secondary instruction. The administrators of one school explicitly opposed the use of HCMSL or signing in Vietnamese word order for instruction. School size and student/teacher ratios varied considerably (see chapter 3 tables and description). Extended ethnographic research is certainly warranted in each of the special schools to provide a more nuanced accounting of organizational and sociolinguistic features.

During the research period the EP, which is located on the grounds of a teacher training university, offered three kinds of educational programming: lower- and upper-secondary (cấp 2, grades 6–9, and cấp 3, grades 10–12); one college-degree track (primary education teacher training); and certificate training in HCMSL instruction.[6] The EP students were adult learners (at least 18 years old) who lived in the student dormitory during their studies. Living at a distance from their family homes, spouses, and children, many students made family visits only during extended holidays, such as Tết, lunar New Year celebrations, and summer breaks. Those students whose first language was a Vietnamese sign language other than HCMSL—such as Hà Nội Sign Language—also learned HCMSL in order to participate in educational programming.

Unlike the special schools and the EP, the HDC—founded and initially exclusively run by EP students and graduates—did not possess a formal rental contract, and it was not provided space by the government. However, it did have a dedicated space for Deaf community organizing that had been arranged by the director of the government-run inclusive-education center for children with disabilities, with whom the HDC had long-standing social and educational ties. This director permitted the HDC's founders to have ongoing use of the ground floor of the inclusive education facility on one

---

6. As of 2013 the EP has also provided formal classes in HCMSL-Vietnamese interpretation to staff members and, in 2015, opened these classes to local aspiring interpreters.

weekend day and for special events. At the time of this writing, the HDC still meets at this center—which is located in a small, fenced-in compound consisting of one main building with three floors and an adjoining two-story building with offices and rooms for audiological testing, speech therapy, and educational services. Between these two buildings is a small courtyard with a few benches, children's playground equipment, and toys. Inside the main building, HDC activities are held on the ground floor in a large conference room with rows of wooden chairs accommodating approximately 100 people and in a small meeting room accommodating 6–8 people. Parking space for attendees' motorbikes is provided at the front and to one side of the building. Members of the HDC also use the courtyard for small-group work sessions and to socialize during meeting breaks or special events.

Both the EP and the HDC are multilingual settings. HCMSL is the language of instruction and interpersonal interaction, along with written/printed Vietnamese. English is also used in both settings. Programming at the EP includes English because it is required by the national curriculum. The EP and the HDC also use English to facilitate interactions with visitors from countries that use English (as a written language) or fingerspelling of English names and proper nouns.[7] Hence, English was not a primary code for either setting; rather, when in language-contact situations, some EP and HDC members wrote or fingerspelled English words in order to clarify a specific concept. Signs from other signed languages were deployed in a similar fashion, such as when HDC members used signs from Japanese Sign Language during a 2009 visit from a delegation from Japan.

The way I have just described the research sites puts this analysis at risk of positioning Deaf education special schools in an extreme dichotomous relationship to the EP and the HDC with respect to language ideologies, language usage, institutional practices, and Deaf social action. However, as ethnographic description throughout this book shows, in everyday practice, distinctions between the research settings, their differing institutional or organizational mandates, and language practices and attitudes, were not so clearly drawn.

During my fieldwork and postdoctoral research, my most extensive contact was with EP students and graduates. These individuals are the first generation of students to attend Deaf education special schools in southern Việt Nam, and their activities placed HCMSL at the center of educational and social aspirations and critique. Over time, the relationships I formed with this constituency of Deaf people gave me an appreciation for the conditions placed on their linguistic participation in institutional and community settings and for related social-change interests. Outside of formal research activities (participant observation, interviews, and surveys), joining this group in a wide variety of activities presented naturalistic opportunities to observe negotiations of language code and social identities in both Deaf-Deaf and Deaf-hearing interactions. These included everyday activities, such as sharing meals, shopping, and socializing in family homes

---

7. During the research period, I observed only one-handed fingerspelling systems used to spell English names and proper nouns. That is, I did not observe Vietnamese Deaf People using two-handed fingerspelling systems, such as those corresponding to British Sign Language or Auslan.

and public spaces, and formal activities such as HCMSL classes conducted for hearing people in Biên Hòa and HCMC, disability-related events, collaborations on workshop presentations, and Deaf community *giao lưu* [cultural exchange events].

As a hearing person who signs, my use of HCMSL and Deaf people's preferential terms of identity reference—DIÉC [Deaf]—often drew comments from both Deaf and hearing/nonsigning people, providing additional sources of insight into dominant-language practices and ideologies. These comments also directly or indirectly referenced other features of my perceived identity—Russian or French heritage (never North American), professional, white, female, and possibly most saliently, non-Việt—belying the naturalistic status of the settings I participated in as well as the contingent nature of my entry into and presence in these settings. In chapter 6 I discuss issues related to my own researcher positionality in connection to postcolonial research and ethical issues involved in transnational Deaf and signed language–related academic and international development work.

The second group with which I had the most contact was current and former Deaf education special school principals and teachers. My interactions with these people took four forms: participant observation at special school sites, formal interviews, interaction at HDC-hosted and other local organizational events, and through email. My introduction to special school personnel was facilitated by my HCMSL teachers, who, in inviting me to attend their HCMSL classes at an organization established by and for people with disabilities, initiated a series of introductions with organizational staff and, later, participation in a conference given by that organization in December 2008, through which I met Deaf education special school principals. Collaborating with the EP and the HDC to host an HCMSL-Vietnamese interpretation workshop for special school personnel in February 2009 facilitated further interactions with special school personnel during both the workshop and school visits, participant observation, and formal interviews. Making multiple trips to Việt Nam to work as an international trainer on an early childhood education project facilitated introduction to a wider range of national special education officials, teacher training faculty, and special school personnel.

Tracing Language and Literacy in Contemporary Vietnamese Deaf Education

When I began preliminary fieldwork in 2007, special schools for students labeled as hearing impaired were well established in and around HCMC, guided by the Vietnamese state's reform strategy for education-led economic development and modernization. In stark contrast to regular education schools, educational outcomes for special schools throughout the country were generally poor (GSO, 2006; NCCD, 2010). The 2009 census data further reported that the national enrollment rate for children ages 6–10 attending regular education schools was 97%, in contrast to 66.5% for all children with disabilities in the same age bracket (GSO, 2009). According to figures from Việt Nam's General Statistics Office (2009), approximately 400,000 Deaf children are of school age. At present no studies have tracked the number of Deaf children not enrolled in school in Việt Nam. Extrapolating from the enrollment disparities reported for regular education versus special education in general, the number of Deaf children not attending school is clearly substantial. Focusing on the circumstances encountered by Deaf people within Deaf education special school settings, school principals and teachers in the five schools where I conducted fieldwork reported that students typically took two or more calendar years to complete one curricular year of study and that many students did not complete primary education or achieve basic literacy (see also Woodward, Nguyen, & Nguyen, 2004; Woodward & Nguyễn, 2012).

Special school personnel commonly explained these circumstances by describing deficits they associated with deafness: The phrase *người Điếc ngược* [lit., person + Deaf + opposite/reverse (of "normal")] appeared at the research sites as both a characterization and an explanation of students' ways of thinking, their spoken and written Vietnamese grammar, and the grammar of their signing. According to school personnel, their expectation was that students should speak, or strive to speak, Vietnamese. If students signed, school personnel expected them to do so in a way that corresponded to Vietnamese word order. School personnel consistently gave two explanations for poor literacy. Frequently asserting their belief in the intelligence of Deaf students, school personnel reasoned that students lacked *ý chí* [will power] or were lazy. They insisted that students could learn to speak Vietnamese if they applied themselves to practicing lip-reading and speaking.

School personnel also faulted their own lack of effectiveness in teaching students to speak Vietnamese. Most school personnel (four of five school principals, current and former teachers) remarked on their failure to devise effective teaching methods. They further described this failure as a result of government inattention to Deaf education, especially the lack of specialized training opportunities. Their explanations thus connected government inaction to a lack of professional training and students' inability to speak Vietnamese. To be clear, staff members also commented on students' difficulties completing one year of the national curriculum within the expected time frame, but their remarks more typically emphasized "overcoming difficulties of being deaf" and learning to speak. Narratives of overcoming were pervasive. Moreover, school personnel connected students' efforts and struggles to their own in ways that extended beyond the classroom and the school to include the broader postcolonial, postwar reconstructive, and future-oriented modernizing moment.

As noted in the introduction, narratives of overcoming have a powerful presence in contemporary Việt Nam and are also reflected in the ways that Deaf groups and organizations of persons with disabilities invoke, comment on, and reformulate "overcoming" as a social mode that centers on their own social action. In mainstream usage, disability would be something to overcome. As invoked by Deaf organizers and disability-oriented organizing, it is social attitudes regarding Deaf people and VSLs, as well as disability broadly, that must be overcome in order for national, social, and economic development goals to be pursued.

In the latter part of the first decade of this century, Deaf education special school personnel also stated that changes in social attitudes were necessary and important; however, their narratives suggested a narrow, if not singular, pathway to broad social attitudinal change: If deafness could not be cured or remediated, then Deaf students must be socialized to perform in a manner consistent with the ways that hearing/speaking Vietnamese people behave.

Despite poor educational outcomes and reports of unsatisfactory communication with students, school personnel asserted the importance of Deaf students attending school and of schools using a speech-based approach, particularly in the first years of school. Spoken Vietnamese, they reasoned, was necessary for Deaf people's human development and especially for inclusion in society. In addition to whatever personal viewpoints special school personnel may have had about the necessity of spoken Vietnamese for social participation, "inclusion in society" also draws directly on educational policy rhetoric connected with the inclusive education movement in Việt Nam.

Worldwide, the inclusive education movement gained momentum in the early 1990s following the undertaking of key international initiatives and statements, including the 1987 UN Convention on the Rights of the Child, the 1990 Jomtien World Declaration on Education for All, the 1993 UN Standard Rules on the Equalization of Opportunities for Persons with Disabilities, the 1994 World Conference on Special Needs Education in Salamanca, Spain, and the Convention on the Rights of Persons with Disabilities (which Việt Nam signed in 2007 and ratified in 2015). In Việt Nam, the Ministry of Education and Training began implementing IE (*giáo dục hòa nhập*, or commonly, *hòa nhập*) in the mid-1990s, primarily via the placement of students with disabilities and Deaf students into regular education schools.

As a set of state initiatives, Việt Nam's implementation of IE did not simply reflect state ratification of international instruments but also drew substantial guidance from core national and legal documents, beginning with the 1992 Vietnamese national constitution (and, later, its successor documents, the 2001 and 2013 amendments), as well as a number of national education and disability-related laws and initiatives. All of these laws, including those pertaining to education and disability draw guidance from the national constitution. In her 2012 reference guide, *Giáo Dục Đặc Biệt Và Những Thuật Ngữ Cơ Bản* [Special Education and Terminology], Dr. Nguyễn Thị Hoàng Yến, Deputy Director of the National Institute of Educational Science (Phó, Viện trưởng Viện Khoa học Giáo dục Việt Nam), foregrounded the importance of the national constitution in securing the rights to education of people with disabilities by making *Vị trí của để người khuyết tật trong hệ thống pháp luật* [the position of people with disabilities in the legal system] the very first section of the book. There she argued the following:[8]

> Một khi vấn về người khuyết tật được đề đến trong hiến pháp có thể hiểu rằng đây là vấn đề cần được chú trọng trong hệ thống luật pháp quốc gia và đòi hỏi *luật pháp cũng như các chính sách kách phảituân thủ các quy định của hiến pháp.*
>
> Once people with disabilities have been mentioned in the constitution, it is understood that the national legal system and laws as well as other policies must comply with the provisions of the constitution. (ibid., pp. 24–25)

In addition to the national constitution, a number of other laws pertaining to education and disability also help shape Deaf education (e.g., the 1998 Law on Education and

---

8. Nguyễn T. H. Y. (2012) provided the English translation herself, as a *sách song ngữ* [bilingual book] in Vietnamese and English.

the 2005 amendment; the 1998 Ordinance on Disabled Persons [no. 06/1998/PL-UBTVQH10], which was followed by the comprehensive 2010 Law on Disabled Persons [notably, the first law to recognize the right to use sign language in education]; the 2001 National Program of Action for Children [no. 23/2001/QD-TTg], which universalized basic secondary education by 2010; and the 2006 Decree no. 01/2006/CT-TTg [On Accelerating the Implementation of New Policies to Assist Disabled People's Economic and Social Development]). However, IE was elevated to an official policy objective with the 2006 passage of Decision no. 23/2006/QD-BGD-DT, Ban Hành Quy Định Về Giáo Dục Hoà Nhập Dành Cho Người Tàn Tật, Khuyết Tật [Regulation on Inclusive Education for Handicapped and Disabled Persons].

Much like their international counterparts,[9] these laws and instruments do not spell out the specific terms, methods, or means by which students are expected to become "integrated" or "included"; they also do not stipulate considerations such as teacher-to-student ratio, teacher language proficiency, or instructional methods. Lê argues that in Việt Nam, as in other world locations, there is "confusion" about the differences between mainstreaming, where students are placed in and expected to adapt to regular education environments, and inclusion, where educational settings and materials are adapted to students (2013, p. 8).

Reilly and Nguyễn's evaluation of IE in six provinces in Việt Nam highlighted the widespread conflation of inclusion with mainstreaming in the nation. They reported that 29,382 "deaf and hearing impaired" students were "placed in classrooms where spoken Vietnamese was the medium of instruction" (2004, p. 25); however, of these students, only one child "shared an effective communication channel with another person" (ibid., p. 7; see also NCCD, 2010). A conference paper given by Lê Văn Tạc, professor and director of Special Education Research at the National Institute of Educational Science (NIES), also reported inadequate placements in the early phase of IE. Lê stated that children with disabilities were "lumped together with other vulnerable children, e.g., 'poor and dirty,' and over-aged children in so-called 'compassion classes'" (2000). A more recent study (Nguyễn T. K. A. & Võ, 2010) finds that "hearing impaired" students in HCMC-based IE settings continue to encounter inadequate learning environments, which lead to educational underachievement and improper assessment; negative attitudes and low educational expectations from teachers; and negative attitudes from *trẻ bình thường* [normal children].

In contrast to Reilly and Nguyễn's (2004) findings, Lê Văn Tạc described the overwhelming benefit of IE for one Deaf student, "Dien," who reportedly thrived because "the teacher was teaching by combining spoken language with fingerspelling and natural signs" (2000). Recent studies of children in IE settings indicate widespread and persistent problems with respect to educational facilities, teacher training, and attitudes demonstrated by teachers and students without disabilities toward those considered

---

9. Precedent-setting national policies on disability include the following: Japan (1970 Fundamental Law for Persons with Disabilities, amended in 2004); the United States (1975 Education for All Handicapped Children Act, PL 94-142; 1990 Individuals with Disabilities Education Act), the United Kingdom (1978 Warnock Report; 1995 Disability Discrimination Act; 1996 Education Act), and China (1990 Law on the Protection of Disabled Persons).

to have disabilities. According to Kham's (2013) analysis of 230 questionnaires and 36 interviews in IE school settings, children with disabilities encounter a number of difficulties at school. To counter these, they "mostly 'do-by-themselves' or try to adapt themselves rather than asking for supports" (p. 103; see also the section beginning on p. 112, *Dealing with difficulties: Voices of CWD;* see also Lê, 2013 and NCCD, 2010).

In addition to whatever programmatic or pedagogical confusion there may have been (and may remain) surrounding IE, a number of other factors facilitated the proliferation of IE in Việt Nam. Notably, these were economic and human capital demands of post–American War reconstruction and a growing accounting of the extent of medical conditions resulting from the U.S. military's use of dioxin that widely contaminated food and water sources. In the context of the pressing circumstances confronted in the immediate postwar period, the Vietnamese state nevertheless managed to prioritize education—in general and in specifically addressing groups previously excluded from education—efforts that have been widely noted throughout the social scientific literatures.

By bringing ethnographic evidence from Deaf education and Deaf social organizing to bear on considerations of educational and social inclusion, this book argues against simple explanations of confusion or economic cost as the determinants of educational structuring and instead illuminates the role that language ideological forces play in the structuring and administration of (special) education. For example, IE policy in Việt Nam allows Deaf education special schools to transfer students to regular education settings, where students find opportunities for higher education and training in specialized fields (e.g., computer technology). However, in order to transfer, students must demonstrate proficiency in spoken Vietnamese. Thus IE policy creates demands on special schools to make students *mainstreaming ready,* able to adapt to the linguistic demands of instruction in spoken Vietnamese (not the other way around). Although these circumstances could be explained in part by Lê (2013) and Reilly and Nguyễn (2004), we must ask why higher education and specialized training opportunities are not available in Deaf education special schools. Allocation of higher educational resources (and so forth) is thus linguistically mediated to include users of spoken Vietnamese and exclude users of VSLs.

Ethnographic examination of these circumstances demonstrates the ways in which linguistic forces shape educational structuring to rationalize and reproduce normative forms of social participation. They also raise a number of questions, especially with respect to the historically deep presence of sign language-based education in Việt Nam: What historical circumstances contributed to the elevation of spoken Vietnamese in contemporary Deaf education? What significance does sign language hold for state agents (educational leaders, school personnel), Deaf students, and Deaf community organizers, especially with respect to national development goals? And what forces facilitate institutionalized notions of Deaf students/persons as a subject category?

To gain insight into these questions I interviewed Ms. Lang,[10] who was, until her retirement in 2011, the director of an inclusive education center in HCMC with more

---

10. All names are pseudonyms, most selected by the research participants themselves. In this case, "Ms. Lang" opted not to create a pseudonym, so I created one for her.

than twenty years of experience in special school administration, training, and evaluation. Ms. Lang described MOET's approach to sign language this way:

> As you know, when there is some new idea, it is often very popular—and nowadays, the people know about sign language. But MOET thinks that it is not the right way for Việt Nam to use sign language. For example, MOET, they have some books about sign language. But it is very difficult to study that. How can people learn sign from the book? . . . And it is just pictures of hands. Just vocabulary. No grammar. So the people who see this book think that sign language is very simple. And it is not.

In her comment, Ms. Lang frames sign language as the site of struggle between two forces engaged in determining "the right way for Việt Nam"—one "popular" and the other, state directed. She also attributes a prominent role to MOET leaders in shaping the perception and distribution of ideas about VSLs. It is worth noting here the significance of Ms. Lang's sharing these ideas with me—a foreign researcher with a professed interest in and an endorsement of signed language as the basis of multilingual Deaf education. Ms. Lang declined to sign informed consent documents because of her concern that MOET officials might obtain evidence of her participation in my research. However, she allowed me to audiotape the interview and said that she was eager to talk with me because "it is important that people talk about what is really happening in the schools and the better way to teach hearing-impaired students." Ms. Lang expressed strong interest in my research project and the hope that it would bring greater attention to education pedagogy for those with a hearing impairment and particularly to the role of signed language in that education.

If we assume that MOET produced sign language books in good faith—and there is every indication that it did—then we have to look for further evidence that helps explain educational structuring and language-related programming. "[L]anguage ideologies represent the perception of language and discourse that is constructed in the interest of a specific social or cultural group. A member's notions of what is 'true,' 'morally good,' or 'aesthetically pleasing' about language and discourse are grounded in social experience and often demonstrably tied to his or her political-economic interests" (Kroskrity, 2000, p. 8).[11] As Ms. Lang described it, the MOET's decisions in the latter part of the first decade of the twenty-first century contributed to Deaf education conditions that limited student educational and social participation—despite highly visible MOET activities to the contrary (e.g., sign language books, social policy). MOET's book production manifested educational leaders' perceptions of sign language as simple, according to Ms. Lang, by representing symbols from VSLs as individual signs without grammar (see chapter 5 for further discussion of these books). The MOET produced

---

11. Kroskrity describes three additional features of language ideologies: (1) Members possess multiple ideologies relative to "the multiplicity of meaningful social divisions (class, gender, clan, elites, generations, and so on) within sociocultural groups that have the potential to produce divergent perspectives expressed as indices of group membership (ibid., p. 12); (2) Members may display varying degrees of awareness of local language ideologies (ibid., p. 18); (3) Members' language ideologies mediate between social structures and forms of talk (ibid., p. 21).

three such books[12] and distributed them primarily to special schools and special education training faculties, thereby concentrating the (mis)characterization of VSLs and Deaf people in the very sites empowered by the state to teach Deaf students. From another perspective, the state concentrated its limited resources in the places deemed by educational leaders to be the most necessary and beneficial. These two perspectives (ideological orientations) are held in productive tension in research participant commentaries, policy, and community organizing action throughout the book.

Returning to the notion of popular and state-directed forces, the distinction Ms. Lang made between these two forces aligned with what I was seeing at my fieldwork sites and during community participation, particularly with respect to the ways that hearing/nonsigning state-institutional and community-organizational agents attempted to structure Deaf people's linguistic practices. For instance, in the five special school sites, school personnel directed Deaf students to speak Vietnamese and, depending on the school and the teacher, discouraged or prohibited signing in classroom activities. While speaking Vietnamese to students, a number of teachers also used some signs in sign-supported speech. *Sign-supported speech* typically involves communication conducted primarily in a spoken language and accompanied by signs. In the five special schools, I witnessed school personnel using sign-supported speech, which they tended to initiate after failed attempts at communicating with students in spoken and written Vietnamese. These methods varied considerably, however, from a few teachers who spoke Vietnamese and signed at the same time fairly consistently (using signs they perceived to be related to the spoken words), to those teachers (most) who occasionally used a few signs. Both practices privilege spoken Vietnamese and force signed language symbols into spoken language grammatical order.

Of approximately twenty-five special school personnel that I observed interacting with students at the five sites, only two school principals and five teachers signed with students on a regular basis. Moreover, these practices typically occurred outside the classroom setting and consisted of speaking in Vietnamese while signing in Vietnamese word order. Signing was thus present at these sites, but not HCMSL, and the signing that was used did not obtain legitimacy or authority as the language of education. School personnel also routinely criticized students' ways of signing (HCMSL or otherwise) as ungrammatical.

By contrast, in settings such as organizations run by and for people with disabilities (Disabled Persons' Organizations, or DPOs) and craft centers, Deaf people used HCMSL during meetings and work activities. Since few hearing people knew how to sign and activities were conducted in spoken Vietnamese without HCMSL-Vietnamese interpretation, Deaf people's input into activities was limited—but not absent—as they conferred with each other to decipher meeting content and used a combination of HCMSL, gesture, and written Vietnamese to communicate their ideas when presenting

---

12. These books were produced through a partnership between MOET, Pearl S. Buck International, and USAID. The books contain basic vocabulary in Hà Nội Sign Language, Hải Phòng Sign Language, HCMSL, and what MOET and partners called "common signs." Each page covers a single concept—such as "girl" or "Monday"—arranged in four rows to a page, with each row containing the signs corresponding to each of the three languages and the so-called "common signs."

to the broader audience. Given that, in the late 2000s, the latter spaces were among the few that explicitly supported the use of sign language, I aimed to understand the popular notions of sign language emerging in these settings.

An interview with the director of the unit for persons with hearing impairment at an HCMC-based DPO clarified one meaning of "popular." "As you see," she stated, "most Deaf people . . . write Vietnamese very badly. Their sentences are in confusion. How can others understand them, especially when they are at work? In some cases, hearing people who studied Vietnamese sign language cannot communicate with Deaf people. Why? Because Deaf people do not follow an ordinary order of sentences; the way they write and sign is quite different from that of hearing people."[13] These remarks resemble those made by school personnel in that both similarly construe "Vietnamese sign language" as a language that should correspond to spoken and/or written Vietnamese.

This initial line of inquiry suggested that *popular/community* and *state/official* discourses on sign language had certain language ideological features in common,[14] particularly with respect to an idealized form of Vietnamese linguistic structure, subject classification, and stratification of Deaf and hearing statuses. One striking difference between Deaf education special school and DPO settings involved the explicit expectation that Deaf DPO members would participate in DPO activities according to the languages that they used; that is, DPO participants' signed languages were not prohibited.

Only two of the fieldwork sites explicitly ratified HCMSL as a legitimate language and attributed authority to HCMSL in relation to everyday decision-making activities: the EP and the HDC. In these settings, HCMSL was not only used freely but also invoked as the basis for Deaf community development, subject group identities, and social change goals. In other settings, even those giving apparent enthusiastic support to sign language, such as the aforementioned DPO, Deaf peoples' signing practices were subject to disciplining and negative commentary.

The inclusive education director, Ms. Lang, explained these circumstances in the following way: "When people look at the hearing impaired person, most people look down on them. Teachers also. They don't think that hearing impaired children *can do* things like normal children. They don't have high expectations for them. And they are also disappointed when their students don't do well, as society judges them [teachers]." According to Ms. Lang and others (e.g., the five special school principals, one EP

---

13. This director stated that she had asked HCMSL instructors to teach classes at the Development Center so that she and other personnel and community members could study it. Nevertheless, she frequently described HCMSL's grammatical differences from Vietnamese as incorrect because, according to her, HCMSL should correspond to the language used by hearing people. Thus, she considered the decision to use Vietnamese and signing in Vietnamese word order at her workplace and in other organizational activities as an "intervention" into "low educational attainment and difficulties in communication."

14. The ethnographic viewpoints described here represent those commonly attested at all of the sites in question. It is not the case, however, that all special school personnel, or non-Deaf/nonsigning persons shared the view that HCMSL (and VSLs broadly) should correspond to Vietnamese word order. For example, chapter 6 describes the aforementioned HCMSL-Vietnamese interpreter training workshop attended by school personnel, in which participants demonstrated differing perceptions of HCMSL.

director), when speech-based methods were first introduced to the special schools in the late 1980s, the fact that they were very new there inspired the hope that students would learn to speak, "but it was not successful, only for some." Such hopes are iconically represented in the naming convention taken up by four of the five major Deaf education special schools in HCMC who use Hy vọng [Hope] + district name or number to identify their schools (e.g., Hy vọng Bình Thạnh, Hy vọng Tám).

In the Deaf education and Deaf Studies literatures, "hope" in new methods and technologies is widely noted in connection to Deaf education regimes that marginalize natural signed languages (Johnson, 2006). In the contemporary Vietnamese context, "new" approaches to Deaf (and regular) education emerge in a political terrain dominated by discourses on *phát triển* [economic and social development] and *hiện đại hoá* [modernization]. Such discourses figure prominently in official rhetoric and media reportage, enlisting citizens to participate in building *một xã hội văn minh hiện đại* [a modern and civilized society] by confronting *lạc hậu* [backwardness] and *cổ hủ* [outdated] conditions and attitudes[15] and by doing one's part to support *tiến bộ xã hội* [social progress]. Scholars of Việt Nam locate the appearance and elaboration of such discourses in the period of French colonial occupation, during which debates over cultural inferiority also grew during the introduction and the spread of social Darwinism, which I discuss later in this chapter (Marr, 1971; Tai, 1992).

Whereas Deaf education is not a new idea in Việt Nam, its consolidation as a national speech-based system during the transition to market socialism and the pressure to move Deaf students to normatively speech-based settings under inclusive education both take shape as modernizing enterprises, which need to be examined in detail. Recalling earlier discussion, my examination of the data takes physical location (sites), temporal moment of events, people (social positions and statuses), and the ideas people express through their signs, words, and extralinguistic action (body movement and identities) as composite formations that are connected to wider social and political milieux or *linguistic landscapes* (Blommaert, 2013). In this examination, the work of a number of key linguistic and anthropological practitioners informs my own thinking on linguistic landscapes (e.g., Agha, 2003, 2006; Ahearn, 2001a, 2011; Ahmed, 2006, 2007, 2012; Dudis, 2011; Duranti, 1992, 1994; Edelman, 2011, 2013; Erickson, 2004; Goodwin & Goodwin, 1992, 2004; Hanks, 1995; Jaffe, 1999; Kusters, 2014, 2015a, 2015b; Lane, 2015; Leap, 2008, 2011).

Examining National Modernization, Language, and Education

The future quality of education, training and research will decide the knowledge and skills of the people and shape the life of every person, and the place of the nation in a globalizing world. In a sense, everything depends on modernizing and improving education. It cannot substitute for good government, smarter industry and productive work, but it helps make them possible. (Lý & Marginson, 2014, p. 4)

---

15. Vietnamese newspapers, academic publications, and political discourses frequently describe backward circumstances. See Phạm Anh Tuấn (2010) and Bui (2000).

In contemporary Việt Nam, discourses on modernization and development circulate widely via official rhetoric, the media, and everyday forms of communication. Such discourses are prominently associated with *đổi mới*, the Vietnamese state's evolving platform for political and economic reform, which has delivered the country from near economic and infrastructural collapse to one of middle-income country status and a rising Asian Tiger economy.[16] The changes that the state authorized in 1986 fundamentally transformed economic institutions and activities by giving a leading role to education and training; despite notable gains, observers also note rising inequality in educational opportunity and class differentiation (Berliner, Đỗ, & McCarty, 2013; London, 2011; NCCD, 2010; Trương, 2000).

The state's education-driven approach to economic and social development is, in part, a legacy of earlier historical developments (e.g., anticolonial struggle, postcolonial state formation), in which literacy in the Vietnamese language coalesced as a national cause and served as a basis for national unity and independence. It also reflects, in the present market-socialist era, Vietnamese state efforts to maintain autonomy in decisions involving national development amid increasing participation in regional economic cooperation (ASEAN), multilateral development-oriented initiatives (Education for All, UN Millennium Development Goals, Convention on the Rights of Persons with Disabilities, UN Sustainable Development Goals), and increasing integration into the global economy via membership in the WTO. Deaf education language policy can be seen as an effect of contradictory demands placed on modernizing institutions and as one of the ways that the Vietnamese state directs national development through educational programming.

An ideological bellwether, modernization discourses and policies tend to be problem oriented, evaluating historical moments, nations, subnational groups, cultural traditions, languages, and language varieties as objects of change. The following section briefly describes the global rise of modernization movements, as well as language and literacy planning as key components of such movements. The remainder of this chapter places Deaf education special schools, inclusive education, and disability policy in the context of broader historical, political-economic, and sociolinguistic transformations to situate language as a highly valued and highly contested element in the ongoing formation, development, and modernization of Việt Nam.

Modernization Discourses and Language Modernization

Addressing modernization from within the discipline of sociolinguistics, Neustupný contends that "the topic of modernization is central to our understanding of society and language" (2006, p. 2209). The emergence of modernization movements is widely associated with the 18th-century industrial revolution in Western Europe and North America and its 19th-century extension through political, economic, and social developments (e.g., rise of modern industrial states, colonialisms). In the post–World War II period, modernization coalesced as an assemblage of (increasingly global)

---

16. Việt Nam achieved middle-income country status in 2011/2012, and its Asian Tiger status has been widely noted in economic reporting, such as Veniez (2013) and Curran (2015), as well as economic studies such as that by Berliner et al. (2013).

capitalist-oriented discourses that emphasized progress through industrialization, secularization, urbanization, and democratization (Margetts, 2012, p. 18). Western optimism of the 1950s and 1960s spurred academic theorizing of modernization's benefits, advocating a normatively liberal form of capitalist economic development as the solution to global ills, colonial transition, the engine of prosperity, and new discoveries and technologies (e.g., Rostow, 1960; Parsons, 1975). Such theories are legacies of the Western philosophical tradition broadly, particularly Enlightenment-era notions of rationalism, individualism, and liberal democratic governance, which brutally bolstered the colonial occupation of peoples and territories that fell on the wrong end of social evolutionism's civilizational divide.

In spite of extensive social scientific critique of social evolutionism and its residual effects with regard to theorizing development and modernization, modernization discourses maintain a strong presence in states' rhetoric and public policies, as well as in economic agendas promulgated by multilateral development-oriented organizations, such as the World Bank and the International Monetary Fund. Three characteristics common to early modernization theories continue to be recycled in reform-oriented public policy-making: (1) emphasis on *economic efficiency*, which links the transition from "subsistence economies to technology-intensive industrialized economies" to "individualism deriv[ing] from an emphasis on individuals and self-orientation, rather than families, communities, and collectivism as the basic unit of society" (Margetts, 2012, p. 26); (2) emphasis on a shift toward economic *integration and interconnectedness*, also increasing social integration through urbanization and industrialization, and national and international integration via standardization within and across states' institutions; and (3) emphasis on "*specialization, scientific advancement, expert knowledge, and technology* in economic, political, and social life" (ibid., p. 27).

In addition to ways of talking about and representing modernization through language, modernization is itself "a common stimulus to language policy, as is authentification of the norms that are devised, invoking nationalism and cultural distinctiveness as key influences" (Lo Bianco, 2001, p. 169). Language policy is therefore a key modernizing mechanism that facilitates the intervention of national language planners in the reproduction or engineering of dominant group interests (Haugen, 1959; Jacobson, 2006, p. 2421).

Language policy and planning have been characterized as organized forms of *language management*, and "discourse management" has been called the process by which "language problems basically originate in discourse (interaction acts) from where they can be (but not necessarily are) transferred to organized language management" (Neustupný, 2006, p. 2210).[17] Literacy in a shared language is a pivotal pre-condition

---

17. Neustupný further identifies five maxims of language management that are central elements in "modern development," quoted here in full: "1) Language must be adequate to the industrializing economy, society and culture; 2) Language must contribute to internal unity; 3) The national language is independent of other languages (However, alliance may be struck with other modernizing languages, or languages that precede on the path of modernization); 4) Relatively equal access to language for all participants is essential; 5) Language is an important symbol of ethnic communities (nations)" (ibid., p. 2212).

for modernizing forms of development, and education the central institution where "language problems" manifest as modernization problems warranting language management. Ethnic minority languages (May, 2008) and nonstandard ("stigmatized") language varieties (Tollefson, 2008, p. 6) commonly confront institutionalized and everyday forms of language management.

Continuity and change in Deaf education language policy in Việt Nam are connected to two prominent modernization epochs in which language management followed from relationships between and transformations in education and state formation: anticolonial/early socialist modernization and market-socialist modernization. During these two epochs, language management and literacy emerge as central concerns connecting national sovereignty with new governance and economic structures, as well as shifting demands for social participation from above and below (i.e., from national political leadership and focal group politics).

Language Management and Literacy in Việt Nam

Whereas the world historic emergence of language management is often associated with the modern formation of European nation-states and European colonialism (Anderson, 1991; Mühlhäusler, 2002), language management in Việt Nam easily preceded European colonialism by more than 1,500 years, beginning with Chinese colonial occupation in 111 BCE and inculcation into Confucian education. Regarding language policy and planning in Việt Nam:[18]

> Việt Nam's history is not unique in its struggle against colonial aggression but it is remarkable in its intensity, duration and also in the diversity of its sources. It is these struggles that frame most of the language policy experiences of the country, which were not mere correlates or reflections of these wider forces but sometimes rose to national importance themselves. (Lo Bianco, 2001, p. 171)

Lo Bianco (2001) places major developments in language planning in Việt Nam in the context of three periods of anticolonial struggle and educational formation: Mandarin education (1070–1883), French colonial education (1861–1945), and Vietnamese national education (with northern and southern systems separated from 1945 to 1975, after which the Communist educational system extended to the whole country). Major developments in formal Deaf education in Việt Nam are concentrated in the French colonial period and the transition to market socialism (officially initiated in 1986). Despite limited growth of formal Deaf education during the intervening 100 years between these periods, these years are extremely significant for shaping decisions about language and literacy, including those shaping the direction that contemporary Deaf education planning would ultimately take. Therefore, the next two sections introduce societal and language modernization by, first, placing the rise of Deaf education in the context of French colonial occupation, as well as nascent anticolonial resistance and the early state-socialist approach to mass language and literacy. The following

---

18. See also DeFrancis (1977) and Marr (1971, 1981).

section then focuses on the transformation and consolidation of Deaf education under contemporary market-socialism.

Anticolonial and Early Socialist Modernization

A mass form of language modernization coalesced in the first decades of the twentieth century as part of broader anticolonial resistance to French domination (DeFrancis, 1977; Lo Bianco, 2001; Marr, 1971, 1981). French colonialism began with conquest of the southern region of the country in 1861. Following the subjugation of the central and northern regions, official rule extended throughout the country between 1887 and 1945. French colonial control made assimilation into the French language the foundation of its *mission civilisatrice* [civilizing mission], which was pursued through the establishment of French-Vietnamese schools (London, 2011; Marr, 1971; Tran, 2009; Trương, 2000). Prior to the arrival of the French, Việt Nam had a long tradition of Confucian education, entrenched for more than one thousand years of Chinese colonialism (111 BCE–939 CE). Continuing in an adapted form for the next 900 years of Vietnamese dynastic rule, classically trained Vietnamese scholars—typically elite and categorically male—continued to use Chinese in education and governance,[19] even after the 13th-century development of the Vietnamese ideographic script *chữ nôm*.[20] Seeking to dismantle local power structures and requiring a literate body that could act as interpreters and clerks in the new colonial bureaucracy, the "first emphasis of the French educational enterprise in Vietnam was the teaching of the national romanized writing system, the *quoc ngu*" (Trương, 2000, p. 27).

Attributed to Alexander de Rhodes, a French Jesuit missionary working in Việt Nam in the mid-1600s, *quốc ngữ* had been developed to aid conversion of the populace to Christianity, but it had not caught on among the people (Marr, 1971). In the first decades of French control many anticolonial activists saw *quốc ngữ* as a "tool of the invaders" (Tai, 1992, p. 3). Others saw French occupation as evidence of Vietnamese cultural, linguistic, and "civilizational" inferiority, "so internalized," Tai reported, that "even revolutionaries referred to themselves by the name given them by their French masters—Annamites" (ibid., p. 7). This was the broader geo- and language-political context in which the formal education of Deaf students began in Việt Nam.

In 1886 Father Azemar, a French colonial missionary, established the *Trường Câm-Điếc Lái Thiêu* [Lái Thiêu School for the Mute-Deaf; hereafter, Lái Thiêu School] in the town of Lái Thiêu, just north of present-day HCMC (Pitrois, 1914, 1916). Azemar

---

19. The distribution of Confucian institutions varied from village to village according to the extent to which local literati accepted the authority of Vietnamese dynastic efforts to control education at the village level, the persistence of village codes whose institutions competed with Confucian precepts, and the prevalance of nonformal education among ethnic groups (London, 2011).

20. When Vietnamese scholars developed *chữ nôm* (Vietnamese ideographic system based on Chinese characters), Vietnamese oral and written traditions were linked for the first time, stimulating literary production in the Vietnamese vernacular. However, lack of standardization, lack of popular access to education, and a position subordinate to Chinese limited its spread. *Chữ nôm* achieved official status for a brief period during the Tay Son Dynasty (1788–1802) (Lo Bianco, 2001; Marr, 1971).

Figure 1.1. Nguyễn Văn Trương teaching catechism to deaf boys. Courtesy of the Gallaudet University Archives.

had sent Nguyễn Văn Trương, a local Deaf youth, to study Deaf pedagogical methods in Rodez, France. After Nguyễn returned to Việt Nam, he and Azemar became the school's first teachers (figure 1.1). In addition, Azemar taught Nguyễn the "Annamite language (for, of course, in Rodez the Deaf pupil had been taught in French). At the same time, he [Azemar] learned the sign-language from him [Nguyễn] and the methods of articulation and lip-reading" (Pitrois, 1914, p. 13).[21]

In photographs from this period, such as the one of Nguyễn Văn Trương in figure 1.1,[22] it is clear that, in addition to signing, other languages were also in use at

---

21. Pitrois was a French Deaf writer who wrote extensively for European and North American audiences; some of her works include biographies of Helen Keller and the Abbe de l'Épée. Pitrois's "most remarkable contribution was her work as the head of an international relief fund for Deaf people displaced by the First World War" (Murray, 2007, p. 89). For more on Yvonne Pitrois and early 20th-century transnational Deaf networks, see Murray (2007).

22. Pitrois (1914) accompanied this photograph with the following caption: "The Deaf Boys Taught by Jacques Cam (They Are Making the French Sign for God)." Jacques Cam may have been the name Nguyễn used while a student at Rodez. "Jacques" is of French derivation, while "Cam" is the Francophone version of *câm* [literally, "mute" in Vietnamese]. The Thuận An Center (formerly, the Lái Thiêu School) identifies him as Nguyễn Văn Trương.

Lái Thiêu. As seen on the blackboard pictured behind Nguyễn, French script appears on the left-hand side of the board, and *quốc ngữ* appears on the right. In the next section I return to issues of language origins and forms as they manifested in language management of VSLs during market-socialist modernization and national institutionalization of Deaf education special schools. Here, these details from Lái Thiêu indicate the scope of French colonial language policy, including that Deaf students were expected to study French and *quốc ngữ* (in its colonial conception as the "Annamite" language). They also used a form of sign language at least ideologically and materially associated with French Deaf education.

During the first six decades of Lái Thiêu's operation, anticolonial opposition gradually grew amid debates about language and about Việt Nam's ability to become a modern and independent nation (see Tai, 1992, p. 20; Marr, 1971, p. 61; DeCaro, 2003, p. 91). According to Tai, the scholar-translator Yen Fu had introduced Herbert Spencer to Vietnamese readers in 1904, and the response was forceful, "a revelation" (1992, p. 20). Tai continues: "[T]he suasive power of Social Darwinism lay in its unfamiliar worldview which, instead of celebrating equilibrium and harmony, exalted the notion of unceasing competition for supremacy and survival among actors endowed with unequal gifts and resources (1992, p. 20; see also Marr, 1971, p. 61). In addition, in this context, the patriotic literati metaphorized colonialism "as a *che do thuc dan* [people-eating system]" and Việt Nam, a "*nhuoc tieu* [weak and small] nation in the process of being swallowed up by a stronger and fitter France" (DeCaro, 2003, p. 91).

Despite *quốc ngữ*'s centuries-long ambivalent status, by the first decades of the twentieth century several factors had converged to elevate *quốc ngữ* among the Vietnamese literati and the mass population alike. Introduction of the printing press gave the writing system wider circulation through popular journalism, literary production, critical works, and educational primers (DeFrancis, 1977; Marr, 1971). After World War I, "a number of educated Vietnamese became excited . . . about the possibility of advancing their country's destiny primarily by means of language development" (Marr, 1971, p. 150). Inasmuch as efforts to conduct education in spoken Vietnamese and *quốc ngữ* were not new, they took on new significance in the colonial context, and by the 1920s a "clear majority of the Vietnamese intelligentsia were committed to the rapid development of *quoc-ngu* as the modernizing solution" (ibid., p. 136).

In the 1920s and 1930s, interest in *quốc ngữ* literacy increasingly expanded throughout Vietnamese society and bolstered the burgeoning anticolonial resistance and nationalist movements (Malarney, 2003; Marr, 1971). "The appropriation of *Quốc Ngữ* to a socially transformative ideology of modernization, a modernization perceived to be an essential ingredient for national liberation, enabled the capture of a discourse not available to *Chu Han* [Chinese characters], nor to *Chu Nom* [Vietnamese characters], nor to French" (Lo Bianco, 2001, p. 202). Whereas *Chu Han* and *Chu Nom* orthographies were associated with elite social statuses, and French was associated with violent colonial domination, *quốc ngữ*, the "Low form in writing and Vietnamese the Low spoken form," enabled discourses on indigenous struggle and indigenous victory from below (ibid.).

By 1945, *quốc ngữ* literacy had become such an important concern that Hồ Chí Minh, revolutionary leader and first president of the Democratic Republic of Việt Nam (DRV), made mass literacy the first war campaign against the French, as well as the foundation for national sovereignty and citizenship:[23]

> If you want to safeguard national independence . . . If you want our nation to grow strong and our country prosperous. Every one of you must know his rights and duties. He must possess knowledge so as to be able to participate in the building of the country. First of all he must learn to read and write quoc ngu. Let the literates teach the illiterates; let them take part in mass education. Let the illiterates study hard. The husband will teach his wife, the elder brother his junior, the children their parents, the master his servants; the rich will open classes for illiterates in their own houses. The women should study harder for up to now many obstacles have stood in their way. It is high time now for them to catch up with men and be worthy of their status of citizens with full electoral rights. I hope young people of both sexes will eagerly participate in this work. (Minh, 1977, pp. 64–65)

Language management initiated in 1945 marked a historic turning point in the collective will to usher in a new sociopolitical order by linking national independence to mass literacy in an indigenous Vietnamese language (that spoken by the largest ethnic group, the Việt Kinh)—even as the written form of the language derived from foreign influence.

In the post–World War II period, "processes of educational development and state formation went hand in hand" (London, 2011, p. 13). From 1945 to 1975 Việt Nam was partitioned into separate northern and southern states with separate educational systems, yet both states worked to institutionalize literacy in *quốc ngữ*. In this period *quốc ngữ* development and dissemination aimed at nothing less than complete social and geopoitical transformation to undo "feudal" (*phong kiến*) attitudes and "backward" (*lạc hậu*) beliefs associated with illiteracy, which had prevailed under the French, as well as social hierarchies associated with Confucian institutions (Malarney, 2011; Marr, 1971). In the north, the DRV conducted guerilla-style literacy training to prepare revolutionary cadres; they also conducted literacy campaigns with non-Việt Kinh ethnic minorities in order to "prove that there was—and had been for centuries—one Vietnamese nation or civilization" (Woodside, 1983b, p. 407).

Five years after the French were expelled from the country, *quốc ngữ* was well established as the language of education and governance in both the northern and the southern educational systems. By 1959 the DRV had declared illiteracy "basically eradicated" in the north (i.e., 93% of persons 12–50 years of age were reported as literate) (Nguyễn, 1994, p. 58). Similar literacy gains were reported for the south following the end of the American War and the reunification of the north and south under the banner of the Socialist Republic of Việt Nam (ibid., p. 59). Although the literature reflects skepticism about the extent to which literacy gains were achieved following the end of French colonial rule, there is no disagreement about the accuracy of, as Woodside phrased it, "the palsied state of education in colonial Indochina" (1983b,

---

23. In the south of Việt Nam, the "transition of the southern curriculum to the Vietnamese language" took place even earlier, with reforms instituted by the first southern prime minister, Trần Trọng Kim, beginning in March 1945 (London, 2011, p. 14; see also Woodside, 1983b).

p. 403) or about popular interest in educational participation. It is worth noting that there were two groups of students who began attending school for the first time under French colonial rule: girls (London, 2011; Luong, 2003; Marr, 1971) and Deaf students. Between 1945 and 1975, prolonged poverty and war certainly "limited the scope of education" in both northern and southern states yet not its formal expansion (London, 2011, p. 13; Woodside, 1983b). Moreover, during the American War period (1965–1975), the fact that the "education system developed as quickly as it did in the context of a war of national independence and amid severe poverty and scarcity is a testament to the determination and mobilizational capacities of national, and especially, local leaders, and to popular enthusiasm for education" (London, 2011, p. 71). It is also a testament to the Vietnamese state's linguistic commitments. Moreover, "Viet Nam's struggle to secure an indigenous national culture free from the influence of foreigners (or more precisely, one in which it was the Vietnamese openly choosing to admit and regulate the nature and extent of these influences) has bequeathed the country an extraordinarily diverse and rich experience of language policy and implementation" (Lo Bianco, 2001, p. 171).

After 1975, the development of a national (regular) educational system in which all citizens were expected to participate prompted increased enrollments—and also succeeded in closing the gender gap in education (Luong, 2003). However, it also placed additional demands on overtaxed state socialist economic institutions and reserves. The provision of education to those either not participating in school or whose participation was limited was one of the new demands emerging at this time. During this period, schools dedicated to the education of Deaf students began to appear—both government-founded schools (*công lập*) and "people-founded" schools (*dân lập*). The first two government-founded schools were established in the northern city of Hải Phòng (in 1975) and in the capital city of Hà Nội (in 1976) (Woodward et al., 2004). People-founded schools followed in the south in the late 1980s.[24] Until the establishment of these schools, the Lái Thiêu School was the only school for Deaf students in operation.

Despite literacy gains achieved by the general population, as well as the opening of education to previously marginalized groups, by 1979 the state had found that "the quality of all-round education was still poor," prompting a substantial program of educational reform (Phạm, M. H., 1994, pp. 33–34). A major result of this reform was the creation of a new national curriculum, which the state instituted in the 1981–1982 school year. The state mandated that *"general education schools have the same duration, the same curricula and the same set of textbooks used in the whole country"* (ibid., p. 36; italics in the original). From 1981 on, instructional content taught in the regular educational system has been designed to follow uniform curricular content and sequencing. For example, every grade 9 teacher of Vietnamese history throughout the country teaches the same lesson on the same day (figure 1.2).

Emphasizing efficiency, integration, standardization, and the scientifically oriented production of knowledge, educational evaluation and reform heralded the central role

---

24. However, no schools for Deaf students existed in the north until after the American War, when the state established the two schools referenced earlier (Woodward et al., 2004).

Figure 1.2. Street sign: "25 Years of Vietnamese Education," HCMC. Caption reads: *Nhiệt liệt chào mừng kỷ niệm lần thứ 25 ngày nhà giáo Việt Nam* (20-11-1982–20-11-2007) [Warmly celebrating 25 years of Vietnamese Education (11-20-1982 to 11-20-2007].

that (1) education would play in the transition to market-socialism and (2) educational evaluation of student subgroup populations would play in structuring educational opportunities. Such goals are periodically revised, such as with MOET's educational improvement directives of 2009. These included the following: (1) no. 4899/2009/CT-BGDDT, which focused on "innovation management and quality improvement" for preschool, general, continuing, and professional education; (2) the corresponding Decision no. 4385/QD-BGDDT, which stipulated the time frame for these activities. Despite such reform initiatives, recent reports, such as the OECD's 2012 Programme for International Student Assessment, as well as a 2013 survey of national scholars conducted by Transparency International, indicate dissatisfaction with the educational system. Of particular concern is the national curriculum's emphasis on "rote memorisation over critical thinking and creative problem-solving," which negatively affects educational quality, and insufficient teacher compensation, which contributes to "corrupt" practices such as student enrollment that is contingent on the ability to pay (M. I., 2013).

Market-Socialist Modernization and Educational Stratification

In the early 1980s, worsening conditions of postwar poverty, poorly performing collective production and state-owned enterprises, and declining infrastructure were exacerbated by loss of aid from the former Soviet Union, embargoes on trade and aid imposed by the United States, protracted occupation of Cambodia, and rising health problems and disability resulting from dioxin contamination and unexploded ordnance (Martin, 2009).[25] Collectivized agricultural production and state-owned enterprises had also failed to produce an adequate supply of food or labor incentives, and differences in subpopulations' access to goods, income, and opportunity increased the general dissatisfaction (Beresford, 2003, p. 58). Market-socialist modernization developed as a response to these circumstances and, bolstered by changes in Vietnamese Communist Party (VCP) leadership, led to the VCP's 1986 decision to pursue political and economic reform during the meeting of the Sixth Party Congress. Đổi mới [lit., "new change," commonly translated as "renovation" or "renewal"] began as a broad platform of political-economic reforms that initiated the gradual process toward a market-socialist economy and integration into the international economic system. "Development of education, science, and technology and improvement of the state management role" were important components of the rebuilding of both society and the state in complementary fashion (Vasavakul, 1997, p. 340; see also London, 2009, p. 381).

According to Phạm Minh Hạc, former minister of education and a revered education scholar and critic, under đổi mới, "education and training along with science and technology [form] the top national policy" (2007, p. 278). This national policy corresponds to the following "four guiding viewpoints" (ibid., pp. 278–279):

1) Education and training is the driving force and the fundamental condition to ensure the achievement of social-economic targets, constructing and defending the country. We should consider investment in education the main investment in development.

2) The education and training's target is to enhance the intellectual standards of the people; to train human resources; to cultivate talents; and to enable people to gain knowledge of culture, science, and professional skills, et cetera.

3) Education and training should be associated closely to the demand for development of the country and in conformity with the progressive trend of the era.

4) Education and training should be diversified; social justice should be ensured in education. (ibid.)

By discursively establishing connections between education, human development, and socioeconomic development, these guiding viewpoints aim to "enable people to obtain comprehensive development, with the sense of independence and socialist ideals, virtue, capability, which will create a human resource strong enough for carrying out industrialization in the direction of modernization, and for defending our country"

---

25. Vietnam Veterans of America reports that the U.S. military "dropped at least 8 million tons of ordnance during the war, of which the Pentagon has said about 10 percent did not detonate," and that, since 1996, Cooperative Vietnamese-INGO action has destroyed about 600,000 bombs (Searcy 2017). (See also Vietnamese Ministry of Defense-Vietnam Veterans of America Foundation *Unexploded Ordnance and Landmine Impact Assessment and Technical Survey* at: http://www.ngocentre.org.vn/files/docs/VietnamUXOLandmineSurvey_PhaseI%20Report.pdf).

(ibid., 282–283). To carry out "industrialization in the direction of modernization," the state began developing differentiated approaches to education and training, or "*specialization, scientific advancement, expert knowledge, and technology*" (Margetts, 2010, p. 27; italics in the original).

One profoundly striking aspect of the *đổi mới* development agenda is the attention given to Deaf education as part of a comprehensive plan for development and modernization. Whereas the Vietnamese state could have chosen—as many governments have—to ignore the educational and social interests of its Deaf citizens, during this period, the state initiated nationalized Deaf education. Other forces, however, were also at work.

For example, the state increased the emphasis on vocational training in order "to steer those with 'intellectual' capability towards careers as 'scientific, technical, and economic cadres,' while equipping the majority of students, those with a 'fixed level of cultural development,' with 'essential appropriate knowledge to step into a life of labour'" (London, 2011, p. 16; internal quotation attributed to Nguyễn Quang Vinh, 1989). This emphasis on *steering* intellectual capacities indicates the Vietnamese state's emerging investment in identifying and assessing forms of ability—which is to say, its investment in classifying supposedly discrete human capacities and plugging these into training and resources development. Related to such classification, in the early reform period the state began to identify "social problems" (*vấn đề xã hội*).[26]

Contending that "social problems did not exist in the Leninist mentality of governance," Nguyễn-võ argues that "what was becoming clear as economic liberalization picked up speed was the need to 'understand' people or 'humans' in their various relations" (2008, p. 88).[27] Exploring the relationships between political-economic restructuring and state handling of prostitution, Nguyễn-võ argues that a liberal form of governance—depoliticized, neutral, outcome oriented, and knowledge driven—emerged alongside the "conception of a society that had to be studied and managed or governed with expertise" (ibid., p. 81).

Việt Nam's campaign against "social evils" (*tệ nạn xã hội*) is another relevant example of state intervention into social problems, whereby certain populations are identified and regulated according to body features and/or practices.[28] The Vietnamese government initiated the social evils campaign in the mid-1990s as an effort to eradicate gambling, prostitution, crime, HIV/AIDS, drug use, street children, and other things the state determined to be social ills (figure 1.3).

---

26. Social problems are the focus of numerous Internet-based and printed publications. Nguyễn Thị Oanh (2012) is one example.

27. Internal quotes are the remarks of Trần Độ, "a high-ranking party official at the start of economic liberalization" (Nguyễn-võ, 2008, p. 88).

28. Human Rights Watch (2006) identifies three key documents establishing social evils activities: (1) Directive 33/CT-TW, "Heightening leadership against social evils" (March 1994); (2) Directive 64/CT-TW, "Enhancing leadership and management, restoring order in cultural activities and cultural services and eliminating social evils" (December 1995); and (3) a Seventh Party Congress document, "Eliminating social evils: Simultaneous implementation of education, economic, administrative and legal methods to effectively combat social evils" (1991).

Figure 1.3. Poster in HCMC (2008): *Ma Tuý Tự Giết Chết Gia Đình!* (Drugs Kill Families!). Photograph courtesy of the U.S. Library of Congress Asian Reading Room and Nhà xuất bản Y học [Medical Publishing House], Hà Nội, Việt Nam.

In 2001, Decree no. 25/2001/ND-CP established social protection centers to rehabilitate those charged with propagating social evils.[29] One Vietnamese researcher described these centers as follows:

> [They] are places for the temporary custody of those who have been picked up by the district authorities during their campaigns. These centers are for people who have not committed any serious crimes, but whose behavior and lifestyle may pose a threat to social order and security. They are, therefore, gathered or arrested without any order from the court or from any judiciary bodies. (Human Rights Watch, 2006)

In addition to these mechanisms, the state's approach to economic development makes an explicit link between poverty and social problems, as defined by the state under the guidance of the Communist Party leadership. The 2002 *Comprehensive Poverty Reduction and Growth Strategy* (Decision no. 2685/VPCP QHQT), for example,

---

29. The Department of Social Evils Prevention administers and regulates the social evils campaign under the auspices of the Ministry of Labor, Invalids, and Social Affairs (*Phòng chống tệ nạn xã hội-Thương binh và Xã hội*).

argues for "see[ing] a harmony between economic growth and measures to solve social problems" (2003, p. 3).

Deafness was one of the areas whose study contributed to the rise of new forms of expert knowledge, classification, treatment, and rehabilitation. Early expertise determined that: (1) Deaf children must learn to speak in order to develop, and therefore, (2) they must be educated in schools that focus on speech (Phạm K., 1984). Marking a significant cultural shift from viewing deafness as spiritual or moral transgression (Pitrois, 1914; Gammeltoft, 2008, 2014, for general discussion of contemporary notions of disability), classification mechanisms emerging in the early reform era nevertheless established the new social categories "handicapped" (*người tàn tật*) and "normal persons" (*người bình thường*), as well as new institutions (special schools, rehabilitation) and social welfare mechanisms (charity events, cash payments, subsidized education).

Phạm Kim's (1984) *Vấn Đề Phục Hồi Chức Năng Cho Người Điếc* [Rehabilitation issues of the Deaf; hereafter, *Rehabilitation issues*]—one of the first books published on Deaf education methods (and still one of just a few books available)—provides a glimpse into the connections forming between medical and educational knowledge in the early political-economic reform period. In the foreword to the book, Professor Trần Hữu Tước, then chair of the Ear, Nose, and Throat Institute of Việt Nam, asserted the following:

Một trong những chức năng chủ yếu đó là nghe: khi không nghe được là không nói được, sẽ không phát triển trí tuệ và tư duy, và chức năng nghe-nói nay được là một chức năng giáo tiếp cơ bản của con người.

One of the main [physiological] functions is hearing: when you do not hear and do not speak, then you will not develop intellectually the ability to think, hearing-speaking is thus the basic communication function of the human being (ibid., p. 3).

However, rather than arguing that Deaf children could not be expected to gain such capacities, Trần proclaimed that a *"một cuộc Cách mạng lớn về khoa học kỹ thuật"* [major revolution in science and technology] would restore their speaking and hearing capabilities (ibid.) (see figure 1.4).

In the book proper, Phạm describes methods for diagnosing and treating deafness, exhorting readers to reject gestural approaches to education and to follow the proposed speech-based methods in order to rehabilitate Deaf children (ibid., p. 212). Throughout the book, Phạm characterizes *điếc-câm* [deaf mutism] as a *những bị khuyết* [plural pronoun + marker for "unfortunate state" + "defects"] (ibid., p. 124):

Điếc-câm là một tàn tật sức nặng nề: trẻ không những bị khuyết đi thế giới âm thanh—hết sức cần thiết để nhận thức được thế giới bên ngoài mà còn bị khuyết luôn cả chức năng ngôn ngữ, công cụ giao tiếp và tư duy!

Deaf mutism is a severe handicap: not only are children with these defects unable to hear sound in the world—and it is very necessary to be aware of the outside world—but also those with these defects do not have functional language, for communication or thinking!

Figure 1.4. Front cover, *Vấn Đề Phục Hồi Chức Năng Cho Người Điếc (Rehabilitation issues of the deaf)*. Photograph courtesy of the U.S Library of Congress Asian Reading Room and Nhà xuât bản yhọc [Medical Publishing House], Hà Nội, Việt Nam.

The word *bị* has been described as an intransitive-passive verb often occurring with "bodily conditions and actions which are viewed as negative" (Simpson & Ho, 2008, p. 832). Examples are *Nam bị mù* [Nam is blind] and *Nam bị tàn tật* [Nam is crippled] (ibid.). Additionally, as my Vietnamese language instructor explained, *bị* is a verb classifier used by speakers to indicate their viewpoint on a situation and enlists listeners to align with such viewpoints—especially in situations in which listeners are unfamiliar with Deaf people. Therefore, a speaker's use of *bị* supplies an authorial cue that deafness be viewed as a regrettable circumstance; the authority of the claim is also connected to the social or situational authority of the speaker, which, in the foregoing passage, is extremely high, given that the speaker is a medical doctor.

Such medico-educational arguments are seen to have a geopolitical dimension, as when Phạm presents the following argument against gestural language:

> Đó là một công trình vĩ đại của trường phái Đờ Lêpê từ cuối thế kỷ thứ 18 mà ngày nay đã số các nuớc không còn dùng nữa nhung lại có một số it nuớc được phát triển và nâng cao lên thành một thứ ngôn ngữ bằng điệu bộ phổ biến cho người điếc vói cái tên mói là

> Measuring the great work of l'Épée's school from the last century, now some 18 countries no longer use this method, but there are some less developed countries who have taken up a gestural language for Deaf people in their countries popularly known as gestuno. (1984, p. 212)

"Gestural language" is associated not only with the supposed failure of sign language-based pedagogy—invoking social memory of the (failed) French occupation in Việt Nam—but also with certain supposed negative impacts of "gestural language" for underperforming economies that unwittingly take up such methods. The emergence of a discourse of *deafness as disability* (negatively construed) is clearly in evidence in Phạm K.'s arguments and the associated research reporting.

Other books circulating in early đổi mới era Deaf education special schools included the 1989 *Mẹ ơi, con không nghe! Hãy giúp con!* [Mother, I cannot hear! Please help me!] (figure 1.5). Also written from what is now referred to as a medical or pathologizing perspective, the parents of Deaf children who founded the first Deaf education special school in HCMC obtained permission from the original French Canadian authors to translate this book into Vietnamese for the purpose of internal circulation at their school.

As in *Rehabilitation Issues*, "Mother, I cannot hear! Please help me!" (hereafter, *Mother*) describes the circumstances of diagnosis and rehabilitation of hearing loss and also includes strategies for effective face-to-face communication with Deaf children through use of hearing aids and speech training. *Mother* and *Rehabilitation Issues* are similar in three other ways as well. First, both texts mark the status of deafness as an unfortunate condition. In the chapter outline of *Mother,* five out of six mentions of đ*iếc* [Deaf] are preceded by the negative marker *bị;* for example, the first chapter's second section is titled *Mấy tuổi chúng ta có thểnghi cháu bị đ*iếc? [At what age can we detect (the unfortunate condition of) deafness?] (lowercase *d* for đ*iếc* in the original) (1989, p. 5). Second, both texts reference *khiếm khuyết thính* [disabling hearing impairment]. A third feature shared by both texts is the description of signs as if they were nonlinguistic, and there is no description of the sociolinguistic practices of Deaf people as members of cultural and language communities. In *Rehabilitation Issues,* signs are described as an inferior compensatory method limited only to "specific concepts," from which its users cannot "abstract or generalize" ("*chỉ đừng lại ở mức khái niệm cụ thể, trực quan mà không*

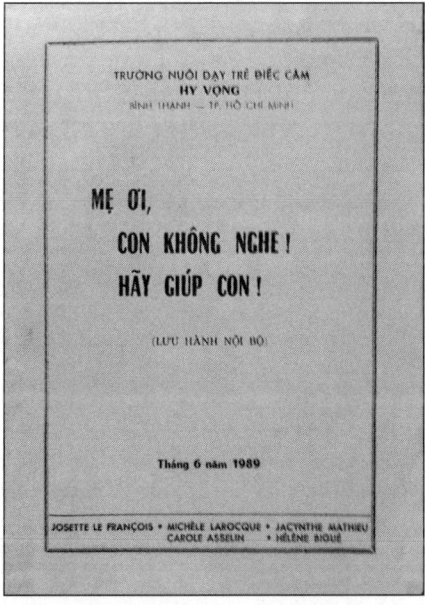

Figure 1.5. Front cover, *Mẹ ơi, con không nghe! Hãy giúp con!* (Mother, I cannot hear! Please help me!). Photograph courtesy of the U.S Library of Congress Asian Reading Room and Nhà xuất bản yhọc [Medical Publishing House], Hà Nội, Việt Nam.

thể tiếp thu được những khái niệm trừu tượng hay khái quát") (Phạm K., 1984, p. 124). In *Mother,* signs (*dấu hiệu*) are described as one method of "allowing children to communicate their own thoughts" (*"Thật vậy, qua những dấu hiệu, trẻ có thể truyền đạt ý nghĩ của mình"*) (1989, p. 97); however, such signs are deemed useful only until "language" (*"ngôn ngữ"*; implying *spoken language*) is "restored" (*"phục hồi ngôn ngữ"*) (ibid.). Both texts provide illustrations of fingerspelling charts, yet, while the illustration in *Rehabilitation Issues* is of Vietnamese origins, *Mother* uses an illustration of an American Sign Language alphabet.[30] Nevertheless, neither of these charts presents fingerspelling as part of a linguistic system but rather as something that stands in for spoken language until it can be developed. These books indicate the ideological circumstances influencing educational decision making in the early years of *đổi mới* political-economic reform.

With *đổi mới*'s open-door policy came an influx of international development organizations focused on disability, among them organizations whose mission aligned with Việt Nam's nascent consolidation of speech-based education. Netherlands-based Komitee Twee was one organization that made an early appearance in Việt Nam (Reilly & Nguyễn, 2004). Partnering with one of the first people-founded schools in HCMC in the early 1990s, Komitee Twee provided teachers with training in speech-based educational methods and students with hearing aids. Corresponding to the approach advocated by rehabilitation experts Trần and Phạm (mentioned earlier), cooperation between MOET and Komitee Twee followed, supporting the implementation of special schools and the establishment of special education teacher-training programs. According to the new national model, the Lái Thiêu School——later renamed the Thu ận An Center[31]—also adopted speech-based methods (figure 1.6).[32]

Rehabilitation Issues differs from *Mother* in one significant way: its argument for speech-only education. In *Rehabilitation Issues,* Phạm Kim argues that the sign-based methods of late 18th- and early 19th-century European educators of Deaf students failed due to their "crude and unsatisfactory method" (*"quá thô sơ và phương pháp chưa thỏa đáng!"*) (1984, p. 79). Whereas the International Congress on the Education of the Deaf had stripped Deaf education sites of Deaf educators and signed languages around the world, it is unsurprising that Phạm Kim considered sign language a "crude" technology, as well as one left behind by a failed political adversary at that (i.e., French

---

30. Neither text contains illustrations of Vietnamese signs. Only *Rehabilitation* contains an illustration of a Vietnamese Sign Language alphabet.

31. After the Hồ Chí Minh City Pedagogic University established its special education department in 1999, the Lái Thiêu School became a training center for special education teachers-in-training. Lái Thiêu subsequently changed its name to Trung Tâm Giáo Dục Trẻ Khuyết Tật Thuận An [Thuận An School for the Education of Children with Disabilities], also referred to as the Thuận An Education and Training Center for Teachers and Children with Hearing Impairment. (See Thuận An's website: www.thuongvevietNam.org/webseiten/ thuanan/html/thuanan_02_en.html)

32. Since 2010 Lái Thiêu/Thuận An's major collaborating partner has been the Global Foundation for Children with Hearing Loss, which promotes hearing aids and speech training much in the manner of Komittee Twee.

Figure 1.6. Trung Tâm Giáo Dục Trẻ Khuyết Tật Thuận An [Thuận An School for Disabled Children's Education]; formerly, Trường Câm-Điếc Lái Thiêu [Lái Thiêu School for the Mute-Deaf].

missionaries). In historical context, it is not only reasonable but indeed commendable that Phạm Kim and other guardians of the state and Communist Party sought to protect Deaf people and the nation from the contaminating effects of sign language, both of which signified colonial domination and prognosticated national vulnerability. Thus, early market-socialist structuring of the Deaf education special school system as a speech-only enterprise may be a reflection of a political-economic evaluation of signed language as not simply a colonial legacy but also an insidious, possibly strategic, external intervention intended to jeopardize Việt Nam's national unity and progress toward development and modernization.

Interviews with Deaf education special school principals—three of whom started working as teachers during the early years of special school formation—reflect Phạm Kim's medical, and threat-invoking, conceptualization of signs, though not necessarily his assumptions about students' intellectual potential. For example, the principals of Hope A and Hope B stated that Deaf students' signing was not "proper"; both principals referred to the grammar exhibited by Deaf students and adult former students as *người điếc ngược* [lit., person + Deaf + opposite/backward]. During interviews, these principals also argued passionately for the intelligence of their students and explained low educational performance with, in the words of the principal of Hope A, "if the students would only try harder." Twelve out of 19 EP adult learners stated that special school personnel viewed them as LỘN XỘN [confused].

The special school system would seem to be the structural equivalent of Phạm Kim's (and other experts) understanding of Deaf students as needing intervention involving auditory listening and speech training. Such a perspective contextualizes the comments by the principal of Hope C, who argued that her school is different from the other special schools: "At [Hope C], we teach by oral language. Parents of Deaf children want them to learn, to get education. The other schools just take care of children" (emphasis in the original). According to this view, special schools that allow sign language fail to address both the biosocial and the state-developmental requirements of *hearing/speaking* in Việt Nam.

Another important feature of this state consolidation of a speech-based approach to Deaf education is that it accompanied economic reforms promoting socialization (*xã hội hoá*) of education and other core social services. In the Vietnamese context, *socialization* refers to processes commonly regarded as privatization in capitalist economies, exemplified by shifting costs for social services away from the state and toward the private sector (London, 2011; Nguyễn-võ, 2008). Socialization thus made it possible, and in many ways necessary, for parents and other concerned citizens to establish people-founded schools for Deaf students. Socialization also contributes to a socialist citizenship contradiction: Everyone is expected to participate in education in order to contribute to Việt Nam's development and modernization; however, only those students whose families can afford to pay school fees and other costs associated with education can achieve educational access. As educational costs are increasingly socialized, many families face these circumstances regardless of whether their children are Deaf or non-Deaf; however, extremely low enrollment of Deaf and hard of hearing students suggests that, in addition to financial outlay, other factors also affect school enrollment.

In this context, the provision of Deaf education had, by the late 1990s, expanded to more than fifty primary-level schools (Woodward et al., 2004); however, Deaf students did not respond to speech-based methods in the manner predicted by *Rehabilitation Issues for the Deaf*. Moreover, because access to Deaf education was limited to the primary, and, in a few locations, lower-secondary levels (in HCMC and also nationally), Deaf students were barred from pursuing higher education. This was the context in which, in 2000, the Education Project established the first program to teach students the national curriculum from sixth through twelfth grade in HCMSL.[33]

Over the course of its decade and a half of operation, the EP has delivered educational programming alongside the national systems of regular education (*phổ thông*) and nonregular and special education (*bổ túc*). In MOET's first few years, research participants reported that the ministry paid little attention to the EP or its instructional methods; however, when the first group of EP students passed the national ninth-grade examination, allowing them to move into upper-secondary education,[34] the EP began

---

33. In 2010 MOET established an educational program based on the EP at the National College for Education in Hà Nội (Trường Cao đẳng Sư phạm Trung Ương, Hà Nội). From 2012 to 2014, special education faculty taught the national curriculum at the lower-secondary level. In fall 2015 the college began offering programming from the tenth to the twelfth grade (*cấp 3*).

34. The national ninth-grade examination is no longer in use. On April 5, 2006, MOET passed Decision 11/2006/QD BGDDT, which discontinued it.

to draw attention from local and national educational leaders. State attention to and cooperation with the EP has grown over the last decade, as several hundred students have completed the ninth and the twelfth grades and as two cohorts of students have graduated with college degrees in primary-level education. The first cohort graduated in 2013 and the other 2014, with seventeen students in total, and the third cohort of students is now poised to graduate.

One indication of the state's interest in the EP's methods and performance outcomes is given in MOET's 2012 establishment of a lower-secondary pilot program in Hà Nội modeled[35] on the EP. This initiative suggested that the state might also be beginning to support sign-based instructional methods for educational settings. Other state activities provide additional evidence for such a turn. In 2013 and 2014 the state undertook a pilot television program called "Teaching Sign Language" (*Dạy Ngôn Ngữ Ký Hiệu*), which was filmed in Hà Nội and featured a prominent local Deaf community leader using Hà Nội Sign Language (the show aired once live and was rebroadcast several times weekly for one year). Then, on December 9, 2014, educational leaders in MOET's National Institute of Educational Science (NIES) and members of the Hà Nội Association of People with Disabilities (Hội Người Khuyết Tật Thành phố Hà Nội) met to discuss ways to *hỗ trợ người khiếm thính hòa nhập cộng đồng* [support the community integration of people with hearing impairment]. During that meeting NIES authorized the teaching of sign language in the continuing education system (*giáo dục thường xuyên*) (Kim, 2014).

In the same period, however, MOET also subsidized, for instance, a large, speech-based, early childhood education project to train teachers exclusively in methods promoting listening and speaking. This project is affiliated with the historic Thuận An Center under the auspices of the HCMC Pedagogic University (Trường Đại học Sư phạm, Tp, HCM) and also carries out training through "mobile mission" teams that travel throughout the country (Global Foundation for Children with Hearing Loss, 2015).[36] Within the system of national Deaf education special schools, speech-based instruction also remains the standard method, and training in the use of bi- or multilingual instructional approaches involving VSLs is not available through MOET (except via short-term and enrollment-limited international development projects such as the one I participated in with the World Concern Development Organization).

With the passage of the 2010 Law on Persons with Disability (no. 51/2010/QH12), the state officially authorized sign language for use in Deaf education and inclusive education. However, disagreement about what sign language is or should be and how it should be used in education and other domains continues to be hotly debated.

---

35. In 2010 MOET established an educational program based on the EP at the National College for Education in Hà Nội (Trường Cao đẳng Sư phạm Trung Ương, Hà Nội). From 2012 to 2014, special education faculty taught the national curriculum at the lower-secondary level. In fall 2015 the college began offering programming for the tenth to the twelfth grades (*cấp 3*).

36. Since 2010 Lái Thiêu/Thuận An's major collaborating partner has been the Global Foundation for Children with Hearing Loss, which promotes hearing aids and speech training much in the manner of Komittee Twee. See the Global Foundation for Children with Hearing Loss website for description of its "Vietnam Deaf Education Program" at http://childrenwithhearingloss.org/projects.shtml

In such discussions, Deaf people have been categorically disadvantaged with regard to structural and symbolic authority, and HCMSL has been disadvantaged with regard to linguistic legitimacy. It is in this context that Deaf education programming and language management continue to privilege both spoken Vietnamese and, more recently, a form of signing that follows Vietnamese word order.

Conclusion

This chapter describes some of the ways in which the modern Vietnamese state views the Vietnamese language and its users: as a vehicle for ethnic and political solidarity, as a mobilizing medium, as a code available for technological invention, but, overwhelmingly, as an instrument of national social reproduction of the socialist citizen. In the early years of state formation, use of a signed language did at least two things. First, it marked Vietnamese Deaf people's *difference,* not so much from individual non-Deaf or HEARING PEOPLE (*người nghe*), and more from the imagined community of nation-builders and defenders, whose fortitude was believed contingent upon a common spoken language. However, it also marked Deaf people's families as contaminating, rather than contributing to, such nation-building (see chapter 4 for further discussion of this point).

In the state-centered phase of *đổi mới,* market-socialist reform, the widespread prevalence of disability as both a natural and a war-related occurrence, as well as the increase in scientific description of deafness and disability, contributed to reframing disability as a medical pathology. Under contemporary market socialism, its political-economic institutions and ideologies, earlier imaginaries are indexed in current practices to authorize a dominant HEARING form of embodiment and sociolinguistic practices as proper national citizenship conduct.

Between the two modernization moments described in this chapter, Việt Nam had succeeded in achieving independence from the French and the Japanese, won the war against the Americans, and reunified the country under a single state system. In the first wave of modernization, Vietnamese—the language used by Việt Nam's largest ethnic group (the Việt Kinh, representing 86% of the population)[37]—was elevated to national-language status along with literacy in *quốc ngữ.* Given the extended colonial context in which ethnic languages were suppressed, first to Chinese and later to French, the advancement of an indigenous Vietnamese language can be understood as a formidable act of resistance. Establishing Vietnamese as the national language and literacy in *quốc ngữ* as the basis of socialist education provided the inspiration from, and the means by which, military encadrement was accomplished and, later, a national system of education and governance in the Vietnamese vernacular. Expert and institutional discourses that emerged during early socialist formation exerted a strong

---

37. According to Vietnamese ethnologists, Việt Nam's ethnocultural diversity includes 54 ethnocultural groups (Đặng Nghiêm Vạn, 2001). If Deaf people were counted as an ethnocultural and a linguistic minority group, as suggested by Deaf participants in the video series *Nghe Bằng Mắt* [Listening by eye], this number would include 55 groups (see https://www.youtube.com/channel/UCMalsiaBTHsWVe87sAOrcXA).

(negative) influence on popular notions about sign language (*ngôn ngữ ky hiệu*) and Deaf people, and the formation of relevant state institutions.

In the second wave of modernization, as expanding market-socialism invested in education as the central driver of economic development, the rise of new forms of scientific expertise facilitated description of newly identified problems, among them the problem of deafness. Aiming to prepare every citizen for participation in the market-Socialist economy, reform-era state investment in education concentrated substantial resources on the universalization of primary education and expanded higher education training in technical, scientific, and vocational fields. Among the groups the state sought to engage in primary education were children with disabilities, whom it addressed by establishing a national system of special schools, including schools for Deaf students. Spoken-language ideologies and hierarchies of idealized forms of national participation figured prominently in official rhetoric and educational planning.

Over the last thirty years, language policies and educational structuring have played a significant role in shaping differentiated forms of educational delivery (academic vs. vocational, regular vs. special) and Deaf people's social participation. Recently, Deaf people's social organizing activities have emerged as a significant force of creativity and a critique of forms of educational and social inclusion and exclusion. Linguistic anthropologists, sociolinguists, and other critical disciplines view language-ideological contests as fundamentally political, in the materially vital sense of everyday struggle over "social goods and their distribution" (Gee, 2010, p. 7), serving particular social group interests (Bourdieu, 1991, p. 167), and as prominent mechanisms in the reproduction of social inequalities (Fairclough, 1989).

2

Putting the Study of Signed Language and State Formation in Perspective

EXAMINATION OF VIỆT Nam's geopolitical history informs analytic understanding of the Vietnamese state's political transformations and its turn toward a market-socialist economy. Such analytic understanding, in turn, informs examination of Việt Nam's educational systems—which I argue are strongly influenced by ideologies related to language and to the body at differing scales, sites, and domains of analytic inquiry. Within late-modern social science theorizing, three major approaches to the study of the state have a bearing on this book: *state as actor, state as effect,* and *state as imagination*. Contributing a fourth approach, *state as embodiment,* I argue that ethnographic examination of microlevel sociolinguistic interactions offers unique insights into macrolevel state formation and change. The significance of the state as embodiment approach—as I discuss in detail shortly—is that it focuses analytic attention on interactions between state agents and (those perceived to be) subjects of the state. State agents are persons whose languages derive legitimacy and authority in large part from their use of the dominant spoken modality and their professional positions in state institutions. State subjects are persons, in this case Deaf students and social organizers, whose languages are often delegitimized in state institutions; moreover, if Deaf subjects participate in state institutions at all, they often hold little to no institutional or situational authority.

The analysis I pursue in this chapter is thereby concerned with the insights such scales and domains provide for generating theory; however, here and throughout this book, I am most interested in the practical implications of these insights for Deaf people's social organizing efforts. That is, my description is oriented toward the ways in which human actors create and transform the nation-state and contestation over the legitimacy and authority of such actors in their sites (or aspirational sites) of sociolinguistic practice.

An example from Việt Nam illuminates the significance (if not the necessity) of ethnography for examining such interactions. A microanalysis of two settings finds that Deaf state subjects achieved legitimacy and authority for their perspectives on HCMSL within a workshop on HCMSL-Vietnamese interpretation (Cooper & Nguyễn, 2015, p. 122). The same was true during a television interview, when Deaf people (state subjects) "invok[ed] knowledge sets connected to signed language linguistic research, deliver[ed] information via specialized terms (grammatical structure, non-manual grammar), [and] shap[ed] discourse in a register recognizable [to state agents] as that of teacher" (ibid.). In these settings, state agents (Deaf education special school principals and teachers) demonstrated changes in attitudes toward HCMSL and Deaf people as evidenced by shifts from referring to Deaf presenters in the third person, and by shifting from referring to them as *khiếm thính* [having a hearing impairment] to *người Điếc* [Deaf people].These state agents asked Deaf presenters direct questions (rather than asking non-Deaf copresenters questions about them) and invited the Deaf presenters to assist with instruction at their schools. Witnessing and video-recording these events facilitated analysis of the ways that non-Deaf people's interactions responded to, indexed, and reflected on the perceived knowledge and capacities of Deaf people to transform the "state" at the level of the situated interaction—and beyond, as evidenced in follow-up interviews, community events, changes in school programming, and so on.

I draw a second example from a 2014 meeting between education leaders and disability advocates, which was widely reported by national media outlets. The interactions reported for that meeting indicate that state intervention into VSLs prevails with respect to characterizations of and lack of training and programming in VSLs—despite official rhetoric supporting 'sign language' in the 2010 Law on Persons with Disability and the 2015 state ratification of the Convention of the Rights of Persons with Disability. For example, Deaf community members' descriptions of their languages and sociolinguistic identities are routinely ignored; indeed, Deaf people may not even be invited to meetings that undoubtedly have a bearing on their institutional participation, language rights, and so forth—as is true for the case discussed next.

On December 9, 2014, Việt Nam's leading education newspaper, *Giáo Dục và Thời Đại* [Education & Era], reported statements made by Lê Văn Tạc, Director of Special Education Research at the National Institute of Educational Science,[1] given at a workshop hosted by the Hà Nội Association of People with Disabilities. The focus of the workshop was the association's proposed new project: Mobilizing Education Policymakers to Include Teaching of Sign Language and Deaf Culture for Hearing Impaired People as One of the Tasks of Centers for Continuing Education (*Vận động các nhà hoạch định chính sách giáo dục đưa việc dạy ngôn ngữ ký hiệu và văn hóa cho người khiếm thính là một trong những nhiệm vụ của các Trung tâm Giáo dục Thường xuyên*).[2]

As one of the highest-ranking special education officials, well known for his leadership in special school and inclusive education initiatives, Lê Văn Tạc's presence signaled the seriousness with which one subset of state-affiliated research partners viewed the association's proposal. Remarks attributed to him then clearly underline the "urgent" need for state commitment to "sign language for deaf people in Việt Nam"(*ngôn ngữ ký hiệu cho người điếc ở Việt Nam*):[3]

> *Việc nghiên cứu, thống nhất và phổ biến ngôn ngữ ký hiệu cho người điếc ở Việt Nam đang là nhu cầu khách quan, bức thiết, cần được quan tâm, đầu tư nghiêm túc về chương trình và chính sách hỗ trợ.*

---

1. The National Institute of Educational Sciences (NIES; Viện Khoa Học Giáo Dục Việt Nam) is located in Hà Nội. See the NIES website, http://vnies.edu.vn

2. The story was reported by Kim Thoa. See http://giaoducthoidai.vn/thoi-su/ho-tro-nguoi-khiem-thinh-hoa-nhap-cong-dong-532871-v.html

3. Note that the journalist does not use the capitalized form of *Điếc* [Deaf], which is preferred by Vietnamese Deaf community leaders and members in this research.

Study of a unified and common sign language for deaf people in Việt Nam are objective needs, urgent, that should be given attention and serious investment in program and policy support.

During the last decade, Vietnamese state attention to signed languages has grown considerably. This is evidenced by the proliferation of positively framed news reportage on deaf people, their talents and aspirations, as well as public interest stories on the love and support Deaf people's families show for them and their use of VSLs.[4] It is also demonstrated by the passage of the 2010 comprehensive disability law (the first law to include sign language and to authorize its use in education); authorization of community-based organizations and INGO projects involving signed language-related training and signing Deaf participants; the 2012 hiring of Việt Nam's first Deaf college graduates as special school teachers; the 2015 ratification of the UN Convention on the Rights of Persons with Disabilities; and statements by eminent state actors such as Lê Văn Tạc.[5]

Foregrounded in these public mediums and sites of interaction and action are relationships between state-directed national and geopolitical agendas, *and* state-directed management of Deaf people's *participation in* and use of VSLs *connected to* such agendas. In state rhetoric and media representation, 'sign language' is commonly referenced as an idealistically singular form, and the state its paramount authorizing medium. For example, in the excerpt given earlier, Lê Văn Tạc does not promote the study of the varieties of VSLs claimed by signed language communities in Việt Nam (Cooper, 2015; Cooper & Nguyễn, 2015) or language researchers (Cooper, 2014; Woodward, 2003; Woodward et al., 2004; Woodward & Nguyễn, 2012). Rather, Lê Văn Tạc's remarks promote the study of a "unified and common sign language." This position has been the official state stance on VSLs since at least 2006, when Vietnamese prime minister Nguyễn Tấn Dũng issued Decree no. 01/2006/CT-TTg, Promoting Implementation of Policies to Assist Disabled Persons in the Current Social-Economic Development Situation. Section three of that decree directed the Ministry of Education and Training to accomplish the unification of sign language in Việt Nam (see *ngôn ngữ ký hiệu* in the following):

Xây dựng trìnhThủ tướng Chính Phủ lược và kế hoạch . . . thống nhất việc sử dụng **ngôn ngữ ký hiệu** [emphasis mine] *cho người khuyết tật/tàn về ngôn ngữ trong phạm vi cả nước.*

Building on the prime minister's strategies and plans . . . unify the use of **sign language** for persons with handicaps or disabilities according to the language of the country.

---

4. An example of positively framed media coverage of Deaf people, their families, and Hà Nội Sign Language includes the October 10, 2015, episode of *"Điều ước Thứ 7"* [Saturday Wishes], a popular Saturday morning program featuring public-interest stories produced and aired by Hà Nội–based VTV3. See http://vtv.vn/video/dieu-uoc-thu-7-10-10-2015-96519.htm

5. In 2012 and 2014 the EP graduated two cohorts (totaling seventeen graduates) who earned college degrees in primary-school Deaf education (*bằng cao đẳng sư phạm tiểu học*). Of these, seven students are now studying to complete their university education.

As an official directive that focused on economic and social development, Decree no. 01/2006/CT-TTg manifests a linguistic imperative for "persons with handicaps or disabilities" as a national strategy. The presence of signed language varieties is not addressed in the decree, nor does the decree specify how the "unification" of sign language is supposed to be operationalized to correspond to "the language of the country." That is, the decree does not indicate how the grammars of VSLs should be transformed in order to take the form of Vietnamese (Woodward, 2003; Woodward & Nguyễn, 2012)—which is an impossible accomplishment for any language to achieve.

In the context of the circumstances just described, languages targeted for modification or management[6] may cease to exist—variously described in the linguistic and anthropological literatures as "language shift" (Fishman, 1971, 1991), "language death" (Crystal, 2000; Mufwene, 2004), and "linguistic genocide" (Skutnabb-Kangas, 2000). Whereas language standardization is an increasingly popular state tactic for (spoken and) signed languages, resistance to such tactics are commonly foiled by signed language communities' own linguistic pleasure in, sociopolitical commitments to, and creativity in maintaining their languages in the face of state pressure (and academic debates).

Oral vs. Manual/Speech vs. Sign Debates

Present in every epoch since the beginning of what has been recorded about the formal education of Deaf students (e.g., circa mid-1600s in England, mid-1700s in France), the *speech vs. sign* debate demonstrates the durability of the notion of language as the externalization of thought, given expression (only) via speech sounds. As discussed in chapter 2, such close coupling of thought with spoken language is recorded in the Western tradition as early as the writings of Aristotle.[7] Worldwide bans on the use of signed languages in Deaf education took nearly two thousand years to consolidate and correspond to mid-to-late nineteenth-century Western-European empire building and the rise of nationalisms that culminated in the resolution endorsing oralism, which was passed at an international meeting of educators and administrators from schools for deaf students in Milan, Italy, in 1880. "The Milan Congress," as it is often referred

---

6. See the discussion in chapter 1 of Neustupný (2006) on language management. Literature from and critique of the field of language policy and planning (LPP) are extremely important here. With respect to signed languages, see Eichmann (2009), Reagan (2010), and Murray (2015).

7. Nearly 2,000 years later John Bulwer, a London-based physician, wrote *Philocophus*, which advocates the education of Deaf people according to a variety of methods, including gestures but particularly through teaching the eye to "heare" (Bulwer, 1648). Among the first sign-based schools for Deaf students was the school established in France 100 years later by Charles-Michel de l'Épée, who created signs for concepts found in the French language. During the next 100 years, Deaf people's increasing access to education facilitated the movement of trained Deaf educators of Deaf students into Deaf educational institutions as teachers in their own right. Just a few years after Herbert Spencer's notion of social Darwinism first appeared in Europe, the infamous 1880 Second International Congress on Education of the Deaf in Milan, Italy, effectively ended the practice of hiring deaf educators of Deaf students by promoting oral methods of instruction rather than manual ones.

to in Deaf studies and Deaf history circles, had a major impact on Deaf education, the status of signed languages, and communication practices between Deaf and non-Deaf people, particularly in European countries and the United States (Lane, 1984, 1992).

The continued relevance of the Milan resolution for language and education debates is marked by activities such as the 2010 collaboration between the British Columbia Deaf community and the International Congress on Education of the Deaf (ICED), which resulted in public condemnation of the Milan resolution at the ICED's 21st meeting in Vancouver, Canada.[8] Moreover, in the late-modern period, the speech versus sign debate is often reinvigorated by technological innovation closely aligned with special-interest groups such as medical providers, surgeons, and device manufacturers (Johnson, 2006). These powerful constituencies, which command access to vast funding streams and lobbying power, periodically trounce the scholarly insights that signed language linguistic and anthropological researchers have managed to establish despite low-priority funding and weak commitments by political leaders.

In Việt Nam the speech versus sign debate is a powerful one; however, it appears that the Milan resolution per se had no direct legacy for Việt Nam. The Lái Thiêu School for the Mute-Deaf was established in 1886, six years after Milan. According to five former Lái Thiêu students with whom I conducted a group interview, Lái Thiêu also continued to operate as a sign language-based school until well "after 1975" and the ongoing reunification of north and south Việt Nam.[9] These interviewees reported that teachers at Lái Thiêu used "sign language well." One interviewee added that teachers at Lái Thiêu used sign language BETTER THAN HEARING PEOPLE [teachers] NOW . . . THE RIGHT WAY. Whatever impact Milan may have had on Việt Nam likely occurred at a later date and via international development partners sought out by the Vietnamese state for the former's demonstrated advocacy of speech-based pedagogical philosophy, which was consistent with the emergent structure of the state's decisions about Deaf education in Việt Nam (Cooper, 2014; Woodward et al., 2003; Woodward & Nguyễn, 2012).

Notwithstanding points of convergence with the emergence of speech-based Deaf education elsewhere, the rise of speech-based Deaf education in Việt Nam is connected to unique social and historical circumstances and has also taken unique directions within state institutions and social change activities. Vietnamese signed languages have never been officially banned, but they were prohibited until 2010 and continue to be both implicitly and explicitly discouraged (Cooper & Nguyễn, 2015).

---

8. Announcement of the ICED decision was covered extensively by Deaf media and academic outlets. Responses by world Deaf leaders include statements by the World Federation of the Deaf (http://wfdeaf.org/news/international-congress-of-the-deaf-iced-july-18-22-2010-vancouver-canada) and then president of Gallaudet University, Alan T. Hurwitz (http://www.gallaudet.edu/news/iced-milan-rejected.html).

9. The five Deaf adults with whom I conducted this group interview were approximately 45 years of age (in 2009) and had been classmates together at Lái Thiêu as children and adolescents. After 1975 they stopped going to school when Lái Thiêu started requiring students to participate in farm production and reportedly discontinued educational programming.

The father of a Deaf daughter, a man who helped cofound one of HCMC's first Deaf education special schools, described the speech versus sign debate in the following way: "There were three groups—and there are still three groups—those who believe in speech only, those who believe in sign only, and those who believe in both. But no one has had any training, so they just keep on doing what they *believe*" (emphasis in the original). This same father went on to describe how, within five years of having established the first special school, he knew the speech-based approach was not working; however, he was, he said, unable to stop it because of people's beliefs, particularly regarding spoken Vietnamese.[10] This father/school founder also explained that, in the mid-1980s, public opinion largely blamed spiritual wrongdoing by the parent(s) for the birth of a Deaf child.[11] Therefore, when the Deaf children who attended his school could turn to their parents and say "*ba, má*" [father, mother], it powerfully suggested to them that their Deaf child might be able to fit into society, remove the family from social stigmatization, and contribute to the growth of the nation.

In the late 1980s, the Vietnamese state pursued speech-based education, institutionalizing it as a national approach within its newly established Deaf education special school system. As mentioned in the introduction, this was followed in the mid-1990s with the implementation of Inclusive Education (IE); IE educational planners determined that Deaf students should be placed in regular education classrooms, by which students were expected to engage in educational activities via spoken Vietnamese. Now, several decades into market-socialist reform, Vietnamese Deaf education special schools and IE continue to variously encourage and discourage VSLs, despite official disability policies that stipulate students' right to use sign language in education. Significant factors contributing to these circumstances include the following: (1) uncertainty on the part of special school personnel as to what HCMSL is, how to use it, and ongoing ambivalence about whether it should be used as an instructional modality; (2) lack of training or retraining in Deaf education instruction; and (3) ongoing state-level debates about language standardization that discourage school personnel from learning a language that they may later be required to abandon in the context of

---

10. In the United States, beliefs that inform educational decisionmaking include things such as the Common Core State Standards (CCSS), which aim to deliver academic excellence through an increasing array of academic assessments (Horvat & Baugh, 2015; McGuinn, 2015) and the Next Generation Science Standards. Other beliefs, especially those prevalent among the general population, include the conviction that use of American Sign Language negatively affects English language literacy. The latter is evidenced in, among other institutionalized practices, educational programming that requires or permits teachers to use spoken English simultaneously with signing (SimCom).

11. An interview with the mother of a Deaf daughter resembled these comments. The mother, a follower of the Đạo Thánh religion, attributed her daughter's deafness to the Buddhist notion of *luật nhân quả* [lit., law of karma]. She explained, for example, that she indulges her daughter's requests for money, even when they are unreasonable, because of the debt she owes to her daughter from a past life.

annual or biannual changes to educational mandates. Related to these circumstances, consider the following comments made by research participant:

> Mây (an EP-trained college graduate and HCMSL instructor): If we raised our hands to sign, they [teachers] would slap our hands and tell us to speak. . . . They told our parents not to sign with us at home or we would never speak. Now we have little communication with our parents. My parents say they are too old to learn sign language.

> Special school principal: If we let them [Deaf students] sign, they won't want to speak. Speaking will give them a better chance in society.

> *Researcher: When students finish school, do they speak?*

> Principal: No. And they can't write—they don't have the words. They can't communicate. We work with Deaf people. . . . we think the government of our country, they don't know what's necessary to work with Deaf people. We have no training. So who would we ask for information? . . . So when we ask questions in class and the students answer the wrong way we don't know why.

> *Researcher: What if students answer using HCMSL?*

> Principal: We have a habit of saying 'người Điếc ngược.' Deaf people are backward. They speak the wrong way.

With respect to the relationships between language ideology, state structures, social and political-economic power (examined in this chapter and in Chapter 3), it is unsurprising that some Deaf communities might advocate signed language standardization as a language right within their own country locations, with international partners, or on behalf of signed language usage groups in other countries (see Chapter 5 for an in-depth discussion of standardization). In the United States, Frances M. Parsons was well known for her staunch advocacy of Total Communication (TC) (1988), and her exportation of TC to countries around the world has received both praise and criticism. American-born Andrew J. Foster established 32 Deaf education mission schools in thirteen African countries using American Sign Language as the language of instruction (Agboola, 2014; Kiyaga & Moores, 2003; Schmaling, 2001) and is widely regarded as the "father" of Deaf education in Africa (Ilabor, 2009). The legacies of Foster's education and missionary work on the African continent are numerous and variously regarded, as indicated in recent critical examination of its features (see Lutalo-Kiingi & De Clerck, 2015; Kusters, 2014, 2015a, 2015b; Moges, 2015).

Soya Mori's work in Southeast Asia provides another example in which he, a Japanese economist specializing in disability and development, advocates a standardized form of Myanmar sign language, which, he argues, resembles the standardized forms of signed languages found "in the United States and Japan" (2011, p. 334). Mori also argues that the supposed standardization of these languages "occurred naturally as part of Deaf community development" (ibid.). Both of these claims are highly contestable and contested.[12] The examples from Parsons, Foster, and Mori indicate the bearing that initiatives have on both (signed) language policy and Deaf education in extranational country locations, as well as on Deaf people and scholars, among others. These circumstances resemble those of Việt Nam, with Komitee Twee's promulgation of speech-based Deaf education soon after the country initiated its open-door policy in 1986.[13] They also resemble contemporary contestation over signed language standardization and varieties in Việt Nam, particularly between those advocating the use of natural signed languages (e.g., HCMSL, Hà Nội Sign Language) and those advocating signing in Vietnamese word order (see chapters 3 and 4 for detailed discussion of these issues).

Exerting influence on those who lack access to citizenship rights, Deaf individuals, social organizers, and their families must navigate engagement with state actors, who may already have affiliations with entities pursuing particular speech- or sign-based agendas. It is the state that then has a strong role in determining the shape of language policies and programming—what Blommaert calls a "conglomerate of form and load" (2005, p. 393); that is, language (usage, identities, ideologies) is an *effect* of both the conventionalized ways that people sign or speak together and the social resources available to them. States, then, are empowered to set the terms—laws, policies, economic appropriations, and so forth—by which certain individuals and groups are included and others excluded. This is not a new observation, but social inequalities have yet to be ethnographically examined in a manner or to the depth that Blommaert (2005) argues is necessary if we are to understand the social distribution of linguistic resources by and within nation-states.

Blommaert's examination of sociolinguistic approaches to language rights is useful for thinking about the ways in which Deaf community leaders develop activist, public information, and research agendas in the context of their membership in particular nation-states and in response to particular state structures and policies. A number of Deaf groups are also conducting such efforts in collaboration with language researchers, including those described in Cooper and Nguyễn (2015), De Clerck (2011), Hochgesang (2015), Kusters (2012, 2015b), Lutalo-Kiingi and De Clerck (2015), and Moriarty Harrelson (2015).[14] Critiquing sociolinguists' fascination with "language

---

12. For a critique of Mori's stance on sign language standardization in developing countries, see Adam (2015), who writes: "[Mori argues that standardization] will increase the human rights of Deaf people and lead to an enhanced respect for Deaf culture and language. This process still raises the questions of who is driving this standardization, whether Deaf people in Myanmar actually have any control over this process, and whether they have any ownership of the language" (p. 437).

13. The Komitee Twee (KT) is a Dutch INGO with various projects in Việt Nam. Previously focusing on training in speech-based instruction and distribution of hearing aids, this work was led by Barry Wright, while much of the teacher training was conducted by Betty Maas. Although KT no longer trains teachers in Deaf education special schools, it still gives periodic presentations and workshops focused on early intervention and "rehabilitation" of children with hearing impairment. For more information on KT's activities in Việt Nam, see http://www.vusta.vn/vi/news/Cac-to-chuc-phi-chinh-phu-quoc-te/Komitee-Twee-of-the-Netherlands-KTwee-BR-Uy-ban-II-Ha-Lan-1086.html

14. See also Harris, Holmes, and Mertens (2009) and Singleton, Jones, and Hanumantha (2014).

names" over descriptions of "differences within the language complex" (2005, p. 391), Blommaert argues that it is not languages that create or dismantle inequality but "how linguistic resources are actually employed, and under what conditions, in real societies" (ibid., p. 410). Thus, it is not naming languages—or in Makoni and Pennycook's (2006) terms, *inventing* or *disinventing* languages—that confers legitimacy but rather the "social load" of value attribution through systematically reproduced language that ratifies normative forms of "groupness" or "identity" (Blommaert, 2005, p. 393). Later in this chapter I return to Blommaert's (ibid.) framework and the analytic importance of ethnographic examination of the relationships between Deaf people's signed language–based action and state formation and change in Việt Nam.

At the time of this writing, HCMSL is one case in which the language—originally named by James C. Woodward (2003) as Hồ Chí Minh City Sign Language—is surviving and is, recently, also appearing to thrive. As the foregoing discussion indicates, the institutionalized life of HCMSL is (along with that of other VSLs) a matter of state-level importance—and it has been for some decades. The social, political, and economic forces that affect HCMSL usage (negatively, positively, or otherwise) are therefore of great consequence to both HCMSL users and to state actors in their ongoing formation and governing of the national state. These forces are also of important analytic significance because, in connecting the examination of signed languages to that of state formation, we gain a perspective on both that contributes to our efforts to understand the features of particular national states and particular subnational populations in previously unexplored ways.

This study then also contributes to efforts to confront notions of states and notions of Deaf populations as monolithic, universal, and ahistoric entities. Hansen and Stepputat's (2006) ethnographic work on states and languages in postcolonial contexts illuminates this point:

> Instead of talking about the state as an entity that always/already consists of certain features, functions, and forms of governance, let us approach each actual state as a historically specific configuration of a range of languages of stateness, some practical, some symbolic and performative, that have been disseminated, translated, interpreted, and combined in widely differing ways and sequences across the globe. (ibid., pp. 6–7)

Applying this conceptual device to research participant commentaries and other ethnographic data in the study, I find it useful to consider the ways in which *languages of stateness* (ideologies) are instantiated by state actors and by Deaf persons and groups, as well as for what purposes. Similarly, we are attentive to the ways in which *languages of deafness*—as well as other terms of subjective or official identification—are instantiated by state actors and Deaf persons and groups and for what purposes.

At first glance, Vietnamese state rhetoric on signed language and Deaf narratives on HCMSL seem to be dichotomous, resembling the ways that some North Atlantic–based Deaf studies and critical disability literatures have theorized, and sometimes valorized, Deaf cultural formation and sociolinguistic perspectives as oppositional consciousness that emerge in response to situations of oppression (Groch, 2001; Woll & Ladd, 2011; Wrigley, 1999). On closer inspection, Vietnamese state rhetoric and Deaf narratives both orient toward mobilization of participation in national development, solidarity, ethnonational culture, and geopolitical sovereignty. Both also emphasize familial and social belonging as key modes of mobilizing participation in development activities (cf. Gammeltoft, 2014).

Resembling Gammeltoft's description of *belonging*—and contrasting with notions of oppositional consciousness prevalent in the North Atlantic Deaf studies literature, which often starkly juxtaposes DEAF and HEARING community identities and goals—the ways that Deaf people in southern Việt Nam imagine, participate in, create, and transform state-society relations via HCMSL demonstrate complex patterns of relationship with both NGƯỜI ĐIẾC [Deaf] and NGƯỜI NGHE [hearing] people. For instance, whereas Deaf individuals and community organizers may disagree with state and media characterizations of deafness and HCMSL (as well as VSLs in general), responses to misrepresentations are often enacted in the context of maintaining and strengthening cherished relationships with Deaf and non-Deaf family members, teachers, and trusted community members—whether such individuals use HCMSL or another VSL or do not sign at all.

Similar examples have been reported for the villages of Bengkala and Desa Kolok in Bali, Indonesia (Branson, Miller, & Marsaja, 1996; Marsaja, 2008; De Vos, 2012), Adamorobe, Ghana (Kusters, 2013, 2015; Nyst, 2007), Ban Khor, Thailand (Nonaka, 2004), a Yucatec-Mayan village (Johnson, 1991), and Bedouin communities in southern Israel (Meir, Sandler, Padden, & Aronoff, 2010). Such examples are also, I would argue, in ample evidence in North Atlantic countries where discourses of polarization between DEAF and HEARING people predominate but which look quite different in everyday sites of interaction.[15]

For the Deaf research participants who collaborated on this study, their responses to misrepresentations of Deaf people and HCMSL centrally involve focusing on educational ambitions and education-centered social organizing (though not necessarily instances of misrepresentation). The remarks of Lưu Ngọc Tú in an interview for the *Tuổi Trẻ* newspaper[16] illustrate this strategy (Trung Tân, 2009):

> Tôi hi vọng khi kết thúc khóa học này tôi sẽ cùng các bạn ở đây xây dựng được một ngôi trường dành riêng cho người khiếm thính học tập bằng NNKH và sẽ học cao hơn, giúp ích nhiều hơn cho xã hội.

> I hope that at the end of this course of study my peers and I will build a school dedicated to hearing impaired students [who wish] to study using sign language, and [by] advancing their educations even further, help society even more.

---

15. Examination of contact between Deaf and non-Deaf persons and groups (those that involve a signed language and those that do not) has yet to receive critical attention by scholars. However, a simple survey of social media sites, videologs, religious organizational newsletters, and other cultural productions clearly indicates that such contact is more than merely oppositional with respect to identity, subjectivity, or material outcomes (e.g., achieving social rights, livelihood sustainability).

16. Hồ Chí Minh City–based *Tuổi Trẻ* is the newspaper of the Communist Party Youth Organization.

According to my analysis of Lưu's text (Cooper, 2014), the journalist's use of "hearing impaired" here is an example of what Pierre Bourdieu termed "an imposition of form" (1991, p. 137). Research participants commonly reported that they informed journalists of their preferential use of the self-identifier ĐIẾC [Deaf] before, during, and after interviews, yet *Điếc* rarely appeared in print. Expanding on Cooper (2014), I maintain that Lưu's strategy demonstrates a focus on the aim, not the name, of a sociolinguistic group or an identity.

Connected to this strategy is the prioritizing of advocacy efforts that call attention to the social conditions confronting Deaf people in Việt Nam. In interviews and community meetings, research participants repeatedly emphasized the tens of thousands of Deaf and hard of hearing children and adults in educational and income-impoverishing situations, whom they hoped to work with in order to change their living conditions (Cooper 2011, 2014; see also NCCD 2010; UNICEF, 2013).[17] To refer to these circumstances, Deaf commentators often used HCMSL KHÔNG ĐỦ ĐIỀU KIỆN [CHO CON ĐI HỌC]. The concept *không đủ điều kiện* can be literally translated as "children ineligible to attend school"; however, such a translation obscures the material emphasis of ĐIỀU KIỆN [lit., means or conditions], which principally indexes a family's financial ability to pay for or subsidize school enrollment (figure 2.1).

The narratives of Deaf research participants also emphasized how society might be restructured to make it not only more inclusive but also more reflective of Deaf people in Việt Nam, particularly with respect to the varieties of VSLs that Deaf people use in the diverse regions of the country. Accordingly, their comments addressed both local and national material realities, and they directed social change activities toward advancing the legitimacy of HCMSL as well as other VSLs. This multilingual affirmative position on VSLs is not shared by most state actors, according to their official statements, from the prime minister, to high-ranking Ministry of Education and Training personnel (such as Lê Văn Tạc, mentioned earlier), to Deaf education principals and teachers. In fact, technological innovation continues to be a significant force in the speech vs. sign debate and in Deaf education language policy and programming broadly. Around the world cochlear implantation (CI) is becoming increasingly affordable, but, especially in the United States, its "benefits" have been mischaracterized by the powerful, financially endowed, and ideologically steeped medical establishment (Johnson, 2006). In performing CI surgeries—whereby a device is implanted into the brain to stimulate the auditory nerve with input from an external receiver—surgeons do not restore auditory functioning but rather, in order to implant the CI, must destroy the auditory apparatus, along with whatever residual hearing an individual might possess.

In Việt Nam, CI is now becoming more available. One doctor in HCMC specializes in CI surgeries, and the media frequently feature stories of CI successes.[18] At the present

---

17. A number of research participants related HCMSL SUPPORT to the Vietnamese concept *ủng hộ*.

18. Articles on cochlear implantation include the following: *Tạo màng nhĩ cho người khiếm thính* [Creating eardrum for the hearing impaired], *Người Lao Đông*, June 15, 2006: http://nld.com.vn/khoa-hoc/tao-mang-nhi-cho-nguoi-khiem-thinh-154316.htm; *300 người thoát đời câm điếc nhờ cấy ốc tai* [300 People Escape life as mute deaf with Cochlear Implant.], *Vietnam Express Online*, December 16, 2016: http://suckhoe.vnexpress.net/tin-tuc/suc-khoe/300-nguoi-thoat-doi-cam-diec-nho-cay-oc-tai-3514641.html

Figure 2.1. HCMCSL for KHÔNG ĐỦ ĐIỀU KIỆN [without the (financial) conditions or means to do X].

time, CI is cost prohibitive for the majority of Vietnamese people. Only one participant in my research study had undergone CI surgery. After the surgery he had no follow-up to learn how to use the device and, finding it a nuisance, decided to stop using the external receiver. However, he has not yet had the internal processor removed because, he said, "It will disappoint my mother. She hopes that I will use it someday and learn to speak." As Việt Nam becomes further integrated into the world market economy, Deaf constituencies and social scientists alike will be attentive to the kinds of technologies the Vietnamese state pursues relative to language policy in Deaf education and employment, training, health and population quality campaigns, and other initiatives aimed at Deaf people's sociolinguistic and body features and practices.

"Western Liberalism," Scientific Racism, and Sociopolitical Displacement of the Body and Language

To put relationships between language and state formation into perspective, this section focuses on the ways in which such relationships have been studied and theorized in the social sciences. This review of approaches to the state and language covers a number of "idealized" cases (Blommaert, 2005, p. 390). It is not my intent to belabor Blommaert's point about the importance of actual versus hypothetical (and often idealized) cases, but signed languages have been so extensively and vigorously described as anything but real language that it is necessary to provide some context for how we got here. In tracing this path, I also scrutinize the notions of a global, shared "we" with respect to signed languages, to a shared Vietnamese Deaf "community" (in southern Việt Nam), and to research relationships established between signed language researchers and research participants and/or collaborating partners (see also Friedner & Kusters 2015).

The state and the "body" both make early appearances in the history of social science theorizing. As heuristic devices and analytic fields, the state and the body have each enjoyed different kinds of theoretical attention and status. Both have been abandoned and taken up again at various points or subsumed under other theoretical projects. However, they are rarely considered in relation to one another, particularly at the level of everyday experience. How do states interact with bodies in everyday life? How might states be conditioned on the features of bodies? To explore these questions, I begin by discussing two foundational notions of the state in Western philosophy and the ways early state formation indexed concerns with the body. I then visit three approaches to the state that were prominent in late-modern social science in order to consider the significance of these formulations of citizenship and sovereignty for establishing criteria of idealized and de-idealized bodies. This allows me to propose a fourth approach to the way in which related concerns might be addressed: a methodology of state embodiment. In each of these approaches, I also discuss their differing implications for education and social change. I do not endorse any one approach over the others; rather, I suggest ways in which each one might be useful to aspects of state analysis.

In the Western philosophical tradition, the state emerges in the sixteenth century as a conceptual object that, for the next three hundred years, takes on the nature of a referentially true thing. The truth of the state, as it is created in the liberal tradition, is its reasoned formation, by which its institutions are governed. According to a system of laws and their rational adjudication, states claimed impartial judgment over and against the unreliability, weakness, and self-interest of the body—notions also powerfully influenced by contemporaneous Christian religious traditions (P. Brown, 1988/2008). Vexed by the body, the early philosophers of the state wrote against it in various ways.

By denying the meaningful participation of the body in reasoning, thinkers of the liberal tradition did not remove the body from the state. Rather, they concealed the body within the state-idea and its various institutions, classification systems, and coordinated activities. Everything that the state did was by definition not body. Body became that which was outside the rational ordering of the state, yet subsumed under it; split off from reason, the body was a thing to be managed and contained. It is with the rationalist project that the investigation of connections between the state and language rightly begins, as the fundaments of many late-modern systems of law, jurisprudence, political organization, and education instantiate very particular inclusions and exclusions founded on notions of body differences and their supposed meanings—especially with respect to assumed language faculties and intellect and their alleged connections to skin colors, body shapes, genitalia, skeletal structures, and so on (Fausto-Sterling, 1995; Gould, 1981; Terry & Urla,1995).[19]

Thomas Hobbes (1588–1679) was among the first early modern writers to theorize the state. In *Leviathan,* Hobbes juxtaposed a brutish state of nature (i.e., war) with that of society conditioned upon a reasoned sovereign state (1651, p. 84). In Hobbes's formulation, mutual adherence to a social contract under the authority of a sovereign ruler allows "Man" to escape "the condition of Man . . . which is a condition of Warre" (ibid. , p. 87). Unlike his contemporary Descartes, Hobbes located reason in a human body, calling into question the "gross errors of certain metaphysicians" (ibid., quoted in the *Stanford Encyclopedia of Philosophy*). However, Hobbes's body was still understood as governed by *jus naturale,* natural law, such that it required the intervention of the sovereign who creates the law in order to prevent man from actions that are "destructive of his life" (*lex naturalis*) (1904[1651], p. 86). Reason in this instance is a political state of affairs in which subjects submit to sovereign rule in order to mitigate the passions of the body and facilitate a defense against enemies—the first of such enemies being "Man" himself. For Hobbes, the state is above its subjects, encompassing them according to a protective agreement by which they are then duty bound. In this agreement, the state of nature (war) is transferred to the state.

Jean-Jacques Rousseau (1712–1778) wrote against Hobbes's proposed state of nature and paternalistic vision of the state to develop his own theory of the social contract, developing a notion of sovereignty expressed as the *general will* of citizens. Accordingly, it is general will that establishes the state "for the common good" (1968[1762], p. 69). The act of sovereignty, according to Rousseau, "is not a covenant between a superior and an inferior, but a covenant of the body with each of its members" (ibid., pp. 76–77). With Rousseau, reason takes the form of a political collective that determines the law

---

19. A complete history of the rationalist project and its implications for sociopolitical orders, languages, and bodies is beyond the scope of this book. For more comprehensive discussions see W. Brown (1995); Damasio (1994[2005]); Johnson (2007); Lakoff and Johnson (1999); and Strathern (2000).

and delegates its application via selection of the agents of government. Sovereignty is thus the act of the free ruling themselves. It is not the law that establishes privileges, admits individuals to classes, or selects a king, but individuals who are each their own sovereign as a "body politic by the social pact" (ibid., p. 80). Here the body is not a specific body, but a mass body whose reality is achieved by agreement and its "*movement* and *will* by legislation" (ibid., p. 80; emphasis mine). In this instance, the state of nature is retained as a positive force in individuals who, "if properly informed, and provided its members do not have any communication among themselves, the great number of small differences will always produce a general will and the decision will be good" (ibid., p. 73). The citizen, in this context, is still characteristically male and French (white).

The development of the modern state thus formed alongside, and indeed was contingent upon, categorization of the body. Such categorization elevated certain body features and practices over others, contributing to increasingly complex classification systems of sexual, gendered, racial, and linguistic descriptions producing socially normative and aberrant typologies, whose foundation supposed binary differences. Men shared nothing in common with women, persons of color with white persons, or signed language users with those of spoken languages. It is in this scientific context that Hobbes's state is authorized, indeed obligated, to kill those posing a threat to the collective, whereas Rousseau's state assigns the obligation to act to the collective. In both instances, state formation centrally concerns forms of normative sovereignty. In the first instance, sovereignty is achieved through the negation of a body given to destruction, and in the second, through the negation of a prepolitical, particularized (normative) body. Both philosophical frameworks provide traces of the emergence of a Western liberal form of modernity that linked together requirements for language and for bodies that authorizes or denies membership in state institutions and identities.

Such frameworks were—and are—but one of many expressions of late-modern sovereignty around the world. Paraphrasing Achille Mbembe's observation, modernity produced multiple notions of sovereignty entailing multiple notions of biopolitics (2001, p. 13). According to Mbembe, it is not modernity but "late-modern political criticism [that] has unfortunately privileged normative theories of democracy and has made the concept of reason one of the most important elements of both the project of modernity and of the topos of sovereignty" (ibid.). Although the sovereignties and biopolitics entailed in Hobbes and Rousseau are distinct, they correspond to a narrow philosophical universe that proved highly influential to worldwide political, economic, and scientific formations. Discussion of Hobbes and Rousseau, as well as their contemporary legibility, demonstrates the powerful legacy these Western liberal conceptions of modernity and sovereignty have had for world sociopolitical organization of states, bodies (persons), and languages. Mbembe's critique thus illuminates the following: (1) the displacement of the body within political and scientific spheres; (2) language as always and already a body-based practice (whether in signed, spoken, or written forms); and (3) that the legacies of Western liberal conceptions of modernity and sovereignty for world geopolitical organization and relations persist in forms we are likely to overlook (i.e., scientific common sense).

With respect to Deaf people and the emergence of the Western liberal tradition, Lennard Davis (1995) reminds us that Rousseau was a beneficiary of seventeenth-century treatises on Deaf people, which mushroomed with the rise in print culture. Publications addressed the nature of deafness, Deaf education, and signed language and included public displays of Deaf people's capabilities. Davis quotes Rousseau, who conjectured that, without speech, "we would have been able to institute laws, to choose leaders, to invent arts, to establish commerce, and to do, in a word, almost as many things as we do with the help of speech" (ibid., p. 59; from Rousseau, 1966, p. 9). In substituting the (then commonly referenced) "dumbness" of the Deaf body with its opposite, Rousseau implicitly accepts the terms proposed by the ideology of a speech-based world, eliminating any difference in social formation emergent in Deaf people's sociolinguistic practices. However—and this, I believe, is important for any examination of similar cases available in the contemporary moment—Rousseau did not attribute radical intellectual difference to deaf people who used signed languages. Davis (1995) locates the latter development in the nineteenth-century rise of nationalist discourses and the increase in expert discourses on deafness, both of which are articulated in the notion that able bodies make an able nation. It was in 1880, at the Second International Congress on Education for the Deaf, held in Milan, Italy, that connections between expert discourses on *deafness* as a medical concern and official rhetoric on nationalisms achieved their apogee in a world ban on the use of signed languages in education.[20]

Over the course of the modern project, reason and spoken languages ascended together to bestow notions of social maturity, moral bearing, and intellectual capacity on those using spoken (and written) languages. The less visible the body during verbal displays, the more refined the *speaker* was presumed to be. The "modern period was marked by a propensity to make difference visible" (Mirzoeff, 1995, p. 71). Mirzoeff continues:

> Prior to the nineteenth century it is reasonable to assert that deafness, in the modern sense, did not exist. There were deaf people, certainly, but their affliction was regarded as an incurable mystery sent by God. For the materialist philosophers of the Enlightenment, deaf people were an interesting case study of the importance of sensory input to the formation of intelligence and rationality.

Over the course of the eighteenth century, the gesticulating body, as well as bodies that used signed languages, increasingly indexed diminished intellectual and moral aptitudes. Such categorizations found reinforcement in other fundamental forms of scientific racism taking shape in Europe and North America at that time, which underwent further elaboration during the nineteenth and twentieth centuries, much as they do today (Baker, 1998, 2010; Farber, 2011; Schafft, 2007; Schafft & Zeidler, 2011; Stern, 2005[2016]).

---

20. Deaf educators were barred from the ICED Milan vote. There was one deaf delegate: James Denison (see Van Cleve & Crouch, 1989, pp. 109–111). Representatives of only two countries voted against the ban: those hailing from the United States and Great Britain (see Branson & Miller, 2002; Ladd, 2003; Lane, 1984; and Van Cleve & Crouch, 1989). See chapter 4 for discussion of the significance of the Milan Congress for Việt Nam.

It is useful to ponder the political circumstances of social science theorizing in the twentieth century that led Nettl, in the late 1960s, to proclaim sovereignty a "dead duck" owing to its status as a "limiting concept" (1968, p. 560). Nettl brackets the end of scientific interest in sovereignty from the period just prior to Hitler's invasion of Poland to the still triumphalist "Vietnam War" era, during which he was writing. Interpreting this contradictory theoretical conclusion (i.e., the negation of sovereignty's analytic and practical relevance) as an instance of social scientific complicity with violent sovereignty (war), it is reasonable to question the turn away from sovereignty *as its occasion*—that is, a historical formation that sacrificed human lives to the ruling political-economic orders that made up—literally and in the constructivist sense—Cold War–era geopolitical engagements.

The circumstances in which there is no ruler, no state, and no entity making the decisions of governance, yet supposedly objective decisions, create a problem for theorizing state governance inasmuch as it makes it difficult to theorize various kinds of local, national, and global relations. This observation brings us back to language.

Theories concerned with the state—such as those addressing state policy, structure of state institutions, and governance practices—often build on theories of language.[21] Furthermore, examinations of language policies and their regulation demonstrate how states and subnational groups employ language ideologies as modes of differentiating and controlling populations (Althusser, 1971; Blommaert, 1999, 2005; Bourdieu, 1998; Irvine & Gal, 2000; Jaffe, 1999; Kusters, 2014; Silverstein, 2000).

Accordingly, language policies and everyday practices give form to sovereignty and citizenship by facilitating the presence and arrangement of language users in space and time. Such arrangements are *semiotic economies*, "where [within globalized capitalism] language, text, and discourse become the principal modes of social relations, civic and political life, economic behavior and activity, where means of production and modes of information become intertwined in analytically complex ways" (Luke, 2002, p. 98; see also Luke, 2003).

Two brief examples from spoken and signed language settings illuminate the material significance of semiotic economies. They also demonstrate the differential logics that have often been applied to language users, particularly those perceived to be different in some way. First, Irvine and Gal describe colonizers' representation of southern African speakers' use of the Xhosa language as "brutal," focusing on the sound of the language's clicks (2000, p.40). Because such characterization depends upon language ideologies, "by which people construct ideological representations of linguistic difference" (ibid., p. 37), Xhosa delegitimation occurred in a political, economic, and, importantly, *intersubjective* context wherein colonizers rejected the unfamiliar sounds of Xhosa along with other aspects of Xhosa speakers' bodies (Mbembe, 2001). The "brutality" of Xhosa language-death is by now understood as a colonial intervention and forcefully rejected.

A second, and clearly contrasting, case is instantiated in debates over oral (speech) versus manual (signed) instructional modalities that continue to pervade "expert" Deaf education debates and popular discourses almost 140 years after the Milan resolution.

---

21. For example, Karl Marx (1973[1857]) employed a notion of language universals. Giorgio Agamben employs a Saussurean topology of rule-based enunciation from the general (*langue*) to the particular (*parole*) (2005, p. 39).

Alexander Graham Bell's work in the U.S. branch of the eugenics movement infamously argued Deaf people to be a "defective variety of the human race" which helped institutionalize the discriminatory practices of the Milan resolution, all done with little protest from social scientific or political leaders (Kevles, 1998; see also A. G. Bell, 2008).

In the contemporary moment, the social and political-economic circumstances of linguistic intervention into signed languages are routinely ignored, replaced by humanitarian arguments inflected with Aristotle's 2000-year-old nativist idea that unintelligible speech demonstrates the absence of intelligence per se (Aristotle, 2004, p. 110; see also Bauman, 2004). Certainly, ethnic-minority spoken languages are often delegitimized in a similar manner (Hinton & Hale, 2001; May, 2008), many of which are spoken in former colonies located in African countries (Bamgbose, 2000, 2011; Mugane, 2006; Spitulnik, 1998). Postcolonial spoken-language politics in African countries also interact with and compel policies related to signed languages and Deaf education (De Clerck, 2011; Lutalo-Kiingi & De Clerck, 2015; Moges, 2015; Nyst, 2007). Similar postcolonization effects have been documented for other world locations, such as Cambodia (Moriarty Harrelson, 2015, 2016), India (Friedner, 2014, 2015), and Việt Nam (Cooper, 2014; Cooper & Nguyễn, 2015; Woodward & Nguyễn, 2012), as well as for most colonizing metropoles that now comprise the world's leading economically developed countries (Branson & Miller, 2007, 2008). Accordingly, it is the erasure of the body in social science theory as a language-making body, as a body that is socially valued in differing ways with respect to differing features, that contributes to the persistence of *spoken language* as the norm, against which *signed language* remains a marked term.

The Social Scientific Turn toward and away from States, Languages, and Bodies

In early to mid-twentieth century descriptions of anthropological "others," structural and structural-functional discussions of human organization, language, labor, exchange, and ritual tended to emphasize description of exotic bodies and body practices yet undertheorized them according to historical, political, and other analytic criteria (e.g., empire building). In arguing for the interpretation of social and political relations of non-Western societies on their own terms, A. R. Radcliffe-Brown (1955[1940], p. xxiii) assailed the notion of the state:

> In writings on political institutions there is a good deal of discussion about the nature and origin of the state, which is usually represented as being an entity over and above the human individuals who make up a society, having as one of its attributes something call "sovereignty," and sometimes spoken of as having a will [law being defined as the will of the state], or as issuing commands. The state in this sense does not exist in the phenomenal world; it is a fiction of the philosophers. What does exist is an organization, i.e.[,] a collection of individual human beings connected by a complex system of relations.[22]

---

22. This quote by Radcliffe-Brown is also referenced, in part or in whole, by Abrams (1988), Arextaga (2003), and Trouillot (2001) in their discussions of the significance of theorizing the state.

Ostensibly dispensing with the state, Radcliffe-Brown nevertheless drew on Max Weber's definition of the state as a "human community that (successfully) claims monopoly of the legitimate use of physical force within a given territory" (1991[1918], p. 78). Omitting reference to the state, Radcliffe-Brown shifted theoretical attention to *society:* "The political organization of a society is that aspect of the total organization which is concerned with the control and regulation of the use of physical force" (1955[1940], p. xxiii). This focus mirrors Marxist theory, except that Marx postulated a repressive state serving the interests of a ruling capitalist economic class. Rather than continue to develop a theory of the state, anthropology replaced the state with something presumably more methodologically material (e.g., institutions, government).

The anthropological turn away from the state—in the same historical period during which many formerly colonized peoples were reclaiming possession of state control—thereby helped usher in a disciplinary concentration on peoples without states, which continued for several decades (Trouillot, 2001). Disciplinary concentration on stateless peoples thus facilitated at least two kinds of divides: (1) a civilizational divide between researchers associated with industrialized states and preindustrial research populations; and (2) an analytic bifurcation of politics (state) and culture (society). For postwar World War II social science theorizing on the state, the effect of this was "not that such phenomena as authoritarianism and totalitarianism were ignored, just that the preferred theoretical explanations were couched in terms of economic backwardness or the unfortunate persistence of non-Western 'traditional' values" (Skocpol, 1985, p. 6). These explanations prominently extended to the various socialisms located throughout the world, limiting social science understanding of the formation of these types of state systems.

The divide between supposedly unstudy-able states yet study-able societies reified society while depoliticizing activities associated with culture. Unwittingly or not, depiction of stateless societies outside urban centers of the North Atlantic reduced such societies, yet again, to their bodies, much as with E. B. Tylor's infamous labeling people who lived outside of urban metropoles as "savages" (1892). Description of stateless peoples extended anthropology's catalogue of body morphologies, which had earlier contributed to the explosion of racial classification systems and eugenics regimes in the nineteenth and early twentieth centuries. In this context, variously gradated theories of human cultural development festered, applied by anthropologists to explain differences within national settings. Oscar Lewis's (1959) "culture of poverty" theory is a particularly pernicious example; Max Weber's (1991[1918]) capitalist-oriented studies of Hinduism and Confucianism are other examples (1958, 1964). Anthropological treatment of human social evolution (e.g., Lewis H. Morgan, Julian Steward) and Marxist theory intersected and reinforced each other regarding evolutionary stages of civilization; however, Marxist theory differed significantly from social evolutionary frameworks, particularly regarding the economic inevitability of society splitting into "exploiting rich and the exploited poor," as well as a view of the state as the instrument of such exploitation (Engels, 1972 [1884], p. 228). According to a most crude comparison, the point of overlap between Max Weber and classical Marxism is the formulation of dominance from "above."

Events extending from the 1960s to the 1980s prompted renewed social science and popular interest in the state. These events included the emergence of postcolonial nation-states eschewing the liberal-democratic model; the growth of diverse socialisms; the U.S.-based civil rights movement and, later, Global North anti–Vietnam War and second-wave feminist movements; and growing interdependencies and competition between states. Neo-Marxist and poststructural theories of the state emerged at this time to challenge the notion of the state as both a concrete unity and simply an object of state repression (Althusser, 1971; Foucault, 1979). The entry of postmodernist theory exploded in activity that nevertheless "reduced the complex phenomena of the state and power to 'discourses' and 'representations,' forgetting that discourses and representations have materiality" (Mbembe, 2001, p. 5).

In context of the contemporary spread of neoliberal capitalism, hypermobility of discourses and representations threatens to further displace the state, along with phenomenological accounts of exploitation and marginalization of actual people in actual places (Mittelman, 1996). Therefore, if a globalized order is truly under way, "if this transformation is indeed epochal . . . it has to engage the most complex institutional architecture we have ever produced: the national state" (Sassen, 2006, p. 1).

Reinvigorating Theorizing on the State: The Significance of Ethnographic Description

Observing trends unaccounted for by theory over the past two decades, social scientists have returned to concerns of the state to address transformation in postsocialist states (Hann, 2003; Makovicky, 2014; Verdery, 1998); new state formation (Vu, 2010); new instruments and locations of state making (Chalfin, 2006); reconfigurations of state and society relations (Bernal, 2006); and state formation in relation to forms of language policy, disciplining, and regulation (Branson & Miller, 2008; May, 2008; Scott, 1990; Tollefson, 1991). Anthropologists are also addressing the effects of globalization on states and the globalized dimensions of state governance (Sharma & Gupta, 2006) and have questioned the extent to which trade, treaties, and other practices labeled as "global" ever take place on a global scale, given that economic trade tends to occur between limited partners exclusive of specific state-to-state arrangements (Trouillot, 2001). Observing the recent resurgence of state control over corporate activities within domestic economies in Europe and Asia, political science is also turning to reconsiderations of state analysis (Bremmer, 2010). These developments notwithstanding, relevant literatures on forms of state organization and governance have yet either to embrace the theoretical, political, and practical potential of ethnographic analyses of language and the body as they might or to sufficiently problematize how power is (re)produced and reformulated through linguistic and other uses of the body.

Four Approaches to the State: The Importance of Language and Bodies to Sociopolitical Analysis

State as Actor

The *state as actor approach* builds on theories that conceptualize the state as the dominant force in sociopolitical life. In the mid-1980s, the release of *Bringing the State Back In* reinvigorated political scientific theorizing of the state (BSBI; Evans, Rueschemeyer,

& Skocpol, 1985). Their research focused on issues such as the autonomy and capacity of states to accomplish set goals (ibid., pp. 347–366), the effectiveness of "weak" (decentralized and democratic) and "strong" (centralized and authoritarian) states (Katznelson, 1985, pp. 257–284), and state coercion and war making (Tilly, 1985, pp. 169–191). One hallmark of BSBI theorizing is the weighing of rational versus irrational decision making and interests, such as Rueschemeyer and Evans's discussion of intervention into state and economic transformations (1985, pp. 44–77). A second hallmark of BSBI theorizing is a concern with domination.

Examination of the state as a rational actor did not include actual persons but rather focused on state institutions and "configurations of organization and action that influence the meanings and methods of politics for all groups and classes in society" (Skocpol 1985, p. 28). With respect to domination, BSBI researchers tended also to focus on state welfare as a positive corollary to domination (Evans, Rueschemeyer, & Skocpol, 1985; Tilly, 1985). Accordingly, this strand of *state as actor* theory viewed the state as *already formed;* therefore, BSBI theorists addressed problems they associated with balancing contradictory interests of governing citizens "internally" and managing forces perceived to be located "externally" (Rueschemeyer & Evans, 1985, p. 48).

Absent in BSBI theorizing is an examination of *protection,* or what feminist political theorist Wendy Brown (1995, p. 15) terms a gendered "technique of domination," which is one of the ways that patriarchal and masculinist structures achieve hegemony over women in particular (in binarized sexual systems). Political rhetoric that ignores gendered and sexual diversity and oppression under conditions of dominance shore up normative structures of dominance—which may explain why BSBI theorists also ignored concerns of language.[23] Although not addressing BSBI theorizing per se, Brown's critique of the liberal political tradition as a masculinist form of dominance, locating "the man in the state," suggests the ways in which political orders anchor dominance through forms of embodiment (1995, pp. 166–196; see also Bourdieu's conception of the male-dominated state, 1998, pp. 371–389).

Relevant here are the *whiteness* and the Anglocentricness of the liberal tradition, by which "the theoretical and practical recognition of the body and flesh of 'the stranger' as flesh and body like mine, *the idea of a common human nature, a humanity shared with others,* long posed, and still poses, a problem for Western consciousness" (Mbembe, 2001, p. 2; emphasis in the original). Also relevant here is what might be called the *hearingness* of the liberal tradition, including a mode of citizenship requiring citizens to "speak" their political interest, to answer the call of duty to the state, and, perhaps most unifying within nationalist imaginaries, to literally speak a common language (Anderson, 1983). The plurality of populations governed by late-modern states raises the question of how consent for such political orders is achieved, particularly given that "state meanings and methods of politics" are both unevenly distributed in and unevenly authorized by populations (Skocpol 1985, p. 28).

The Marx-Althusser strand of *state as actor* addresses the issue of how states reproduce themselves over time by introducing the notion of ideological *interpellation.*

---

23. Laitlin's examination of political and religious conflicts in Yorubaland, Nigeria, is one exception (1985, pp. 285–316).

Expanding on Marx's notion of the capitalist mode of production, Althusser theorized social formation as that which "must reproduce the conditions of its production at the same time it produces" (1971, p. 128). In addition to certain skills and knowledge, capitalism must therefore reproduce "submission to the rules of the established order" (i.e., "the ruling ideology") (ibid., p. 132). Interpellation describes a situation in which ideological state apparatuses (ISAs)—such as religious organizations, family, and, especially in Althusser's view, the educational system—inculcate individuals as subjects to particular categories and later interpellate or "hail" them as such. Interpellation adds an element of multiplicity and difference to the ideological field such that, according to a person's particular inculcation experience, that person may answer "yes" to the hail (as a "good" subject) or "no" to the hail (as a "bad" subject). Or, according to Pechéux (1982) and Muñoz (1999), the person may do something altogether different, to "disidentify" with the constraints of centering institutions that fail to embrace the full human diversity of lived experience (Silverstein, 1998, p. 404).

In state theorizing that centers on education as a set of institutions charged with instruction in a "pure" language, theories of language may themselves facilitate synergistic connections between language and power that bolster forms of dominance concentrated in the state (Althusser, 1971; Bourdieu, 1998, p. 123). This would include educational mandates that penalize multilanguage learning and usage, including sanctions against the use of signed languages.

State as Effect

The *state as effect* turns *state as actor* on its head or, as Foucault famously argued in his critique of political theory, sought "to cut off the king's head" (1990, pp. 88–89). A number of people have contributed to theorizing the state as effect—Arextaga (2003), Hall (1985), Mitchell (1991), and Trouillot (2001), to name just a few. Given Foucault's broad influence on the social sciences, in this section I focus solely on his ideas.

Contra contemporaneous political theory, Foucault did not locate power in the state but within persons constituted as certain kinds of subjects of biopower. *Biopower* is a term used to describe the modern rise in enumerating and sorting mechanisms, the effect of which has been the creation of populations via expert discourse (e.g., heterosexual sexuality). Subjects are then, first and foremost, kinds of body (soldier, factory worker, teacher), which Foucault theorized as "docile"—that is, someone that "may be subjected, used, transformed and improved" according to technologies of knowledge and power (1979, p. 136). These technologies imply but are not limited to formal institutions of education as they contain a range of "techniques human beings use to understand themselves" (Foucault, 1988, p. 18).

Among these techniques are "technologies of the self," which Foucault closely linked to his theory of *governmentality*. In cutting off the king's head, Foucault developed a theory of power extending beyond institutions of the state and traditional forms of political analysis (law, sovereignty, right) to describe the origins of the modern European state. With *governmentality*, Foucault argued for a historically contingent notion of state formation and decentered regimes of governing. According to Foucault, the centerpiece of state formation concerned the *art of government*. The central problem of the art of government "is how to introduce the economy—that is to say, the correct manner of managing individuals, goods and wealth within the family (which a good father is expected to do in relation to his wife, children, and servants). . . into the management of the state" (1991, p. 92).[24] As "tactics" of government, *governmentality* defines (1) differentiated populations, (2) particular forms and apparatuses of government, and (3) the gradual emergence of the administrative state (Foucault, 1991, pp. 102–103). Government is therefore that set of entities that produces a problem, which then "offers certain strategies for managing or solving the problem" (Lemke, 2007, p. 44).

Governmentality does not explain, however, how the economy, the law, the educational system, and other apparatuses are coordinated. For instance, how is it that, if I do not appear for court, the police come to arrest me? "This is exactly the step," argued Stuart Hall, "that Foucault refuses"—what Hall termed "articulation"—which Hall found in Althusser's useful contradictory coupling of state ideological and repressive apparatuses (1985, p. 93). As a number of scholars have commented, governmentality acting on a docile body creates a problem for theorizing agency by limiting its theoretical scope (Ahearn, 2001; Bartky, 1995). As with *state as actor*, in *state as effect*, theorizing the significance of specific body experiences—differing in the ways in which they encounter, interact with, and create forms of power—disappears in a universalist wash of indistinction (Hayles, 1999). In such a theoretical universe, the circumstances that condition the emergence of subject categories that index specific physical attributes (yet paradoxically ignore the salience of such attributes) is often lost to history—such as when social scientists (and others) discuss deafness while ignoring signed languages. Orisanmi Burton's (2015) *Black Lives Matter: A Critique of Anthropology* is among our guiding forces here in arguing anthropology's ethical obligation to address the ways in which "bodies matter," countering the tendency to claim the socially constructed idea of race (in Burton's potent examples), yet eliding the very real biological effects that racialized bodies (persons) endure.

By emphasizing the absorption of the state within discourses, Foucault nevertheless convincingly challenged two troublesome notions in BSBI political theorizing: the notion of a concrete and unitary state, and the notion of a state separate from society. At the same time, by ignoring powers assembled in institutions—the differential authority of the jurist, the police officer, and the teacher—the state appeared to be nowhere and to comprise no particular gendered, ethnic, racial, sexual, or other human features. This is productive of a tension in Foucault's theorizing, which Agamben addresses by asking "What is the point at which the voluntary servitude of individuals comes into contact with objective power?" (1998, p. 6) and what is the "locus" of power (2005, p. 24)? To these questions I add another: How is power transformed by particular people, in particular locations, with the bodies and the languages they possess (or are attributed with possessing)?

---

24. Foucault argues, for instance, that governmentality could not take hold in the seventeenth century because of the repressive force of the "reasoned state," in which "institutions of sovereignty were the basic political institutions and the exercise of power was conceived as an exercise of sovereignty" (1991, p. 97). However, by the nineteenth century, economic rationality had sufficiently permeated the institutions of the state such that direct police and military control were no longer as necessary to maintain the desired behaviors of subject populations (Foucault, 2009, p. 354).

State as Imagination

> *Instead of talking about the state as an entity that always/already consists of certain features, functions, and forms of governance, let us approach each actual state as a historically specific configuration of a range of languages of stateness, some practical, some symbolic and performative, that have been disseminated, translated, interpreted, and combined in widely differing ways and sequences across the globe.* (Hansen & Stepputat, 2006, pp. 6–7)

State as imagination is an approach that concentrates on theorizing everyday practices that address the state, even when state agents are not present or an individual's actions might not be readily perceived as connected to the state. Admittedly, outside official venues, the state is not easily locatable; as a consequence, state influences in everyday life can be difficult to identify. It is this tension of the *everywhere- and yet nowhere-ness* of the state, the absent locus of power, that the third approach to the state addresses. Philip Abrams's (1988) "Notes on the Difficulty of Studying the State" surveyed the major political-sociological obstacles to the study of the state. In that article Abrams argues that it is the way that theorists' have conceptualized the state that has interfered with the study of the state and state power—namely, through attempts to locate the "hidden reality" of the state (ibid., p. 61). Rather than taking the tack of reaffirming its existence or abandoning its study, Abrams proposes that "we should recognize that cogency of the idea of the state as an ideological power and treat that as a compelling object of analysis" (ibid., p. 79). He continues:

> The state is not the reality that stands behind the mask of political practice. It is itself the mask, which prevents our seeing political practice as it is. . . . There is a state-system . . . a palpable nexus of practice and institutional structure centered in government. . . . There is, too, a state-idea, projected, purveyed, and variously believed in different societies at different times. (ibid., p. 82)

The authors in *States of Imagination*, a coedited volume by Thomas Blom Hansen and Finn Stepputat (2001), expand on Abrams's analysis (see also Mitchell, 2002, and Trouillot, 2001).

From the perspective of *states as imagination*, ongoing state formation has less to do with what a state *is* and more with how citizen-subjects conceptualize it. Ideas of the state appear in languages that are, in Bakhtin's sense, dialogic, shared, yet also specific to their locations of usage.[25] Bakhtin's perspective has been extremely influential in

---

25. Bakhtin described language as a dialogic relationship between speakers and listeners, including the multiple dialogic forms, genres, and styles available to speakers and listeners in discourse (1981, p. 272). Bakhtin's theory of language does not prespecify either meaning or the combinations that meaning may take but rather directs the researcher back to the context of utterance. In his translation notes to Bakhtin's work, Holquist, synopsizes Bakhtin's theoretical emphasis thus: "Language, when it *means*, is somebody talking to somebody else, even when that someone else is one's own inner addressee (1981, p. xxi). Moreover, the context of utterance is interwoven with relations of power and authority, which are relations of "living human beings moving through space and not merely a physical body" (ibid., p. 105).

sociolinguistic and linguistic anthropological examination of social power and has significant implications for theorizing sovereignty and citizenship. For example, Seider's discussion of postwar Guatemala eschews the classic notion of citizenship as a fixed set of rights, which in everyday life are frequently unrealized. Rather, Seider considers how citizenship emerges in a dynamic process between differing social groups (in Hansen & Stepputat, 2001, p. 204).

In a more purely theoretical essay, Dean (2001; also in Hansen & Stepputat, 2001) considers the changing meanings of and relationships between citizenship and sovereignty within biopolitical liberalism. Dean provides a description of citizenship and sovereignty as working synergistically (ibid., pp. 62–63):

> The liberal arts of governing though freedom . . . always contains a divide between those capable of deserving of the responsibilities and freedoms of mature citizenship and those who are not. For those who are not, this will often mean despotic provision for their special needs with the aim of rendering them autonomous by fostering capacities of responsibility and self-governance.

Dean suggests, but does not name, the importance of the marked body—the "minority" ethnic, racial, gender, sexual, linguistic, or other phenotypically suspect body—to theoretical projects that aim to decipher the processes by which states establish and maintain sociopolitical regimes. Such examination is useful in deciphering mechanisms of inclusion (and its mirror—diversity) that increasingly appear in social policy and specialized programming, which, despite whatever good intentions, leave structures of inequality firmly in place (Ahmed, 2012; Urciuoli, 2010). Implicated here are Deaf education special schools and inclusive education settings around the world that deny students access to natural signed languages.

Situated within postcolonial theory, Hansen and Stepputat's approach focuses on ethnographic examination of particular sites wherein "languages of stateness" appear. They argue that "a state exists only when these 'languages' of governance and authority combine and coexist in one way or another" (2001, p. 8). However, paraphrasing Hansen and Stepputat, to theorize postcolonial forms of governance is to be continually confronted by Western notions of governance and their central concerns, highlighting the need to understand the historically specific nature of differing postcolonial state formations. By attending to languages of stateness, Hansen and Stepputat and coauthors employ Foucauldian and classical perspectives to pursue the "ambiguities of the state . . . as both illusory as well as a set of institutions; as both distant and impersonal ideas as well as localized and personified institutions; as both violent and destructive as well as benevolent and productive" (ibid., p. 5). This includes examination of connections of ideal-type official state rhetoric, as well as the ways in which the state actions are ratified by particular communities, resisted, or both.

I am inclined to the *states of imagination* model as it acknowledges that political orders have, resembling Hall's description of Althusser, a certain "structuration" in terms of both institutions and ideologies. Questioning the limitations of theory to sufficiently explain differing postcolonial political orders is also an extremely important aspect of that model—which is to say, this questioning challenges the theoretical insistence on normative liberal democratic notions of "freedom" and "rights."Fiona Wilson's (2001) examination of interaction between the Peruvian state and a rural Andean province involving schools, teachers, and students is particularly relevant to my own examination of education in Việt Nam, so, in the following paragraphs I discuss her case in detail.

In the late 1990s, Wilson recorded the narrative of a teacher who described his role in arranging schoolchildren's participation in the annual celebration of the national myth of origin, the Fiestas Patrias parade. Taking the form of an antistate narrative, the teacher constructed the parade as a form of popular subnationalism that contrasted with the form of state nationalism familiar to participants, who were also well aware of the state's failure to provide adequate educational opportunity to their children. At the same time, this teacher made decisions about which children would join in the parade, clearly making "the choice of which children are allowed to march and carry flags, pennants, batons, or swords . . . a social issue, for not all in the community have the resources allowing them to present their children *in a suitable way*" (ibid., p. 337; emphasis mine). Ultimately, the parade did not take place because of repression by antistate militants (the Sendero). Wilson uses this example to make the argument, with which I agree, that the relationships teachers engage in with each other, students, and community members are extremely significant to state formation. These kinds of relationships are also significant for students' own sociopolitical strategizing and related organizing efforts, as I discuss in chapters 3, 4, and 5.

The issue of suitability is important to consider in more detail, as it relates to questions of citizenship—considering this book's focus on everyday and small-scale citizen action—and sovereignty. In the case of the Fiestas Patrias parade, suitability involves small-scale contestation of subnational status against the national state, which yet seeks ratification by community members and state representatives with respect to both appropriateness of appearance and ways of *performing* appearance. For example, subnational members' fleshly animation of the state's ineffectual batons and swords must still convincingly deliver the state's revered songs. It is by appropriating state markers (e.g., flag, sword) and using them with precision that parade participants might challenge the state regime by outperforming it. In wielding the sword, they are not filled with state fervor, as Pascal's kneeler is said to believe in God (Althusser, 1971) or Bourdieu's mime feels grief (1998). Indeed, in order for this instance of resistance to be effective, in order for the set of social relationships that describes the nation-within-a-nation to go on living, resistance must go unrecognized as such, as much as the marchers' subjectivities must remain *tacit* (Decena, 2008).

A useful concept here is Agamben's "state of exception,"which he describes as an "inclusive exclusion" that arises not in accordance with the rule, but in the suspension of it (1998, p. 21). To paraphrase Agamben, by our making a determination about that which the rule does not contain, the rule radically includes that which it excludes. That the Andean provincial nation exists in a relation of exclusion to the state is given in the state's refusal of its subnational communities' actual conditions of living. The parade marks the Andean provincial nation's difference from the state, highlighting the withdrawal of the state from the promise of universal provision of education. The inability of the Sendero to distinguish the parade as an antistate formation is further clarified by Agamben's discussion of the condition of "inclusive exclusion," whereby the inclusion precludes "every possibility of clearly distinguishing between membership and inclusion, between exception and rule" (ibid. , p. 25). It is also clarified by the important role that teachers, in addition to other state agents not under the everyday surveillance of the state, may play as "tricksters who challenge in myriad ways the extent and nature of the state" (Wilson, 2001, p. 317).

As Wilson's case demonstrates, citizenship in the state does not preclude exclusion from the state. Furthermore, official modes of citizenship do not exhaust the forms and expressions given to citizenship in specific social contexts.[26] Following from the reinvigoration of social scientific interest in citizenship that began in the 1990s, a rich archive of citizenship practices now demonstrates that numerous forms of citizenship may or may not be reflected in official state institutions, histories, or policies. These forms include group identification (Young, 1990; Kymlicka & Norman, 1994), cultural solidarity (Ong, 1996; Taylor, 1992), intimacy (Plummer, 1995), and sexuality (Bell & Binnie, 2000). Particularly useful to analysis of the politicized body is Beasley and Bacchi's examination of "citizen-bodies," which argues that the body "materializes the operations of power in social life" (2000, p. 344).

Regarding the exercise of sovereignty, Wilson's case demonstrates that the police and the military are not the only figures empowered by the state to enforce social inequalities. To paraphrase Ernest Gellner, it is increasingly likely that it will be the professor who "stands at the base of the modern social order" (1983, p. 34). In Wilson, it is not the state but the Sendero and the teacher that impose their will on the bodies of the parade-goers: The Sendero use the threat of violence, and the teacher uses the promise of self-determination. Both are examples of what Hansen and Stepputat term "de facto" forms of sovereignty, which take the body "as the site of, and object of, sovereign power" (2006, pp. 296–297). In Wilson, students are inducted into sovereign power through the teacher's revered handling of the batons and swords, as well as through the song of the mother-fatherland—which is dialogically embodied along with modes of tacit resistance. So how does the teacher shape a resistance narrative within the movements, gestures, and song tones of nation-state celebration? And how do students translate and transform such knowledge for their own purposes? Significantly, all of this took place within a mere few hours, as the whole community prepared to march in the parade, which, in this case, was called off and so never happened. Nonetheless, through Wilson's ethnography, we have evidence of the Peruvian state's body (at a particular historical moment), its sovereign enforcement of bodies that look and act in particular, idealized, ways, and people's resistance to such discriminatory conditions.

Ethnographic manifestations of the state such as those just discussed indicate the presence of not only diverse state "languages" of the state but also diverse state *bodies*. Accordingly, each state must be examined with respect to the bodies they normatively authorize or discipline. Bodies that fail to satisfy states' requirements are those most often marginalized, whether they be included or excluded from state institutions or, following Agamben (1998), excluded via inclusion. Sassen submits that "today's

---

26. For Agamben, citizenship "names the new status of life as the origin and ground of sovereignty," and thereby citizenship preconditions the nature and extent of the inclusive exclusion (1998, p. 129).

citizenship practices have to do with the production of 'presence' of those without power" (2006, p. 315). Examination of citizenship thus requires going to where citizenship is least apparent. Rethinking issues of sovereignty and citizenship is therefore vital to the refining of social science theory. Particularly in light of Brook and Luong's critique of the entrenchment of the "Weberian view of capitalism," which attributes economic development to culture (1997, p. 3).

Unlike *state as actor* and *state as effect*, *state as imagination* makes no assumptions about what languages of stateness are in operation; rather, this approach invites researchers to document them. Returning to Mbembe's (2001) observation that modernity produced multiple notions of sovereignty entailing multiple notions of biopolitics, which theory conceals, it is through the continued structuration of *reason* in late-modern political-economic systems that social scientific theorizing is so often able to proceed without reference to actual bodies that think and feel, assent or dissent, in an interactional context. To put this somewhat differently, and much more elegantly, Mbembe writes that "It should be noted, as far as fieldwork is concerned, that there is less and less. Knowledge of local languages, vital to any theoretical and philosophical understanding, is deemed unnecessary" (ibid., p. 7). Turning next to consider the *state as embodiment*, it is the interactional body, the body that signs or speaks with others that is the central concern of this approach.

State as Embodiment

> *Form is the very appearance of the world and not the condition of its possibility; it is the birth of a norm and not realized according to a norm; it is the identity of the external and the internal and not the projection of the internal in the external.*
> (Merleau-Ponty (1962, pp. 60–61)

The three approaches to the state surveyed earlier include characterizations of the state as a dominant force in *state as actor*, a diffuse force in *state as effect*, and a discursive force with material repercussions within the *state as imagination*. Incorporating insights from the previous three approaches, this section explores the ways in which the state is formed and governed in relation to particular embodied experiences and interests.[27]

In the early 1990s, linguists and anthropologists who were rediscovering the phenomenology of Edmund Husserl and Merleau-Ponty and utilizing new technologies (e.g., brain imaging) began to explore embodiment as shared fields of attention, perception, and attunement (Csordas, 1990; Duranti, 1992; Farnell, 1995; Lakoff & Johnson, 1980, 1999). This renewed interest in embodiment as the "ground" of linguistic cultures, social organization, and human-environment interactions—not simply as representational or symbolic canvas—spurred numerous research projects. Such scholarship

---

27. I am indebted to a number of ethnographers whose work contributes to my own ongoing formulation of the *state as embodiment* approach: Ahearn (2001, 2003); Ahmed (2006, 2007, 2012); Blommaert (2005, 2013); Duranti (1994); Edelman (2011, 2013); Jaffe (1999, 2009); and Leap (2008, 2011), among others.

addresses various dimensions of embodied interaction and intersubjectivity (Csordas, 2008; Hanks, 1995, 2005; Turner, 1995; see also Leder, 1990, 1992; and Weiss, 1999, for perspectives from philosophy), as well as the salience of ethnography to new analytic insights into embodiment for particular sociocultural contexts (Edwards, 2012; Enfield, 2003, 2009; Hanks, 2010; Scheper-Hughes, 1993).[28]

For instance, Nancy Scheper-Hughes's classic work *Death without Weeping*—her 1993 study of the political economy of child death in the Brazilian favela of Bom Jesus de Mata—is remarkable for ethnographically demonstrating how the body becomes a "battleground," a site of political struggle, and how linguistic practices are the medium through which mothers interactively shape conventionalized expectations of and explanations for child death. Under direct threat of state violence, illness emerges as a primary mode of political protest and revolutionary potential.

Work by Ahmed (2007) and Leap (2008) provides other significant examples of the importance of particular bodies to particular state-mediated contexts. Ahmed's phenomenological consideration of whiteness as orientation and likeness demonstrates how we come to experience our circumstances as "familiar," "the world we implicitly know, as a world that is organized in specific ways" (2007, p. 155). Ahmed continues:

> To think of this implicit knowledge as inherited is to think about how we inherit a relation to place and to placement: at home, things are not done a certain way, but the domestic "'puts things" in their place. Whiteness is inherited through the very placement of things (ibid.).

Leap's (2008) investigation of connections of sexuality and geography in postapartheid Cape Town similarly demonstrates how certain white South Africans in the city center invoke sexuality to regulate race and/or class within privileged white and comparatively affluent gay clubs. In the city-center gay clubs, one intersubjective reading of embodiment (race, sexuality) and display (class markers such as clothing) may be played against another as colonially codified forms of regulation and disciplining are reworked through the diversity discourses of the New South Africa as they appear in particular spaces (e.g., city-center gay clubs, gay-friendly Cape Flats *shebeens* (local gathering places serving food and drinks). Leap argues, in order to understand narrative description of sexual geographies, that we must undertake a social reading of the circumstances and related experiences (ibid., p. 259); moreover, doing so "forces confrontation with a legacy of social structures and descriptive practices which date from the apartheid years and before, and which discourses of citizenship, reconciliation, and nation-building were just beginning to emerge in the late 1990s" (ibid.).

Leap's and Ahmed's respective attention to the organizing features of geography and place both illuminate forms of ordinary domestication. Body experiences and the values we attribute to bodies are always already historically rooted in complex privileging processes.

Recent work in nonformalist (i.e., non-Chomskyian) cognitive linguistics (Dancygier & Sweetser, 2015; Evans & Green, 2006; Kovecses, 2010, 2015; Langacker, 2000, 2009)

---

28. See Asad (2003), Lock (1993a), and Farnell (1999) for surveys on the anthropology of the body and embodiment.

and cognitive science (Gallagher, 2005; Johnson, 2007) contributes to insights into language usage, embodiment, and social organization by exploring the nature of viewpoint and meaning. Taken together, such research demonstrates that what is commonly referred to as "human knowledge" fundamentally involves the experiences of our bodies.[29] Cognitive linguistic researchers who are examining signed languages are making major contributions to this area of research by analyzing the complex relationships between spatial, temporal, kinesthetic, conceptual, and semantic properties of signed language usage (Armstrong & Wilcox, 2007; Dudis, 2004, 2011; Janzen, 2015; Liddell, 2003; Taub, 2001; Wilcox & Shaffer, 2005).[30]

Accepting that language is always an embodied experience—whether signed, spoken, written, typed, texted, emojied or imagined—how are we to understand the body's erasure from much of language theorizing and, thereby, from other domains of the social? Johnson (2007) provides both insight into these circumstances and support for the significance of language and bodies to state formation.

Johnson establishes his thesis on embodiment in the context of the social and scientific repercussions of dualist notions of *mind* as separate from *body*.[31] *Representationalist* accountings of the mind, Johnson argues, characterize mental entities as independent from the world; in this paradigm, thought corresponds to or represents things in the world but has no meaningful interaction with the world. He goes on to demonstrate how the dualist notion is not just an idea (in the dualist sense, separate from the world) but stems from neurobiological mechanisms that mask how the body is part of thought. One such mechanism Johnson terms "bodily disappearance," drawing from Leder's (1990) "focal disappearance": In order for an object to be drawn out of the perceptual field, for example, the body must function in a manner such that "our bodily organs and operations recede and even hide in our acts of experiencing things in the world" (Johnson, 2007, p. 4). Johnson gives the example of seeing: "I see *with* my eyes (which undergo focal disappearance), but that seeing would be impossible without those eyes' existence in a body that makes a number of fine adjustments, such as holding the head in a certain way, keeping the body erect and pointed in a certain direction, and moving the body in ways that ensure a clear line of sight" (ibid., p. 5; emphasis in the original). The constitution of an object from the perceptual field, what Edmund Husserl (1931) called *horizon,* itself requires the disappearance or peripheralizing of nearby objects.

---

29. I put human knowledge in quotes here to mark the fact that, since the human species does not have a sole claim on body experience, then knowledge cannot be singularly associated with the "human." Such cognitive scientific research supports examinations of meaning undertaken by anthropologists and those in related fields of inquiry to broaden the scope of how knowledge is conceptualized.

30. Anthropological scholarship on ethnicity has also explored the role of embodied cognition relative to how "ways of seeing" influence ethnic formation, social categorization, and stereotyping (Brubaker, Loveman, & Stamatov, 2004, p. 45).

31. For philosophical critique of empiricism generally and Descartes's specific impact on scientific notions of mind and body, see Merleau-Ponty's (1962) discussion of traditional prejudices (chapters 3 and 4). For neurobiological critique of Descartes's theory of mind and body, particularly the role of emotion in decisionmaking, see Damasio (2005).

Paraphrasing his "big babies" argument, Johnson posits that our ways of understanding the world are, from the first moments of life, ways of qualitatively *engaging with* the world. Accordingly, *knowing* the world is primarily mediated by body-based experiences and not by conceptual knowledge sets or things we are taught. According to Johnson, *meaning* "is not just what is consciously entertained in acts of feeling and thought; instead, meaning reaches down into our corporeal encounter with our environment" (2007, p. 26). Interaction-based experiences thus give rise to conceptualization but cannot be reduced to conceptualization. Johnson further argues that conceptual objects do not exist per se but are constituted from "our perceptual and motor capacities, our interests, our history, and our values" (ibid., p. 76). Merleau-Ponty phrased this somewhat differently: "The life of consciousness—cognitive life, the life of desire or perceptual life—is subtended by an 'intentional arc' which projects round about us our past, our future, our human setting, our physical, ideological and moral situation" (1962, p.136).

In his examination of relationships between embodied experience and sociolinguistic interaction, Johnson's work also establishes a framework for exploring connections between body experience and sociocultural and political organization. Johnson's emphasis on environment and Merleau-Ponty's emphasis on "situation" both highlight the historical nature of body-based interactional experience; that is, *meaning* does not remain constant across space and time but continuously undergoes change. According to the latter perspectives, even habitual body experience is always under formation not only in relation to things such as changes in setting and situation, aging, and illness but also in relation to conceptualizations reconfigured through new instantiations of activities perceived as habits. This viewpoint complicates Bourdieu's notion of bodily *hexis* to reframe even repetitive movement patterns as open to change situationally and as a force in both social formation and change (1984).

In accordance with focal and bodily disappearance, as well as bodily hexis, our accumulated embodied-environment practices feel right to us—not only on physical, emotional, and communicative levels but socially and politically as well. The sense of rightness connected to ordinary ways of doing contributes to both naturalization and normalization of the features of our bodies and our body practices. Within institutions of the state, body ideologies are embedded in commonsense endorsement of certain expert opinions about institutional design, social policy, disciplining of groups perceived to be deviant, and other forms of intervention into nonnormative body appearances and practices. As a methodological tool, *state as embodiment* contributes to investigation of what Collier and Lakoff term "regimes of living," or "situated configurations of normative, technical, and political elements that are brought into alignment in problematic or uncertain situations" (2004, p.31).

Regimes of disappearing, disciplining, regulating, and excluding bodies—or including, promoting, and joining in body practices—are empirical matters, replete with ideological attachments and state-level imperatives. It is when we consider the *state as embodiment* that sovereignty, what Foucault called "the ancient right to *take* life or *let* live . . . replaced [in modernity] by a power to *foster* life or *disallow* it to the point of death," comes into clearer view (Foucault, 2003, p. 80; emphasis in the original).

Following the propositions outlined in *state as embodiment* we might turn Hansen and Stepputat's (2001) focus on the ways in which "states acquire reality in everyday life" in the other direction to ask the following: How do linguistic embodiments acquire their particular realities in institutional life? How do institutional agents (policymakers, principals, teachers) use their own languaging/experiencing bodies to set the terms of institutional interaction? This study is primarily concerned with persons whose actions and interactions are engaged with sites of education and social organizing.

Conclusion

In chapter 1, Reilly and Nguyễn's (2004) evaluation of inclusive education in Việt Nam emphasized that both the structuring of universal primary education on the national level and the decisions about instructional language policy and management are contingent on *government policy*. As the following chapters demonstrate Deaf education language policies are heavily influenced by varying forms of expert information, which also facilitate the production of educational assessments and other regulatory frameworks that school administrators, vocational training administrators, and, increasingly, employers are expected to comply with in everyday practice. Chapter 3 focuses on the relationships between state and educational structuring, the sites and practices wherein teachers and students interact with each other, and the ways that *adult learners cum social organizers* analyze their sociolinguistic circumstances, both retrospectively and within the immediate moment of particular situations. In this ongoing analysis, Vietnamese Deaf signers might be best understood as ambivalently regarded nationals, that is, as *citizen-bodies* that bring national scrutiny to bear on both state policy and practices.

Significantly, such national scrutiny directed toward Vietnamese Deaf people who use HCMSL (and other VSLs) occurs in the context of other emergent forms of inequality in which the state has played an important role. London argues as follows:

> The development of a quasi-universalist formal education system in Vietnam under centrally planned state-socialism was a project built on stable class alliances, produced historic gains in literacy and primary education, and enabled the CPV [Communist Party of Việt Nam] to achieve major political imperatives, including the promotion of welfare, social order, and political legitimacy. But over time, state-socialism generated new class hierarchies, and education policies and their conduct promoted major educational inequalities, many of which were due to state-socialist mechanisms of distribution. Vietnam's transition from centrally planned state-socialism to an internationally linked market economy enabled rapid increases in the scale of formal education and—in important respects—improved the quality and accessibility of education. But the emergence of a new economy transformed the character of class relations—both within and outside the state. This phenomenon in combination with new education policies and other factors, contributed to the emergence of new inequality-generating mechanisms, which in some cases replaced, and in others, added to the inequality legacies of state-socialism. (2011, p. 92)

As the remaining chapters of this book demonstrate, the system of Deaf education special schools and inclusive education are two of the "new inequality-generating mechanisms" in Việt Nam. Seemingly paradoxically, some—not all—of the Deaf education special schools are also places where *new equality-generating mechanisms* are emerging. I take up these two concerns in the next chapter.

3

Deaf Education and Deaf Social Organizing

Sites of Social Inclusion and Exclusion

It is not the cultural, linguistic, and political expression or mobilization of (minority) ethnicities and nationalisms which are the cause of so much contemporary mayhem in the modern world, but their disavowal. We ignore their ongoing influence and purchase at our peril. (May, 2008, p. 301)

IN THE PREVIOUS chapter I argued that what is commonly referred to as "the state" is better conceptualized as: (1) human actors who embody and express particular environment- and situation-related viewpoints on their historical, sociolinguistic, political-economic, and other circumstances, who (2) share and conventionalize viewpoints via language, which then (3) iteratively and continuously form and transform "the state." Accordingly, analysis of state formation and change in contemporary Việt Nam would be incomplete without an accounting of Deaf people's experiences of and viewpoints on their conditions of living. In the second half of this chapter I focus directly on these in the context of three ethnographic vignettes and continue that focus in the remaining chapters. Before turning to these three vignettes, I discuss the role of the Vietnamese state system and transformations in leadership structure and national objectives during the period leading up to and including initiation of the political reform period (1986 to the present).

State Formation, Education, Deaf Bodies, and Notions of Disability in Việt Nam

In chapter 1, I discussed London's argument that, beginning in the post–World War II period, "processes of educational development and state formation went hand in hand" (2011, p. 13). Consistent with London's analysis, Dang and Beresford's (1998) description of authority relations in Việt Nam provides a detailed look at state formation following World War II and throughout the first decade of political-economic reforms. Covering the period from the establishment of the socialist Democratic Republic of Việt Nam (DRV) and extending approximately 10 years after the initiation of *đổi mới* (1945–1998), they describe three phases of state formation: (1) establishment of core DRV institutions (1945–1955); (2) "partification," whereby the Vietnamese Communist Party (hereafter, the Party) led in matters of state (1955–1986), and (3) "statification," whereby the role of the Party diminished as the role of the government and the legislature increased under *đổi mới* reforms (1986–present) and the establishment of a market-socialist economy.

The first two phases of state formation occurred in context of ongoing war. In the first phase, the government carried out operations with a "reasonable degree of autonomy" by members who were both communist and noncommunist, and the "main task of the Party was to provide analysis" (Dang & Beresford, 1998, p. 21). During partification, the Party moved to build a fully socialist state, assuming a primary role in directing civil resistance, securing and maintaining sovereign independence, while establishing a state-socialist framework for economic development and modernization. It was also during this phase that "fence breakers" (*phá rào*) began to experiment with economic activities outside the centrally planned economy, achieving various degrees of success and official recognition (ibid., p. 60). During the statification phase, still ongoing, concerns regarding participation in international trade and the demands of competitive production have taken the place of concerns about the external threat of war (see figure 3.1).

Begun as a state-administered restructuring of the economic system, the early political and economic transformations witnessed in the early *đổi mới* reform period included authorizing market-based activities, decentralized production and gradual reduction of state-owned enterprises, and implementation of a more expansive openness akin to Gorbachev's glasnost. Externally, openness included initiation of transnational trade agreements, increase in foreign direct investment (FDI), and relaxation of travel restrictions (mostly) to and away from the country. Internally, openness included gradual liberalization of the media, growth in entrepreneurship, a burgeoning civil society sector (Thayer, 1992), and reprivatization of, for example, education and health care (London, 2003). During the early to mid-reform period, organization and administration of production changed tremendously because of market-oriented reforms and related legal structures. As a result, between 1990 and 2007 the GDP grew at an annual rate of 6.5–8%, and the poverty rate decreased to 15.5%.[1]

In 1990 Việt Nam was a food-importing nation; by 2005, Việt Nam had become a leading exporter of rice, cashews, tea, coffee, rubber, wood, and other agricultural products. Việt Nam is now fast becoming one of Southeast Asia's industrial hubs, particularly via export-oriented processing plants (Cao, 2007).[2] As a result of such changes in economic structuring, Việt Nam achieved middle-income country status in 2012. Despite impressive economic gains, over the course of *đổi mới* social issues have grown. The quality of education has also declined despite increasing state expenditures on

---

1. According to the World Bank, in 1986 Việt Nam's GDP was approximately $14 billion with per capita Purchasing Power Parity (PPP) approximately $437 USD. Just over two decades later (2008), Việt Nam's GDP grew to $99.13 billion and in 2012 jumped to nearly $156 billion, moving the country to lower middle-income status. The World Bank's most recent calculation (2015) put Việt Nam's GDP at $193 billion, and PPP approximately $1,684 (See World Bank data at http://data.worldbank.org/country/vietnam).

2. Export-oriented, "just-in-time" processing plants (e.g., Khu Công Nghiệp Biên Hòa-1 and -2 and Amata Industrial Park) are concentrated in southern Việt Nam. These form part of the long string of industrial parks bordering the Hà Nội Highway throughout Đồng Nai province.

Vietnamese State System

The *VCP* meets every five years to determine National goals and formalize policy.

The *National Assembly (NA)* consists of 498 members who hold positions in the Standing Committee, seven legislative committee, and the Ethnic Council. The Na holds legislative and executive powers, and is also responsible for electing the President and Prime Minister.

The *President* is the official head of state.

The *Prime Minister (PM)* is responsible for the day-to-day operations of the government.

The Government is the highest body of the state administration, and reports to the President and the NA. Government ministries can propose policy which then must be approved by the NA.

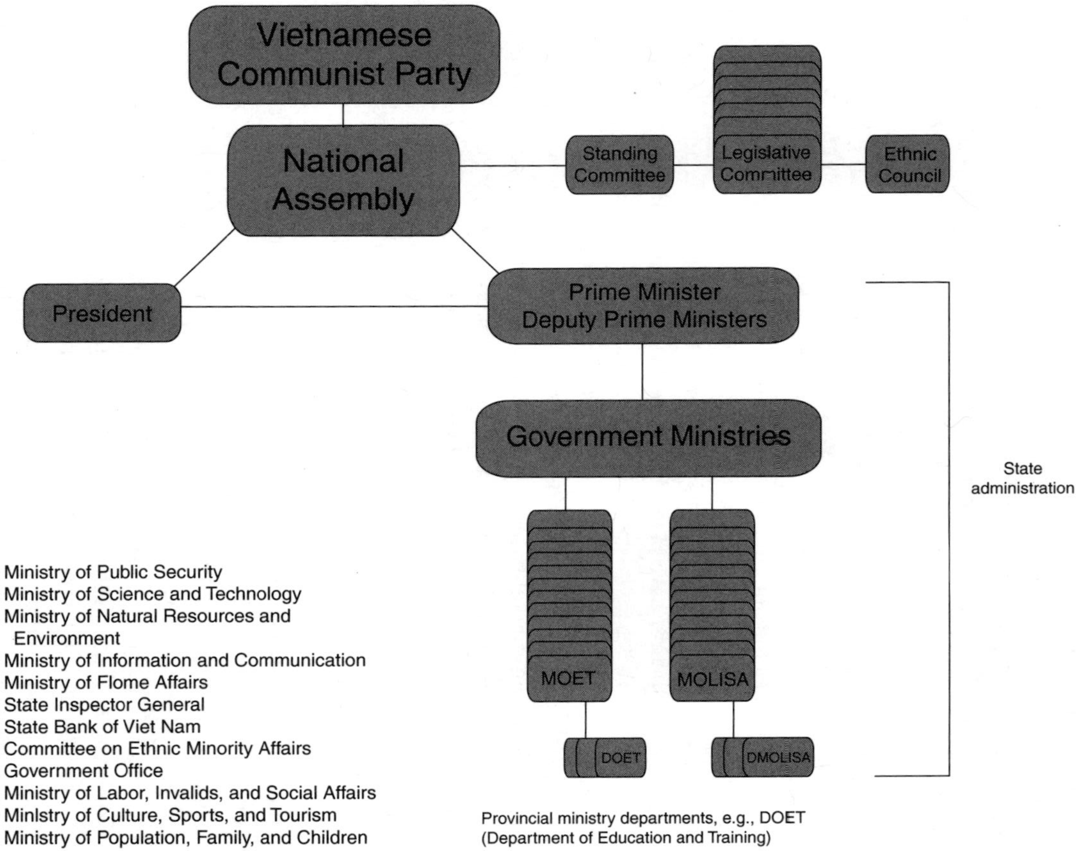

Government Ministries:
1) Ministry of National Defense
2) Ministry of Foreign Affairs
3) Ministry of Justice
4) Ministry of Finance
5) Ministry of Transport
6) Ministry of Construction
7) Ministry of Education and Training
8) Ministry of Agriculture and Rural Development
9) Ministry of Industry and Trade
10) Ministry of Planning and Investment
11) Ministry of FHealth
12) Ministry of Fisheries
13) Ministry of Public Security
14) Ministry of Science and Technology
15) Ministry of Natural Resources and Environment
16) Ministry of Information and Communication
17) Ministry of Flome Affairs
18) State Inspector General
19) State Bank of Viet Nam
20) Committee on Ethnic Minority Affairs
21) Government Office
22) Ministry of Labor, Invalids, and Social Affairs
23) Ministry of Culture, Sports, and Tourism
24) Ministry of Population, Family, and Children

Provincial ministry departments, e.g., DOET (Department of Education and Training)

Figure 3.1. Vietnamese state system (contemporary market-socialist period).

Sources: SRV Government website: www.chinhphu.vn, 2) Vietnamese Embassy to the U.S. website: www.vietnamembassy.us.org. 3) mcCarty(2001).

education, which—unlike public health—have gone up proportionately with the annual rise in gross domestic product (London, 2008, p. 119).

Concerns over educational quality are hardly new. In 1950, 1956, and 1979 the Vietnamese state implemented educational reforms to "establish a democratic, popular education in the interests of national construction" (Phạm, 1994, p. 31). With the 1982 establishment of a national curriculum, national socialist education aimed to integrate practical training with academic instruction in specialized technical fields believed to be most necessary to national development. Accordingly, the aim of education was to "enable people to obtain comprehensive development, with the sense of independence and socialist ideals, virtue, capability, which will create a human resource strong enough for carrying out industrialization in the direction of modernization, and for defending our country" (Phạm, 2007, pp. 282–283).

Despite official reports of near-universal literacy rates, deficits in the quantity, quality, relevance, and labor desirability of education continued to be observed during the second decade of the reform period. MOET official reports such as *Education in Vietnam 1945–1991* (1994) and *Education in Vietnam: Situation, Issues, Policies* (1994) addressed these concerns directly, as did outside assessments, including the 1992 joint UNESCO/UN Development Programme's *Education and Human Resources Sector Analysis, Synthesis Report,* as well as social scientific reporting (Doan, 2004; Duggan, 2001; Kolko, 1997; London, 2011; Marr, 1988; Woodside, 1983b) (figure 3.2).

Explaining these circumstances, Doan argues that, unlike economic reform, đổi mới educational reform left the structure of the general educational system relatively intact, including centralized management mechanisms and personnel, uniform "one-size-fits-all" policies, and rote learning according to nationalized curricula (2004, p. 148).[3] Recently, critics of educational socialization (xã hội hóa giáo dục; see chapter 1) further argue that the state is retreating in its commitment to educational provision and that the state's investment in education phải được coi là đầu tư cho hạ tầng quốc gia [should be treated as an investment in national infrastructure] (Giáp, 2010, p. 15).

Under economic liberalization, market rationalities such as cost-benefit analyses exert influence on other domains, adding the force of rationality to seemingly natural circumstances. For example, in her study of post-đổi mới prostitution practices in Việt Nam, Nguyễn-võ observes that liberalizing mechanisms contribute to "the depoliticization of governance" via expert knowledge and "the possibility of privatization (called 'socialization' in Việt Nam) of governing functions" (2008, p. 80). Through such logics and institutional processes, the state separates practices (persons) perceived to be social problems, such as sex work or disability, into programmatic and spatial niches. For those persons presumed to be sex workers, such niches have included reeducation facilities, often involving punitive treatment practices (Nguyễn-võ, 2008). For Deaf people, these niches include seemingly affirmative special school and education settings,[4] as well as new business niches such as signed language–based tourism (Cooper, 2015;

---

3. See http://tuanvietnam.vietnamnet.vn/2010-03-22-giao-duc-lac-hau-chi-cach-giao-duc-hien-dai-mot-buoc-chan

4. *Education for the disabled needs more attention: Hồ Chí Minh City* (Thanh Niên News, August 2009).

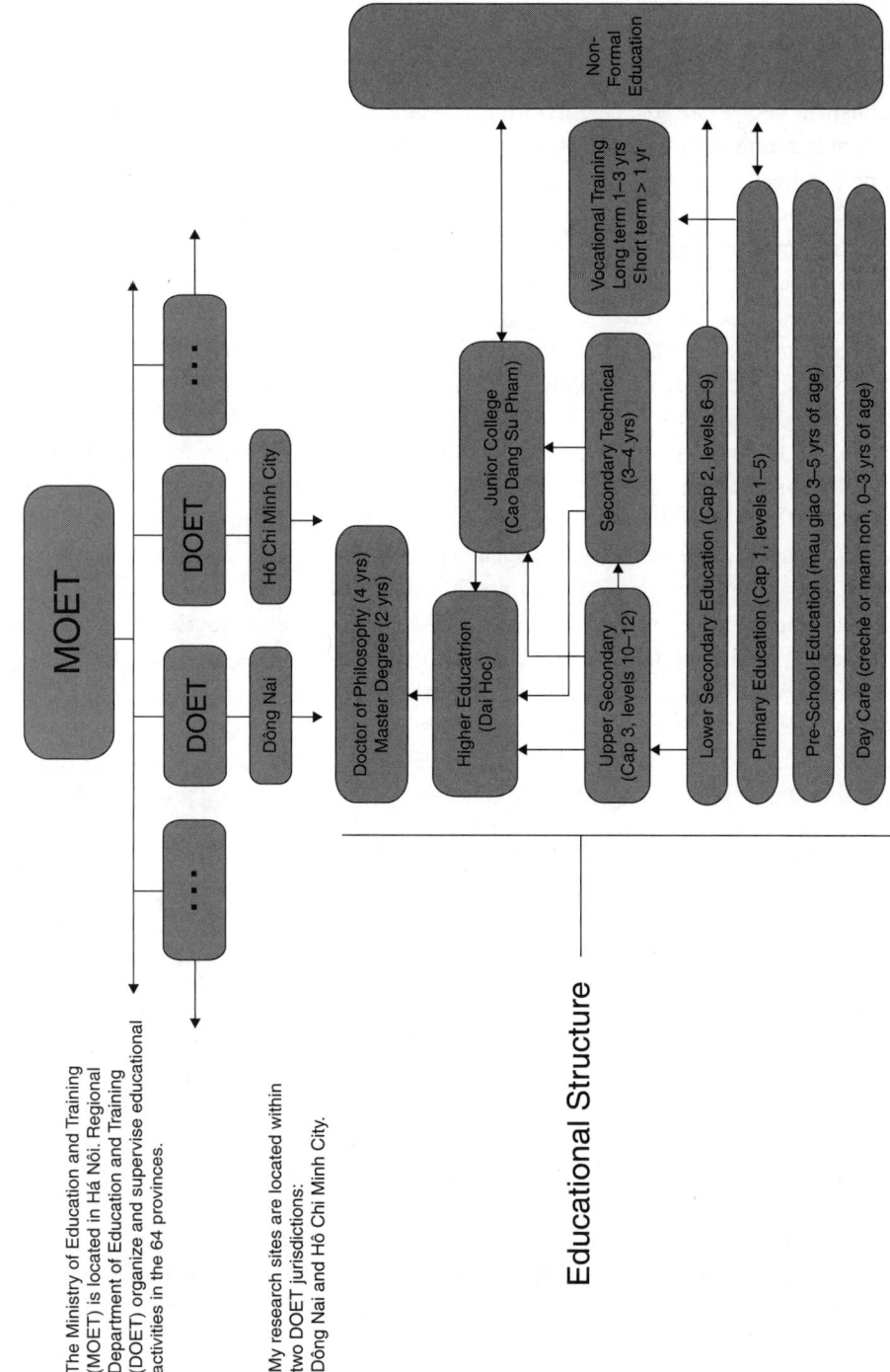

Figure 3.2. Vietnamese educational system (contemporary market-socialist period).

Source: 1) Ministry of Education and Training website: en.moet.vn.gov, 2) research participant description.

see chapter 6 for an in-depth discussion of tourism). However, whereas neither special school education nor tourism in southern Việt Nam is based on the use of VSLs, VSLs often remain relegated to the margins of academic and entrepreneurial spaces.[5]

Bracketing *regular* and *special* education into separate domains is one of the ways that gaps between the respective educational systems are masked, including differences in educational programming, expectations, resources, outcomes, and related labor productivity. Since the initiation of *đổi mới*, London argues, the "education system has changed considerably." He observes three broad trends, quoted here in full: "(1) large and sustained increases in education spending; (2) shifts in the principles and institutions governing the provision and payment for education; and (3) continuous if uneven expansions in the scale of the education system, as indicated by enrolments and other measures" (2011, p. 22). The universalization of primary education is one area of seemingly clear achievement, with census and survey data consistently indicating high rates of child enrollment and completion for students "in their age-appropriate grades" (ibid., p. 35). However, to the extent that state reporting and researcher analyses do not include students who fall outside the regular education system, such characterization of contemporary educational performance is, at the very least, inaccurate.

Until recently the Vietnamese state had concentrated its tracking of educational outcomes exclusively on *người bình thường* [normal people]. With its 2006 *Vietnamese Household Living Standards Survey*, the state for the first time included *người khuyết tật* [people with disabilities] in its national census instrument. Documenting discrete categories of hearing "disability," the survey reported that an astonishing 3.3% of the total population (84.1 million in 2006), or some 2,775,300 persons, had some kind of hearing "disability" (GSO, 2006, section 4.25). Language data on persons within these identified groups were not reported.

In the demographic section of my 2009 survey of the five special schools in this study, principals reported a total of approximately 761 students (for all five schools combined; see the tables in this chapter). If we add to this figure Deaf students attending other special and inclusive education schools in Hô Chí Minh City and the surrounding area, a rough estimate of the total number might be in the range of 1,500–2,000 students. Thus, if the *VHLSS* figures are correct, the vast majority of Deaf and hard of hearing persons in Việt Nam do not attend school—a situation also borne out by the government's own survey data on school attendance (NCCD, 2010). Findings from the 2009 Population and Housing Census downwardly adjusted disability figures to less than half of the original number, reporting 7 million persons with disability, of whom 1 million are reported to have hearing disability (GSO, 2009). These new figures still put the number of eligible school-aged youth at 400,000, with 20,000 students seeking entry to special schools each year, a situation made dire by the limited number of schools, lack of appropriate teacher preparation, and teachers who lack bilingual proficiency in a VSL (Mỹ, 2015; NCCD, 2010).

---

5. One exception to the use of ASL in Vietnamese tourism is *Deaf Travel Vietnam*, a Deaf-owned and -operated touring company. Established in 2015 in northern Việt Nam (Hà Nội), Deaf Travel Vietnam uses Hà Nội Sign Language as the primary language of their touring services. See https://www.facebook.com/deaftravelvietnam

The ways in which the Vietnamese state has addressed Deaf education and disability in the đổi mới reform period is extremely interesting. Importantly, unlike many countries, including those with equivalent and substantially higher economic reserves, the state has devoted a great deal of attention and resources to the growth of special school education. Nevertheless, as the earlier discussion indicates, Deaf educational structuring has been mired in negative ideological notions of deafness as a disabling condition and of Deaf people's sociocultural practices and use of VSLs as evidence for disability. This is the context in which Deaf people's emergent social organizing efforts for HCMSL and culturally affirmative recognition of Deaf people have been taking place. The situation is certainly complex, particularly given the reasonable connections made by Vietnamese state leaders between colonial legacies of signed language–based education in Việt Nam and late-modern humanitarian development projects involving pedagogically and linguistically distinct approaches to Deaf education.[6]

Geopolitics, Economics, Disability: State Alignment of Special Statuses

In the contemporary moment, the Vietnamese state devotes considerable resources to domestic concerns (education, health, economic growth and sustainability, independence) and the ways these relate to geopolitical concerns and competitiveness. Writing more than a decade into the đổi mới reform period, Dang and Beresford posited independence as "the most difficult problem today" (1998, p. 105). They continued: "Integration of the Vietnamese economy into the world market system threatens the ability of the Vietnamese state to direct the development process in a way that it has not experienced before" (ibid.).

Between 1998 and 2015, the Vietnamese state demonstrated its dexterity in directing the development process, as well as in weathering regional crises, such as the Asian economic crisis (1997–1998) and ongoing maritime disputes with the Chinese state over control of the Biển Đông [East Sea]. Yet, "the sheer rapidity of change . . . presents some serious challenges concerning the way forward. The Vietnamese state must grapple, not only with new demands arising from its own population, but aid donors and foreign investors" (Beresford, 2008, p. 222).

When it was proposed, there was some indication that the Trans-Pacific Partnership might put some of Dang and Beresford's (1998) and Beresford's (2008) concerns to rest as a number of observers predicted that Việt Nam would enjoy a comparative advantage with respect to many of the eleven participating countries (Boudreau, 2015; Bradsher, 2015; Nguyễn, 2015; VIR, 2015). Following the Trump administration's decision to withdraw from the TPP, however, Việt Nam joined other ASEAN member states in pursuing the Regional Comprehensive Economic Partnership (RCEP). It is still too early to tell what impacts the RCEP might have with respect to international cooperation and national development. For now, the most prominent demands arising from Việt Nam's own population remain calls for increased access to and improvements in education and training programming. The demand for improved health-care

---

6. See Ferguson (1994) and Jackson (2007) for similar discussions of depoliticizing trends and processes in what Jackson terms the international development "industry."

infrastructure is also a major concern, particularly in the area of services for persons with multiple disabilities—in connection to which the vast human and environmental magnitude of dioxin contamination is only now beginning to be understood (Gammeltoft, 2014; Kimmons, 2014; Martin, 2009, 2012).

It is in the context of education and health demands that economic development—the primary driver of state policy (Phạm M. H., 2007)—is increasingly linked to the development of the domestic population. In 2000 the state responded to the "poor quality" of the population by initiating Decision no. 147/2000/QD-TTg, a national population strategy with the following overarching goal for the 2000–2010 period:

> To build families with fewer and healthier children, aiming to stabilize the population's size at a reasonable level for a prosperous and happy life. To improve the population's quality and develop a human resource of high quality in order to meet the requirements of industrialization and modernization, making a contribution into the rapid and sustainable development of the country. (Ministry of Justice, 2000, section 2, part a)

Gammeltoft (2014) describes the increased availability of prenatal technologies and selective abortions in this same period, which have facilitated the rise of low-cost, street-level clinics that families utilize as a way of avoiding live births of children suspected of having disabling conditions. Moreover, according to the foregoing statements and Gammeltoft's study, it is clear that the labor required to produce a "high-quality" population falls disproportionately on women.

Unlike the war veteran and the war widow of earlier times, or even the dioxin baby of post–American War[7] sequellae, deafness has no direct link to a heroic national past or a modernizing future. From a classic socialist perspective, the domestic vulnerability (or burden) of the Vietnamese Deaf population marks these individuals as a concern not distinct to Việt Nam but available to an internationalist solution. Đổi mới reforms occasioned not only the articulation of the Vietnamese state with multilateral trade partners but also development-aid discourses on disability. Combined with state emphasis on producing a modern and knowledgeable citizenry, as well as the role of Vietnamese language-centered education in such national aims, Vietnamese Deaf people are overwhelmingly constituted as figures of dependency, particularly within educational domains that report Deaf student educational underachievement. Ideologies of dependency facilitated interventions structured at making Deaf students (people) more like people with normatively construed abilities to hear and speak, so that they might access and demonstrate knowledge and productive capacity in a manner resembling the latter.

Economic growth has also facilitated other kinds of body-oriented intervention into a range of domestic development arenas and issues. For example, infrastructural demands such as road and bridge building have not kept pace with the increased transportation of goods and daily commuters. The sharp rise in the sale of motorcycles and,

---

7. For the Vietnamese perspective on the war that began with the partition of North and South Việt Nam, which took place after the 1954 Geneva Conference and lasted until 1975, see Hayslip (1993); Kwon (2006); Schwenkel (2006); Turner and Phan Thanh Hao (1998).

more recently, cars has exacerbated traffic conditions on already overburdened roadways. Consequently, in October 2008 the Ministry of Health issued a new law that, for the first time, put formal requirements on the minimum height (4'9"), weight (minimum of 88 lbs.), chest circumference (28.35"), and medical conditions of motorcycle drivers.[8] In response to a wave of calls and editorial publications by journalists and bloggers, the Ministry of Health omitted certain requirements, notably the chest-circumference test.[9] During the same period, Deaf people were still denied access to drivers' licenses (for motorcycles and automobiles), although the government agreed to offer a "pilot training course on road traffic rules for the hearing impaired" (Viet Nam Net Bridge, 2008).[10] At the time of this writing, the Vietnamese state continues to deny Deaf people access to drivers' licenses.

The state also controls economic access according to other kinds of body-based tests, such as the March 2009 ruling on gender assignment surgery, which authorized surgery only for "those with congenital defects" (Van Lien-Chau, 2008).[11] Also frequently in the news, homosexuality, framed medically as *đồng tính luyến ai* [English translation], is often associated with violent incidents, prostitution, and negative implications for Vietnamese families and society. Recently, following the publication of several books by same-sex-identified persons, same-sex-based organizing, and the appearance of sympathetic gay characters on television, positive reporting on same-sex-identified people is increasing in the media.[12] Yet, in a study reviewing 502 stories published between 2004 and 2008, the Institute for the Study of Society, Economy, and Environment reported that "Vietnamese newspapers continue to discriminate against lesbians and gay men" (Bao Anh, 2009). Remarkably, in 2012, the state issued a statement in support of *cộng đồng người đồng tính, song tính và chuyển giới* [gay, bisexual, and transgender] citizens after the latter

---

8. Nam Sơn (2008).

9. A tongue-in-cheek editorial-style article exhorted *Vú To Mới Được Ra Đường* ["Big breasts permitted to go outside!"], indirectly chiding the government for the differential burden the law would place on small-breasted women. Asking how the police would operationalize this law, the writer offered to be a chest measurer (Nguyện, 2008).

10. This article reports that the pilot training course was conducted in Hà Nội with 88 trainees. It does not say how such training was accomplished, given the lack of Hà Nội Sign Language interpreters.

11. On November 26, 2015, Việt Nam passed a new law that took effect on January 1, 2016, supporting citizens' rights to access gender assignment surgeries and allowing individuals to officially register new names and gender statuses with the government—however, only *after reassignment surgery is completed*. As critics point out, the new law violates principle 3 of the Yogyakarta Principles, which states that "no one will be required to undergo medical procedures, including sex reassignment surgery" (Paulat, 2015).

12. In 2006, one periodical asked, *Đồng tính luyến ái: Khiếm khuyết về thể chất hay tâm lý?* [Is homosexuality a physical or psychological defect?] (Việtbao.vn.com, July 7). In 2009, Lao Động news (news of the Vietnamese Worker's Party) printed a sympathetic article on the prevalence of attacks on homosexuals: 4,5% *đồng tính nam từng bị tấn công* [4.5% of homosexuals get attacked] (laodong.com, September 8). In 2009, positive portrayal of gay relationships and the formation of gay culture began appearing (e.g., "*Thế giới thứ ba*" *trong phim Việt* [lit., "Third-world gay and lesbian sexuality" in Vietnamese film]) (N. V.).

and their supporters hosted the first Việt Pride parade (now an annual event), during which they rode bicycles through the streets of Hà Nội on August 5 (BBC, 2012a, 2012b).[13]

Chapters 4 and 5 discuss relationships between state representation of language, bodies, and notions of disability in more detail. The examples I discuss in this chapter mark, first, the ideological circumstances of state institutions and policy in Việt Nam, and, second, the historical and emergent possibilities for a domestic social movement for Deaf education that is founded on instruction in VSLs. As an economically driven entity, the state must transform its historical understanding of economic capacity as contingent on hearing-speaking into one that also includes economic capacity as an affordance of seeing-signing. Barriers to such a transformation include forces involved in contemporary Việt Nam's *semiotic economy* (Luke, 2007). In the postwar reconstruction and market-socialist eras, Deaf and signing bodies have often been enlisted as bodies recalcitrant to the promise of Vietnamese progress; the visual nature of signing facilitates representation in media outlets, for better or for worse, including those that use images of signing to index problems with Việt Nam's overburdened social welfare system. Importantly, from 2010 to 2015, such representations have been joined by positive accounts of Deaf people as Deaf social organizers have taken on increasingly public roles in social campaigns, as well as in education and employment domains, demonstrating expertise in social leadership and communication—albeit in unfamiliar and, to many, ambiguous modalities (i.e., VSLs).

The ability on the part of state agents to come to terms with VSLs as national resources is, according to a number of observers, of great consequence to the state's economic development goals. For example, Buckup's analysis of the 2006 *VHLSS* data suggests that Việt Nam's economic future may depend, in part, on also solving the communication barriers historically consolidated between Deaf and non-Deaf people. In an International Labour Organization working paper titled *The price of exclusion: The economic consequences of excluding people with disabilities from the world of work,* Buckup estimates the loss of economic productivity for working-age persons with disability in various countries. His analysis of Việt Nam showed that exclusion of these persons from labor activities, some 13.92% of a total population of 7 million, accounted for losses in GDP of US $1.82 billion in 2006 (2009, p. 15). Buckup further estimates that the "largest losses occur in the group of people with moderate disabilities" and that "through adequate policies, an untapped potential of US $1,221 million could be mobilized in this group" (ibid., p. 16).

In June 2010, Thanh Niên News announced that Việt Nam's Institute of Labor Science had issued a report in collaboration with the ILO, finding evidence of both job growth and yet poor job generation. The report recommended that Việt Nam improve "investment in the social security system" to "protect vulnerable citizens from falling through the cracks" (Bao Van, 2010). Buckup's (2009) extensive analysis for the ILO also shows that many persons perceived to be "vulnerable citizens" are in fact available and qualified for gainful employment.

---

13. In Vietnamese news reports, the acronym LGBT (lesbian, gay, bisexual, transgender) is used, often accompanied by *viết tắt bằng tiếng Anh* [abbreviated from the English].

Marazzi contends that language and communication are central to the service-oriented "new economy," in which human resources predominate over industrial production, which is, in turn, contingent on *"general intellect entrepreneurship"* (2008, p. 46; emphasis in the original). Fairclough's argument complements Marazzi's in underlining that "language is becoming more central and more salient in New Capitalism" (2002, p. 163). Fairclough argues that "there is a sense in which language (and more broadly semiosis, including 'visual language') is becoming more salient and more central in the New Capitalism (ibid.). According to Marazzi, the rise of information and communication services and technologies, as well as financial language, facilitate "bodiliness," whereby market transactions "presuppose the *negation* of the body of the speakers," who, by selecting whatever financial convention they wish to pursue, align as a "community" (2008, pp. 35–36; emphasis in the original).

If we accept Marazzi's and Fairclough's arguments and pair these with Buckup's data set, then it becomes rather more pressing to examine language policies and practices, which can be understood as geopolitical contests that majority-language speakers leverage in their attempts to gain or maintain social and political-economic opportunity for themselves. Among the available leveraging mechanisms is the pathologization of minority-language users. Opportunities for social equity in education are directly linked to such opportunities outside it (Phạm, 2007). Among the more significant barriers to implementing social changes that promote Deaf people's participation in education, employment, and other institutional and market domains, is the Vietnamese state's reluctance to acknowledge social inequalities.

In a study of class dynamics in Việt Nam, "Vietnamese scholars and commentators have been unable, politically, to address such manifestations of inequality, although research on the communist experience in other countries has clearly shown the salience of inequalities linked to political capital and the access to resources and power under communism" (Nguyễn-Marshall, Drummond, & Bélanger, 2015, p. 4). As the introduction to this chapter demonstrates, scholarly criticism of inequality is an active force in Việt Nam; however, it is often framed as recommendations, reforms, or program initiatives related to development and modernization, not social inequalities per se.

Schools and individual classrooms are significant sites of social change efforts in which educational inequality and related language contests predominate. Language contestation indexes the struggle between conventional and alternative interpretive models, which also powerfully presuppose "the body of the speaker" (Marazzi, 2008, p. 36):

> In a strongly linguistic system, therefore, the crisis of a convention means the explosion of the body of the multitude, of the plurality of the individual differences which, once again, must face the, if you will, historical task of producing/electing a new convention. (ibid.)

By Marazzi's formulation, the 2006 *VHLSS* and its successor instrument, the 2009 Population and Housing Census, consolidate the hegemony of the category "hearing disability" by masking both Deaf people's actual sociolinguistic practices and state-institutional language agendas (e.g., policies, laws). Through the very format of such instruments, which focus on functional impairments and ignore functional capacities,

Deaf individuals and groups may be presumed "languageless," implicitly evaluated through the normative rhetoric of survey authors and analysts. This masking of one set of features of human diversity and sociolinguistic practices for another (HCMSL for Vietnamese, for example) contributes to the reproduction and naturalization of spoken Vietnamese sociolinguistic practices as normative—for bodies and society as a whole.

Extending the argument begun in the previous section, displacement of one set of sociopolitical practices for another highlights one of the terrains in which language contests in Việt Nam are being waged: the body of the Deaf signed language user. For Deaf students at school, these contests take place predominantly in the classroom. For Deaf social organizers, they take place within Deaf organizations themselves, among and between Deaf and non-Deaf organizations. As I explain later, a significant force in Deaf social organizing concerns gender. Language contests also take place in market-oriented locations, as I discuss in chapter 6, with varying effects for signed language users and for representations of HCMSL (and VSLs in general).

The body's centrality to language contests is indicated by states' attempts to control signed language usage. Such regulation constrains the sociolinguistic expression of individual and group-collective bodies and is also implicated in language loss in Việt Nam. According to Marazzi, language loss is not accidental or unintended; rather, the "necessary cost of production becomes *the life itself of the linguistic community*" (2008, p. 50; emphasis in the original).

Blommaert's (2005) examination of the state helps put costs of production into better context. As decisions about production costs also involve decisions about linguistic communities imposing and bearing such costs, Blommaert would not only place these decisions within the jurisdiction of the state but also "attribute a special position to the state as an actor in the construction and reproduction of orders of indexicality within stratified polycentric systems, enormous differences between states with regard to effectiveness, scope, and range of activities notwithstanding" (ibid., p. 397). Blommaert builds this argument in relation to three observations on the paramount importance of the state as an "unavoidable actor" in processes of language policies and rights (ibid.):

(1) The state is a switchboard between various levels. In particular, it is an actor that organizes a dynamic between the world system and a "locality." The state often orients towards transnational centering institutions: capitalism, democracy, an international work order, transnational images of prestige and success, models of education, and so forth. It often also orients to transnational models of language and language use: literacy, the relative value of "local" languages versus "world" languages and so forth. This dynamic is two-way, contrasting between "us" and "the rest of the world," and it is at the core of many state activities. (ibid.)

(2) Related to (1) the state organizes a particular space in which it can establish a regime of language perceived as "national" and with particular forms of stratification in value attribution to linguistic varieties and forms of usage. Thus, the state is one of the main organizers of *possible contrasts* within a particular space: it allows others to create differences between their norms and those that are valid nationally (e.g., those that are transmitted through the education system). Civil society, for instance, will typically organize itself in contrast to (or modelled on) the state. The state is, wherever

it exists, a centering institution with a considerable scope and depth. And the state is very often the actor that uses "language" in the sense of "language name" (English/French/Chinese, etc.) as its "central value."

(3) The state can contribute a materiality to its role as a centering institution in a way hard to match by others. The state has the capacity to provide an infrastructure for the reproduction of a particular regime of language: an education system, media, culture production—each time a *selective* mechanism which includes some forms of language and excludes others. The state, in other words, has the capacity to exert substantial control over the two dynamics of access discussed in the previous section: access to forms and access to spaces of interpretation. The state has coercive instruments usually exclusive to the state: the legal system and the law enforcement system. So the state is often a determining force in the sociolinguistic landscape, in contrast to other centering institutions whose effect can best be described as dominant (ibid., pp. 396–397; emphases in the original).

Blommaert's framework demonstrates the analytic importance of ethnographic examination of relationships between actual language practices, state-institutional infrastructures, and the nature of engagement between interactants in specific sites. In this study I follow Blommaert in considering units of person-site-language-institution or organization in relation to the wider sociopolitical context.

Although much can be learned from historical, macrolevel, and theoretical accounts of states and state institutions, such accounts cannot illuminate particular lived experiences and responses to the conditions people encounter. The remainder of this chapter takes the theoretical points established in chapter 2, and, linking them to the historical and political-economic circumstances described immediately above, ethnographically examines them in the context of the research sites. In doing so, this chapter extends the conversation about the institutionalized organization of languages and bodies—or, to put it another way, and more specifically—the sociopolitical disciplining and regulation of signed language usage within and in connection to state institutions. Thus, in this chapter I apply and extend my examination of the socially and politically managed body, demonstrating the ways that Deaf and non-Deaf people deploy, index, and transform ideologies of language and the nation-state within sites of Deaf education and Deaf social organizing.

STUPID, CRAZY, LAZY, and GAY: HCMSL and Body Appearance as Social Provocation

On a Saturday evening in June 2007 eight EP students invited me to join them for dinner at a restaurant across from the grounds of the teacher's college, where they studied and lived in Biên Hòa. Approaching the end of the spring term, which would bring a much-anticipated, month-long summer break, the mood was light and playful as we conversed in HCMSL. It was also punctuated by a sobering discussion of the events of the last two days. I had met these higher-education-aspiring students two weeks earlier while I was staying in faculty housing near the student dormitory. This living arrangement facilitated my joining EP students for a range of activities, including most lunches and dinners, during which times I observed a range of responses to Deaf people and their use of HCMSL. These reactions were mostly of a negative or an ambivalent sort. As we ate our *cơm* dishes of rice topped with fish or pork, we talked about the situation that had happened the night before, in which a variety-store clerk had nearly forced one of the students out of her shop.

Lan, an EP student of about 20 years of age, had entered the open-air, street-front shop while the rest of us had stayed on the sidewalk. Continuing to sign with us as she perused the store's merchandise, Lan had taken some laundry detergent from a shelf, then gestured for the clerk to get some yogurt from a refrigerated case that was behind the counter. The clerk's facial expression reflected anger. She was clearly repulsed, her eyes darting back and forth between Lan and us. Her expression continued to harden as Lan waved away the plain yogurt she was handed and pointed toward a different flavor, the passion fruit. After taking Lan's payment, the shop clerk motioned for Lan to leave, practically pushing her out of the store. The group's explanation of this incident was that such occurrences were commonplace and that it was their use of signed language that prompted insults such as "crazy" and "stupid." As if to seal this point of their collective analysis, a few minutes later two men approached our table and smacked one of us, Tân, on the head, then mocked his use of HCMSL.[14] This led to an altercation, in which the restaurant owner, much beloved by these EP students, intervened. Eventually the two men left.

When I asked about their understanding of such negative social reactions to signed language, the EP students immediately related these to their early educational experiences, focusing on the inaccessible classroom languages and the language attitudes of teachers and society in general. Although these students hailed from different parts of the country (four were from the capital city of Hà Nội; one was from Vũng Tàu [south of Hồ Chí Minh City]; and three came from Hồ Chí Minh City), their narratives recounted many of the same details: teachers who required them to speak Vietnamese and forbade them to sign; their attempts to conceal signing from teachers and, when caught, being scolded for exhibiting IMPROPER BEHAVIOR or LAZINESS; school principals and teachers who instructed their parents not to sign at home, thereby limiting the students' communication with their family members. Contrasting these experiences were the rewards that came from producing a few syllables of spoken Vietnamese, oftentimes despite their lack of understanding of the meaning of these utterances.

As they described these classroom interactions, the EP students made repeated reference both to teachers WORKING HARD (*công sức*) to communicate with students and to students WORKING HARD (*công sức*) to communicate with teachers. Nonetheless, both failed to achieve the intended results. They also described the primary institutional and classroom-based aim of education, which was to teach Deaf students to speak and then to master educational content, in that order. As instances of *retrospective narratization* (Kleinman, 1988), these commentaries profiled participation in a shared project (communication, education), the failure for which fell asymmetrically on students, who were either unwilling or unable to apply themselves to learning Vietnamese.

---

14. The circumstances surrounding each of these events warrant further analysis as the central actors provided additional interpretation of the reason their ways of signing and bodily presentation had made them the target of attack.

Commentaries instantiated in interviews, daily conversation, and Deaf social organizing activities often took the form of retrospective narratization as focal research participants (Deaf adults who use HCMSL) reflected on their early family, school, community, and work experiences. I follow Leap (2011, p. 193) in viewing the use of retrospection as a narrative device that allows speakers (here, signers) to do the following:

> emphasize certain features of the past, and to downplay other features, so that they can make a point about the lessons they have learned from personal experiences while telling stories to others, and it is easy to see that personal narratives are constructed, fabricated documents, whose fictive qualities leave little room for presentations of objective, unbiased presentation. (ibid.)

Leap argues that retrospective narratization—along with other narratives devices such as the use of "false starts, flashbacks, abrupt scene-shifting, addition of forgotten details" (ibid.), to which I would add repetition and social confirmation (both solicited and unsolicited)—imparts significance to immediate exchanges, including those involving research. Leap foregrounds the constructed or fabricated nature of narrative as a powerful aspect of its expression and analysis. To make this point, Leap draws from historian Allesandro Portelli, who argued, with respect to the fabricated nature of narrative, as follows: "Rather than being a weakness, this is, however, their strength: errors, inventions and myths lead us through and beyond the facts to their meanings" (Portelli, 1991, p. 2; in Leap, 2011, p. 193).[15]

Another connection between Leap's analysis of gay men's use of retrospective narratization and the act of seemingly random violence that took place in a public restaurant in Biên Hòa is the role that gender attribution and sexual statuses play in contemporary Việt Nam. According to an analysis I did of this altercation (for an unpublished paper presented at the 2008 TransSomaTechnics Conference), the recent visibility of HCMSL in public spaces may be viewed as a provocation, particularly where, under conditions of market socialism, social positions based on normative gender, sexual, and body appearances and practices are undergoing rapid transformation. In this particular instance, after his attackers left the restaurant, Tân provided three explanations of what prompted the attack: "They think deaf people are not equal to hearing people; deaf people are ridiculed for their facial expressions and signing in Việt Nam," "They think I'm gay," and "Vietnamese people don't wear earrings or style their hair. But I do what I want." Tân's analysis of the cultural and sociopolitical motivations of his attack is compelling. It suggests a commonality in the ways his body was negatively interpellated, which was in the context of other signing but none so "fashion[able]" bodies, as

---

15. I extend my thanks to William L. Leap for his (2011) use of Kleinman's retrospective narratization in *Homophobia as moral geography* and related conversations with him, as well as conversations with American Unversity undergraduate students in Anth 225, Anth 215, and Anth 254 classes. All of these exchanges extended my appreciation for the methodological usefulness of retrospective narratization and critical analysis of texts involving retrospection.

Tân remarked later. Central to two of these interpretations—gay and fashionable—are mechanisms of transgressive sexuality and gender nonconformity.[16]

Tensions between such state-authorized linguistic and body-based requirements and emergent forms of social participation based in shared signed languages are a central concern in the narratives produced by this study's focal participants (HCMSL users). In the following introduction to the primary research settings, forms of social inclusion and exclusion are indicated as follows: (1) formal language policy and programming; (2) informal langauge practices; (3) language attitudes and ideologies; and (4) sociolinguistic, educational, and other aspirations.

Introduction to the Three Primary Research Settings and Implications for Sociopolitical Formation

Deaf Education Special Schools

As chapter 1 explains, parents of Deaf children living in HCMC were among the first people to establish Deaf education special schools in southern Việt Nam in the mid-1980s. In the early 1990s, various institutions of the Vietnamese state, including the Ministry of Health and the Ministry of Labor, Invalids, and Social Affairs, began to exercise jurisdiction over the special schools. In the late 1990s and early 2000s, this jurisdiction was transferred to the Ministry of Education and Training. With the establishment of college-level special education training at the Hồ Chí Minh City Pedagogic University in 2002, a formal relationship connected special education teacher-trainees with positions of employment in the special schools. Of the special schools in which I conducted participant observation in 2008 and 2009, three were funded by the state, while two were privately funded by parent tuition payment or other support (e.g., Catholic church). However, all Deaf education special schools require families to subsidize student education in some way—through the purchase of textbooks, supplies, and various school fees.

Three of the Deaf education special schools in this study are located in separate districts of HCMC. The other two are situated outside HCMC: one in a peri-urban setting close to HCMC, and another in a peri-urban setting in Đồng Nai province. As explained in chapter 1, the three HCMC-based schools follow the southern Vietnamese convention of labeling Deaf education special schools according to this formula: Hy Vọng [lit., "hope"] + district number or name. Following this convention, I call the three HCMC-based schools in this study Hope A, Hope B, and Hope C. The two schools located outside HCMC do not follow the Hope + district number/name formula because they use a variation on Trung Tâm Khuyết Tật [lit., Disability Center]. I refer to them as Disability Center 1 (DC1) and Disability Center 2 (DC2). All of the schools offered primary-level instruction; four also offered lower-secondary instruction (table 3.1).

---

16. For more information on social inequality related to gender identity and sexuality in Việt Nam, see USAID and the UNDP's cooperative 2014 report, *Being LGBT in Asia: Viet Nam country report, a participatory review and analysis of the legal and social environment for lesbian, gay, bisexual, and transgender (LGBT) persons and civil society*.

Table 3.1. Special School for Deaf Children and Educational Project Instructional Levels Offered (2009–2010).

Schools	Preschool/ Kindergarten (mẫu giáo)	Primary (Levels 1–5)	Lower-Secondary (Levels 6–9)	Upper-Secondary (Levels 10–12)	Junior College
Hope A	X	X	X	o	o
Hope B	X	X	o	o	o
Hope C	X	X	X	o	o
DC 1	X	X	X	o	o
DC 2	o	o	X	o	o
EP	o	o	X	X	X

Table legend: X = established program; o = no established program.

Table 3.2. Special School for Deaf Children and Educational Project Student Census.

Schools	Number of Deaf Students	Age Range of Students	Gender Ratio (M)/(F)	# Students with Deaf Parents	# Students with Deaf Siblings
Hope A	97	2–31	40/57	1	2
Hope B	43	1–17	25/18	1	1
Hope C	157	2–22	not available	2	1
DC1	285	1–35	not available	1	9
DC2	130	5–25	57/73	1	6
EP	49	16–33	28/21	0	2

At the primary level (cấp 1; grades 1–5), students typically remain in the same classroom all day. One teacher is responsible for teaching all subjects; these subjects are expected to be the same as those taught in regular education classrooms and include Vietnamese, Vietnamese history, mathematics, geography, moral and civic education; however, MOET has allowed Deaf education special schools to modify their curricula such that certain lessons may not be taught, either in part or at all. At the lower-secondary level (cấp 2; grades 6–9), each teacher is responsible for two areas, which include at least two additional subjects: Vietnamese literature and English. In cấp 2, students change classrooms and/or teachers throughout the day. In the five schools in this study, the student census ranged from 43 students at the low end (Hope B, a day or nonresidential school) and 285 students at the high end (DC1, a residential school). Four of the schools also offered preschool (mẫu giáo) classes. Student ages at these five sites ranged from 1 to 35 years. Students with whom I had the most contact at the special schools and the EP ranged from approximately 16 to 32 years of age (table 3.2).

In terms of teacher characteristics at the five special schools from 2008 to 2012, content area teachers, whose responsibility it was to teach the national curriculum, were all non-Deaf and predominantly trained at the junior-college level and above;

Table 3.3. Special School for Deaf Children and Educational Project Teacher Census (2009–2010).

Schools	Total Number of Teachers	Number of Teachers with Junior College or University Training	Number of Teachers with University Training in Special Education*	Ratio of Teachers Male/Female
Hope A	16	12	2	6 m/10 f
Hope B	10	10	2	1 m/9 f
Hope C	16	10	5	0 m/16 f
DC1	36	36	2	1 m/35 f
DC2	26	25	8	5 m/21 f
EP	16	16	0	5 m/11 f

*The number of teachers with special education training includes the total number with junior college or university training. For example, for Hope A, the total number of teachers with any kind of training is 12 out of 16 teachers. Of that number, two teachers have additional credentialing.

however, a small but growing proportion of teachers held or had returned to school to pursue special education credentialing (figure 3.3).[17]

In many of the Deaf education special schools I visited, posters illustrating various kinds of educational content hung on the walls of the classrooms and hallways. However, in the five (speech-based) special schools in this study, I observed no posters of speech production anywhere, including the classrooms. Given the emphasis on spoken language in the special school system, it would be reasonable to expect to see speech-articulation charts similar to those produced and circulated among medical experts.

Figures 3.3a and 3.3b give two examples of oral production charts produced circa mid-1980s for speech training and rehabilitation. Although the images are faded in these illustrations,[18] it is possible to discern mouth shape, tongue placement, and other features of vocal articulation. Some special school teachers reported that tonal production charts are still used in regular education classrooms; however, I did not see any in the classrooms or offices of the special schools where I conducted participant observation or in the EP or the HDC.

Until 2009, none of the five special schools in my research offered teacher training in HCSL. In early 2009, DC2 invited the EP to provide HCMSL instruction to its teachers twice a week. Between 2009 and the time of this writing, HCMSL classes for teachers and interested community members has expanded by means of the following initiatives: (1) MOET's hiring of five Deaf teachers with college credentialing (through the EP) to teach primary-level education in Deaf education special schools;[19] (2) HCMSL

17. These data were drawn from survey results provided by the principals of the five special schools and the EP for 2009 and 2010 only.

18. The condition of this book is such that, even when holding it in one's hands, the print-type and images are obscured due to fading.

19. In these situations, providing HCMSL instruction to teaching colleagues is an additional duty on top of their regular teaching responsibilities.

(a)

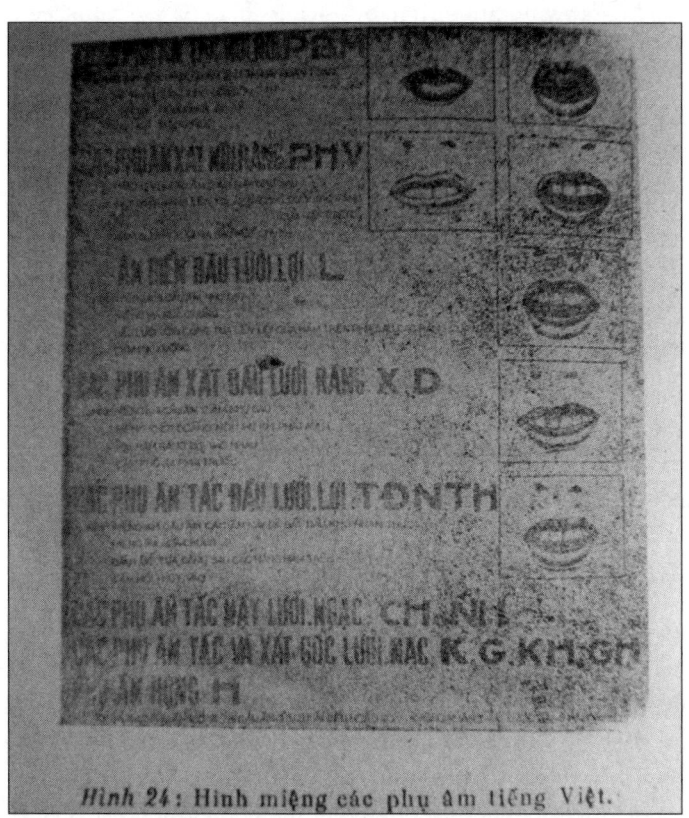

(b)

Figure 3.3. Two oral production charts from Dr. Phạm Kim's (1984) *Vấn Đề Phục Hồi Chức Năng Cho Người Điếc* [Rehabilitation issues of the deaf]. Figure 3.3a is titled *Hình miệng các nguyên âm tiếng Việt* [Oral form of Vietnamese vowels], and figure 3.3b is titled *Hình miệng các nguyên âm tiếng Việt* [Oral form of Vietnamese vowels]. Photographs courtesy of the Asian Reading Room of the Library of Congress and also of Nhà xuất bản Y học [Medical Publishing House], Hà Nội, Việt Nam.

classes offered by the HCMC Deaf Club (HDC), as well as the teaching of other VSLs in Deaf clubs around the country, and through community *giao lưu* [cultural exchange events] hosted by Deaf social organizers; and, most recently, (3) the National Institute of Educational Science's 2014 authorization of sign language classes through the national continuing education system [*giáo dục thường xuyê*].

In all of the schools, class size was smaller in the three located in HCMC (4–10 students), while class size was appreciably larger (12–20 students) at DC1 and DC2. The smaller class censuses at Hope A, Hope B, and Hope C facilitated the arrangement of desks in semicircles, thereby allowing students better visual access to the teacher and to each other. At DC1 and DC2, students' desks were arranged in rows, such that the students often had to crane their necks to see the teacher's instructions. In all of the classrooms, desks faced the front of the room, which commonly contained a teacher's desk and, behind that, a blackboard.

Classroom communication at the sites varied from school to school and from classroom to classroom. In each classroom, the activities I observed were categorically teacher centered. According to Deaf and non-Deaf research participants,[20] such arrangements corresponded to Vietnamese educational design in general (i.e., oriented toward teacher transmission of content). A typical class proceeded according to the national curriculum: Teachers began classes by writing the first section of the day's lesson on the board, which students then copied into individual notebooks. Teachers would then ask students to use spoken Vietnamese to recite the lesson they had just written on the board, or they would read the lesson aloud, and the students would then recite it. Next, the teachers would write the next section of the lesson on the board. Each section of the day's lesson unfolded more or less in this manner. In larger classes, such as those holding 150–200 students (which I occasionally observed due to their location on the same college campus as the EP), lessons were conducted in a similarly unidirectional manner with little direct student-to-teacher interaction.

In all of these schools, students typically sat facing the front of the room and watched while the teacher—usually, "she," though occasionally "he"—wrote on the blackboard and spoke to the class. Sometimes the teachers I observed used the blackboard as a visual cue, pointing to words as they said them. They also instructed students to read passages from the board or their textbooks. They rarely asked the students questions. Occasionally, a teacher asked a student how to sign a concept that the teacher had written on the board or that appeared in the textbook.

Until 2012 the southern Deaf education special schools had no Deaf content area teachers. Prior to 2012, two Deaf teachers worked at Hope C; however, their specialization was arts and crafts production. In 2012, Hope B hired two Deaf primary-level teachers who earned college degrees in primary-level education through the EP, both of whom use HCMSL and written Vietnamese in the classroom. Except for the latter two Deaf teachers—and several more with college credentialing in other areas of the country (one each in Đà Lạt, Cần Thơ, and Hà Nội)—non-Deaf and nonsigning teachers

---

20. The research participants who either explicitly or implicitly described Vietnamese pedagogy as teacher directed and/or centered included special school principals, EP directors and staff, and one director of an inclusive education center.

are responsible for nearly the entire Deaf education special school and IE systems. Thus, in the absence of teacher training in VSLs, VSL proficiency assessments, and credentialing requirements, VSLs remain tacitly prohibited in educational institutions. Moreover, one of the Deaf teachers now employed in a special school reported to me that they experience ongoing pressure to speak in Vietnamese while signing. This is an important point—one that is significant for the changing sociopolitical terrain in which Deaf social organizers are engaging in social change action.

With respect to communication, none of these schools used HCMSL for instruction. Described in more detail later, they used spoken Vietnamese simultaneously with anywhere from a few to many signs in Vietnamese word order and/or with pointing and gestures. Only the EP used (and continues to use) HCMSL as an instructional language and the core of its other programming.

A thorough linguistic description of the differences between VSLs, signing in Vietnamese word order, and spoken Vietnamese is beyond the scope of this chapter and this book, although a few points should suffice to distinguish these modalities: VSLs are distinct from spoken Vietnamese with respect to modality as well as to grammatical structure. So, whenever a person speaks Vietnamese and signs at the same time, that person is not using a VSL. To speak and sign is to attempt to express two distinct symbol and grammatical systems simultaneously—which is not only impossible but also results in utterances not sanctioned by the conventions of either language. Figure 3.4 shows the way that Deaf people in southern Việt Nam refer to the fluent use of HCMSL and signing in Vietnamese word order.

In the final section of this chapter I return to a discussion of Deaf people's confrontations with pressures to sign and speak at the same time, commonly referred to in Deaf education circles as simultaneous communication or Sim Com and, here, Sign-Supported Vietnamese (or SSV).

At Hope A and Hope B, the school principals alternated between using spoken Vietnamese alone and in combination with signing in Vietnamese word order when interacting with students both inside and outside the classroom. At Hope A, two teachers also communicated with students in this manner. At Hope B, no teachers signed with students in full sentences—either in HCMSL or in Vietnamese word order—but they did use individual signs. At Hope C, the principal did not sign and prohibited teachers from signing in the classroom; however, when the principal was not around, I observed one teacher signing proficiently with students (i.e., the teacher was able to engage in extended conversations, as well as ask and answer students' questions). Three other teachers at Hope C used individual signs sporadically, often in combination with spoken or written Vietnamese.[21] At DC1, although the principal did not use HCMSL (according to her own and student reports), she encouraged teachers in their attempts to use sign

---

21. My descriptions of proficiency are offered with the caveat that I am neither fluent in HCMSL nor trained as a sign language assessment expert in any language. These observations are intended merely to differentiate between broad types or instances of signing represented by HCMSL, signing in Vietnamese word order (either accompanied or unaccompanied by spoken Vietnamese), sporadic use of signs, and those who use do not sign at all.

(a) SIGNING FLUENTLY IN THE MANNER OF VIETNAMESE DEAF PEOPLE

(b) SIGNING IN VIETNAMESE WORD ORDER

Figure 3.4. These different signs show the way that Deaf people in southern Việt Nam refer to the fluent use of HCMSL versus signing in Vietnamese word order.

language in the classroom. Two teachers appeared quite comfortable using signs, although they alternated between using signs in combination with spoken Vietnamese, signing in Vietnamese word order, and signing in a manner resembling adult users of HCMSL. Finally, at DC2, the principal and the assistant principal did not sign, nor did the teachers use sign language. Communication in DC2 classrooms has, since 2009, undergone changes since the introduction of HCMSL classes taught by EP-trained teachers; evidence for this comes from research participants, as well as from videos available on YouTube and through social media sites (e.g., Facebook) (see table 3.4).[22]

In interviews with Deaf education special school administrators and teachers, comments on Deaf people's language use and literacy centered on the double notion that *speaking demonstrates understanding and signing demonstrates lack of understanding*. A former Hope C teacher described her perspective of students in the mid- to late 1990s this way:

> If I saw them sign, I would say, "No, don't sign." I would ask them, "No, don't sign." And, yeah, I remember [that] some [students], when they come to class, and they have to learn some story, and when I ask them to come speak for me [in front of the class] and they do like this [shows fingerspelling behind back]. I would get angry and say, "No signing!" At that time I didn't understand why they do like this . . . đánh dấu tay [lit., fingerspell; again shows how students fingerspelled behind their back while speaking]. Just I know that they don't like to speak, and just they like to sign. And it's not good for them. And I was a little angry, and I said to them, "*No, no! No sign!*" (speaker's emphasis)

The results from a survey I conducted with 47 former special school students attending the EP in 2008 and 2009 mirrored this teacher's assessment (see table 3.5).

---

22. As of this writing, my former HCMSL teachers report that a few teachers at DC2—those who have studied HCMSL with teachers from the EP since 2009—are now signing with their students.

Table 3.4. Special School and Educational Project Instructional Languages (2009–2010).

Schools	Schools in Which HCMSL Is the Mandated Instructional Modality	Schools That Use Some Signs in Vietnamese Word Order (Sign-Supported Vietnamese or SSV)	Schools That Train Teachers in the Use of HCMSL (Not State Funded)
Hope A	o	At lower-secondary levels if teachers know some signs. Principal uses SSV with older students.	Principal taught sign language (SSV) to content-area teachers on an intermittent basis and SSV to students twice a week.
Hope B	o	For some assembly meetings and ad hoc groups conducted by the principal (only the principal knows some signs).	Principal held occasional meetings with teachers to practice signing.
Hope C	o	Students were allowed to use signs on their own 1 day per week for 2 hours during the school's Deaf club. Neither HCMSL nor SSV was permitted in the classroom (although I observed 2 teachers using SSV).	o
DC1	o	Three teachers signed in the classroom, using a combination of SSV and HCMSL.	o
DC2	o	o	X (HCMSL teachers from the EP taught classes twice a week).
EP	X	The majority of teachers (14 out of 16 teachers) used SSV, either while speaking or subvocalizing in Vietnamese; approximately half, or 7 teachers, also used some HCMSL. Two teachers consistently used HCMSL in the classroom. Two teachers did not sign at all; in the latter classes, instruction was conducted via an HCMSL-Vietnamese interpreter.	X

Table legend: X = contains programmatic feature; o = does not contain programmatic feature.

Table 3.5. Educational Project Survey of 47 Students' Former Special School Experiences (2009).

	Lóp 6*	Lóp 7	Lóp 9	Lóp 10	Lóp 11	First year of college	Total
Class size	4	8	3	16	6	10	47
Age & gender	17–24 years 4 male	16–25 years 5 males/3 females	20–23 years 2 male/1 female	16–33 years 7 male/9 female	21–26 years 3 male/3 female	25–33 years 5 male/5 female	16–33 years 26 male/21 female
Instructional modality at former school**	Vietnamese and fingerspelling	Vietnamese and "gesture"; some sign with older students	Vietnamese and some sign	Vietnamese, fingerspelling, and some signing in VN word order	Vietnamese and fingerspelling; Grades 1–5 "must speak"	Vietnamese "100%"	47/47 Vietnamese 26/47 (Vietnamese &) fingerspelling, some gesturing and signing with older students
Communication mode at home	¾ "none" ¼ "try to teach, family forgets"	7/8 "none" 1/8 two Deaf siblings at home—communicates only with siblings	2/3 mother fingerspells and gestures, "interprets for father"	15/16 "none" 1/16 Deaf older brother	6/6 "none"	10/10 writing, some speaking and gesturing	32/47 "none" 47/47 reported that their school principal discouraged parents from signing at home
Communication mode with peers	4/4 sign	8/8 sign	3/3 sign	16/16 sign	6/6 sign	10/10 sign	47/47 sign
Sign allowed in class	4/4 no	7/8 no 1/8 yes	3/3 no	16/16 no	6/6 no	10/10 no	46/47 no
Teacher response to signing	4/4 told to stop, hands and head slapped	8/8 told to stop, punished	3/3 told to stop, made to stand against wall, knees bent or head in corner	16/16 told to stop: 11/16 hit with ruler, ear pinched	6/6 teacher "angry," told to stop signing	10/10 told to stop; 8/10 hit on hand with ruler, kneeling in corner with hands overhead	47/47 told to stop signing
How students learned sign language	4/4 from older students	7/8 from older students 1/8 from sibling	3/3 from older students	15/16 from older students 1/16 from older brother	6/6 from older students	10/10 from older students	45/47 learned sign from older students
Job training	sewing, handicrafts	sewing, handicrafts, stone-cutting	"art"; one student completed computer training but never received certificate	sewing, handicrafts, bamboo production, cake decorating	sewing and embroidery; 2 students completed computer classes but never received certificates	sewing, art, embroidery, making greeting cards	47/47 low-wage craft and physical labor
College readiness training	4/4 none	8/8 none	3/3 none	16/16 none	6/6 none	10/10 none	47/47 none

* Lóp 6–11 is roughly equivalent to U.S. grades 6–11. Lóp 12 is not included because there were no students studying at the grade 12 level in the 2009–2010 year.

** 34 out of 47 students in the survey previously attended one of the five special schools included in this research: 2 students attended Hope A; 1 student attended Hope B; 19 students attended Hope C; 4 students attended DC1; and 8 students attended DC2.

Representing twelve special schools from the southern, central, and northern regions of the country, 46 of 47 respondents (97.8%, 34 of whom were from the five sites in this research) reported that they were not allowed to sign in class. All 47 respondents reported that their special school teachers had also verbally ordered them to "stop signing." In addition, 34 reported teachers' use of corporal punishment to try to force them to stop signing, including the following: slapping heads and hands; ordering them to stand with their back to a wall with knees bent for extended periods; standing with their head facing toward a corner; pinching ears; and hitting various body parts with rulers. One former Hope C teacher said she did not observe corporal punishment but that teachers in the special schools may have done these things to "help" students learn to speak.

Deaf Education Special School Outcomes

When students demonstrated "good" speech, they were sent to nearby regular schools for inclusive education (IE, or *hòa nhập*). However, principals and teachers reported that it was the rare student who was able to attend a regular education class and perform satisfactorily. One former Hope C teacher stated the following: "The teachers there talk so fast, and the [Deaf] students can't follow. At [Hope C] it was different because students could take the same class for two years." Repetition of courses was, as she explained, expected for Deaf students. The principal of Hope B described IE in a similar way: "Sometimes students go to *hòa nhập*, but they always come back [to Hope B]. They cannot succeed in *hòa nhập*."

The comments of one director of an IE center, herself a former special school principal, further illuminates these circumstances:

> In the lower levels the teacher may be aware that there is a Deaf student in the class. But at the high-school level, class size may be 40–45 students, and the teacher often does not know the Deaf student is there. Also, because the teacher must follow the national curriculum, it's very difficult for the teacher to have extra time with the [Deaf] students.

In their descriptions of IE, former teachers, principals, and the IE director agreed that Deaf students' success in regular education environments is hampered by multiple factors, including the lack of teacher training in general and instructional language in particular; pace of instruction; and visual barriers and seating arrangement. Nevertheless, IE settings were the environments to which they—and the other special school principals—encouraged Deaf students to aspire because these were places where, according to their educational mandate and their social aims, Deaf students would speak and associate with hearing students.

Reflecting further on special school practices, one former Hope C teacher (the same person who earlier described her attempts to control student signing by telling them not to sign) characterized instruction at Hope C in the following way (circa 1990–1999):

> The way we teach is *thụ động* [lit., passive]. We would often say *cách dạy và học rất thụ động*, that teaching and learning are passive with Deaf students. This means, for example, that today we teach a lesson and we write the lesson on the blackboard

and we teach the students how to speak. Then after that, the students have to learn by heart. Even they don't know the meaning, yet they still have to learn it by heart. Then after that they memorize the paragraph, they just write down all the words they remember. But they don't have any idea what words they are saying or writing.

This description is reminiscent of the example of the civics lesson at Hope C given at the beginning of this chapter, in which students were not evaluated on their comprehension of the content but rather on their reproduction of words and phrases.

An interview with Mĩ, who, prior to coming to work as a staff member and an HCMSL-Vietnamese interpreter for the EP, also worked as a teacher at Hope C, offers an incisive evaluation of the comparative effectiveness of her former method of communication with Deaf students and her current sign-based practices:

Right now, when I remember, I think this way of teaching is so stupid! So stupid! At that time I *believed* that the students could *hear* [speaker's emphasis]. Because when they come to class and sit in front of me, I—[pausing, seeming embarrassed]—well, I *really* speak Vietnamese. I speak the whole lesson—*like talking with hearing people* [speaker's emphasis]. At that time I believed that the students can hear me. But it's not like that! They learned by themselves. They learned so hard! They learned so hard. And just they wrote what they remember. I would say the words in Vietnamese. Then they write. But they don't hear me. In fact, they can't hear! . . . When the teachers talk, the students can't recognize. Or they do something else—they get bored or something. I think they get bored because they don't understand. Then they just keep silent. They don't do like this in the class [raises her hand]. They never raise their hand.

In the regular education system, students typically complete primary education (*cấp* 1) at 10 years of age and lower-secondary education (*cấp* 2) at 14 years of age (see figure 3.1 of the Vietnamese Educational System on p. 70). By contrast, it was not uncommon for Deaf students in primary and lower-secondary classes to be above the age of 17. Accordingly, special school students in their 20s—and, in fewer numbers, their 30s—shared classes with younger students. According to the principals, the special schools followed the national curriculum; however, students are not able to complete the coursework in one year, so they commonly repeat grade levels for multiple years. Students may opt to leave school in order to work or to acquire vocational training where it is available; however, most students do not go on to higher-secondary classes because few are available to them.

Unlike students in regular education schools, special school students are tracked toward classes in vocational training (*đào tạo nghề*), which may include painting, sewing and embroidery, making quilled paper greeting cards (*sự làm thành ống giấy*), masonry, bamboo production, and other handicrafts. Training in handicrafts and physical labor for Deaf students is a historically entrenched practice in Việt Nam, going back as least as far as the French colonial period. Contemporary Deaf educational structuring therefore bears a disconcerting resemblance to the training Deaf students received at the Lái Thiêu School for the Mute-Deaf more than 100 years ago (see figures 3.5 and 3.6).

Figure 3.5. Deaf girls at manual work (Lái Thiêu School for the Mute-Deaf) (Pitrois 1914). Courtesy of Gallaudet University Archives.

Figure 3.6. Boys and girls at work on the coffee plantation (Lái Thiêu School for the Mute-Deaf) (Pitrois 1914). Courtesy of Gallaudet University Archives.

Once Deaf students leave school, they are often tracked into "disability-specific enterprises" and vocational training, the majority of which "are very small and [involve] working in low profit-margin industries such as handicrafts, sewing, massage, etc." (International Labour Organization, 2008, p. 6). One example of such handicraft production comes from an HCMC-based center for children with disabilities: a packet of postcards featuring photographs of silk paintings by "hearing impaired children," typically given to institutional partners, funders, and visitors (figure 3.7). I discuss the second example of the way Deaf people are enlisted in art and handicraft production in chapter 6 as it provides a clear case of the contemporary legal and political-economic circumstances related to what I term the emerging "disability marketplace" in Việt Nam (Cooper, 2015).

A 2008 ILO report revealed that, although a large number of services and programs exist for people with disabilities in Việt Nam, the latter are "very poorly mainstreamed into the vocational education, employment and enterprise development sectors" (p. 6). The report mentions "Deaf and hearing-impaired" people in a number of places, as students or employees within settings specifically established to train them using a local sign language (e.g., café service); otherwise, Deaf people and those with a hearing impairment were listed as recipients of services also delivered to people with multiple disabilities and Down syndrome (ibid., p. 33). Although the report does not explain such circumstances, the implication is that these populations share the use of sign language—which they may—but the implication seems to be that both populations share intellectual deficits.

Until 2010, only Hope A and the EP included computer training in their curricula (e.g., data entry, use of various software programs). My 2009 survey of EP students' previous special school experiences also found that 3 out of 47 students had taken community-based, computer-training courses but had never received certificates they had earned. As of 2015, computer training was much more common for the special schools in general and particularly for schools in urban locations and for students in the upper grades. In southern Việt Nam, the EP is the only place where Deaf students may attend high school and a college or university. In the fall semester of 2015, Deaf students attending the Trường Cao đẳng Sư phạm Trung ương (National College of Education, Hà Nội) received access to the high-school curriculum in Hà Nội Sign Language for the first time. Prior to 2015, therefore, Deaf students who wished to attend high school had to attend the EP in the southern province of Đồng Nai. Otherwise, as an aggregate, Deaf students in Việt Nam were barred from pursuing or completing a high-school education at that time.

The Education Project

Established in 2000, the EP is the first sign-based high-school and college program for Deaf adults in Việt Nam. Located in the southern province of Đồng Nai some 35 kilometers northeast of HCMC, the EP rented classrooms at a provincial university during its first year of operation. In 2001, space constraints at that university and growing student population prompted the EP to relocate to a college of education (lit., *cao đẳng s ư phạm*) also in Đồng Nai. From 2001 until the time of this writing, the EP has rented

Figure 3.7. Front cover, postcard packet titled Tranh lụa do học sinh khiếm thính sang tác(silk painting by children with hearing impairment).

space and dormitory rooms from the college, which, in August of 2010, was approved for university status (*đại học*). The university now also subsidizes the EP's programming.

As were two of the special schools in this study, the EP was initially established and supported solely via private funding.[23] Whereas the Đồng Nai People's Committee approved the EP's educational plan, the day-to-day operations of the EP must comply with MOET mandates under the jurisdiction of the provincial-level Department of Education and Training (DOET), as well as with university policies. Therefore, any programmatic changes to the EP must undergo review and approval by the university and the DOET.

The EP was established as the result of a collaboration between a local educator and a linguist from the United States who specialized in signed language research. Prior to coming to Việt Nam, this linguist had directed the first higher-education program for Deaf adults in another Southeast Asian country. In 1996 and 1997 he conducted linguistic research in Việt Nam, an experience that convinced him, in 1999, to propose the EP, which is similar in mission and in its multilingual programmatic approach to the program he had previously directed. He chose Việt Nam because, as he stated in an interview, he was determined that such a program should be established in a place where "the indigenous sign language was pretty well preserved." Việt Nam was also a place, he believed, that could serve as a model for other countries in the region with

---

23. The EP received an initial commitment of support from a major international nongovernmental organization for a 10-year period; subject to periodic review, it received extended support.

similar economies and Deaf educational interests. At some point this linguist met an enthusiastic collaborator—a former Deaf education special school teacher and assistant principal who became an early advocate for sign language–based education after attending presentations given by this linguist. The two then decided to work together as project codirectors. According to its intended design, the EP included three tracks: high-school completion and college readiness (i.e., upper-secondary coursework granting eligibility to take the 12th-grade national examination); training in signed language linguistic analysis and HCMSL instruction; and HCMSL-Vietnamese interpreter training. The first two tracks were implemented immediately and were expanded, in 2008–2009, to include a college track in primary-education teacher training. The third track, interpreter training, was implemented on an in-house basis in 2012 for staff members who were interpreting for EP courses and related program events and in 2016 for working interpreters in southern Việt Nam.

With the exception of the American linguist, all of the EP teachers and staff were Vietnamese. Most of the employees were also non-Deaf, and many of them studied HCMSL at the EP. Prior to 2010, HCMSL instructors who had themselves taken and then taught HCMSL courses at the EP also held ongoing work, but these jobs were not secure, salaried positions. Non-Deaf students at the college who wanted more intensive HCMSL instruction sometimes subsidized HCMSL-instructors' wages by taking individual classes or tutoring, as I did when I took classes from these instructors in 2007, 2008, and 2009. In 2010, the EP hired one of its Deaf graduates for a salaried position in the administrative office. The EP now has several salaried Deaf employees working in various capacities, including as HCMSL instructors, curricular teachers, and interpreter trainers.[24] Another significant programmatic feature of the EP during the first decade of its operation was the participation of Deaf scholars from the United States—those specializing in signed language instruction and curriculum design—who taught for the EP on a voluntary basis, usually during seasonal breaks from their own academic institutions.

Unlike the Deaf education special school system, the EP directors based their instructional program on the use of HCMSL. The HCMSL instruction track was fundamental to the operationalization of the EP's objectives as it provided a foundation for all other aspects of the program. When the EP began, it employed no credentialed subject-area teachers who were proficient in HCMSL. Therefore, the EP codirectors asked that the first cohort of *lớp* 6 (grade 6) students train their subject-area teachers in the use of HCMSL prior to, and in tandem with, subject-area coursework. The codirectors also arranged for a specialist in sign language instruction and curriculum design from the United States to train the first cohort of students in HCMSL instruction. After this first group of HCMSL instructors developed instructional materials and began opening classes to the teaching college, the EP encouraged subject-area teachers to continue their formal study of HCMSL. However, whereas most of the EP content-area

---

24. Through a cooperative arrangement between the EP and a U.S.-based university, Deaf teachers credentialed in primary-level education and possessing certificates in HCMSL instruction participated in interpretation studies training, along with the EP's non-Deaf interpreting staff.

teachers held more than one job, it was difficult for them to stay late after the instruction day had ended to take evening classes in HCMSL. Therefore, most of the EP teachers continued to acquire HCMSL during classroom interactions with EP students but not through formal study.

In 2008 and 2009, the EP had approximately fifty students and sixteen teachers. Class size at the EP ranged between 4 and 15 students, depending on the grade level and the content area. In the lower- and upper-secondary educational program, the EP offered the same curriculum as did the regular education schools. These courses covered topics such as Vietnamese, Vietnamese literature, Vietnamese history, mathematics, geography, moral and civic education, English, and physical education. The EP also used standard-issue instructional materials, such as course textbooks—that is, the same materials as those used in regular education classrooms. Deaf students participating in the HCMSL instruction track also took additional courses in signed language structure and analysis, lesson planning and curriculum design, and world Deaf histories and cultures. After completing high school, those students who were permitted to study primary-level education took courses at the EP, as well as theory and practice courses required by the teaching college (now university). These included child development, legal aspects of childhood education, teaching methods and design, practicum, and internship.

The Deaf education special schools and the EP have four major structural and programmatic differences. First, the special schools use spoken Vietnamese as the primary mode of instruction and, where teacher language proficiency allowed, some use of either HCMSL but, more commonly, signing in Vietnamese word order. By contrast, the pedagogical approach at the EP is based on HCMSL. Second, the special schools do not require students to complete instructional levels within one curricular year, whereas the EP requires its students to complete and pass all required coursework within a curricular year. Third, in the special schools, teachers of lower-secondary courses are responsible for teaching two subjects. By contrast, teachers at the EP are hired for their expertise in one subject, and they are expected to teach courses only in that area. Finally, special schools typically train students to work in low-wage-earning activities such as arts, crafts, and physical labor, whereas the EP provides full access to the subjects included in the national curriculum, trains interested students for a specialization in HCMSL instruction, and offers one college program in primary-level Deaf education teacher preparation.

The EP's impact on educational outcomes has been remarkable (Woodward et al., 2004; Woodward & Nguyễn, 2012). In 2003 the EP announced that the first group of Deaf students ever to take *lớp* 9 classes (grade 9) had passed the Vietnamese 9th-grade national examination.[25] Moreover, not only had all ten students in that group passed the exam, but two had also passed with honors.[26] In 2006, four of Việt Nam's first Deaf

---

25. Around 2006, MOET discontinued the 9th-grade national examination.

26. Prior to 2006, Việt Nam required 9th- and 12th-grade national examinations that mediated, respectively, promotion from primary- to secondary-level education, and entry to higher education and secondary technical studies. Examinations are now no longer required; instead, the country now assesses academic capability according to academic performance in the classroom and grading (*quy cây*).

high-school graduates then passed the 12th-grade national examination, which, like the 9th-grade exam, is an anonymous examination that identifies test takers only by number. By 2008, around 19 EP graduates had passed the national examination, and 12 of these went on to study primary-level Deaf education through the EP's newly implemented college-level program.[27] In 2012, the EP graduated its first cohort of nine students credentialed as primary-level Deaf education teachers. In 2014 eight more students graduated from this program, and a third cohort is set to graduate in 2017.

With respect to the EP's third original programmatic track—HCMSL-Vietnamese interpretation training—the EP codirectors had intended for interpreter training to parallel student academic training such that, as students graduated and were ready to enter college and the workforce, a pool of trained interpreters would be ready to interpret in these settings. According to one of the EP codirectors (the American linguist), this component was not implemented because so few hearing students wanted to continue beyond the first year of HCMSL studies that the HCMSL teachers reportedly said, "No, we can't teach just one student." In chapter 5 I discuss some of the factors that created barriers to student participation in HCMSL classes and the nascent establishment of interpreter training in the latter part of the 2010s. However, this situation began to shift in the early 2010s, facilitating broader social and state-level interest in HCMSL and VSLs generally.

Unlike the Deaf education special school system, the EP designed its instructional program around the use of HCMSL. Subject-area teachers were not expected to be immediately fluent in HCMSL; however, they were encouraged to study with EP-trained teachers and use the grammar of HCMSL. One of the EP codirectors described the EP's approach to instructional language use this way:

> We basically told them [the subject-area teachers] at the beginning that they had to learn signs from Deaf people and that they had to try to sign as much like Deaf people as they could in class. Giving a lot of visual information . . . We don't require, we encourage, the teachers not to use their voice. But we don't fire them if they do use their voice. But we encourage them not to.

If, after giving teachers an opportunity to practice teaching using HCMSL, the EP's adult learners were unable to understand a particular teacher, that teacher was terminated. According to the EP codirector quoted in the preceding paragraph, two of the early content-area teachers had a great deal of difficulty learning HCMSL and teaching through visual methods. These were teachers from the special school: "They were signing in word-by-word fashion, and the students said 'we can't understand them,' so we let them go." This approach gives considerable weight to Deaf assessment of linguistic and instructional efficacy, as well as participation in institutional decision making.

At the same time, the aforementioned EP codirector continued: "We have encountered problems with teacher retention." Additionally, most teachers work part-time at

---

27. The outcomes of EP student academic performance were provided by one of the EP codirectors from a report submitted to EP project funders detailing the first nine years of academic performance (publicly available).

the EP, maintaining full-time jobs elsewhere; in one interview, the EP codirector surmised that this might be due to interest in maintaining government benefits, as well as teacher concerns over the longevity of the EP.

According to EP adult learners, replacement teachers were hard to find and equally hard to train. This situation led to the retention of some teachers who were not proficient in HCMSL but who had acclimated to the programmatic objectives and pedagogical features of the EP. Therefore, although some teachers may not be proficient signers, their willingness to make repeated attempts to understand student communication or to ask for assistance from an EP interpreter makes retaining them worthwhile. The teachers that have worked with the EP for an extended period of time (5–15 years) have learned to accommodate a new language, a new model of classroom discourse, and new socialization practices even if they themselves have not developed fluency in HCMSL.

The Deaf education special schools and the EP have three major programmatic differences: focus on content; peer-to-peer instruction; and emphasis on Deaf sociolinguistic practices. First, by making sign language the route of academic transmission and knowledge of the subjects taught its goal, the EP set an institutional mandate that teachers and students focus their interactions around acquisition and use of the diverse subjects taught.

In everyday practice, my observation of EP classrooms found that teachers did focus on lesson content; however, I did not observe many extended teacher-student exchanges about the content. A typical class involved teachers lecturing and setting up activities for students to report answers, yet limited interaction about content implications or alternative perspectives. Teacher comments were typically directed at "right" and "wrong" answers. This may be secondary to teacher proficiency in HCMSL. It may also be an example of a kind of instructional method increasingly critiqued within education scholarship in Việt Nam (e.g., teacher centered, examination oriented) (Doan, 2004, p. 148). One of the EP codirectors offered this explanation of teacher focus:

> In the primary and secondary levels education is very traditional. Teachers lecture and may call students to the board. More than 12 years ago, MOET said we should not lecture all the time, that we need to focus on the learner, that the focus should not be on the teacher, that students should have a chance to interact in small groups. A few years ago we got a new minister of MOET, Nguyễn Thiện Nhân,[28] and he is encouraging teachers to be flexible and creative. When I meet with the teachers here I tell them this. But they don't know how to change their way of teaching. I tell them: I am the person responsible here and I want you to do it. I want the students here to write their ideas and to write them in Vietnamese with correct grammar. It will not be good now. But it can be in the future. Many Vietnamese say that Deaf people cannot write well. So they [teachers] just worry about how to finish the [lesson] book, how to

---

28. In 2006, Nguyễn Thiện Nhân was appointed minister of the Ministry of Education and Training. Studying in Germany, he earned a BA and a PhD in technological cybernetics. As a Fulbright scholar, he also studied at the University of Oregon, earning an MA in public administration. He then studied international development and government at Harvard. While working within the current system of education, he is perceived as being dedicated to educational reform and ethics (Lucius, 2009).

finish the curriculum. To pass the test. Memorization is fine for the test. But, for real life, I want them to learn.

Here, the comments of one of the EP codirectors point up concerns about educational reform and calls for training in the nation. They also connect to prevalent notions about Deaf people and Deaf capacity.

As a rule, teachers in Việt Nam are charged with teaching a variety of subjects. Adult learners at the EP pose a double challenge to non-Deaf teachers' customary use of the national curriculum because their educational histories vary enough from student to student to challenge teachers' ability to presume a degree of mastery of materials from earlier grades. Moreover, cultural materials routinely encountered by non-Deaf students at a young age—such as the lyrics to songs used in *mẫu giáo* [preschool] classes for civic education or other content—demand contextualization in order to establish a strong cultural-conceptual foundation for instruction in more advanced material (e.g., Marxist-Leninist economics). Students at the EP often asked teachers to explain the meaning of songs and other popular texts, which they only knew by name and/or by heart but did not understand. In the latter instance, it is the EP—a state-regulated but non-state subsidized international development project—which introduces students to the meaning of socialist and traditional Vietnamese texts long unavailable to them in national speech-based special school education.

Teaching students with HCMSL and print/written Vietnamese thus poses a translational challenge. In addition to language usage, language fluency also involves culturally-rich semantic and pragmatic information, as well as ease in moving and observing body movement. Symbolization and comprehension are thus closely connected with how conceptual properties are shaped by sociolinguistic and experiential resources. Lack of teacher proficiency in HCMSL creates an instructional challenge for teachers and a learning challenge for students: Students may possess textbooks in written Vietnamese, yet classroom instruction must extend their understanding of these texts. Moreover, EP students demonstrate variable proficiencies with written Vietnamese (for the reasons just discussed), creating an added challenge; often, teachers must explicitly clarify grammatical and compositional elements of Vietnamese-language texts and prompt students to provide an appropriate sign in HCMSL with which to symbolize a concept's meaning in subsequent course activities.

During the classes I observed at the EP, whenever teachers encountered difficulty with either expressing a concept in HCMSL or providing a complete answer to a student's question, peer interactions typically took place. During these exchanges, the students' understandings were collectively assembled, often guided by a student known either to perform well academically or to possess a high status among the other students. A study of learning strategies in a residential primary school for Deaf children in Thailand charts similar territory, documenting a tradition of peer-initiated instruction, which is the basis for language acquisition and academic performance (Reilly & Reilly, 2005).

Similar to the findings in the Thai data, I routinely observed instances of student discussion and debate both inside and outside EP classrooms. Within EP classrooms, student use of peer-initiated instruction connects to strategies likely employed in their previous special school settings; however, unlike those settings, the EP's educational environment explicitly endorsed communication in HCMSL. Moreover, teachers sometimes leveraged these peer-instruction strategies by asking one student to explain some aspect of the lesson to another student. Giving peer-instruction strategies a place in the classroom seemed to help bridge translational divides between teacher and student, with key students serving as a translational and/or a subject-content bridge for other students. The peer-initiated instructional exchanges I observed at the EP typically ended when students arrived at an understanding sufficient to continue the lesson, agreed to discuss it further after class, or the teacher interrupted to continue the lesson. Outside the classroom, peer-instruction exchanges took place in informal meetings between classes, over meals, or when gathering in dorm rooms for study sessions.

From one perspective, a sociolinguistic and translational divide exists between teachers and Deaf adult learners at the EP due to the differing and characteristically low level of content area-teachers' proficiency in HCMSL and the students' limited exposure to academic Vietnamese earlier in their education. From another perspective, it is the very existence of this divide, combined with the particular EP programmatic features (i.e., endorsing use of HCMSL, soliciting adult learners' expression of their own ideas, and so forth) that promotes Deaf adult learners to discuss academic materials in HCMSL in the classroom. Accordingly, these structural features of the EP legitimized Deaf people's learning strategies and HCMSL as appropriate to both academic work and intellectual leadership.

If content area-teachers monitor these exchanges, they may improve their own understanding of how ideas are expressed in HCMSL, while also evaluating student accuracy. However, the content area-teachers I observed did not consistently monitor student exchanges; rather, they often used these peer-consultative exchanges as opportunities to move the lesson forward by writing a new section of the lesson on the board; sometimes they even stepped out of the classroom to attend to other business. Observing students' peer exchanges is a significant act on the part of the content area-teachers, particularly in the context of the long-standing devaluation of Deaf sociolinguistic practices. To allow students to work out their own understandings of lesson content, including accessing well-developed visual modes of exchange (e.g., prompting, challenging, cajoling, encouraging, elaborating), is to give value to these activities within the activity and the institution.

In nearly every class that I observed at the EP I saw content area-teachers using sociolinguistic practices conventionalized among southern Vietnamese Deaf people, including various uses of eye gaze and gesture to get and direct student attention. How closely these teachers' sociolinguistic practices correspond to those conventionalized among Vietnamese Deaf people is an area that warrants further research. Interviews and surveys with EP students indicate that they perceive differences between the communication practices of EP and Deaf education special school personnel. At the EP, 19 out of 19 interviewees referred to communication within the EP as fundamentally different from that at special schools. Rồng described the differences this way:

> If you compare the special school and the [EP], what the [EP] does is better. Because we learn so rapidly using sign language. Learning through speech methods, we did

not learn very well—like with writing—I was the worst. I would write the lesson, but then when I approached the teacher for help, I could just as easily have turned my notebook sideways. The meaning was always unclear. It was like not being able to see. I couldn't write. Then I came here [EP], and the teacher used sign language to explain the meaning of the lesson, and I started to get it. Not immediately. It took time. Learning word-by-word, sentence-by-sentence, practicing writing, getting it wrong and receiving the teacher's corrections, again and again, before I started to write better. Searching for meaning, talking with other students, going back to the teacher and asking for more explanation, and finally the meaning started to become clear, and I understood. Signing is so important. Signing [as modality of instruction] beats speech. You can't learn through speech. [Rồng laughed]. It's impossible![29]

During a survey of EP students' prior special school experiences, students made additional comments that pinpointed the EP as the first school where they could freely use a sign language.

Respect for language difference and teacher variability in acquiring HCMSL also facilitates EP use of HCMSL-Vietnamese interpreters in the classroom. Despite not having established their program for training interpreters until 2012–2013, the EP co-directors conducted in-house training sessions and also traveled to other countries (e.g., Malaysia, the Philippines, the United States) to participate in interpreter-training workshops. Moreover, the EP codirectors and Mĩ (the EP's first dedicated staff member and interpreter, who, until 2016, had worked for the EP continuously for the first sixteen years of its existence[30]) each improved their own HCMSL proficiency through the course of daily program operations. Moreover, whenever a new teacher is hired or college courses need to be interpreted, Mĩ usually interpreted because of the advanced level of the content and terminological specialization. The EP's use of interpreters in the classroom is a significant programmatic innovation in Deaf education in Việt Nam. Moreover, by hiring interpreters, parents, teachers, university administrators, the provincial-level Department of Education and Training, and other partners become exposed to their use and grew accustomed to engaging with EP adult learners through an HCMSL-Vietnamese language intermediary.

The effectiveness of HCMSL-Vietnamese interpreters in facilitating interactions between Deaf and non-Deaf persons is also demonstrated in the activities at the HCMC Deaf Club. Using HCMSL to conduct club activities, which HDC leaders refer to simply as FLUENT SIGNING (see discussion earlier in this chapter), the club's leaders established the organization as a place that welcomes the sociolinguistic practices of Vietnam-

---

29. Cooper (2011) attributes this quote to "Quân." The change in attribution reflects ongoing work with this research participant who, in 2015, asked me to change his psuedonym to Rồng.

30. The EP's ability to maintain a high level of programming stemmed in part from Mĩ's long-standing dedication to the EP, which is not simply an expression of her own commitment but also the EP's skillful use of loopholes in government policies that allow international development entities to devise their own compensation arrangements. The latter constrained Mĩ's ability to save enough money to further her own education and thereby improve her own career opportunities. For example, Mĩ worked for the EP for 14 years before receiving a raise in salary or social insurance.

ese Deaf people. Through use of HCMSL-Vietnamese interpreters, they also welcome HDC members' families, community partners, and other visitors.

The Hồ Chí Minh City Deaf Club

The HCMC Deaf Club was initiated in December 2008 by a group of senior EP students, among them approximately ten students who had trained in HCMSL instruction. When they established the HDC, only three other such clubs existed in the country: the Thái Nguyên Deaf Club (est. 1997), the Hà Nội Association of the Deaf (est. 2000), and the Hải Phòng Deaf Club (est. 2003). With the support of one of the EP's codirectors, the HDC secured a meeting space in a central location of HCMC: a government facility that provided early intervention services to children with disabilities. This facility is in one of HCMC's central districts and is close to major bus routes and thoroughfares. Its convenient location permits HDC members who live in the city's other districts to attend meetings and events. The meeting space allotted to the HDC is located on the main floor of the facility's largest conference room and holds about 60 chairs. During the meetings I attended in 2008 and 2009, weekly membership attendance varied from approximately 75 to 110 attendees; those meetings with the smallest attendance typically occurred during holidays and summer vacation periods. The age range of HDC members ranged from approximately 18 to 60 years of age.

From 2008 to 2010, the HDC held general membership meetings, which lasted approximately 2 hours, at this location on Saturday mornings; on Saturday afternoons and Sunday mornings they also offered HCMSL classes to the community, free of charge. In 2010, the HDC changed their general membership meeting to Sundays to accommodate the scheduling needs of the early intervention center as well as to allow members who worked on Saturdays to attend HDC meetings.[31]

At the time of this writing, the HDC has not been recognized by the Vietnamese state, nor has the state recognized any of the country's Deaf clubs, which now number more than 25 in the northern, central, and southern regions. As discussed in the first section of this chapter, Việt Nam's political structure is that of a one-party state whose government comprises ministries, over which the Communist Party has ultimate authority via the National Assembly (see figure 3.1). There is no popular vote, nor is political organizing allowed; however, several decrees stipulate the conditions under which citizens are permitted to associate, which are periodically updated to reflect state concerns. The 2007 Decree on the Organization and Operation of Cooperative Groups (no. 151/2007/ND-CP) authorized groups to assemble under officially recognized *câu lạc bộ* [clubs], "people's associations," and community-based organizations and to pursue activities such as weight training, foreign language study, computer programming, cultural and performing arts, and any number of *nonpolitical* activities.[32] Decree no.

---

31. At the time of publication, the HDC continues to hold its general membership meetings on Sundays.

32. Prior to enacting the 2007 Decree on the Organization and Operation of Cooperative Groups, the state passed the 2001 Law on Government Organizations, the 2003 Decree 88/2003/ND-CP, and the 2005 Civil Code.

151 was followed by the 2010 Decree on Associations (no. 45/2010/ND-CP), which includes "one major change" (from prior legislation) (Wischermann, 2011):

> [I]n the new decree [no. 45, 2010] and in a new chapter 6, so-called "specific associations" (*Hoi co tinh chat dac thu*) are introduced. Without mentioning them explicitly, it is clear that here the "umbrella organizations" are meant. The right to select those organizations belongs exclusively to the prime minister. The decree stipulates that these "specific associations" will receive funds from the state that should help them to cover costs for personnel, offices, "duties associated with state functions," and "assignments of state management tasks" (Article 35). Article 34 of the decree states that those specific civic organizations have specific rights (*quyền*) as well as certain obligations (*nghĩa vụ*). (ibid., p. 392)

With the exception of mass organizations that fall directly under the auspices of the Vietnamese Fatherland Front, "all other groups, societies, associations, and organizations must be registered with and approved by the state or people's councils" (Thayer, 1992, p. 111; see also Thayer, 2008; Lucius, 2009, pp. 31–33). In order to associate as an organization, groups must petition the state for official status. Until the state grants official status, unofficial groups are vulnerable to being disbanded. At the same time, the proliferation of associative groups in the *đổi mới* reform period makes state monitoring and regulation of group activities increasingly difficult (Norlund, 2007; Thayer, 2009, p. 5) (figure 3.8).

Despite the HDC's unofficial status, its founders modeled the structure of the group on that of other officially recognized organizations. Accordingly, the HDC leadership includes a chair (*chủ tịch*); two vice chairs (*phó chủ tịch*)—one who attends to outreach in Việt Nam (*ủy viên đối nội*) and the other, to outreach outside Việt Nam (*ủy viên đối ngoài*); a secretary (*thu ký*); a treasurer (*thủ quỹ*); a commissioner of activities and entertainment (*ủy viên thể thao-văn nghệ*); a commissioner of membership information (*ủy viên thông tin*); and a commissioner of social relations (*ủy viên xã hội*). From 2008 to 2010, HDC leadership positions were held exclusively by then current or former EP students. After 2010, the HDC membership began to vote for persons not affiliated with the EP who had demonstrated leadership initiative through their participation in HDC activities. Another significant aspect of the HDC organizational structure is that formal roles are evenly divided between self-identified male and female club members. In the 2014–2016 term, the position of chair was held by a (male) EP graduate, and the remaining positions were held by a combination of EP and non-EP-related community members.

Although the HDC is not officially recognized, it has assembled as a group for more than seven years without interruption. Members of the HDC and other HCMC-based and provincial Deaf clubs have also, individually and as groups, participated in a number of state-sponsored activities. These include national meetings, such as those hosted by the National Coordinating Council on Disability (NCCD) and the National Institute of Educational Science (NIES); transnational meetings, such as those held in Bangkok, Thailand, by the Asia-Pacific Development Center on Disability (APCD); international conferences and training sessions in Hong Kong, Malaysia, Japan, and the United States; and international development projects such as Malteser International's training in Disaster Relief and the World Concern Development Organization's Intergenerational Deaf Education Outreach Project.

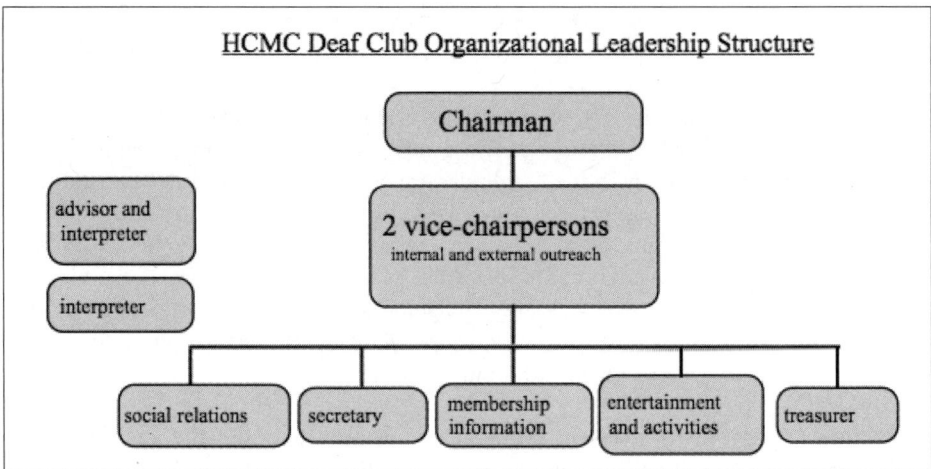

Figure 3.8. HCMC Deaf Club organizational leadership structure.

These circumstances notwithstanding, until it is granted official recognition, the HDC cannot appeal to the government for financial or in-kind support, nor can it join international organizations such as the World Federation of the Deaf. In chapter 5 I describe initiatives undertaken by the HDC and its affiliate Deaf clubs and associations throughout Việt Nam to petition the Vietnamese state for official *câu lạc bộ* recognition and, more broadly, for recognition of the newly forming Hiệp hội quốc gia của người Điếc [National Association of the Deaf].

In the meantime, the HDC continues to pursue a broad range of activities, all related in some aspect to HCMSL usage, training, and policy change. These activities include promoting social awareness and state recognition of HCMSL as a language in its own right; promoting and teaching HCMSL instruction and community-initiated interpreter training; promoting women's leadership in HDC activities; hosting community events at which Deaf and non-Deaf community members can meet and socialize using HCMSL; partnering with international nongovernmental organizations in Việt Nam; and partnering with Deaf associations in other countries, either through Internet-based platforms or by sending and receiving delegations to training sessions and meetings.

Understanding that the HDC has no financial support, the government facility that provides the space to the HDC does so free of charge. The leaders and members of the HDC do, however, pay membership dues every month (in 2010 this fee was $10.00 VNĐ, or approximately $0.50 USD; in 2015 the fee was $15.00 VNĐ, or $0.75 USD). This fee covers the cost of providing club activities and materials, printing (as yet unofficial) membership cards and T-shirts, hosting community events, and making videos about HDC events to circulate via social media.[33] All other aspects of organizational life are voluntary and involve no fees. For example, one of the EP codirectors and one EP staff member often volunteer to interpret for the HDC when requested, such as

---

33. In the early and mid-2010s the most commonly used social media platforms used by HDC leaders (and other Deaf clubs and associations around the country) were Facebook and YouTube.

during major workshops, training sessions, newspaper and television interviews, and presentations given by invited guests.

A typical meeting of the HDC consisted of five activities: greetings and presentation of the meeting agenda; small-group discussions; small-group reports on those discussions; arts and entertainment; and discussion of one or more current Deaf Club action items. To begin each meeting, statements of greeting were given either by the Deaf Club chair or another leader, welcoming everyone and outlining the agenda. This was followed by the first activity, which involved breaking the larger group into smaller ones with a topic for discussion.

Early in the HDC's formation, Deaf Club leaders and members decided on the census of each small group and named these according to the members' interests; a total of ten small groups have the following names: Trông trọt [Growing]; U60 ["Under 60," to designate older club members]; Bóng đá [Football]; BIG (loanword from English); STAR (also a loanword from English); Chim bồ Câu [Pigeons]; Hòa bình [Peace]; Ánh nắng mặt trời [Sunshine]; Đại đoàn kết [Solidarity]; and Vượt qua [Overcoming]. Regular attendance at the club entitles one to become a club member, to whom the HDC issues (again, unofficial) membership cards, an assignment to one of the established small groups, and the opportunity to purchase a shirt emblazoned with the club logo. Organizing members into small groups has allowed HDC leaders to more easily keep track of attendance and small-group responsibilities. During the small-group discussions, HDC leaders typically sit with one of these groups and, when its members seem unclear about the topic, help facilitate the discussion.

After the small-group discussions, club leaders routinely asked the group facilitators to bring the attention of these members to the front of the room, where a platform (approximately 6 feet deep by 8 feet wide and one foot off the floor) had been set up. The club leaders typically facilitated most of the activities from this platform, and after the small-group discussions, they typically asked the group leaders to present the attendance for their groups. Next, participants were called to the platform to share their ideas on that day's discussion topic. The leaders also facilitated turn taking among the participants and called on individuals who had made comments in the small groups but had not come forward on their own.

Following the small-group reports, the director of activities and entertainment, a gifted storyteller who used humor to encourage participation, would tell jokes or stories and/or enlist members in the building of a group story or activity. This part of the club meeting often succeeded in getting some of the newer or more reserved members involved in activities: Because their participation was framed as "fun" and not as serious discussion, they could contribute a story or joke for the amusement of the others without feeling any pressure to represent knowledge on a subject. Regardless of their explicit or implicit purposes (e.g., core social organizing or entertainment), club activities always contained the signers viewpoints on their everyday circumstances and the issues they encountered as they navigated social life. The HDC participants often told stories about miscommunication in their families, difficulties getting or keeping a job, and differences between Deaf and non-Deaf ways of signing and the pressures to, if not actually be like, then to appear and act like, non-Deaf people.

The final activity usually involved discussion of the status of current HDC objectives and reports by the HDC leadership with respect to furthering them. All of the five

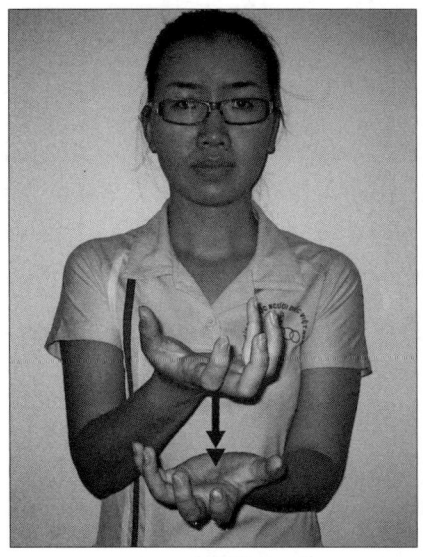 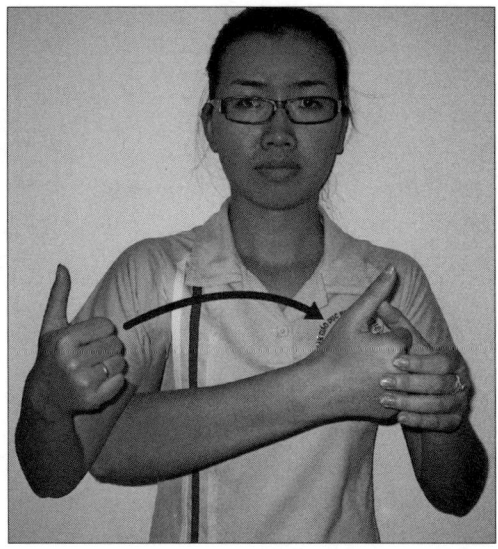

SOCIETY   INCLUSION

Figure 3.9. These two HCMSL signs together represent the concept hòi nhập xã hội [social inclusion].

sections of the club meeting were conducted in HCMSL, as well as Vietnamese, such as when information was written on the whiteboard at the front of the room or when members took notes in each of the small-group activity books.

Unlike the special schools and the EP, the activities of the HDC are all organized and run by Vietnamese Deaf people. Indeed, the historic emergence of the Deaf Club was premised on this desired organizational feature, along with a requirement that HDC leaders and members use HCMSL—that is, not signing in Vietnamese word order (as most HDC members had encountered in the special school system) or in a foreign signed language (which were prominent in northern Việt Nam but becoming increasingly visible in southern Việt Nam, particularly via tourism). When visitors from other provinces attended HDC meetings, HDC leaders welcomed the other varieties of VSL. They also welcomed delegations from countries who used foreign signed languages, with the expectation that communication would be interpreted by one of the HDC leaders into HCMSL. HDC leaders' actions and commentaries demonstrated their interest in establishing a broad network of national and international alliances to support HDC aims—particularly with respect to signed language recognition and sociolinguistic inclusion of Deaf people in the wider society.

The HDC meetings addressed issues of social inclusion from a number of angles, including attention given to HDC leadership structure and meeting facilitation; community-based campaigns and advocacy (petitions, awareness raising); and international Deaf social networking.[34] In chapters 5 and 6 I discuss HDC initiatives in more depth

---

34. From 2012 to 2016, the number of Deaf clubs has grown significantly. From 2015 to the time of publication, the HDC has partnered with another organization in an effort to strengthen its membership and boost social-change actions. The membership of the HDC's partnering organization consists of younger persons (18–30 years of age) known for their use of creative and fun activities and social organizing methods.

and focus on some of the challenges to organizational legitimacy and authority that the club has encountered in its efforts to maintain and develop both sustainable local Deaf organizations and a national Deaf association.

Emergent Sociolinguistic Identities and Sociopolitics

The circumstances surrounding the formation of the HDC illuminate issues related to contemporary notions of Deaf embodiment, language ideology, and the sociopolitics of signed language usage emergent during the latter part of the 2010s. Prior to establishing the HDC, the club's leaders had participated in the Development Center,[35] an HCMC-based organization run by and for persons with disability that had a membership group I am calling the Hearing Impaired Club (HIC). In March 2007 the Development Center created a Hearing Impaired Unit (HIU) and hired its first director to coordinate training, job placement, and counseling for Deaf and hard of hearing people and their families on issues related to deafness. This HIU director then hired several EP students with training in HCMSL instruction to teach HCMSL classes at the Development Center. During this time, the HIU director established the HIC, which the HCMSL instructors and other EP students also attended. During a meeting of the HIC in December 2008, a pivotal event occurred that prompted the HCMSL instructors to discontinue their association with the HIC.

The pivotal event concerned the selection of new leadership for what the HIU director referred to as alternately "*my* hearing impaired club" or "*my* Deaf club" (emphasis mine). When selecting the HIC's club leaders, the HIU director appointed the club's hearing interpreter (who is a former special school teacher and signs in Vietnamese word order) as the new HIC president. The HIU director also appointed herself (a self-identified hard of hearing person with limited knowledge of signs) as the new HIC vice president.

As former members of the HIC described it, this event prompted a subsection of the HIC to form a new club (the HDC) because the Hearing Impaired Unit director's appointment of herself and the interpreter to lead the club did not allow club members to have a say in guiding the organization's issues and activities. Another significant issue was the fact that the HIU director and the interpreter also did not use the preferential language of the HIC membership (i.e., HCMSL).

The use of spoken Vietnamese and signing in Vietnamese word order by the HIU director and the interpreter often caused confusion during membership meetings; on several occasions that I witnessed, HIC club activities were unable to proceed, and members were certainly not able to participate in the activities as much as they might have, had the venue been language accessible (see later discussion). Ultimately, when the EP-affiliated HCMSL instructors raised the issue of holding a vote, the HIU director ejected them from the meeting. They then appealed directly to the Development Center's executive director to facilitate a "real" vote (i.e., anonymous and with multiple candidates), but the executive director refused to get involved. At the next HIC meeting, the HIU director told the HCMSL instructors that they were not welcome at future HIC meetings. At this point, the group of HCMSL instructors decided to form a

---

35. As with the special schools and the EP, "Development Center" is a fictitious name.

separate club (the HDC), which comprised Deaf and hard of hearing leaders who used HCMSL or other VSLs.

The tensions that emerged between the HIC leadership and its (former) members reflect these individuals' responses to a number of social changes taking place in HCMC in the latter 2010s, particularly with respect to the use, teaching, and recognition of both HCMSL as a language and signing Deaf people's social organizing. At that time, the Development Center was the only place in HCMC that offered HCMSL classes, so that site was significant for the consolidation and contestation of language identity and related sociopolitical work.

The HCMSL teachers whom I studied with at the EP initially introduced me to the personnel, classes, and activities of the Development Center in 2007. In 2007 and 2008 I went to the Development Center on approximately ten occasions and observed students in ten HCMSL classes (each consisting of two and a half hours of instruction, including breaks) and four HIC meetings (lasting approximately two hours each). I also met with the HIU director on four occasions, interviewed her face-to-face and via email (at her request), and met with the Development Center executive director twice (30–45 minutes each time). After the HDC was established, I continued to go to the Development Center to meet with the HIU director and the executive director and was invited by them to present at a conference titled "Living with Hearing Loss" in December 2008; however, subsequent meetings with the HIU director became increasingly tense as she believed that I, as she put it, "belonged to" the EP and represented its interests—particularly the use of HCMSL and Deaf people's leadership. Although I had originally intended to make the Development Center a more substantial part of my research, I decided not to do so due to the distrust expressed by the HIU director and the HIC vice president with regard to my intentions, especially after the latter expelled EP-affiliated Deaf members from their club. Nonetheless, the data I collected there illustrate certain dynamics not only between Deaf and non-Deaf persons but also between Deaf and hard of hearing persons and social hierarchies involving those who sign and those who do not.

The first time I went to the Development Center, the HCMSL instructors told me to be on the outlook for the HIU director as she might attend one of the classes. They variously described her as "hard of hearing" and as "Deaf." These HCMSL instructors also told me the HIU director did not know how to sign, but they had not described her communication. Hence, I was not quite sure who and/or what kind of language practices to be on the lookout for.

The HIU director was not present at the first HCMSL class I attended at the Development Center. During that class I observed several interesting patterns, particularly those common to second-language instruction settings, wherein students may revert to their first language when they are having trouble understanding the instructor, which prompts the instructor to redirect them to the target language. In this class, students sat at tables arranged in a large circle facing their teacher, Công (see chapter 4 for more on Công's background and activities). The students intermittently looked away from Công, dropping their eye gaze to the floor and leaning in toward their tablemates, speaking softly in Vietnamese. Sometimes they giggled while pointing at their instruction sheets. To get their attention, Công waved his hand in the students' direction or asked an attentive student to tap the shoulder of those conversing in Vietnamese. He then directed them back to the lesson: Using humor and pantomime to mirror the students' behavior, Công signed to the students that they must ask him for clarification when they did not understand the materials (figure 3.10).

In the other HCMSL classes I attended at the Development Center, students engaged in similar compensatory strategies, turning to each other and speaking when they did not understand; however, in the second class that I attended, rather than immediately redirecting the students, the instructor, Mỹ Uyên, waited and watched. She then turned to me and, pointing to one of the students, signed discreetly: "That is the director of the Hearing Impaired Unit." The HIU director continued talking in Vietnamese and did not see our communication. I was surprised by the HIU director's behavior, given the powerful example that she was setting (for the novice HCMSL students in particular).

In Vietnamese society, teachers hold an honored position within the social hierarchy. They are so respected that, at Tết, the Vietnamese New Year, after first paying one's respects to one's family elders, students go to the homes of current and former teachers

Figure 3.10. Deaf instructor teaching HCMSL at the development center (2007).

to thank them.[36] In the organizational hierarchy of the Development Center, the HIU director also held a high position as the person who instituted initiatives related to Deaf and hard of hearing people and especially as the person who controlled access to resources and opportunities (training, employment, international networking). The HIU director's decision to speak Vietnamese in front of HCMSL instructors thus not only demonstrated disrespect for the instructor, and implicitly the subject matter, but also marked her authority both in the classroom and as the language model for the students and other HIC members. After observing for a few minutes, Mỹ Uyên politely intervened (as Công had in his class on the day the HIU director had not been present), redirecting the class to the immediate lesson.

At the Development Center I also observed meetings of the Hearing Impaired Club. These meetings were facilitated in two ways. The first involved two hearing people standing at the front of the room on a small platform, one speaking in Vietnamese and signing in Vietnamese word order while the other paraphrased the content, writing it in Vietnamese on a blackboard. The second format involved a hearing person speaking and signing in Vietnamese word order while the HIU director either spoke or wrote on the board. When the HIU director was not presenting, she sat very close to one of the Development Center's volunteers, who repeated all of the content to her, maintaining eye gaze with the HIU director and mouthing each Vietnamese word at a slower pace (i.e., a form of oral interpretation). At the meetings of the HIC that I attended, 35–40 Deaf and hard of hearing people were in attendance. At these meetings, communication between HIC leaders and members appeared very similar to a formal presentation: The HIC leaders talked and the HIC members watched, sitting at tables arranged in rows, as if at school. Occasionally they nodded their heads or signed with each other, but they seldom contributed to the activities. The communication between HIC leaders and members was predominantly unidirectional, allowing little opportunity for club members to contribute their own ideas or to ask questions. The primary barrier to such participation, according to my observations, were linguistic in nature but also related to social and organizational hierarchies. Readers will recall that the HIC president (a non-Deaf former special school teacher who signed in Vietnamese word order) and the HIC vice president (a hard of hearing identified person who knew only a few signs) ran the HIC meetings. In this context the HIC members rarely came to the front of the room to address the whole membership; in other words, they were rarely invited to do so.

The few times I observed HIC members addressing the whole audience were when they literally "took the stage" to clarify the presentations by HIC leaders. Lane's (2011) work on *Black women queering the mic* is helpful here; in that work Lane recounts how, in the context of male-dominated hegemonic heterosexual masculinity, black women have literally and metaphorically grabbed the mic for their music and video productions, which are simultaneously claims to visibility and self-representation of their bodies, sexualities, racial and class politics, and a variety of other social interests.

---

36. In addition to honoring teachers at Tết, Teachers' Day is a national holiday in Việt Nam, celebrated annually on November 20.

"[I]n the hands of the Black heterosexual male, the mic is particularly potent. In hip-hop culture, the microphone represents duty—to speak, to act—on behalf of one's self and community. It also represents power for the one who holds it, because it is their voice that is heard at the party, in the car, on the block, and on the radio far beyond the city limits" (ibid., p. 776).[37]

As I describe in the book's introductory chapter regarding Trang's participation in "310 Years of Đồng Nai," in southern Việt Nam during the latter 2010s, Deaf people rarely appeared on any stage. When they did, their presence was brief—often limited to assembling on stages during charity events to receive gifts and to have their photographs taken for charity organizations or government publicity. That is, they did not address audiences directly (see chapter 5 for discussion of charity events). The only exception I observed to this pattern, until around 2010, were EP-hosted events and ceremonies at which Deaf people presented on stage. At events typically organized by the EP codirectors and staff, EP students often delivered presentation content, either in whole or in part. In the context of non-Deaf people's control over Deaf people's social visibility—and the broader sociocultural context, in which the sharing of ideas and experiences with people in large audience events is highly valued (*chia sẻ ý kiến là điều cần thiết của mỗi cá nhân trong xã hội*)—Deaf people's self-determined participation assumes great significance. In the situations I observed in southern Việt Nam, Deaf social actors did not grab the mic but rather took the stage in a polite yet self-assertive manner; these instances nevertheless resemble Lane's political notion of "linguistic gestures of grabbing the mic" (2011, p. 779).

The gendered and linguistic power dynamics related to Deaf people "taking the stage" are addressed later. Lane's (2015) theorizing of queer black women's "scene spaces" in Washington, DC, is also an extremely compelling model for thinking about the ways in which Deaf people created shared spaces of HCMSL sociolinguistic vitality within otherwise HEARING-controlled or -dominated settings, such as the HIU, cafés, restaurants, and museums (see chapter 6).

In HIC meetings Deaf participants "took the stage" from the HIC leaders, typically in order to translate the meetings' communicative interactions for one another. Recalling that these meetings were conducted in either a form of signing in Vietnamese word order or Vietnamese (with someone interpreting into Vietnamese word order), instances of Deaf participants "taking the stage" typically involved one or more members *interpreting for the interpreter,* that is, translating from Vietnamese word order to HCMSL.

In the meetings I attended (approximately ten), the only HIC member to routinely take the stage was someone I am calling Nam (a Deaf man who appeared to be about 50 years old, one of few male participants and also one of the eldest) occasionally interrupted the proceedings to make sure that the other participants were following the HIC leaders' information exchange and decision making. Nam's translational interruptions tended to follow a common pattern: HIC leaders gave

---

37. I am grateful to Nikki C. Lane for her theorizing on "grabbing the mic," her scholarship on "scene spaces," and conversations over the past four years, which have greatly contributed both to the ways in which I think about space and to the gendered, sexual, racial, and class politics of bodies as material forces in the creation of spaces.

monologic presentations, followed by Nam's translations, after which HIC members asked Nam clarifying questions; that is, members did not ask the HIC leaders these clarifying questions, even though they were the ones who had generated the original content. Following Nam's translation work, HIC members tended to engage in socializing until Nam provided the next chunk of translated information.

During the HIC leaders' presentations, Nam watched intently, occasionally interrupting them to ask a question, then getting to his feet, and facing the audience to back-translate the HIC leaders' comments. After each translated segment, the room would spring into motion with requests directed at Nam, including questions about content, implicit meanings, clarification of sign vocabulary, and the potential impact of the information for HIC members. Some HIC members also shared their personal experiences of the topic with Nam. While these conversations transpired between Nam and the other members, the HIC leaders observed but did not respond to his presentation of the material; neither did they link the clarifications, concerns, and interests that Nam and the other members discussed to their own subsequent statements. It was as if these instances of Nam "taking the stage" did not happen at all; the HIC leaders seemed to simply indulge them but not see them as central to the HIC's activities.

In repeated observation of these exchanges it was not clear to me whether the HIC leaders understood Nam's comments or his interactions with HIC members; in general, it appeared that the language Nam used—which he shared with the signing members of the HIC—was not accessible to the HIC leaders.[38] Despite this lack of mutual communication, the HIC leaders maintained their manner of presentation throughout the meetings I observed.[39] Moreover, this communication format was explicitly endorsed by and participated in by both the Development Center executive director and the HIU director.

---

38. In interviews with the HIU director, she explained that she had become Deaf at the age of seven and grew up speaking both Vietnamese and English. She neither attended a special school nor learned a VSL; rather, she had attended regular schools and later a university, both of which she graduated from by reading the lips of her instructors and using other self-adaptive strategies (e.g., notetakers). Because of these experiences, the HIU director described herself as "hard of hearing." Having trained in a professional field and neither a social worker nor a rehabilitation expert (both new fields in Việt Nam), she was nevertheless extremely passionate about her work. In an interview conducted in spoken and written English, she described two challenges in working with Deaf "clients": "I must be patient and recognize that they [Deaf clients] don't understand me due to their low educational attainment or difficulties in communication. And one more challenge is studying sign language [myself]."

39. One Volunteer Service Overseas (VSO) volunteer working in an inclusive education center attended meetings of the HIC and shared with me her informal survey of HIC members' communication, literacy, and employment circumstances (communicated to her in English by the HIC's club president and interpreter). Of 43 respondents, self-reports included the following: None had completed primary education; six had steady employment (as mechanic, hairdresser, tailor, dishwasher, printer, makeup artist); three to five persons sold state-sponsored lottery tickets; approximately 35 lived at home with parents and had no salary; six reported using sign language to communicate with family; 10–15 reported confidence in reading newspapers.

The circumstances just described immediately, as well as those surrounding the eventual split between the HIC members who left the HIC to establish the HCMC Deaf Club and those who stayed, illustrate some of the ways in which signing Deaf people[40] negotiate ideologies and identities related to HCMSL usage. They also illustrate the ways that embodiment practices (e.g., taking the stage) facilitate citizenship-related claims to self-determination, which clearly also take place in sites ostensibly established on Deaf people's behalf and whose mission it is to include and represent them (e.g., Deaf education special schools, Development Center Hearing Impaired Club). Accordingly, such negotiations aimed at citizenship participation are neither specific nor limited to sites that are naïve about VSLs and Vietnamese Deaf people's cultural practices.

Whereas these negotiations are likely an aspect of every site and every interaction Deaf people in contemporary southern Việt Nam engage in, they are doubtless most prevalent for high-stakes interactions with state agents and others in positions of power, such as national and international nongovernmental organizational interactants. Whether they are interacting with state agents or NGO actors, Deaf people's sociolinguistic negotiation practices have significant material consequences for access to resources, power, or both. Accordingly, Deaf people's social organizing practices involve *infrapolitics*, "the strategic form that subjects must assume under conditions of great peril . . . [and by which] all political action takes forms that are designed to obscure their intentions or to take cover behind an apparent meaning" (Scott, 2005, pp. 71–72). These circumstances put into better context Nam's polite yet assertive approach to clarifying the communication by HIC leaders, his tolerance for so little access to information and organizational recognition, and his willingness to translate and interpret without compensation.

Conclusion

This chapter focuses on the historical context and description of the primary research sites, particularly with respect to language policy and language socialization inasmuch as they contribute to experiences of social inclusion and exclusion at those sites. Arguing that the research participants' sociolinguistic practices are instances of infrapolitical interaction at the sites, the chapter demonstrates the ways in which Vietnamese Deaf people's sociolinguistic practices orient toward collaborative and self-determined social participation. In addition, it demonstrates the ways in which HCMSL legitimacy and authority are related to access to other forms of social resources and power. Prohibitions on the use of HCMSL, demands to sign and speak at the same time, and the disciplining of signed language usage are all instances of Agamben's "inclusive exclusion" (Agamben, 1998, p. 21), in that Deaf students—their bodies—may be nominally included in educational institutions even as their valued experiences and practices are excluded.

---

40. By "Deaf people," I am specifically referring to the 31 people who participated in individual and group interviews, the 47 people who participated in my survey at the EP (related to prior special school experiences), as well as other Deaf community members with whom I interacted at HDC meetings and community events, as well as through my consultancy and training activities for the World Concern Development Organization's Intergenerational Deaf Education Outreach Project (IDEO-VN).

Designed according to state policy and MOET guidelines, the special school system does not allow Deaf students to pursue upper-secondary-level studies—unless they can either hear and speak well enough to attend regular education classes through inclusive education placement or are able to attend the two sign-based high-school programs via the EP or MOET's Hà Nội–based school, which is modeled on the EP. Unlike regular education students, the majority of Deaf students are trained in handicraft production and tracked into vocational occupations and trades that involve physical labor. The architecture of both the special school and the IE systems is built on inclusive exclusion: Deaf students may attend school; however, to do so they must forfeit many of the valued aspects of Deaf sociolinguistic practices and body-based social interactional conventions. Accordingly, in order for Deaf students to attend Deaf education and IE schools, they must cross a threshold beyond which they are no longer, in the proper service to national education, Điếc [Deaf].

Such circumstances bear the mark of political sovereignty, where state language policy and programming mechanisms—and, related to these, the actions of school personnel, students' families, and even the students themselves—coalesce in an assessment of crisis regarding Deaf sociolinguistic practices. The "'sovereign' structure of the law," or, in the case of the special schools, their language policy and programming structure—"its peculiar and original 'force' has the form of a state of exception in which fact and law are indistinguishable" (Agamben, 1998, p. 27). The actual lives of Deaf students are thus a problem that demands an exception to established (regular education) practice, such as waiving the mandated completion of each curricular grade level within one calendar year. Were Deaf students regarded as other students, they, too, would be subject both to compulsory education through the 12th grade and to educational promotion through the national curriculum, which is on pace with their non-Deaf, age-cohort peers. In spoken language, a HEARING-normative embodiment is the fact that authorizes the laws, policies, and practices of exception. And the Deaf education special school would be, in Agamben's terms, the localization or locus of one form of state exception (see 2005, pp. 24–25).

In order to meet the demands of the settings in which such exclusions prevail, Deaf students must forfeit the "very life of the linguistic community itself" (Marazzi, 2008, p. 50). Following from this exploration are two significant analytic insights that establish the foundation for chapter 4: (1) that ideological notions about Deaf people and HCMSL (or sign language) that are circulating within the primary research sites reflect and respond to the hierarchical valence of language codes in Việt Nam broadly, and (2) that such ideological notions include implicit and explicit references to state agents and power, particularly in connection to the national goals of development, modernization, unity, and sovereignty.

Being Vietnamese and Điếc Tủy

Negotiating Sociopolitical Visions through Active Citizenship

4

THE CONCERNS OF adult members of the Deaf community related to linguistic access to education, as well as their aspirations for education as a path to social participation and contribution, are the key themes in the narratives that open this book. These themes also appear in the narratives and commentaries shared with me at the research sites earlier. Việt Nam's establishment of a national system of Deaf education special schools was an innovation that allowed many Deaf students to attend school for the first time. From their inception as part of the political-economic reform of the mid-1980s, the design of the special schools corresponded to expert medical recommendations that connected the ability to speak Vietnamese to the ability to think and to properly conduct oneself in Vietnamese society.

Negative ideological descriptions of sign language as an impediment to individual cognitive and social development prevailed in the first decades of market socialist reform (1986 to 2006). Educational leaders throughout the country vigorously discouraged the use of VSLs, and school personnel implored families not to sign with their children at home, advising them that these children would abandon spoken Vietnamese for sign language as an easier form of communication. Until the early 2000s, MOET capped student access to Deaf education at lớp 5 (grade 5). The reason for this was that "in 2000 most government agencies and schools did not feel that Deaf people were able to study at the sixth-grade level" (Woodward & Nguyễn, 2012, p. 21). By 2008, a few schools in southern Việt Nam began offering access to lớp 6, 7, and 8. However, with the exception of the EP, no schools offered classes for Deaf students beyond lớp 8 (grade 8) unless they were enrolled in inclusive education classes.

According to the southern Vietnamese Deaf adults whom I interviewed, as they grew older their efforts to succeed in speech-based schools were as dissatisfying to them as their educational experiences were disappointing. They therefore often turned away from education only to encounter discrimination in their attempts to obtain gainful employment. These experiences took place in the context of the sociolinguistic ideologies discussed in chapter 3, such as STUPID, LAZY, CRAZY, and also possibly GAY. Additionally, they reflect the lack of familial and social ties that would facilitate introduction into family businesses and employment. Moreover, as I also described in the introduction to chapter 3, use of HCMSL often provoked negative social commentary from non-Deaf people, strangers and familiar community members alike. Such Deaf adult commentaries demonstrate metalinguistic awareness of HCMSL (and other VSLs) as a potential (1) incitement against spoken Vietnamese sociolinguistic ideals; (2) flashpoint for debates about what it means to be a contributing member of Vietnamese society; and (3) barrier to social participation.

Công: Educational Aspiration, Peer-Learning Strategies, and the Foundation of Deaf Social Change Organizing

Công was one of my first (and ongoing) HCMSL instructors. The stories he shared with me illustrate the effects of language ideology on educational design and aspiration and on Deaf social change initiatives.[1] They are also illustrative of the nature of Deaf socialization and peer-learning strategies that foster natural language acquisition, Deaf people's sociolinguistic identities, and Deaf sociopolitical formation. When Công was ten years old, his parents enrolled him in the Hà Nội–based Xã Đàn School. In 1988 Xã Đàn was the only school for Deaf students in the country's capital city.[2] After Công had spent three years there, his parents were dissatisfied with his educational progress. Công explained: "My teachers signed a little, mostly speaking Vietnamese to teach lessons. Some students signed well with each other (while other simply pointed to objects) but could not understand the teachers. Unprepared to move to the next level, we were held back in school." When a second school was founded that relied exclusively on a speech-based instructional model, Công's parents enrolled him there.[3] After nine years at the Trường Dân lập dạy trẻ điếc Nhân Chính–Hà Nội (Nhân Chính Private School for Deaf Children–Hà Nội), Công had completed *lớp* 5 (grade 5), advancing approximately one grade every two years.

Seeing no value in his continuing school, Công's family secured him a job working for a garment manufacturer, and so, at age nineteen, Công left school in order to work. Around the same time, Công attended a meeting of the Hà Nội Association of the Deaf and learned of another opportunity that attracted him more: an adult education program founded on a signed language–based model of instruction (the EP). Công appealed to his parents to let him interview for admission to the EP, but his parents refused, concerned about the 1,700 kilometers that this would put between them, as well as their doubts about the effectiveness of sign-based education. So Công worked for one year at the garment factory.

When a friend in the EP's first student cohort returned to Hà Nội describing a very positive experience there, Công approached his parents again: When he pleaded his case using spoken and written Vietnamese, his parents relented, allowing Công to interview for admission. After the EP offered Công admission for the second cohort of students, Công's father made the trip south with him and—seeing presentations by the

---

1. This is the same "Công" mentioned in chapter 3; all references to "Công" throughout the book are to the same individual.

2. Xã Đàn School was established in 1975. Prior to this time the only other school for Deaf students was the Lái Thiêu School for the Mute-Deaf in southern Việt Nam (see chapter 1).

3. This school, often referred to simply as *Nhân Chính*, was founded in 1990 by the Red Cross of Hà Nội, a nongovernmental organization. Nhân Chính opened its doors in September 1991. See: http://khiemthinhnhanchinh.edu.vn/home/thu-ngo.html

EP's directors, staff, and students—returned to Hà Nội, satisfied that sign-based education was an approach worth trying, if (Công recalled his father saying) his son was "to have an opportunity in life." So in 2001, at twenty years of age, Công began lớp 6 (grade 6) and, for the first time, studied with teachers and students who all endeavored to share the same language. To do so, Công had to first learn HCMSL, as his native language was Hà Nội Sign Language (HNSL).[4]

When we met in June 2007, Công was nearing the completion of his secondary education. His plan was to continue to the highest level available to him, hoping to someday earn a college degree so that he might play a role in educating young Deaf students. Whereas in the early stages of my research most of the Deaf research participants expressed early and ongoing doubt about ever achieving their educational goals, by the summer of 2012, nine of the more than 40 Deaf adult education students I interviewed had graduated from college (including Công). By the summer of 2014 a second cohort of graduates brought this number to seventeen. A third cohort of college students is, as of this writing, now pursuing undergraduate degrees at the EP.

I interviewed Công a number of times from 2007 to 2015 and worked alongside him as a cotrainer for the World Concern Development Organization's Intergenerational Deaf Education Outreach Project (IDEO; 2012–2014). Công's commentaries often revisited his own and his EP peers' educational and social opportunities and lamented the limited opportunities available to most Deaf students in Việt Nam to pursue higher education. Công credited his own educational achievement to two sources: participation in signed language–based educational programming with other Deaf people and involvement in community-based Deaf associations.

As my description of Công's account of his educational experiences shows, Công's high-school and college studies at the EP, as well as his own teaching practices, are starkly different from those he encountered during his twelve years in speech-based Deaf education special schools (from 1988 to 2000). In a 2008 interview with Công and one of his EP cohort members (Rồng, who also hailed from Hà Nội), Công described his special school experiences this way:

> So from 7:30 to 9 o'clock in the morning we sat at our desks and used speech. The teacher would ask each of us to stand up independently and read clearly. When we did, we always signed discreetly as we read aloud. . . . That's how we would memorize the lesson, by signing. So when we got up to demonstrate, we always signed whatever we said aloud. Always one hand moving from the wrist down. The teachers never saw us signing; they weren't paying attention to our hands, just our voices. Outside the classroom we [students] always signed with each other, and anytime a teacher came by, we would immediately stop signing, hoping not to be caught. Because we had learned from signing to each other in the past that the teachers would always approach us and say, "You are supposed to speak, not sign; signing is not good." We would say to the teachers: (looking doubtful) "Speaking is good?" (teachers: yes!). So we tried that—just speaking to each other. But that was impossible!!! [laughed]

---

4. This description of shared language is intended to illustrate that it was Deaf students' aspiration to share a language, not necessarily their actual language use, that provided the favorable conditions for student engagement in the classroom.

I would sign [to classmate], then ask in sign language: "Did you understand me?" They would answer: "No, nothing." Then we would sign . . . until the teachers came along again. . . . This happened every day, repeatedly, on and on, until the teachers could not control for it. There was nothing they could do but let us Deaf students do whatever we wanted. We are D-I-É-C T-Ủ-Y [fingerspelled; lit., Deaf to the marrow].

Also demonstrated in Công's narrative is the way in which Deaf interactants coordinate their responses to language disciplining and regulation. Throughout his interview, Công's *retrospective narrations* (see chapter 3) repeatedly evidenced looking to his peers—literally shifting his eye gaze in their direction during his narrative, depicting the way he and his peers had mutually determined the best course of action.[5] Practices of coordinated action and decision making were also evident in the immediate space of the interview—with Công and Rông engaging in coordinated action in the presentation of certain facts (e.g., years of shared school attendance), as well as to affirm or express contrasting viewpoints on their individual experiences. I return to these features of coordinated action and shared decision making in the following sections, particularly in the one on the Hồ Chí Minh City Deaf Club.

Natural Language Interaction as Active Citizenship

In this study I follow Reis (2013) in discussing participation in education and community-based organizations as forms of *active citizenship* (cf. Kearns, 1995, and Miraftab & Wills, 2005; see also Emery's 2006 and 2009 examinations of Deaf citizenship in the United Kingdom). In Việt Nam, "since there is no binary idea of state and society as separate spheres," the public "must be viewed as a sphere of education," which is itself a part of the party state (2013, p. 84); all active engagement in Vietnamese society thus takes place within the "boundaries of the party state" (ibid., p. 87).

Commentaries by Deaf research participants (as newly credentialed teachers) trace the boundaries of the socially conceived state, and the state-related society, when they describe their difficulties in obtaining teaching positions at the special schools and language policy requiring Deaf teachers to deliver classroom instruction through spoken Vietnamese and signing (Sign Supported Vietnamese). Attending to citizenship as a sociopolitically specified concept in Việt Nam illuminates Vietnamese Deaf people's modes of linguistic citizenship as practices that connect Deaf social interests to broader national and geopolitical interests. Gammeltoft's examination of the uses and meanings of prenatal diagnostic technologies in Việt Nam further illuminates the basis of active citizenship practices in Việt Nam:

> Citizens are expected to relate to themselves as subjects of obligation and to respect and comply with standards and norms defined by authorities—whether school teachers, medical doctors, or population cadres. Within this political community, concern for others is expressed by overseeing and taking care of them, rather than by setting them free. (2007, p. 160; see also 2014; cf. Milwertz, 1997)

---

5. See Dudis (2011 for a discussion of depiction versus other frameworks (e.g., constructed action; cf. Metzger, 1995).

Seeing active citizenship as a useful formulation, particularly in the context of value placed on coordinated social action and belonging, the present analysis diverges in two ways from Reis (2013) with respect to her conclusions. First is the degree of Vietnamese state control over its citizenry. Whereas Reis's formulation describes the state's near absolute control of its population, this study demonstrates the various modes by which Deaf (and non-Deaf) citizens accommodate, negotiate, and resist pressure from majority-group members with respect to HCMSL. Second, Reis (ibid.) does not address the significance of linguistic practices as forces of social control or as analytic units for examining such control. Chapter 2's extensive discussion of Blommaert's (2005) formulation of states as organizing regimes of language via state bureaucracies and "centering institutions" provides a better accounting of how individuals come to inhabit differing social statuses and to repesent differing ideological positions vis-a-vis the national state.

Given the Vietnamese state's platform, which makes education the primary vehicle for ensuring national economic development, and literacy in the national language the primary medium of instruction,[6] claims to languages other than Vietnamese implicitly challenge national development agendas. The state's varying involvement in Deaf education- and Deaf community-based organizing during the 2000s and early 2010s nevertheless allowed Deaf people's signed language-centered sociopolitical interests to gain wider circulation, evidencing what some scholars of Việt Nam term "change from within" (Wischermann, 2011; cf. Fforde, 2011, and Thayer, 2009).

In this context of the state's differing approaches to its Deaf citizens, language politics connected to VSLs have been productive of distinct ideological positions related to signed language variety (addressed in depth later in this chapter). Such differing ideological positions involve forms of *evaluation* (Thompson & Hunston, 2000), *stancetaking* and alignments between *stancetakers* (Du Bois, 2007), which also serve to "establish the relative authority of interactants . . . situat[ing] the sources of that authority in a wider sociocultural field (Jaffe, 2009, p. 7).

Deaf and non-Deaf people made direct and indirect commentaries about each other's language use (evaluation), expressed viewpoints indicating how their language usage, attitudes, or identities related to or were distinguished from each other (stancetaking, alignments, or disalignments),[7] as well as how, through such attributions of value, they established and leveraged situational and institutionalized forms of power (claims to legitimacy and authority). During interviews with EP students and Deaf social organizers, signers' commentaries generally aligned with HCMSL, HNSL, or another VSL (e.g., Hải Phòng Sign Language). The commentaries of special school administrators and personnel generally aligned with spoken and written Vietnamese, though two school principals were outspoken advocates of signing in Vietnamese word order while speaking Vietnamese (see the discussion in chapter 3 of Sign-Supported Vietnamese) and MOET's efforts to standardize VSLs in all regions.

---

6. English-language instruction obtains the next critical language position, with English-language proficiency a requirement for high-school completion, and service-sector employment increasingly contingent on spoken English-language ability.

7. See also Levinson (1988) on *affiliated* and *disaffiliated* utterances.

Between 2007 and 2014, a third ideological position came into clearer view: consolidation of stances aligned with signed languages other than VSLs, especially, but not limited to, American Sign Language. Interviews with Deaf and non-Deaf people indexed commentators' perceptions of foreign signed languages as superior to VSLs or, as commonly expressed by the Deaf social organizers in my study, concern over the sociolinguistic and economic implications of such perceptions of superiority. For instance, Cooper (2015) describes the impacts of American Sign Language–based tourism in Việt Nam on VSLs. Whereas Deaf people lack access to VSLs in education, the appearance of ASL in the market realm provides jobs and social opportunities not available elsewhere. This is a consequence of the participation of INGOs and other international entities in what I term the *disability marketplace,* which explicitly or inadvertently promote ASL as an idealized language. Social media platforms such as CamFrog, ooVoo, and Facebook play a significant role here as well, in that people meet in Web-based video chat rooms using ASL and compare Deaf people's social access in the United States and Việt nam. During the last decade, according to interviewees, we have seen a steady increase in Vietnamese Deaf community members who preferentially use ASL. Meanwhile, social and economic opportunities related to VSLs remain limited (see chapter 6 for a detailed discussion of ASL-based tourism).

In Công's narrative (given earlier), Công clearly aligns his communication experiences at Nhân Chính with (his recollection of) the way he and his Deaf peers signed at that time. His closing remark—*There was nothing they could do but let the Deaf students do whatever we wanted. We are* ĐIẾC TỦY *[Deaf to the marrow]*—gives powerful expression to his and his peers' sociolinguistic desires and convictions (stancetaking).

Taken as a whole, Công's commentary is also an excellent example of retrospective narratization deployed in the production of Deaf social agency. That is, Công (1) positions himself and his peers as social agents collectively engaging in preferred sociolinguistic practices and social organization, and (2) indexes his and his peers' responsiveness to—yet ultimately also their refusal to conform to—institutionalized language policies and disciplining. Such positioning and refusal are striking in this instance and other commentaries like it if we consider the opportunities actually available to Công and his peers in the 1990s. This chapter focuses on ethnographic circumstances taking place in the late 2010s that facilitated increasing state and mass attention to southern Vietnamese Deaf people's social projects and recognition of them as social agents in their own right. I relate three vignettes illustrating the kinds of action Deaf students and social organizers undertook in the late 2010s. Chapters 5 and 6 then focus on state and mass media attention to such initiatives.

Linguistic Self-Determination and the Sociopolitics of Place

As I discussed earlier and throughout this book, the Deaf educational terrain that Deaf students such as Trang and Công encountered in Việt Nam in the late 1980s is situated within (1) world histories of language ideologies that have privileged spoken languages over signed languages, and (2) the particular sociolinguistic, political-economic, and pre- and postwar reconstruction circumstances that Việt Nam faced. With respect to (2), Việt Nam's achievement of middle-income status in 2012 is a strong indication of the fortitude of Vietnamese society members and the Vietnamese state's commitment to national development. However, as indicated by the circumstances explored in this chapter, Việt Nam's ascending economic status has not only failed to result in economic integration of Deaf people (and people with disabilities) but has also created or exacerbated forms of social inequality. These have long been of concern to scholars and society members alike, particularly with respect to educational access (London, 2003, 2011; Kham, 2014; Phạm & Fry, 2004; Woodside, 1983b; Woodward & Nguyễn, 2012); gender equity (Drummond, 2005; Luong, 2003); and connections of disability and poverty, particularly for rural areas (International Labour Organization/Irish Aid, 2013; Mont & Nguyễn, 2011; NCCD, 2010; Phạm et al., 2013); as well as what Berliner et al. term the "middle-income trap" (2013).

Three Vignettes: Language Use, Ideology, and Social Critique in Special School and Education Project Classrooms and at Hồ Chí Minh City Deaf Club Meetings

In this section I present a vignette from each of the three primary research sites: a special school class, an Education Project class, and two meetings of the Hồ Chí Minh City Deaf Club. I selected these examples for their representativeness of participant observation at the sites. That is, the practices I observed at each site (and at the special schools) took on a familiarity as the "way things are done here." In the remainder of the chapter I refer to these examples of language and embodied practices to analyze connections and contradictions in the speakers' and signers' evaluation of institutional conditions.

Special School Classrooms: One Class Session on Citizenship Education

I observed a lớp 8 [grade 8] class on *giáo dục công dân* (citizenship education), which includes topics such as respect for others, law and discipline, moral behavior, social voluntarism and creativity, and health. This particular lesson, which took place during the second semester of early 2009, concerned HIV/AIDS and drug use. Fourteen students, ages 16–25, sat in two rows facing a blackboard, onto which the teacher had copied passages from a textbook. After the teacher wrote a segment on the left-hand side of the board, she stepped to her right and started writing a new section on the blackboard while giving instructions in Vietnamese. Facing the blackboard to write, the teacher's back was to the students; therefore, her lips and facial expressions were not visible. The students, presumably well accustomed to the structure of these activities, began copying the first segment from the board, craning their necks in order to see around the teacher's body. While she wrote, the students alternated their gaze between their notebooks and the blackboard, occasionally signing to each other to discuss the spelling or meaning of a word. The teacher then wrote the following on the blackboard: 10 phút, 14g30–14g40 (10 minutes, 2:30 to 2:40).

As the students worked on the lesson, they focused either on their writing or on one another. One student discussed his answer with a tablemate. When the tablemate asked the first student to repeat a fingerspelled term, the teacher approached them. Apparently perceiving this exchange as one in which the first student was having difficulty, the teacher said to the student in spoken Vietnamese, "*Em đã quên hả?*" [younger person pronoun + past-tense marker + verb "forget" + interrogatory; trans. "You forgot?"].

As she spoke, she produced only one sign: FORGET. The student appeared slightly confused, then smiled at her, and turned back to converse with his peer. This interaction resembles Công's narrative (earlier in this chapter), particularly his description of Deaf students' signing practices as D-I-É-C T-Ủ-Y [Deaf to the marrow]; that is, in the context of little *meaningful* communication with their teacher, these students pursued sociolinguistic practices that were the most meaningful for them. This scenario also included another practice that I observed students engaging in at the five special school sites and in family homes—which were also consistently reported by EP-associated research participants: obedience and feigning comprehension via smiling and head nodding (see later discussion and figure 4.1).

After about 10 minutes, the teacher called out "mười" [lit,. ten] and proceeded to count backward in Vietnamese. Arriving at the number "tám" [eight], she also signed EIGHT; she then continued in Vietnamese without signing until she reached the number "hai" [two], at which point she also signed TWO. Speaking in what seemed a natural manner, the teacher completed the countdown in Vietnamese with no other signs, gestures, or other visual cues. She then looked at a student and called on him to report his answer in Vietnamese. The students each took turns standing up to give their answers in spoken Vietnamese, once again appearing either to have understood her direction or to have known what was expected of them from repetition of this type of activity.

When the students spoke, I often could not understand what they said, even though many of the words were written on the board. The teacher nodded after each student took a turn, sometimes asking them to repeat. She did not correct either the students' pronunciation or the content of their answers. After the students finished reporting all of the answers (some of them incorrectly), the teacher dismissed the class. There was no teacher-student discussion of content.

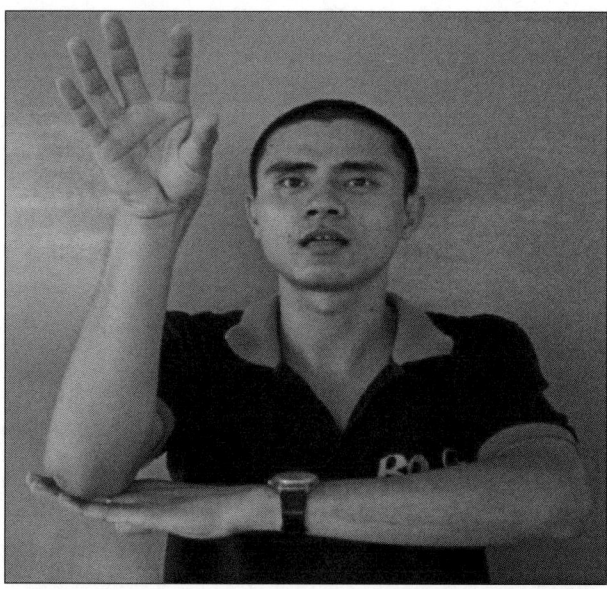

Figure 4.1. HCMSL for FEIGNING COMPREHENSION.

During the ten-minute work period, however, the students had carried on an energetic discussion in HCMSL about the content of the lesson, which, as mentioned earlier, centered on the consequences of drug addiction. While several of the students appeared to have difficulty with some of the terms and focused on their meanings, others discussed how drug use and HIV were related. Some shared personal stories about persons they knew with HIV. During the break that followed the class, I asked several of the students to tell me what the lesson was about. Even those students who had discussed the materials enthusiastically during class had misunderstood much of the content: "You can get HIV from people coughing on you," one student told me. In effect, although the teacher had moved through the required sections of the lesson, the actual content was lost to the students. The teacher's inability to sign or otherwise communicate with the students created a barrier to the students' educational progress—which in this case, could also result in compromising their health. Moreover, given that the primary goal of special school education was oriented toward teaching students to speak Vietnamese, having received no feedback on their individual word pronunciations, it is unlikely that the students gained useful feedback.

Student strategies of smiling, nodding, relying on peers (rather than on teachers) for feedback, and resisting asking questions or otherwise interacting with teachers were patterns I observed repeatedly at each of the five special school sites. Smiling and nodding were among the most common strategies students used, which Cooper (2014) analyzes as a form of social accommodation coordinated between Deaf students in situations of linguistic inaccessibility. These circumstances resemble the peer education strategies documented in Deaf boarding schools in Thailand (Reilly & Reilly, 2005).

The distribution of these strategies in southern Việt Nam is also indicated by Deaf adults' self-reports of having used, and continuing to use, such techniques for diverse settings. In interviews, one HCMSL sign was commonly employed to describe classroom strategies, appearing in every interview I conducted as well as during participant observation (figure 4.1).

This sign's descriptive label, NODDING-AS-IF-UNDERSTANDING, reflects the interviewees' descriptions of their use of the sign in class as a way of telling one another that they could not understand teachers' spoken Vietnamese (Cooper, 2014):

> Deaf interviewees explained that when they were younger they often strained to understand teachers by using lip-reading techniques. Lip-reading spoken Vietnamese is complicated by the fact that, as a tonal language, tones and tone patterns do not have visual counterparts. Thus, by the time they reached the upper-primary grades, failing to comprehend teacher communication had become so routinized that they simply waited for class to end so they could socialize with their peers in signed language. NODDING-AS-IF-UNDERSTANDING thus describes the practice of feigning comprehension by literally nodding their heads to whatever teachers said. This sign is also used to represent an internal state of resignation to one's circumstances. (ibid., p. 322)

To be clear, this sign is not used in direct interactions with teachers; it is used only between Deaf interactants to describe or report on their experiences and is often followed by strategizing the handling of demands in a given immediate situation.

According to interviewees and my own observations, special school students tended to engage in "safetalk," in which interactions between teachers and students involve "cued responses and chorus-like answers, with students often repeating key lexical items after the teacher" (Hornberger & Chick, 2001, in Jean-Jacques Weber, 2014, p. 46; see last section for discussion of "caretaker-" and "school-talk").

Education Project Classrooms: One Session on a History Lesson

The EP classrooms I observed were similar to the special school classes in a number of ways: typically 4–12 students seated in one or two rows facing a blackboard, in front of which was the teacher's desk; formal greeting of instructor at beginning and end of class; and teachers writing lessons from the national curriculum on the board while students copied them in their notebooks. The instructional environment of the classroom, however, was quite different from that of the special school classrooms.

Establishing instruction in the national curriculum as its goal and HCMSL the medium of transmission for subject-area content, the EP set an institutional mandate that teachers and adult learners coordinate their activities around a particular focus: the teaching and learning of knowledge sets. In the everyday practices that I observed, teacher comments were largely directed at lesson content. Unlike at the special schools, the EP teachers that I observed did not, for the most part, correct learners' speech and signing or otherwise comment on learner language practices. One exception included teacher requests for students to supply the signs needed to appropriately express a concept. When learners did not possess a conventionalized sign for a concept, they typically talked among themselves and agreed on a sign, which they then supplied to teachers. This practice resembles and likely draws on practices I described earlier for the special school settings. Although the EP adult learners did not direct class activities, they were nonetheless actively involved in and invited to contribute to the creation of a clear communication environment. Description of a lớp 9 [grade 9] class on *lịch sử thế giới* [world history] conducted in the first semester of the 2008–2009 school year illuminates some of the features of EP classroom engagement.

On this day, the topic was postcolonial national independence.[8] Focusing on three time periods—1945–1960, 1960–1970, and 1970–1980—the classroom activities and discussion involved comparison between decolonization processes in Việt Nam and those in other formerly colonized countries. After copying questions from the board, the teacher, who, like all of the EP content instructors was non-Deaf and not fluent in HCMSL, called a student, Trường, to the blackboard. A world map hung to the right side of the blackboard.[9] The teacher asked Trường to explain the events that took place

---

8. This lesson (Lesson 3) was based on the 9th-grade Vietnamese history book (*sách giáo khoa lịch sử lớp 9*) (Bộ Giáo Dục Đào Tạo, 2008), where it is found in chapter 2, "Asia, Africa, and Latin America, 1945–present" (Chương II: Các nước Á, Phi, Mỹ La Tinh từ năm 1945 đến nay). Lesson 3 focuses on "The development process: People's liberation and the dissolution of the colonial system" (orig. Bài 3: Qúa trình phát triển của phong trao giải phóng dân tộc và sự tan rã của hệ thong thuộc đ̦ia).

9. Unlike most maps produced in the United States, the map used in this lesson has the United States located on the far right (not the center) of the map and is much smaller in proportion to the Asian continent.

during the first time period (1945–1960). Answering in HCMSL, Trường explained that this was the period in which Việt Nam achieved victory over and independence from the French. The teacher, subvocalizing in Vietnamese and signing, asked Trường to explain the nature of this independence: "Việt Nam độc lập như thế nào?" He stammered, making several false starts in his attempt to answer the question. The teacher waited, then asked him again. Appearing exasperated, Trường stammered once more, then said to the class, "I knew what I wanted to say, now I forgot everything!" Several students raised their hands, while others rapidly spelled or signed suggestions to him.

The teacher smiled and watched these exchanges; however, she did not shift her eye gaze to watch individual students during the exchange. Sometimes she looked in the direction of Trường's communication partners rather than at him; at other times, she looked out the door toward the hallway. Eventually she asked whether another student wanted to try giving the answer. A student seated in the front row looked at Trường, who still had the floor, and signed to him "French control." This apparently jogged his memory, as Trường then rallied to a description of how French control had left the country very poor and the Vietnamese people uneducated. He explained that after "Uncle Hồ" (Hồ Chí Minh) led the war, he created programs to feed and educate the Vietnamese people. He pointed to Tanzania on the world map and fingerspelled the country name. He then stepped away from the map and depicted the map in the space in front of his body, indicating the relative locations of and distance between Việt Nam and Tanzania.[10] As Trường did this, the teacher seemed impatient, as if his spatial description was unnecessary. Trường glanced at her, catching her expression, but continued his comments, adding that, although Việt Nam achieved its independence during this period, other countries such as Tanzania still struggled for theirs. The teacher nodded to Trường, then asked another student to come to the board, after which a similar process unfolded for discussion of the second period of independence (1960–1970).

Before the next student could start her comments, another teacher came to the door of the classroom, and the two teachers stood in the doorway, speaking in Vietnamese for about three minutes while the students looked on. When the history teacher finished her conversation, she did not summarize the conversation she had just had in front of the students or otherwise comment on it; rather, she signed to the student who had been waiting: "CONTINUE."

Except for classes conducted in Vietnamese and interpreted into HCMSL (discussed later), the majority of the classes I observed at the EP were conducted more or less in the same manner as in this history class. On the most fundamental level, the differences I observed between EP and the special school classrooms were facilitated by the use of HCMSL and the use of socialization practices conventionalized among Vietnamese Deaf people. It is significant that these practices took place regardless of teacher proficiency in HCMSL. That is, despite lack of teacher proficiency in HCMSL, learner multilingualism (in HCMSL, Vietnamese, and English), as well as the EP program requirement that classes be conducted in HCMSL, facilitated learners' academic

---

10. This is an example of "spatializ[ing] relational terms" in sign language (Emmorey & Falgier, 1999, p. 12). See also Winston (1995) for a discussion of what she terms "spatial mapping."

socialization, including the use of preferential learning strategies, such as peer prompts. The deployment of such learning and communication strategies was, in turn, contingent on these adult learners' individual and collectively shared sense of self-determination and aspirations connected to their use of HCMSL. During interviews, EP students frequently invoked one sign to index positive changes in self- and Deaf cultural group understanding: TƯ NHÌN LẠI MÌNH [lit., in retrospect] (Cooper, 2014) (figure 4.2).

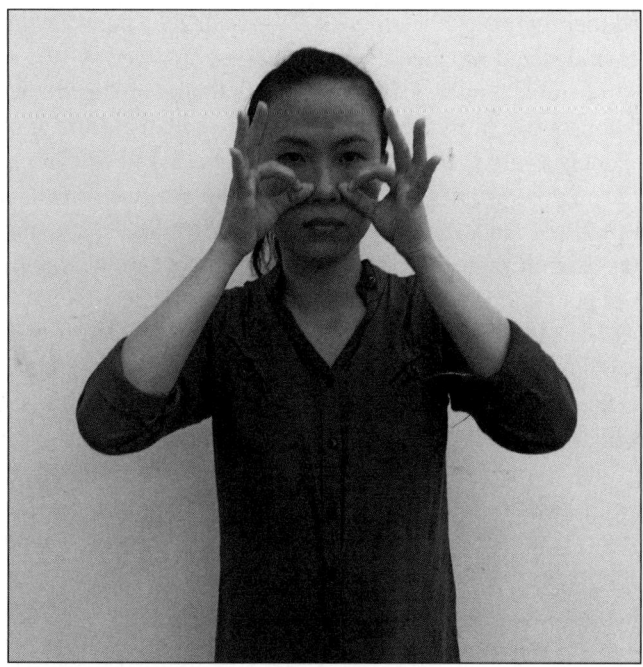

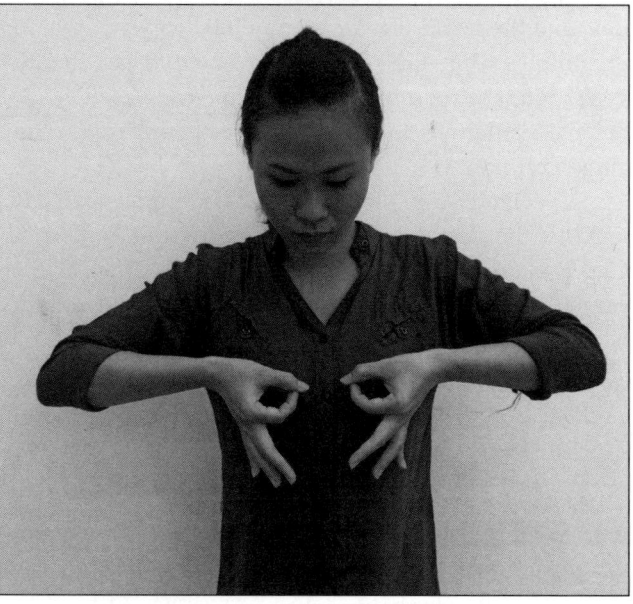

Figure 4.2. HCMSL for RETROSPECTION *[tư nhìn lại mình]* (parts 1 and 2).

The translation of this concept into Vietnamese, which I solicited from Deaf and non-Deaf signing research participants, does not capture the full meaning of the concept as it is expressed in HCMSL, or even quite the same concept. As figure 4.2 shows, the HCMSL sign depicts looking inward, indexing the experiencing self; thus, the Deaf and non-Deaf (signing) research participants' connection between this sign and the spoken Vietnamese concept of retrospection seems to emphasize reflection on inner experience.

The meaning of this sign is clarified by looking at Tấn's comparison of the institutional opportunities he encountered in a special school and those he encountered at the EP:

> At school [special school] I used to talk with the teachers in Vietnamese. They always told me I could speak well. So anytime we had a school ceremony with visitors, the teachers would pick me to read something for the audience. I signed with students, too. I did both. But I thought speaking was better. The teachers said we should speak. When I came here [EP] and learned about sign language and Deaf people, I IN RETROSPECT realized that, at [special school], they didn't teach me about being Deaf. They just rewarded me when I talked like them.

Here, *retrospection* is an effect of an ideological universe that prominently foregrounds not only individual insight but also a complex form of collective self-awareness: awareness as a Deaf person and user of a Vietnamese signed language that draws on Deaf and HCMSL-based sociality to reflect on relationships with non-Deaf Vietnamese persons. The full meaning of the signed concept therefore contains additional meaning not found in the Vietnamese expression *tunhìn lai mình*.

In my interviews with EP adult learners and HCD leaders, HCMSL RETROSPECTION frequently collocated with the sign WAKE UP; research participants connected this HCMSL sign to the Vietnamese concept *nhận thức* [lit., to recognize], which they signed and occasionally followed by fingerspelling N-H-ậ-N T-H-ứ-C (figure 4.3).

As the research participants explained it to me, to WAKING UP is one outcome of the labor of RETROSPECTION. By examining and developing insight into one's experiences, one has an opportunity to WAKE UP. Thus, WAKING UP also entails transformation with respect to one's perspective, or *quan điểm*, of oneself and one's relationships to the world.

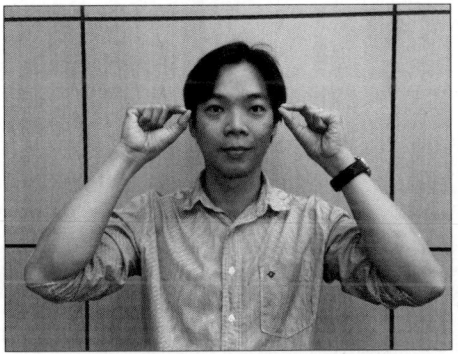 

Figure 4.3. HCMSL for WAKE UP *[nhận thức]* (parts 1 and 2).

130   Chapter 4

WAKE UP and its relationship to self- and collective insight (as southern Vietnamese signers explained it to me) resemble Flemish Deaf people's cultural rhetoric on SLEEP-ING and WAKING UP:

> It is important to SPREAD information about deaf culture and deaf people and fight for deaf rights. Deaf people have to ACHIEVE-GOALS. Both deaf and hearing people SHOULD KNOW: they should WAKE UP from their SLEEP so that deaf people can have better lives. (De Clerck, 2005, p. 119)

According to my analysis of HCMSL WAKE UP and my reading of De Clerck (2005), I argue that Vietnamese Deaf people's instantiation of WAKE UP is a concept that indexes *sociopolitical* understanding in that it marks recognition of both self and community as social agents and prompts social change action. This argument is supported by Hồ Chí Minh City Deaf Club leader commentaries analyzed in the next section and also includes, like De Clerck (ibid.), an emphasis on both ĐIẾC [Deaf] and NGƯỜI NGHE [hearing people] knowing about HCMSL (and VSLs broadly), Deaf culture, and the knowledge and skills that Deaf people possess.

Language similarities and variation are not only sociolinguistically compelling but also deeply politically and intersubjectively meaningful in their differences—from individual to individual and from community to community. Figures 4.4 shows an example of WAKE UP (*nhận thức*) as it is symbolized in Hà Nội Sign Language. Earlier, HCMSL WAKE UP is produced in what might be considered citation style, that is, without nonmanual markers. Here, the HNSL sign for the same concept is shown with nonmanual markers that indicate a negative state of being (initial position) and a positive state of being (final position).

It is important to note that, although both the HCMSL and the HNSL signs for WAKE UP take a slightly different but related form, the meaning of both signs (as discussed earlier) involves a depiction of opening the eyes, metaphorizing *seeing as understanding* (Lakoff & Johnson, 1980; see also Kovecses [2010] and Taub [2001] for an examination of metaphor in ASL). The upcoming HDC leader commentaries illustrate the ways in

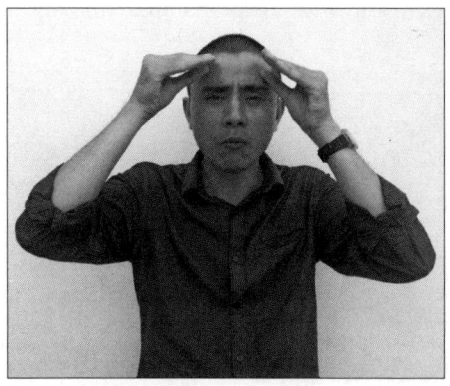 

Figure 4.4. HNSL for WAKE UP *[nhận thức]* (parts 1 and 2).

which seeing, understanding, and acting are connected in southern Vietnamese Deaf social organizing.

A significant area of WAKING UP for adult Deaf users of HCMSL involves reflection on (predominantly) speech-based educational experiences, particularly the ways that teachers did or did not engage them using sign language. In the five Deaf education special schools and the EP, I observed a practice that surprised me: Despite the prohibition against signing, teachers commonly prompted students to provide signs for content area concepts, in the manner of "What's the sign for X?" Eliciting signs from students is not necessarily inappropriate and can often demonstrate respect for them (or other interactants); however, in the case of Deaf education special school teachers, who are entrusted to instruct students in content area subjects, it is absolutely inappropriate to prompt students to symbolize concepts, particularly where (1) students have been prohibited from signing and thereby may not have the available lexicon to produce an answer that is felicitous with the HCMSL, but, possibly more important, where (2) teachers have not yet taught students the content area materials.

As described earlier, EP adult learners often consulted one another on the creation of a sign to symbolize a concept they encountered in their higher-education studies. These peer consultations were thereby based on an understanding of the relevant topic and the particular concept under review.

By contrast, in the special schools, students invented signs based on minimal exposure to concepts. This—and teachers' varying personalities and communication proficiencies—contributed to the construction of distinct ecolects in each classroom setting. These events reflected teacher commentaries: When I inquired how they had learned to sign, teachers typically answered, "I learned from my students" [Học sinh của chị (cô/anh/tôi) cho chị (cô/anh/tôi) biết]. As already noted, MOET does not provide systematic training to Deaf education special school teachers or personnel in the use of HCMSL (SSV or other communication systems). Not surprisingly, in the absence of teacher training and Deaf adults to model HCMSL, idiosyncratic communication practices (and lexicons) developed wherever teachers tried to communicate with Deaf students. In the absence of language training and modeling, it is also not unexpected that teachers sought to learn from students.

In the special schools, therefore, teacher acquisition of HCMSL or SSV occurs on a classroom-by-classroom basis in the direction of children to adults, from those still acquiring fundamental conceptual categories to those for whom such categories are presumably well established. Unless they have Deaf parents, Deaf children are not likely to have exposure to HCMSL by adult users of the language until they reach an age at which they can begin attending an HCMC Deaf club or other Deaf-centered social activity.

As already noted, at the EP, students also teach their teachers sign language; however, the EP is explicitly founded on such a model. The significant difference between the special schools and EP formats with respect to teacher language-training is that EP students *cum-HCMSL-instructors* are adults, and they are also the very people who developed instructional materials based on their own work on the linguistic description and analysis of HCMSL.

Hồ Chí Minh City Deaf Club Meetings: Addressing a Social Change Objective

In chapter 3 I described the typical structure of an HDC meeting, which comprised five sections: greeting and meeting agenda; small-group discussion; small-group reports; arts and entertainment; and discussion of an HDC action item. Here I describe the entertainment section of the August 2, 2008, meeting and the discussion section of the August 9, 2008, meeting. In these two meetings, HDC leaders structured the activities around facilitating the participation and leadership of women club members.

To begin the entertainment section of the meeting, Bùi Huy—who was then the director of activities and entertainment for the HDC—got everyone's attention by waving to members, most of whom were seated in two long sections of chairs some 10–12 rows deep along either side of a long, rectangular room. As he made eye contact with individuals, they would then tap the shoulder of the person seated next to them, and both would turn toward the front of the room. Within a few seconds the room was visually fixed on Bùi Huy, expecting something surprising in store.

On the day from which I draw this first example, Bùi Huy began the entertainment with a lighthearted and somewhat self-deprecating description of men's participation in the club. He followed this with a rhetorical question: "But what about women's participation?" Bùi Huy continued by listing certain skills and knowledge possessed by the women members, including the work they did in their households, their paid positions of employment, their art activities, and their use of the Internet for communication and information gathering. When he then invited the women to come forward to share their stories of such activities, the room went very still. Bùi Huy looked on, pressing his gaze and broad smile into the audience as club members looked at each other and, with nods of the head or physical jabs, prompted one or another female club member to stand up and tell a story. After a few minutes, Thuận, a woman of about 25 years of age, stood up and walked to the platform.

Bùi Huy clapped his hands in apparent anticipation and stepped to the side of the platform to make room for her. He then asked audience members to pay close attention; returning his eye gaze to Thuận, Bùi Huy nodded to her, indicating that everyone was now paying attention. Everyone waited. Thuận told a story involving an episode from a Vietnamese television sitcom. As she did so, using what appeared to be a fluent form of HCMCSL, replete with fully depicted "scenes" of constructed action and dialogue, the attention of the club membership was rapt, and her own comedic timing was so finely tuned that the membership laughed at the various mishaps she related in her rendition of this episode of the sitcom. Television programming in Việt Nam is not closed captioned in Vietnamese or interpreted into VSLs; therefore, Thuận's retelling was built solely of her own observation of the interactions between the sitcom's characters.

When Thuận had finished, Bùi Huy—who had also watched her story closely—remarked to the club membership about her storytelling skill. He then asked the members whether they recognized the television program. A preponderance of members raised their hands, indicating that they had. Bùi Huy went on to then ask them questions about some of the details contained in Thuận's retelling. When members answered, he checked the accuracy of their responses with the storyteller; although he had watched the story and knew the answers himself, he deferred to her as the "author" of the story to evaluate the audience's comprehension. At the end of this exchange, Bùi Huy once again addressed the club membership and invited other women members to bring stories about their home life or work to the next meeting.

At the next meeting (August 9, 2008), instead of breaking into small groups, club leaders opened the gathering by continuing with the previous week's central activity. Opening the floor to women members to share their stories of life and work, two women came forward. Both appearing to be in their early 20s, the first participant opened her statements with, "I have no skill," then continued to describe working multiple jobs, none of which pays well, and that it is hard to find work. The second participant then described her work doing "street art," drawing pictures of tourists near Chợ Bến Thành [Bến Thành Market], in HCMC's famous District One. She stated that her job does not pay well but that it is steady work that she enjoys. She added that she might find better employment if she could communicate with potential employers but explained that she is repeatedly turned away because she is Deaf. After the two women returned to their seats, one of the female club leaders, Lê, took the platform. Lê related the two women's narratives of striving to find good employment to the common Vietnamese Deaf experience of attempting to get an education in environments that are full of barriers. Lê then addressed the membership at greater length:

> We have all had the experience of teachers telling us sign language is bad—we internalized that. But sign language is the language of Deaf people. If hearing people see Deaf and hearing people communicating in sign language, then they will have to "engage in retrospection" and reevaluate their opinion of sign language. In the future, society will change when hearing people see that Deaf people who sign can be a part of society.

After Lê had finished her comments, four more women asked to share their experiences. The final speaker began her comments by apologizing for her signing skill; she explained that she had not attended school with other Deaf people. The club leaders and audience encouraged her to use the signs she knew; she did that, and as she continued to sign, her confidence seemed to grow as she told her experience of looking for work. When she completed her narrative, the club chair said to the audience, "She is a good signer, isn't she?! She hasn't come forward before. This is her first time. But now she has and it's wonderful, isn't it?" The audience responded enthusiastically, and she smiled as she returned to her seat. The club chair, Su, closed this section of the meeting by signing the following:

> Vietnamese Deaf women are important to society. You work. You help your families. And you also come to the Deaf Club. We need you to keep coming to the Deaf Club and practice presenting about your knowledge and experience, so that you can tell people about your skills. But we also need you to practice these skills so you can start to share your ideas [with hearing people] about Deaf people, about sign language, and what Deaf people can contribute to society.

To this Lê added: "And we need you to teach your family and friends how to sign. Because, if more Vietnamese people knew sign language, we could work together so easily to help Việt Nam develop."

Figure 4.5. Hồ Chí Minh City Deaf Club, foregrounding women's leadership (HDC).

At the HDC meetings just described, I was struck by two observations, beginning with the focus on women's participation. Taking this focus, HDC leaders addressed an issue of concern within the wider Deaf community: specifically, that many families kept their Deaf daughters at home, believing that they would be at risk if allowed to go outside, nor could they benefit from education, and were therefore best suited to do household labor. During the late 2010s (non-Deaf) women's social participation was also of general concern in the public media as women's participation in political leadership and economic production had notably declined during early market socialism (as opposed to during and following both the French Anticolonial and American wars). The HDC leaders were clearly attentive to the circumstances of their women members. They were also concerned about Deaf women's absence from Deaf leadership and the significance this had for for the HDC's organizational efficacy, as well as for both broader Deaf social contributions to society and national development (figure 4.5).

The second thing that struck me about the activities at these two meetings was the detailed planning and role differentiation involved in facilitating them. During the previous four to five weeks, HDC leaders gradually moved women's participation to the forefront of club activities. Then, after telling the membership on August 2, 2009, that women members would be expected to address the group the following week, they followed through on that stated expectation. Finally, with the exception of Bùi Huy's role as entertainment and activities director, women HDC leaders facilitated many of the club's other activities (as indicated by Lê's presentation to the HDC membership, mentioned earlier). Moreover, all of the HDC leaders modeled giving social affirmation (legitimacy) to the members' various knowledge and skills.

Taken together, these activities indicated that HDC leaders had an explicit agenda regarding women's leadership. In an interview with the club chair, I asked about this agenda. Su stated that promoting women's leadership had been a recent focus of club planning. He went on to describe how, in their weekly planning sessions, club leaders discussed different ways to enhance women's participation:

> In school [special school] Deaf students never share their own ideas or tell their own stories in class. Well, first, they are not allowed to sign. But even in classes where the teachers let them sign, the teachers only ask them questions based on the lesson. Deaf students don't have opportunities to develop presentation skills. Girl students are often more reserved than boys. Since we started the [sign for HDC], I noticed that women members sat together and rarely addressed the whole group. Anytime we asked a question, it was man, man, man, man, man. The club leaders and I talked about it together and decided that Deaf women needed particular encouragement. Many of them work, in and outside the home, but are not recognized for their ideas. Now we are focusing on simply encouraging them to sign in front of the group. When they sign in a stilted way, we praise them and encourage them, or we may ask questions to help them develop their story . . . By doing this, they will develop their presenting skills. I tell them "The [sign for HDC] needs you to develop your presenting skills so that you can present information to hearing people and help lead Deaf people's inclusion in society."

Reflecting Su's description of differential participation of female and male HDC members, in interviews with the four female club leaders, each described the protectiveness of her parents. Mây stated that her parents rarely allowed her out of the house by herself, other than for school or Deaf club meetings, because her parents were worried something might happen to her. Lê's situation was similar, though she was allowed somewhat more freedom of movement because her family lived closer to the center of HCMC and she was very familiar with the city. By contrast, Mỹ Uyên reported a certain independence in going to and from her parents and her grandmother's home. All four female HDC leaders reported that they had almost no communication with their families. Consequently, they had no opportunity to make their family members aware of their academic or organizing acumen, a recognition that might have encouraged families to have confidence in their daughters' abilities.

The circumstances of the gendered nature of opportunity in Việt Nam anticipate that the language of Deaf women's leadership may either go unnoticed or become a focal point for social scrutiny and/or interest (Drummond, 2005; Nguyễn, A. P., 2004; Luong, 2003).[11] Other research on civil society action in Việt Nam is consistent with these findings (Norlund, 2007; Wischermann, 2011). In addition, INGO-based research evaluating the inclusion needs of people with disabilities at all levels of Vietnamese

---

11. As Việt Nam achieved middle-income status (in 2012), observers have continued to draw attention to the increasing gender disparities in live births of babies counted as either male or female. On September 24, 2014, for instance, *Tuổi Trẻ* (newspaper) reported that "Gender inequality in Vietnam [is] rising, expected to continue," centering on an announcement by Nguyễn Văn Tân, deputy head of the Department of Population and Family Planning. He stated that Việt Nam's "gender ratio had increased to 1:14. It has also been predicted that there will be 2.3 to 4.3 million more men than women in Vietnam by 2050." Such trends do not bear out predicted declines in gender inequality and the centrality of patrifocal systems under socialism (cf. Luong, 1989; cf. Luong 2003).

society is also consistent with these findings. For example, Catholic Relief Services and USAID report that "among the communities [evaluated] there is a tendency to regard similar disabilities among girls/women more severely than those of boys/men" (2010, p. 7).[12]

In the context of limited opportunities to express oneself both at home and at school, the HDC's promotion of Deaf women's participation in club activities and leadership building can be understood as criticism of the gendered features of Deaf social marginalization. Conducting activities that aim to change Deaf women's exercise of social authority is therefore an intervention into gendered structures of power that have negative differential impacts on Vietnamese Deaf women. At the same time, it is an intervention into social and political economic organization that attaches to language broadly and VSLs specifically: To promote Deaf women's perspectives is to promote female sociopolitical agency in a language that is not the national language. Trang's two television appearances within a six-month period and especially her use of those opportunities to represent the Deaf community's perspectives on educational and social marginalization are examples of sociopolitical agency (see the Introduction).

Among my inspirations for focusing on the two HDC meetings discussed earlier is my desire to also show how communication within the HDC, as well as HDC objectives, both hinged on an appreciation of HCMSL and related sociolinguistic practices as *social resources*. In weekly meetings, HDC leaders demonstrated their respect for the sociolinguistic practices and values of HDC members. These leaders could have ignored members' access to communication, for example, by signing their presentations in a way that required members to adapt to conditions on their own. In a crowded meeting space, this might mean dealing with poor visibility, getting clarification from one another, or moving to another place in the room in order to see the HDC leaders better. The fact that HDC leaders themselves valued the members' full access to information, practices (e.g., routine requests to shift body orientation or to repeat information when a signer's message was visually obscured) facilitated the incorporation of these practices into the structuring of HDC activities. Not only did this promote clear communication between HDC leaders and members, but it also gave HDC members authority in structuring communication. Similar to spoken language users' practice of saying "Speak up!," HDC leaders and members continuously negotiated visual needs to ensure active participation in meeting activities.

The HDC activities were thus structured by the particular social and linguistic interests of the Deaf membership at each meeting. Such structuring facilitated the transformation of a meeting *place* into a "disclosive space" (Spinosa, Flores, & Dreyfus,

---

12. Exacerbating the circumstances of gendered inequality, a workshop hosted by Dương Quốc Trọng, phó, Tổng cục DS-KHHGĐ [General Directorate, Ministry of Health Population and Family Planning Department], *Tuổi Trẻ* (newspaper) reported the latter discussing a "cultural preference for sons" and that attendees also commented on "easy access to abortion and high-tech gender detection tools" (*Tuổi Trẻ* staff writer, 2013; see also 2013 report by Dương Quốc Trọng). In December 2016, VN Express News reported these circumstances still unabated, headlining with, "Gender imbalance threatens Vietnam's social stability: experts." (see http://e.vnexpress.net/news/news/gender-imbalance-threatens-vietnam-s-social-stability-experts-3513922.html)

1999, in Escobar, 2001, pp. 167–168), in which HDC participants experimented with expressing and negotiating knowledge that centrally also involved "dealing with oneself, other people, and things" (ibid.). Carrying out HDC activities in HCMSL connected HDC knowledge sets to HCMSL and to the intellectual and sociopolitical labor of southern Vietnamese Deaf people more broadly, regardless of whether they had had an opportunity to attend school. The "things" that such activities addressed during the meetings I observed were, as Lê and Su noted, Deaf people's contributions to society.

In addition to promoting the advancement of women's leadership within the HDC and Vietnamese society at large, the HDC actively pursued the promotion of Deaf leadership and community building generally; HCMSL teaching; cooperation with other local and national Deaf clubs to build support for official state recognition of Vietnamese Deaf cultural associations; establishment of a Vietnamese National Deaf Association—which would also permit them to apply for membership in the World Federation of the Deaf. Now in its eighth year, the HDC also sponsors and participates in events with local special school personnel to promote understanding and acceptance of HCMCSL. Many HDC leaders and members have also participated in INGO projects with related aims.[13] The following are four major outgrowths of HDC activities: (1) HCMSL training and advocacy; (2) HCMSL-Vietnamese interpreter training; and (3) national and international partnerships that facilitate state recognition of Deaf Clubs throughout Việt Nam. I address these three areas of the HDC's social organizing work in detail in chapters 5 and 6.

Multilingualism: Institutionalization of Fluency and Dysfluency

For the school administrator, school might be characterized as students' "home away from home." Althusser theorized the school as a primary institution of ideological inculcation, a domesticating place par excellence. It is useful to consider the ways in which spoken language sociolinguistic practices and HEARING embodiment are institutionalized and deployed as mechanisms. These are then used to inculcate and discipline Deaf students in normative spoken language practices. Such mechanisms—often referred to under umbrella terms such as *language management, language planning,* and *language rehabilitation*—create the conditions for Deaf student fluencies and dysfluencies in schools and other settings of HEARING (non-Deaf and usually nonsigning) control. Next I discuss four mechanisms: misinterpreting student sign production; misinterpreting student metacommunication; teacher sign language production and reception errors; and teacher eye gaze practices.

---

13. The HDC is involved in INGO activities such as the Asia-Pacific Development Center on Disability (cross-disability policy and leadership training); Central Deaf Services (signed language training center); Malteser International (disaster reduction and relief training); Nippon Foundation (Deaf leadership training); UNICEF (capacity-building funding); and the World Concern Development Organization (family-to-school training introducing VSLs in early childhood and school readiness).

Descriptions of student-to-student and student-to-teacher communication clearly demonstrate how a Deaf child's body literally becomes visible to his[14] peers and teachers as sense making and contextually appropriate (i.e., as a legitimately normative student, or, in Altusser's (1971) terms, a "good subject") (Ramsey, 1997). Furthermore, teachers' "ability to correctly predict the points at which they should intervene, to recognize strategies that did not work, and to support strategies that did" are anchored in the ability to employ linguistic and embodied knowledge to distinguish between student performance and actual understanding (ibid., p. 80).

For example, a teacher in a self-contained classroom asked a Deaf student, Paul, a follow-up question after the student had accurately labeled a drawing "scared" but had difficulty explaining the word (ibid.). In classrooms predicated on speech practices, apparently accurate yet incomplete performances such as Paul's may be misinterpreted as demonstrating satisfactory comprehension and go unexplored by the teacher.

In environments where teachers possess metacommunicative knowledge about the signed language in use, shifts in eye gaze, pointing, and signing to oneself are all sociolinguistic features of an engaged student. However, in institutional settings where teachers do not understand these practices—even where teachers do know how to use the local signed language at the novice level or higher levels, as the mainstreaming teachers in Ramsey's study did—meaningful communicative behaviors may be overlooked or misconstrued as off task. Indeed, Ramsey found that, when Deaf students signed to themselves, hearing teachers often misconstrued such engagement as off task and interrupted the students' learning process. Ramsey argues that these students were recipients of an instrumental form of communication, a "functional repertoire—directives and evaluations," which she calls "talk" (ibid., p. 68; cf. Mather, 1989, for discussion of "school talk").

Regarding teacher sign language production and reception errors, a U.S.-based study (Johnson, Liddell, & Erting, 1989) of Deaf preschool children found markedly different language practices instantiated by a hearing teacher who used English as the basis for sign-supported speech and by a Deaf classroom aide who was bilingual in American Sign Language and an "English form" of signing (according to school policy). From this study the authors concluded that "both the form of the language and the content of the conversational interactions are important in the socialization of Deaf children" (ibid., p. 83). Ultimately, Johnson et al. found that it was the Deaf aide who had fewer mistranslations of English concepts and more complete representations of English in her sign production with respect to the meaning of the sentence. This was due to the fact that the aide was not using a spoken language as the foundation for her socialization practices.

More recent work on second-modality acquisition suggests that non-Deaf educational professionals may face additional challenges in their acquisition and use of signed languages (or, more pertinently, languages of a modality different from that acquired in their own language communities) (Chen Pichler, 2009; see also Rosen, 2004). Early work on second-modality acquisition—then framed as second language acquisition (among hearing learners of ASL)—found that students had difficulty producing facial

---

14. In this section, Ramsey (1997) described the interactions with a focal study participant whom she described as male.

markers such as those indicating "yes/no questions, *wh*-questions, both sentential and lexical negation, and adverbials" (McIntire & Reilly, 1988, p. 373). Since most Deaf education teachers are nonnative signers, they learn the signed language later in life, that is, after spoken language sociolinguistic patterns and other uses of the body have been well established.

Chen Pichler describes the situation in this way: "The categories we are used to seeing as hearing people—the gestures one might be able to call up as belonging to a particular cultural population—are not as refined or as numerous as those produced by the local sign language" (pers. comm.). Among the findings in her study of handshape accuracy among hearing adult learners of sign language as a second language, Chen Pichler found that subjects consistently made errors producing unmarked handshapes (B, A, S), I, C, O, 5) that resembled but were not identical to handshapes they already knew. One subject consistently produced an A or "fist handshape" whenever the prompt included an S handshape. Chen Pichler analyzes this production error thus: "Whenever she sees signs or gestures with the A and S handshapes, she perceptually assimilates them . . . to the *fist* category she already possesses" (2009, p. 45). Chen Pichler's analysis is consistent with another analysis of nonmanual (facial) signals that proposes that "adults use . . . their preexisting knowledge of standard communicative and universal affective facial signals to interpret ASL linguistic markers" (McIntire & Reilly, 1988, p. 373).

Chen Pichler's findings have implications for the education of Vietnamese Deaf students, whose teachers are primarily both second-language and second-modality learners of sign language. Even when teachers believe they are using HCMSL correctly, their signing may contain production errors that students have to negotiate. Moreover, when students sign to teachers, errors in the reception of HCMSL (and other VSLs) may result in errant teacher assessment and intervention into student learning (as discussed earlier in Ramsey [1997; see also Mather, 1989]).

Eye gaze is another salient feature of both linguistic and nonlinguistic gesture/posture repertoires practiced by Deaf people, near-native hearing signers, and hearing nonsigners, albeit in markedly different ways. As a linguistic feature, shifts in eye gaze not only accompany pronominal reference but also are conventionalized in a broad range of linguistic (e.g., lexical, syntactic) and intersubjective functions (e.g., turn taking, cueing an interlocutor to objects or persons in the environment). Shifts in eye gaze also facilitate a variety of attention-sharing and conversational practices, such as checking to see whether the audience is still with the speaker and regulating turn taking (Bahan, 2004, p. 21), as well as collaborative sharing and organization of the conversational "floor" (Coates & Sutton-Spence, 2001, p. 519). Eye gaze can play a deictic role in direct and depictive sign-acts, where gaze functions as pointing. Eye gaze also participates in the construction of imagistic gesture and pantomime and also provides navigational cues to the signer who has the floor while doing things such as locomoting and conversing. Bahan's theorizing of Deaf peoples' distinct "sensory orientation" includes meanings and values placed on things such as linguistic and discursive uses of eye gaze, as well as social uses of eye contact during communication exchanges (2004). In addition to signaling comprehension, interest, and affect, eye gaze behaviors constitute a register of signer investment in the communicative exchange and the ideas expressed.

The evidence also suggests that uses of eye gaze can either promote or disrupt classroom activities. One study finds that a native and fluently signing Deaf teacher used eye gaze to control turn taking, eye gaze with nonmanual markers "to nominate a student to respond to a question," to direct classroom attention to particular speakers, and to maintain compliance by making eye contact with individual students (Smith & Ramsey, 2004, p. 53; see also Singleton & Morgan, 2005, on "visual attunement"). Mather's study of two classrooms, one with a native signing teacher and the other with a nonnative signing teacher, found that the former skillfully used two forms of eye gaze: One involving "mutual eye contact between a speaker and an individual addressee" Mather termed I-GAZE, and the other, involving a speaker addressing a whole group, she called G-GAZE (1987, pp. 15–16). In Mather's study, a nonnative (signing) teacher produced nonfelicitous eye gaze behaviors and other nonmanual errors. For example, in one classroom interaction the teacher misdirected her eye gaze toward an individual student while delivering general comments to the whole class. To that individual student, this behavior appeared to be an accusation, and the student responded accordingly (1989, pp. 22–23).

Among native users of signed languages, changes in eye gaze entail various kinds of explicit negotiation, particularly when removal of eye gaze is involved. For example, in the case of noncomprehension, an interactant might interject a question or request clarification (rather than removing eye gaze). If eye gaze is removed, conventionalized practice entails addressing the situation explicitly by apology and/or explanation. Novice signed language users are often unaccustomed to varied uses of eye gaze and their social negotiation. When teachers (hearing and/or second language/second modality learners) remove eye gaze from students without negotiating such changes, embodiment practices conventionalized to speech and/or aural listening make a significant site of analysis. As a person who began to study my first signed language (ASL) in my early 20s, I learned such lessons (and continue to learn them) the hard way: by shifting my eye gaze away from interactants (friends, colleagues, family members) at the wrong time, thereby missing a part of the conversation and likely appearing distracted, uninterested, or noncomprehending. When I receive feedback on such behaviors, I have an opportunity to learn about the sociolinguistic patterns I acquired among my spoken language communities in Cincinnati, Ohio, and to make conscious choices with respect to the kind of relationships I want to develop among the signed language communities I interact with.

Taken together, the foregoing discussion sheds further light on forms of sociolinguistic practice and HEARING embodiment that influence teacher production and reception errors. An excellent example of these types of errors is found in a description of the erroneous substitution of DEVIL for BUNNY: While producing the utterance "You were a good Easter bunny" in English, the teacher used the accompanying signs GOOD EASTER DEVIL (Johnson et al., 1989, p. 81). Teacher sign production and reception errors have implications for both classroom management and educational efficacy. For example, a "teacher who fails to use [appropriate nonmanual] signals when asking a question and gets no answer may think that the student does not know the answer and proceed to supply it" (Mather, 1989, p. 14).

Johnson et al. (1989) also found that it was not only what the Deaf aide signed but also the way she signed that had implications for Deaf linguistic socialization. Thus, "the choice," they argue, "of a particular form of signing—ASL, fluent English signing, or sign supported speech—in particular situations with particular people carries social meaning in and of itself" (ibid., p. 83). Accordingly, both teacher choice of and proficiency in a language code have implications for student understandings of social reality and their place in relation to it. It is in this context that Kannapell's study of Deaf college students ultimately argued that "language planning means identity planning," underlining the importance of language planning as a "powerful tool" in Deaf people's school-based sociolinguistic development and experiences (1985, p. 297).

Conclusion

In reflection with Nguyễn-võ's (2008) analysis, state attention to Deaf education special schools and Deaf social organizing (or lack thereof) can be understood as a form of governance directed at caretaking, informed by a paternalistic logic. In a book with a title of the same name, Lane (1992) described this logic as a "mask of benevolence." In the Vietnamese case it is possible to see sovereignty at work not only in cases of war or conflict but also in cases involving imagined need and care. Deaf students are required to study the national curriculum in Vietnamese instead of another Vietnamese language (e.g., HCMSL); yet, by the very design of the special school system, they are allowed to repeat grade levels and are widely barred from studying beyond the 5th, 8th or 9th grade, depending on the particular school, and may not have an opportunity to attend school at all. Because poor student performance is not recognized as an indication of a problem with the educational system itself, the special school system is actually underwritten as a caretaking institution. This, consequently, facilitates a wider social reproduction of Deaf people as "special," thereby authorizing the intervention and institutionalization of state structures centered on "helping" Vietnamese Deaf people—which I address in the next chapter.

Even though the daily practices of special school teachers are not monitored by MOET, the social reproduction of the *inclusive exclusion* (see chapter 3) persists according to the practices of *teachers cum state agents*, even where educational leaders and school personnel recognize the ineffectiveness of classroom teaching practices and the students' lack of linguistic access to core content. Indeed, we might ask how transnational initiatives such as the EP gained entry into the Vietnamese educational system in the first place. It may be that the latter's ability to set up programming in Việt Nam was facilitated by state agents who, at least initially—and for a long time (Woodward & Nguyễn, 2012)—perceived the EP as easing the state's caretaking burden for a population the latter perceived as "unable to study at the sixth-grade level" (p. 27).

The EP is premised on the establishment of a reinvigorated paradigm in Việt Nam: Deaf education in a sign-based environment. Taking students from all over Việt Nam,[15]

---

15. The EP student census includes students who hail from Hà Nội in the north, Đà Lạt in south central Việt Nam near the highlands, and Vũng Tàu several hours south of HCMC, as well as other locations.

the EP directors assessed applicants according to proficiency demonstrated in their *local* sign variety. Upon coming to the EP, students who hailed from other regions of Việt Nam were then expected to learn the southern variety of sign, principally HCMSL. Already possessing the skills of fluent signers discussed earlier in this chapter, students from outside the region nevertheless went through a period of acclimatization, yet quickly became conversant and then fluent in their second sign language. Teachers fared less well learning sign language. Even the most dedicated teachers, beloved by EP students, have some difficulty communicating with EP students as, the teachers reported, their schedules do not allow for ongoing classroom study of HCMSL or sufficient time for interacting in and getting feedback on their signing practices. Moreover, while EP teachers used HCMSL or signing in Vietnamese word order in the classroom, outside the classroom teachers often return to spoken language practices.

Programmatic structuring of the EP thus contributed to making its programming a Deaf and sign language affirmative space, which is yet HEARING controlled and whose sociolinguistic practices are still dominated by the use of spoken Vietnamese (and, in some instances, English), except when such practices are made to shift. For example, EP students occasionally challenged Mĩ to sign rather than speak whenever she interacted with EP teachers and administrators. Because Mĩ is an EP staff member and an HCMSL-Vietnamese interpreter, her professional status is notably lower than that of the EP codirectors and teachers, and her gregarious personality also seemed to invite student contact and open feedback. Accordingly, the EP could be understood as a *bridging institution*. Premised on what might be called a paradigm of inclusive-inclusion, the EP achieved its objective of providing higher education in the national curriculum on pace with non-Deaf students. In other ways, the EP's instructional environment resembles students' previous special school experiences of *inclusive exclusion* (Agamben, 1998), particularly with regard to instruction provided by non-Deaf teachers with rudimentary HCMSL proficiency. The significant difference between the EP and the Special Schools is that, within the EP, students were permitted to consult with each other (e.g., peer instruction) and to use HCMSL to establish conceptual anchors to the content and/or in classroom activities.

Of the three sites, the HCMC Deaf Club demonstrated the most inclusive form of institutional inclusion of Deaf and hard of hearing language and embodiment practices. All of its activities are conducted in sign language, and all local varieties of sign languages are welcome without the requirement that they be standardized, whether regionally or nationally. The HDC leaders facilitated club activities with an emphasis on collective comprehension and maximum participation by all HDC members. Moreover, HDC leaders devised ways to involve members who tended to be reticent (e.g., Deaf women) and supplied discourse tools to inexperienced presenters. In doing so, the HDC makes an *inclusive exception* for those Deaf and hard of hearing members who are either still acquiring HCMSL (or some other VSL) or who sign in Vietnamese word order/SSV to HCMSL (in the hope that they will naturally acquire HCMSL during their participation in the HDC and choose to use that language over the communication methods previously encountered in school.

By contrast, according to descriptions of their lives outside of HDC activities, many HDC members and several HDC leaders' home lives could be characterized as places of "exclusive exclusion." According to several interviewees and narratives of family life presented by HDC members during routine club activities, many southern Vietnamese Deaf people feel that they are basically boarders in their family homes; without jobs, their families see them as noncontributors to family life and family economics. These two extremes—the inclusive inclusion of the club and the exclusive exclusion of outside places—make the HDC a place of bonding. At the same time, within this place of seemingly optimal inclusion, both HDC leaders and members direct their activities toward activities (and imaginaries) centered on *biến đổi xã hội* [social change], particularly the reconfiguration of those laws and other social structures presently limiting Deaf and non-Deaf people's ability to freely associate with one another in HCMSL.

The HDC leaders promote the expansion of HCMSL language learning among hearing people and the development of an interpreting profession as two ways to facilitate this transformation. Such efforts are diametrically opposed to the notions of Deaf social inclusion that prevail in most Deaf education special schools: that is, inclusion as an outcome of speaking Vietnamese. Even as special school personnel acknowledged that "speaking doesn't work," the reluctance of special school administrators and other personnel to relinquish or substantially modify speech-based methods indexes the significant obedience that school personnel demonstrate toward state mandates (both formal and informal ones). The distance between these two distinct action-oriented agendas is far from being depoliticized or neutral; rather, the epistemological, ontological, and sociolinguistic foundations and entailments of these agendas are highly charged with political-economic meaning and implication. The circumstances that Công encountered as he made multiple attempts at earning—truly, in every sense of the word, *earning*—his education illuminate such intersubjective and political-economic entailments and implications. In the next chapter, I put Deaf education and social organizing initiatives in the context of disability-related development to explore relationships between the two.

5

Postreunification Deaf Marginalization, Deaf-Led Social Change, and Disability-Oriented Development

What is "development"? It is perhaps worth remembering just how recent a question this is. This question, which today is apt to strike us as so natural, so self-evidently necessary, would have made no sense even a century ago. It is a peculiarity of our historical era that "development" is central to so much of our thinking about so much of the world. (Ferguson, 1994, p. xiii)

Người Điếc là mồi. Các công ty và tổ chức là người đi câu cá. Và nhà nước là còn cá.

[Deaf people are the bait. The companies and organizations are the people who fish. And the state is the fish.] (Interview with HCMSL-Vietnamese interpreter)

Market-Socialist Transition

Postreunification Problems and Transnational Encounters

FOLLOWING FROM EXPANDED transnational diplomatic and trade relations established under early market-socialist reforms, NGOs offering development assistance to "vulnerable populations" proliferated in Việt Nam (USAID, 2004, p. 7). In 1986 a Dutch NGO, the Komitee Twee, was the first to focus on Deaf concerns. Because it sponsored "a teacher training program in Deaf education . . . it had a great impact" (Woodward, Nguyễn, & Nguyễn, 2004, p. 235). The Komitee Twee promulgated speech-based methods of instruction for Deaf students and also trained teachers at Lái Thiêu. In 2003, there were more than 50 Deaf education special schools in Việt Nam whose pedagogy was speech based (ibid.). By 2014, that number had risen to more than 70 schools, representing differing approaches to instructional language and pedagogy, depending on the language policies of individual school principals and the language proficiencies of individual content-area instructors. To a person, nearly all of those whom I interviewed—whether they identified as Deaf or non-Deaf, signer or nonsigner—invoked the Komitee Twee, the "Committee Two," or "the Dutch" as the reason that speech-based education gained a foothold in Việt Nam in the early 1990s. These commentaries resemble the argument that "because the Dutch-sponsored teacher training program in Deaf education was the first of its kind in Viet Nam, it had a great impact" (Woodward et al., 2004, p. 235).[1] However, only those who had directly participated in either procuring and/or undertaking training from the Komitee Twee—including one director of inclusive education, two special school principals, one of the codirectors of the Education Project, the EP administrative assistant/interpreter, and the special school founder introduced in chapter 1—put their comments in the context of historical precedent, especially state initiatives that predated collaboration with the Komitee Twee. According to these commentators, partnering with Komitee Twee brought in additional funding for hearing aids, classroom materials, and training; however, the Vietnamese state had long been engaged in a project of growing domestic literacy via the Vietnamese language, which included the education of Deaf students. Thus, the analysis I pursue here diverges from the individual commentators and from Woodward et al. (2004) to emphasize the perspectives of Vietnamese educators, educational administrators, and parents who organized to found the first Deaf education special school in Hồ Chí Minh City.

One of the things that a speech-based approach provides (to those for whom such enterprises are of interest) is the *hope* that students will achieve some measure of spoken Vietnamese with their families and communities. In the context of a national shortage of Deaf education infrastructure—schools, teacher training, and signed language pedagogical resources—the speech-based approach also facilitated (and continues to facilitate) educating students in their local communities. Enabling students to attend schools near their home may also be more culturally appropriate than requiring them to migrate to a single site, where teachers using sign methods might concentrate, because it "keeps the children at home and connected to their commune and society" (Reilly & Nguyen, 2004, p. 34).

The rationale often given for the "suppression of sign language [is that] . . . it 'isolated people from the national community'" (Davis, 1995, p. 83). My examination of the Vietnamese language ideological views of VSLs that predominated during the first two decades of Deaf education special school language policy and programming is consistent with that of Davis (1995). Accordingly, state structuring of the early speech-based Deaf education system reflected a view of deafness as a national problem that demanded a national solution in both language use and language modality. This followed from and is reflected in the instrumental suppression of HCMSL (and all VSLs) in Deaf education special schools, and in language policy and programming.

Beginning in the early reform period, the Vietnamese state passed laws on and received developmental assistance targeting both disability and education. Việt Nam first received support from the U.S. Agency for International Development (USAID) in 1997 for the purposes of trade and investment; however, this was preceded (six years earlier)

---

1. Dutch-led international aid projects have historical depth and complexity, beginning with the increasing Dutch presence in the country in the latter 16th century, and later their intervention in the Trịnh-Nguyễn War by taking the side of the Trịnh lords in the north. A "comparison with British, American, and Dutch colonies in South and Southeast Asia reveals that the French continued to occupy a much higher percentage of middle- and low-level bureaucratic, entrepreneurial, and technical positions" into the early 1930s (Marr, 1981, p. 24). Accordingly, when the Vietnamese state determined to "open the door," the Dutch presence may have been perceived more favorably, or at least may have been more easily tolerated than other transnational and international partners.

by assistance to vulnerable groups, including persons with HIV/AIDS and persons with mental and physical handicaps (USAID, 2004, p. 7). In the same year, 1991, Việt Nam also passed the "Law on the Protection, Care, and Education of Children ... affirm[ing] the principle of non-discrimination against disabled children" (Reilly & Nguyen, 2004, p. 20). In the USAID mechanism of disability categories, Deaf people were listed as a vulnerable group, and monies were allotted for "inclusive education" and "training to assist hearing-impaired and Deaf children and their families" (USAID, 2004, p. 8).

However, USAID documents from this period do not specify what is meant by "inclusive education" or what "training" Deaf children and their parents should (or did) receive. Further, such USAID reports do not indicate the rationale for inclusive education, nor do they mention any critique by signed language linguists, Deaf studies scholars, or Deaf constituencies around the world (Brueggemann, 2009; Emery & O'Brien, 2014; Harris, Holmes, & Mertens 2009; Singleton, Jones & Hanumantha, 2014). However, other documents from this period, such as UNESCO's 1994 *Salamanca statement and framework for action on special needs education,* explicitly encouraged national signatories to recognize signed languages and to "ensure that all deaf persons have access to education in their national sign languages" (section II, article A.21: 18).

The Salamanca Statement (hereafter, Salamanca) is credited with formalizing the tenets of inclusive education, a trend begun, most visibly, in North Atlantic disability advocacy as a result of the Americans with Disabilities Act (1990).[2] Disability-rights constituencies around the world heralded Salamanca for providing learners with disabilities with their first-ever access to regular education environments and curricula. By contrast, responses to Salamanca by worldwide Deaf education scholars and Deaf constituent groups represent a continuum from wariness to outright rejection.[3] This is

---

2. The majority of national disability laws now in force were enacted during the 1990s. They include the Americans with Disabilities Act 1990; the Australian Disability Discrimination Act 1992; the Nigerian Disability Decree 1993; the Sri Lanka Protection of the Rights of Persons with Disability 1996; and the Guatemalan Disability Discrimination Ordinance 1997. Many countries (e.g., Việt Nam) include protectionist language in their national constitutions. Also see Lord and Stein (2015) for an excellent discussion of worldwide disability law and the specific terrains in which Deaf African constituencies advocate for education, economic, legal, social, and political rights. The Disability Rights Clinic of the Syracuse University College of Law is also a wonderful resource on national, regional, and international disability rights laws: http://law.syr.edu/academics/clinical-experiential/clinical-legal-education/disability-rights-clinic/ [retrieved February 26, 2017].

3. The Salamanca Statement on Special Needs Education called for attention to sign language, however, not standardization. Section II, part A, item 21, states that "sign language ... should be recognized and provision made to ensure that all Deaf persons have access to education in their national sign language" (1994, p. 18). Eighteen years later the Biwako Millennium Framework for Action (section F, part 1, item 43, and part 2, targets 19 and 20) addresses the following: Item 43, "sign language, Braille, finger Braille, and tactile sign language have not yet been standardized"; it also says that persons "maybe [sic] deprived of the basic human right to language and communication in their daily lives." Target 19 centers on development and dissemination of a standard sign language, and Target 20 addresses the role of governments in training and employing "sign language interpreters, Braille transcribers," and so on (2002, p. 19). The implicit assumption in these two documents is that each country contains only one sign language variety and that, where multiple varieties exist, they should be made into a single, uniform code.

because the effect of Salamanca was to expeditiously facilitate a practice already known as *mainstreaming,* which removes Deaf students from their natural language acquisition environments (i.e., from one another, from signing Deaf adults, and from signing non-Deaf people) Moreover, in referring to sign language in a general way, Salamanca and its successor documents contribute to misconceptions about a universal signed language and notions of singular national sign languages—which misrepresents the nature of language in general (not just signed ones).

In the United States, mainstreaming facilitated the development of an array of new services and technologies designed to augment teachers' ability to interact meaningfully with Deaf students—contributing to the growth of, among other industries, the signed-spoken language interpreting field. Interpreters now working in mainstream settings in the United States may even pursue a unique national interpreting credential of education certification: ED: K–12, kindergarten through grade 12. A national system of Deaf education, both day and residential schools, has continued to operate in tandem with the mainstream system; however, over the past 20 years, major investments in the mainstreaming system (directly and via political lobbying) have facilitated the ascendancy of both mainstreaming and IE schools over the once vital Deaf education system in the United States.

During the first two decades of market-socialist reform, the Vietnamese state could have followed international recommendations to educate children in their natural or, at least, their national signed languages. The Vietnamese state took a different tack when it chose to implement a national system of Deaf education that incorporated the teaching of speech and listening practices. The ultimate goal of Deaf educational leaders at that time reflected a medical view of deafness, which aimed to cure students of deafness or at least train them to speak like "normal" people, after which students could be transferred into regular education schools (Nguyễn T. H. Y., 2012; Nguyễn T. K. A. & Võ, 2010; Lê, 2000).

When Việt Nam first initiated its open-door policy, the development apparatus was just getting established (Ferguson, 1994; see Jackson, 2007, for a related analysis of the development industry). Today, there are thousands of smaller and larger development-oriented NGOs, and the U.S. is channeling substantial development aid dollars into investment in Việt Nam (Norlund, 2007; Thayer, 2008; Wischermann, 2011). In 2013, the last year for which figures have been fully reported (at the time of this writing), USAID alone invested $131,476,659 US in Việt Nam.[4] Also that same year, the large-scale *Disability Projects Review Assessment and Analysis Report* for USAID provided feedback from self-identified persons with disabilities, domestic and international NGOs (including those established and run by persons with disabilities, often referred to in the development literature as *Disabled People's Organizations,* or DPOs, and ministry officials in various sectors (e.g., education, employment, health) (Lynch & Phạm, 2013). Recommendations from that report contributed to USAID's 2015 unveiling of six new projects "serving persons with

---

4. USAID's inventory of its foreign aid distributions to Việt Nam is accessible at its online *Foreign Aid Explorer* database, at https://explorer.usaid.gov/cd

disabilities in Vietnam aimed at promoting health, social inclusion, and disability rights" (USAID, 2015).[5]

Several of my research partners and colleagues in Việt Nam participated in the meetings that USAID conducted and reported their consternation at reading the *Disability Projects Review Assessment and Analysis Report* (Lynch & Phạm, 2013). Of greatest concern to these approximately 10 people were the characterization of sign language and Deaf people's "needs." Whereas sign language is mentioned in the report, it appears only in the context of the following sectors and in the following ways:

1. Section I, Key Findings, Health: "With five Sign Language interpreters in the country, access to information and communication for the Deaf community will remain extremely limited." (ibid., p. ix)
2. Section I, Key Findings, Education: "Need to improve the capacity and availability of specialized learning approaches and supports, such as in classroom aids, sign language interpretation, braille . . ." (ibid. p. x)
3. Section I, Key Findings, Access to Key Needs Opportunities: "Some options to consider are to support the development of a nationally useful sign language, or support sign language interpreter training programs. According to the Hanoi Deaf Club, there are only five qualified interpreters in the country." (ibid., p. xiv)
4. Section IV, Government of Vietnam, Ministry of Education and Training: "Regulate national standards on sign language and Braille for the persons with disabilities." (ibid., p. 11)
5. Section V, Services for Persons with Disability, Education Sector: "Challenges . . . that need to be addressed as IE becomes more fully incorporated in the education system"; "Lack of a standardized sign language as well as a lack of sign language interpreters. However, most culturally deaf individuals prefer to be educated in deaf schools where teachers themselves use sign language." (ibid., p. 20)

Of grave concern are several significant errors or elisions that informed USAID's recommendations and funding decisions. First, the report contains a notable methodological problem in its reliance on a report by a single Deaf association to characterize the nature of sign language interpreting for the whole country as limited to "five" interpreters (points 1 and 3 in the foregoing list). The characterization of the interpreting situation is patently false as, in 2013, Việt Nam possessed nearly 20 Deaf clubs or associations, each with at least one or two non-Deaf people who were bilingual in a VSL and Vietnamese, as well as several special school teachers and family members with similar proficiencies. USAID's characterization was inconsistent with Deaf social organizing and in the early 2010s, and more accurately reflects data from five years—such as my own reporting of an interview conducted with two HCMSL-Vietnamese interpreters (who were also Deaf education personnel), Cooper (2009, p. 18). In that

---

5. USAID announced these projects in a press release on September 11, 2015 at https://www.usaid.gov/vietnam/press-releases/sep-11-2015-us-supported-project-enhances-educational-and-social (last updated on October 20, 2016). For more information about USAID's work in Việt Nam see https://www.usaid.gov/where-we-work/asia/vietnam (last updated April 5, 2017).

interview, the nature of VSL(s)-Vietnamese interpretation in Việt Nam was described in the following way:

> There are not many people doing interpreting in VN. In the north, only four or five people work as interpreters—not officially like me—but as teachers in the school. In the south, there are more people who interpret, maybe more than 10; this is because in the south the society is more willing to teach SL. However, there are only two people who earn money as interpreters, and they work full-time for the Ha Noi Deaf Association [in the north] Even though they work full-time, they have not had any formal training.

Thus, while VSLs-Vietnamese interpreting was an emergent practice in the late 2000s, by 2012, Deaf Clubs and Associations were actively teaching courses in VSLs, engaging local bilinguals in ad hoc interpreter training, and World Concern Development Organization's Intergenerational Deaf Education Outreach Project-Vietnam (IDEO-VN) had already begun implementing Family Mentorship training that included a core component in VSLs-Vietnamese interpreting for family settings. Moreover, by the time of Lynch and Phạm's 2013 report for USAID, the EP had also begun offering HCMSL Vietnamese interpreter training with university partners from the United States,

Possibly even more powerful evidence disputing the aforementioned USAID claims comes from the World Concern Development Organization's ability to implement its IDEO-VN Project, for which it initially selected approximately thirty (and later added a second cohort of similar size) non-Deaf people who were bilingual in a VSL and Vietnamese (from novice to advanced proficiency levels), hailing from four provinces in the northern, middle, and southern regions of Việt Nam.[6]

Second, the report also demonstrates an analytic failure to consider the role of signed languages, or the absence thereof, in educational settings (point 2 in the list). The education and other sections in the document have at least four mentions of the importance of hearing aids and eleven mentions of assistive devices and technologies. This suggests, at the very least, that the USAID research team had no knowledge of the Deaf education situation, its extraordinary history, and the extremely contested nature of Deaf educational language policy and programming.

Third, the USAID report makes a powerful claim positing the need for a "nationally useful sign language" (point 3 above). This recommendation is not supported by signed language linguistic research; moreover, no linguistic specialists participated in USAID's data collection or analysis. Related to this claim are points 4 and 5 in the list: positing the need for regulating standards for sign language and braille, as well as repeated reference (in point 5 and elsewhere in the document) to a national and/ or "standardized sign language." Point 4 thus lumps 'sign language' together with a system for representing language (braille) and Deaf people with blindness, as if both

---

6. See the description of the outcomes of the World Concern Development Organization's *Intergenerational Deaf Education Outreach Project-Vietnam* at the World Bank: http://www.worldbank.org/en/news/press-release/2015/08/10/helping-deaf-children-in-vietnam-communicate-and-access-education-through-sign-language. Also see mass media press on IDEO-VN outcomes at: https://www.vietnambreakingnews.com/2016/06/innovations-help-deaf-children-better-prepare-for-formal-schooling/

groups (rather, subject categories—and also DeafBlind people) possessed similar sociolinguistic experiences and interests. And, as already stated, linguistic scholarship does not support language planning for standardization in the manner suggested in this report. These recommendations nevertheless bear a striking resemblance to those put forth by Lê Văn Tạc, director of Special Education Research at the National Institute of Educational Science, which I discuss in the opening section of chapter 2.

Absent from the USAID report is any discussion of the importance of training families and teachers in VSLs, as well as the importance of using VSLs in homes, communities, and educational settings, recommendations that are strongly supported in both Deaf education and signed language linguistic literatures. The report also does not mention Vietnamese Deaf people's leadership in capacity building programmatic, research, or training recommendations; nor is there any mention of Deaf people's employment.

These concerns could become grave realities for Vietnamese Deaf individuals and groups in the implementation of recently funded USAID programming, which, according to USAID's Việt Nam mission director, Joakim Parker, is oriented toward "persons with disabilities," "development," and transnational partnerships between the United States and Việt Nam (USAID, 2015):

> "Persons with disabilities can play an important role in Vietnam's continued development," said USAID Vietnam Mission Director Joakim Parker. "USAID's support is designed to help them realize their potential with involvement of family, government and civil society, which will contribute to the broader goal of a more inclusive Vietnam. Cooperation [in] supporting persons with disabilities is also an important element of the Comprehensive Partnership between our two countries."[7]

In such statements the work of state agents and their transnational counterparts is very clear—at the cost of millions of US dollars per year; yet, with recommendations based on incomplete data and analysis, the potential of such dollars to influence Deaf communities in the ways that they desire is manifestly limited, and limiting. That is, the Deaf constituencies I spoke with had little hope that USAID funds will be directed toward their concerns, and they were especially incensed by the repeated references to hearing aid distribution.

The findings of a white paper, *Inclusion of Disability in USAID Solicitations for Funding* (Hayes, Swift, Shettle, & Waghorn, 2015), jointly conducted by representatives from the Perkins School for the Blind, the U.S. Council on Disabilities, and CBM U.S., suggest that the concerns of southern Vietnamese Deaf constituencies are likely well founded:

> Based on the study findings, it is clear that the inclusion of people with disabilities in USAID's projects begins with solicitation language that calls for inclusion in a significant way. Furthermore, only if the solicitation uses significant language around disability will the implemented work be inclusive of people with disabilities. In developing solicitations, donors need to be aware that disability inclusive language

---

7. See USAID's press release at https://www.usaid.gov/vietnam/press-releases/united-states-broaden-support-persons-disabilities-vietnam (retrieved February 27, 2017).

must be clearly stated and required within all components of a project in order for people with disabilities to be fully included. With this new data, the Disability Working Group recommends that USAID include a strengthened disability policy in solicitations for funding and that USAID continue to train staff on best practices for including disability language. USAID cannot achieve its mission of "ending poverty and promoting resilient, democratic societies" unless society as a whole, including people with disabilities, are [sic] a meaningful part of USAID's global strategy and policy as well as fully included in USAID work. (ibid., pp. 2–4)[8]

As should be clear by this point in this book, the signifier *inclusion* reveals very little about the models on which Vietnamese state agents predicate their design of Deaf education or inclusive education, or of the conditions warranting their systematic expansion.

Whereas, since the 2010 passage of the Law on Persons with Disability and the 2015 ratification of the Convention on the Rights of Persons with Disability, the Vietnamese state has generated a marked increase in official statements demonstrating *sự cởi mở* [openness] toward VSLs, the directions in which such openness might lead are highly contingent on how state agents view and respond to national development concerns. And they are also contingent on how state agents interact with transnational partners within broader networks of epistemic, political-economic, and sociolinguistic commitments. As this discussion indicates, such viewpoints, responses, and interactions are highly contradictory, particularly with respect to the notion of signed languages as bona fide languages and to the multiple varieties of VSLs that Việt Nam's Deaf signed language communities actually use. This is the context in which the HDC—and other Deaf clubs and associations in HCMC and around the country—are carrying out their social organizing work. So, although it is striking that the USAID report contains many errors and misrepresentations of Deaf communities' interests, these must also be considered in the context of the influence that state agents have, particularly at the international level.

Focusing on Deaf commentators' reactions to the USAID disability recommendations illuminates the circumstances under which HDC leaders and members pursue initiatives to promote HCMSL training and advocacy, HCMSL-Vietnamese interpreter training, national and international partnerships facilitating state recognition of nationwide Deaf associations, and social change advocacy promoting Deaf people's access to education and employment. The HDC also pursues INGO relationships, including those with USAID and its partners, yet it does so while also advocating for HCMSL-related aims (i.e., contra the major recommendations of recent USAID analysis).

Background on Việt Nam's Disability-Related Development Industry

Việt Nam joined ASEAN in 1995, two years into its Decade of the Disabled (1993–2003) and a year after Salamanca. At that time, disability was "on the radar," and many countries and regions were organizing to emulate North Atlantic disability policies. When consulting these new development entities and frameworks, Vietnamese state

---

8. For paragraph quotation, the authors cite the United States Agency for International Development (USAID) website: www.usaid.gov.

officials would have encountered transnational discourses on disability and on deafness. Of course, the way in which they reviewed and evaluated the available discourses cannot be viewed as simple; rather, all discourses are intersubjectively constituted according to the circumstances of an individual's early sociolinguistic acquisition, professional or group-specific inculcation, as well as to the immediate context of an interaction. "All words have the 'taste' of a profession, a genre, a tendency, a party, a particular work, a particular person, a generation, an age group, the day and hour. Each word tastes of the context and contexts in which it has lived its socially charged life" (Bakhtin, 1981, p. 293). Put somewhat differently, state agents evaluate the information they receive about Deaf people (e.g., signed languages, VSLs, disability) according to a variety of knowledge sources and resources, which are, according to their roles within the state hierarchy, significantly related to their obligations to defend national interests.

The interests expressed by contemporary state agents take place in the context of Việt Nam's recent colonial past, its ongoing commemoration of heroic anticolonial figures, intermittent threats of geopolitical intervention—such as China's repeated attempts to claim Biển Đông (Eastern Sea)[9]—and national and international development mandates. To approach Deaf education and disability-related development decisions from another direction (were the Vietnamese state simply, in a cynical framing, implementing disability-related policy and initiatives in order to appease transnational counterparts), Deaf education and inclusive education in Việt Nam might look quite different—or might not exist at all. The point I want to underline here is that state agents build epistemic spaces and social influence by interacting with each other regarding their own concerns and interests: Ideas about Deaf people circulate and recycle through formal and informal daily interactions, often without the participation of Deaf people themselves (Hayes et al., 2015; NCCD, 2010) and rarely with the participation of signed language linguistic, cognitive scientific, or anthropological scholarship. In this context, one misconception about signed languages and literacy continues to circulate widely in Vietnamese education circles: Learning signed language interferes with the acquisition of spoken language (Cao & Đỗ, 2007; Đặng, 2010).

One scholarly description of producing a CD for the purpose of teaching children with hearing impairment to speak is extremely influential in the contemporary context, especially given the authors' status as faculty members of HCMC's Pedagogic University (Cao & Đỗ, 2007). The authors make the following claim (ibid., p. 152; cf. Cao's description of sign language as a "communication method" that "*cộng đồng người khiếm thính phải sử dụng*" [the hearing impaired community must use] [2013, p. 181]):

Trẻ khiếm thính là những trẻ bị suy giảm chức năng nghe, dẫn đến hậu quả là không thể, hoặc khó có thể hình thành ngôn ngữ, từ đó làm hạn chế khả năng giao tiếp và ảnh hưởng đến quá trình nhận thức. Vì thế, nhiệm vụ quan trọng trong giáo dục trẻ khiếm thính là hình thành và phát triển ngôn ngữ cho trẻ. Ở trường học, môn Tiếng Việt đóng vai trò

---

9. The Eastern Sea—which the Chinese government calls the South China Sea—is a strategically important and natural resource-rich area.

quan trọng trong việc thực hiện nhiệm vụ này. Thông qua môn Tiếng Việt, trẻ khiếm thính sẽ chiếm lĩnh được ngôn ngữ, biết sử dụng ngôn ngữ như một phương tiện để giao tiếp, công cụ tư duy như mọi thành viên khác trong xã hội.

Hearing impaired children's unfortunate deficits in hearing make it impossible to achieve good results or to form language [implied spoken/written] without difficulty, thereby limiting their ability to communicate and negatively influencing cognitive processes. Therefore, the important task of hearing impaired children's education is language formation and development for these children. In schools, the study of Vietnamese plays an important role in the implementation of these tasks. Through the study of Vietnamese, hearing impaired children will seize upon [spoken/written] language, know how to use [spoken] language as a medium for communication, investing in thinking tools as every other member of society.

The worldwide propagation of such notions is widely attributed to Alexander Graham Bell (1884–1969), whose ideas influenced not only the Milan resolution (see discussion in chapter 2) but also the eugenics movement, which was spreading throughout North Atlantic countries in the late 19th century. One of the early vehicles for disseminating such ideas among education and medical leaders was *Vấn Đề Phục Hồi Chức Năng Cho Người Điếc* [Rehabilitation issues of the deaf] (Phạm K., 1984) (see discussion given later and in chapter 6). These ideas, which many education scholars (e.g., Cao & Đỗ, 2007; Cao, 2013; Đặng, 2010) attest, are still powerfully active in Vietnamese educational circles.

Interviews with special school principals and teachers, ministry personnel (i.e., Department of Labor, Invalids, and Social Affairs, or DOLISA), and family members of Deaf people also instantiated this notion. This notion also crops up in transnational disability-centered development work. For example, a 2002 press release of the Dutch Coalition on Disability and Development, reporting the events of a meeting convened to discuss Vietnamese progress toward the 2015 UN Millennium Development Goals, states the following: "Scientific research has demonstrated the complexity of simultaneously learning spoken language and sign language . . . [therefore] using sign language to support spoken language could be a way out of the dilemma" (Jonker & Raijmakers, 2002, p. 1). While advocating sign language, albeit only to *support spoken language*, experts maintain that signing can be an accompaniment to spoken language when, in fact, the grammatical structure of sign languages is distinct from that of spoken languages and cannot be performed at the same time (see chapter 3 for discussion of this point).

Such discourses on supportive approaches to Deaf education, in which there is a "dilemma" to be solved, not only misrepresent the linguistic status of signed languages, but also Deaf persons themselves as analytic units for social welfare, as opposed to, say, one of social leadership or economic development. The foregoing discussion underscores that the presence of these discourses in the Vietnamese context is—while misinformed—likely a factor of their alignment with preexisting social categories and institutional structures than of either national or international manipulation, opportunism, or malice.

In the Shadow of Disability: Language Standardization and Deaf Collective Self-Determination

Returning to southern Deaf social leaders' language-related concerns and initiatives which opened this chapter, HDC leaders and members frequently commented on the effects of misinformation and debates about HCMSL for their social change–oriented work. Possibly most pressing in the 2012–2015 period were their concerns about the state's interest in standardizing VSLs, as well as a related concern, the encroachment of foreign signed languages—especially American Sign Language. Later in this chapter I address each of these in turn.

The national curriculum is printed in Vietnamese and structured around the use of spoken and written Vietnamese. With the exception of EP teachers and staff and HDC leaders and members, interviews with five Deaf education special school principals and teachers, the staff of one community-based organization run by and for people with disabilities, a director of an inclusive education center, a deputy administrator in DOLISA (in HCMC), a journalist, and families of Deaf students all reached the consensus that, as one principal stated, "Everyone uses a different form of sign language." MOET took one approach to the issue of language variation, while the EP took another approach: the former was problem formulation, and the latter linguistic documentation, description, and analysis.

MOET initially addressed circumstances of signed language variation by holding regional meetings of special school principals and teachers to determine the signs used in their schools. According to the principal of Hope A, the IE director, and one EP codirector, Deaf people also participated in these meetings; however, as the EP director noted, neither the Deaf nor the non-Deaf participants in these meetings had linguistic training. The EP codirector further explained that some signs were "invented on the spot" during these meetings, while other signs were replaced with the signs from another region to facilitate standardization among regions. Moreover, these meetings involved young Deaf students who, like my descriptions of Deaf education special school classrooms in chapters 3 and 4, had had little contact with signing Deaf adults. The resulting sign "documentation" thus involves both attested signs (signs actually used by deaf people) and invented signs, catalogued in three reference books: *Ký Hiệu Của Người Điếc Việt Nam, Sách 1–3* [Signs of Deaf People in Việt Nam, Books 1–3]. The principal of Hope A gave me the copy of *Sách 2* [Book 2], shown in figure 5.1.

Produced by MOET with funding from Pearl S. Buck International and USAID, these reference books include a single vocabulary item per page. Each page is organized into four rows, representing regional signs for each word as symbolized in Hà Nội, Hải Phòng, and HCMSL. The fourth row contains what the text's authors termed "common signs" (*ký hiệu chung*). According to the foreword of Book 2, the goal of these texts is to do the following:

> *Giúp cho trẻ khiếm thính theo học hòa nhập [hệ thống Giáo dục Hòa Nhập], tiếp thu tri thức một cách dễ dàng hơn; đồng thời tạo thuận lợi cho giáo viên, trẻ nghe, các bậc cha mẹ và những người có liên quan giao tiếp được với nhưng trẻ khiếm thính này (2003, vi)*

Deaf Marginalization, Deaf-Led Social Change and Disability-Oriented Development 155

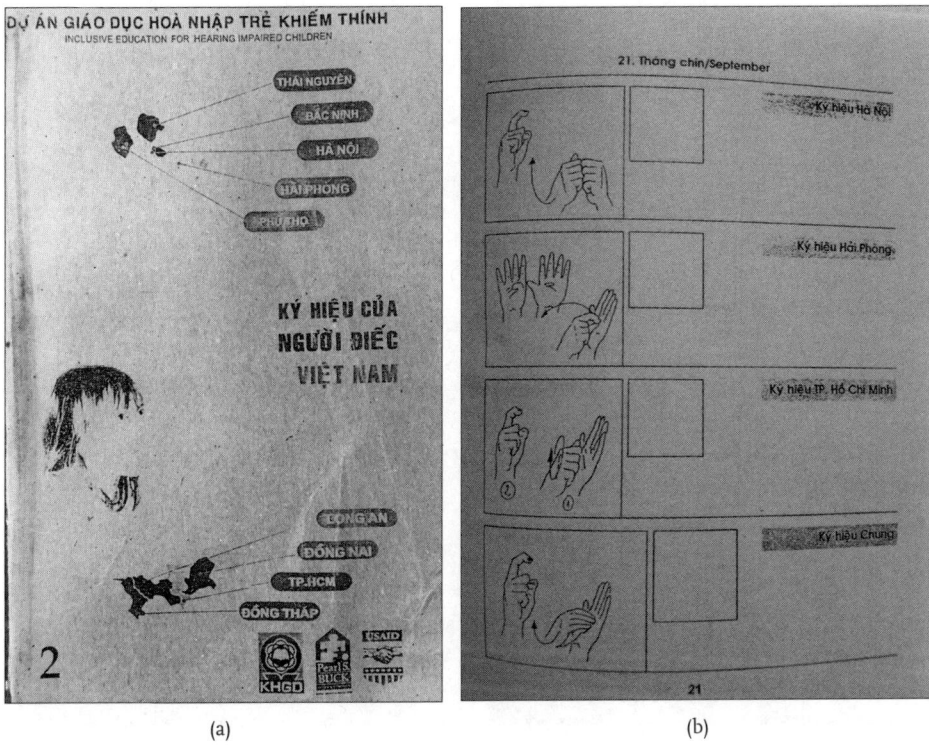

(a)   (b)

Figure 5.1. *Ký Hiệu Của Người Điếc Việt Nam, Sách 2* (Signs of deaf people in Việt Nam, Book 2). 5.1(a) is the front cover and 5.1(b) is a page with signs symbolizing Tháng Chin (September).

> Help hearing impaired children enroll in [the system of] inclusive education to acquire knowledge more easily and, at the same time, to enable teachers, hearing children, and parents and concerned people to be able to communicate with these hearing impaired children (2003, p. ix).

Focusing on the urban centers where Deaf people in Việt Nam have developed "gestures and signs," the foreword goes on to state that "these gestures and signs are often natural, spontaneous, or imported from overseas and have not been systematized yet" (ibid., p. ix). The implication is clear: Such "gestures and signs" are not language, which is also indicated by the absence of *ngôn ngữ* [language] preceding *ký hiệu* [signs] on the covers of Books 1–3. Quite significantly, these books contain no description whatsoever of the grammars of VSLs.

Another book produced in this same period (1999)—*Từ Điển Truyền Thông Đa Ngôn Ngữ với Ngôn Ngữ Ký Hiệu Mỹ* [Dictionary of multilingual communication with American Sign Language], by Nhà Sách Trẻ [Children's Book Publishers] of HCMC—also presents signs in list fashion without grammatical description (figure 5.2). However, unlike *Signs of Deaf People in Việt Nam*, this dictionary does not make pejorative reference to "spontaneous" signs; rather, it is a compilation of various signs from American Sign Language presented alongside print language entries.

As Figure 5.2b shows, the book has headings in English and Vietnamese, followed by illustrations for individual ASL signs (four per page) and a list of (supposedly)

 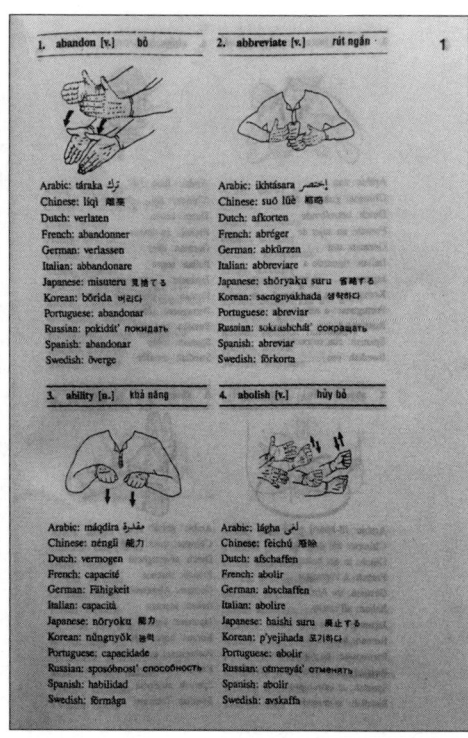

(a) (b)

Figure 5.2. *Từ Điển Truyền Thông Đa Ngôn Ngữ vời Ngôn Ngữ Ký Hiệu Mỹ* (Dictionary of multilingual communication with American Sign Language). 5.2(a) is the front cover while 5.2(b) is the first page of dictionary entries.

corresponding lexical equivalents in twelve print languages. Altogether, the dictionary contains 2,500 entries in ASL, which, with the 14 print languages, gives a total of 35,000 entries. The immediate inside cover of the book also contains fingerspelling charts for American Sign Language and International Sign Language (the latter is represented as a one-handed fingerspelling system). The multilingual and, indeed, international cachet of the book may be one of the reasons it is still widely available in bookstores all over Việt Nam. Just to be clear: The bookstores I have visited in HCMC, Đà Lạt, Hà Nội, Huế, and Nha Trang do not offer primers on VSLs, but I have easily located—as recently as 2016—the *Dictionary of multilingual communication with American Sign Language.*

Since the publication of *Ký Hiệu của Người Điếc, Sách 3* (Book 3), MOET has not produced further sign language books. It has, however, attempted to. For example, in 2013, personnel from the National Institute of Educational Sciences personnel (NIES; under the direction of MOET) created a draft of a book of signs for use in mathematics instruction. *Ngôn Ngữ Ký Hiệu Dành Cho Các Cấp Học Phổ Thông, Quyển 1* [Secondary-level sign language, Book 1], which was never published. This draft effort contained one or more vocabulary items per page, organized into between one and four rows representing the signs supposedly used in the *bắc* [north], *nam* [south], or *trung* [central] regions of Việt Nam, or *chung* [common].

In January 2013 I happened to be present at the informal unveiling of this book in Hà Nội. Deaf leaders immediately rejected the premise of the book. None of these college-educated and/or long-time community leaders from around the country had participated in either the data collection for or the production of the book, which they identified contained many errors. For instance, where there are fewer than four rows per mathematics term, it appears that the regions that are not represented "lack" signs to express these concepts.

The most glaring problem with the book, however, is its cover, which contains an illustration of the American Sign Language fingerspelling alphabet (figure 5.3).

In figure 5.3a, readers will note the form of the fingerspelled letter F as one that corresponds to ASL. Whereas fingerspelling in VSLs correspond to Vietnamese orthography, there is no letter *f*, except when it is used to spell loanwords, and then VSL fingerspelling systems produce the letter *f* in a horizontal position, not in the vertical position seen in figure 5.3a. Here, the use of F is infelicitous with respect to VSL fingerspelling systems as well as written and printed forms of Vietnamese. Note also the shape of the ASL fingerspelled letter H: In figure 5.3b, the bottom figure (representing the central region's sign for *hàm số*) clearly shows the fingerspelled form H, which is commonly used in the northern region and in some parts of central Việt Nam (left-hand side of the illustration, the signer's right hand [this looks like an 8, not an H]). Another error, immediately above the illustration just discussed, involves the form of

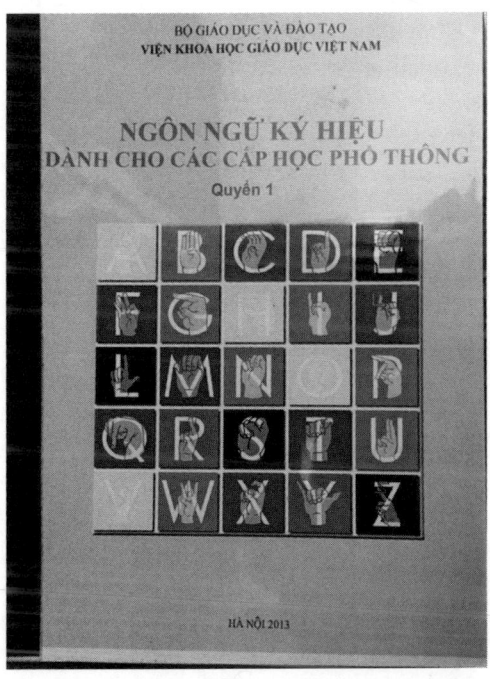

(a)

(b)

Figure 5.3. *Ngôn Ngữ Ký Hiệu Dành Cho Các Cấp Học Phổ Thông, Quyển 1* (Secondary-level sign language, Book 1). 5.3(a) is the front cover and 5.3(b) is a page showing signs for Tỷ lệ nghịch (inverse) for the central and southern regions. sample page.

hàm số that is used in the northern region (*bắc*). Whereas the illustration shows the southern form of the fingerspelled letter H, this sign form is erroneously labeled.

Forcefully rejecting *Ngôn Ngữ Ký Hiệu Dành Cho Các Cấp Học Phổ Thông, Quyển 1*, HDC and other provincial-level Deaf club leaders requested a meeting with NIES to discuss the former's critique of the book. To their credit, NIES personnel met with these national Deaf leaders and decided not to move forward with production of the book.

Another area involving both materials targeting Deaf education instruction and transnational development-aid partners has to do with the production of CD-ROMs. In 2008, the Samsung Corporation was an early supporter of Việt Nam's Special Education Training, contributing $40,000 USD for the production of a signed language–based CD-ROM.

In an interview with an assistant director of the Special Education Teacher Training Program at Hồ Chí Minh City's Pedagogic University, I learned that, from 2008 to 2010, special education teacher trainees did not take sign language classes while studying Deaf education. Instead, they were given the Samsung-sponsored CD-ROM of vocabulary items to use; moreover, once they graduated, they were sent directly into Deaf education special school classrooms, where they were expected to acquire sign language from the students—in those schools that permit sign language usage in the classroom, whether HCMSL or as Sign-Supported Vietnamese. Such practices deviate from standard training provided to regular education teachers. Moreover, in the regular education system, students begin learning English in cấp 2 (grades 6 through 9). These classes are offered according to specific targeted varieties of English, including the forms spoken in the United, States, the United Kingdom, and Australia. Therefore, MOET has a system for systematically differentiating between and hierarchically ordering the study of languages other than Vietnamese. However, MOET has approached teacher training in sign language quite differently. It has only recently recognized VSL varieties, but, as ongoing state efforts to standardize VSLs indicate, such "recognition" is ambivalent and contradictory.

The Special Education Teacher Training Program's assistant director gave me a copy of the CD-ROM. In 2009, Deborah Chen Pichler—a linguist at Gallaudet University in Washington, DC, who specializes in signed language acquisition, including signed language acquisition among second-modality learners—agreed to review the CD-ROM for me. According to Chen Pichler's assessment, the CD-ROM contains individual signs and signs in sequence; however, no information is given about how these sequences relate to one another (i.e., as a symbolic system) or how they relate to or are different from spoken Vietnamese. Therefore, it is not clear from the CD-ROM what grammatical structure the signs are supposed to represent. Moreover, the CD-ROM contains no metalinguistic information that might support second language and second-modality learners' receptive and productive accuracy, that is, how to use the signs as they are represented (pers. comm.).

Chen Pichler describes second language acquisition as a dynamic process that demands live interaction; hence, she also notes that some CD-ROM–based language programs, such as the Rosetta programs, now offer more dynamic feedback, such as the audiographic rendering of words spoken into a microphone and comments about the intelligibility of the user's production (pers. comm.). Similarly, signed language instruction benefits from modeling. Accordingly, in its present iteration, the Samsung-sponsored CD-ROM is not an instructional tool; rather, it is simply a more technologically sophisticated version of the vocabulary list approach to presenting VSLs, such as that seen in *Ký Hiệu Của Người Điếc Việt Nam, Sách 2*.

The EP has produced the first—and, to date, the only—linguistic description of HCMSL grammar; moreover, it is the only program to have trained HCMSL instructors. Because MOET has jurisdiction over the EP, MOET agents are aware of the EP's HCMSL instructional materials. Nevertheless, MOET has not adopted the EP's model for use in the special schools or in the special education teacher training programs. In an interview, one of the EP codirectors evaluated these circumstances in the following way:

> The idea is that Deaf people are somehow different from hearing people, so it's okay, maybe, maybe, for hearing people in different places to speak differently sometimes. Although, in the curriculum—of course—it shouldn't be. But Deaf people *need* [emphasis in the original] a standard sign language, according to MOET, because it's felt that they can't communicate with each other. But the problem is not with Deaf people. The problem is with hearing people; so they [MOET] still haven't realized the fact that if they use this "standard" sign, who's going to teach it to the teachers? No one uses it. And if you are going to interpret on TV with this, which Deaf people are going to understand it? So they haven't come to that point yet, because they think that if they develop the model, well, then Deaf people will just follow, and it will be better for them. Rather than letting Deaf people make their own decisions.

Despite the program's lack of training materials and methods, the assistant director of the Special Education Teacher Training Program at HCMC Pedagogic University reported during the aforementioned interview that interest in their program is growing, along with their student census. This is, in part, facilitated by the benefits MOET introduced in the late 2000s, which increased special school teachers' salaries to 70% greater than those of regular education teachers.[10] Such an institutionalized order suggests that the Vietnamese state views VSLs—and possibly all languages—as instruments that can be modified at will by government decree and financial incentive.

Nevertheless, evidence from those with career-long investments in the Deaf education special school system indicate that a number of ongoing structural, training-related, and language ideological issues continue to interfere with teachers' ability to interact with students effectively and to achieve desired educational outcomes. In an interview following her participation in an interpreting workshop described in the next chapter, the principal of Hope A described the circumstances of teaching in the special schools thus:

---

10. Newspaper articles often mention the 70% differential pay for special school teachers. UNESCO Bangkok's draft Vietnam Country Report, Case study and manual on guidelines for action to include children and youth with disabilities in school systems and the EFA monitoring process, also notes this pay differential (UNESCO, 2004, p. 11).

> The problem is that, until now [interpreting workshop], we do not talk together all of us [teachers from different schools]. So I know many signs, but 50%, half of the signs, I don't know—each school has their own signs. When we teach—all of us—here at [Hope A, at DC1 and DC2]—we all sign, but then when the students sign, we don't know what they are signing. We don't understand. If they don't explain to us, we don't know. So if they say [sign] something, we don't know what they are saying [signing].

Later in the interview, the principal of Hope A said the following:

> We saw [at the interpreting workshop, in a presentation given by one of the EP codirectors on the structure of HCMSL], how Deaf people say [sign] the sentence—it's not the same way we say the sentence [Vietnamese word order], but we [teachers] don't know anything about the grammar of sign language. But all the Deaf people know—they all say the sentence the same way—say the same thing.

The comments of one person, who was then the IE director and former special school principal, further encapsulated the frustration expressed by principals and teachers, who reported struggling to communicate with their students:

> Yeah. Yeah. I see, in the special schools, they don't know exactly how to use sign language, and so how about the teachers in the [inclusive education] primary school?! The people in the ministry [MOET], they don't answer about that—about how hard it is for the teachers. And how can they [teachers] do two things at the same time?! They have two levels—one level is Vietnamese, and one level is sign language, and how can they do that [at the same time] [speaker's emphasis]?!

When I asked the IE director where the regular education IE teachers were expected to learn methods for communicating with Deaf and hard of hearing students, she answered:

> Some people in MOET. But they never came to train me . . . and they [MOET trainers] haven't had training either. . . . I don't know [laughs], but I know the way we do in Việt Nam . . . The hearing impaired children in the normal classrooms don't even have hearing aids.

She went on to explain that it is these same "people in MOET" who are responsible for the new special education training programs. "Therefore," she continued, "the people who work with me in early intervention from the Ministry of Education . . . they have no idea about special education. They have no idea about hearing impaired education. So they just *do a job* [emphasis in the original, with tone of derision]!"

In the same interview, this IE director explained that, as of 2005, special school teachers have been further restricted by the requirement to attend monthly district education departmental meetings. Prior to 2005, teachers from the special schools—all of which are located in separate districts—met on a monthly basis and shared teaching methods and experiences related specifically to special education.

When I asked what prompted this change, the director explained that, before 2005, a number of schools were still administered by the Ministry of Health and the

Ministry of Labor, Invalids, and Social Affairs. Thus, in 2005, MOET shifted all of the schools under their jurisdiction and established district-level educational meetings. Special school teachers attend these meetings, and, in the words of the IE director, "they come there and listen to other teachers, but nothing is related to their work."

The examples included in this section demonstrate instances of certain ministry-level structuring that imposes requirements on Deaf education special school administrators and teachers without providing the practical and programmatic resources they need to make the special schools efficacious. The IE director gave financial and attitudinal reasons for these circumstances: (1) "MOET does not have money [to support special education]," and (2) "They think that hearing impaired children are very different from the normal. They don't think that the hearing impaired children can *do like the normal*. They don't have the high expectation for them" (speaker's emphasis).

At the same time, certain administrators, such as the IE director and the special school principals, have committed their careers to Deaf children's education in the belief that these young people can learn more than performance outcomes suggest. Over time, these administrators have shared with each other their instructional methods, periodically changing their approaches or seeking resources from outside Việt Nam. For instance, the principals of Hope A, Hope B, and DC1 have found different ways to use sign language in their schools and to offer training to teachers. The principals of Hope A and Hope B described their efforts to teach sign language to their content-area teachers. The principal of Hope B established a sign language-based life-skills class for older students, and the principal of DC2 paid for HCMSL instructors to teach content-area teachers at her school twice a week. And at both Hope B and DC1, the principals encouraged teachers to attend the HCMC Deaf Cultural Club in order to practice HCMSL.

In some respects, the practices I observed at the EP provide a contrast here. The EP student commentaries on their own practices rarely occurred in the immediate setting of the EP; rather, EP learners chose to discuss these issues outside the EP setting and to further expand on aspects of their own and EP personnel's practices during interviews. These differences appear to be salient to Deaf imaginaries and experiences, which they associated with ĐIẾC [DEAF] and NGƯỜI NGHE [HEARING] sociolinguistic identities. The EP student descriptions of the latter two identities indexed particular concerns about the potential negative implications of sociolinguistic viewpoints on educational and other opportunities. Given that such concerns are also salient for Deaf self-determination, I address these here, focusing on linguistic access and decision-making authority.

In EP classrooms and other settings involving the formal participation of Deaf adult students (e.g., EP assemblies and meetings), I observed EP teachers and personnel using either HCMSL or SSV (or some combination of the two). However, in informal settings, such as chance meetings in the hallway or when interrupting a class or a meeting to ask a question (see chapter 4's vignette about the world history lesson), these same non-Deaf EP personnel often spoke without signing and concluded these conversations without describing to Deaf onlookers the nature of the exchange. That is, EP personnel did not translate the exchange or otherwise reference the communication, such as by summarizing the content to the (Deaf) people present.

These practices were not unique to the EP. I observed similar practices in all five special schools, the Development Center, and other locations where Deaf and signing/

non-Deaf people were both present, such as social events, conferences, and homes. However, witnessing these events at the EP—the mission of which was to be a bilingual educational setting founded on the use of HCMSL—admittedly surprised me. Observing such exchanges frequently during my first visit to Việt Nam in 2007 and throughout the research period, I wondered whether EP learners' responses to these situations had something in common with my own.

My own personal and professional experiences with Deaf ASL users in the United States and with sign-proficient hearing people have been that they observe conventions that aim to ensure that everyone present is a full participant in the communication interaction. As in other bilingual settings where conversation tends to take place in predominantly one language, ASL is the predominant language when Deaf people are present (and when non-Deaf persons choose ASL). Unlike spoken language bilingual settings, if English is selected as the language of interaction, then Deaf people have almost no access whatsoever to the conversational content. Thus, if I did not speak a given language but were aware that everyone in the room knew my language and chose not to use it, then I would wonder about the circumstances that determined their choice. To be absolutely explicit about my own perspective here: I believe that signed languages should be used whenever interacting directly or indirectly with Deaf people (i.e., whenever they are present), and also that non-Deaf signers can choose to use signed languages with each other just as they would any other language that they share. Moreover, I do not view Simultaneous Communication (SimCom) as a language but rather as a method that can be useful for brief exchanges when at least one conversational partner is not bilingual in a signed language; however, given the impossibility of employing two languages simultaneously, the use of Simultaneous Communication demands explicit negotiation between the communication partners about how SimCom is to be used—and never as an instructional modality (for the reasons just stated; also see chapter 3 for discussion).[11]

Non-Deaf people's use of spoken Vietnamese when in the presence of Deaf people was a practice I observed in all of the research settings (especially when the latter were not directly engaged in an activity with non-Deaf persons). This suggested to me that these non-Deaf people's use of HCMSL was motivated by the fact that *they* had something to communicate directly to a Deaf person; otherwise, they used Vietnamese. Interviews conducted with EP teachers and personnel later confirmed this impression. As one teacher expressed it, "We sign in class. If I need to talk to a student, then I sign. When I talk to other teachers or to the directors, then I speak." Positional requirements and/or authority hierarchies are invoked in this explanation, which also indicate that choices about language code are made relative to the immediate interactants, privileging the need or aim on the part of the non-Deaf person. Such practices also reflect

---

11. For example, when Deaf friends and I are attending social functions together, they may ask me to speak and sign at the same time so that, when conversing with a non-Deaf person who does not sign, the conversation will have the feeling of a dynamic, real-time exchange in the manner of English-language usage and hearing discourse practices (rather than one that pauses for consecutive interpretation). Such situations often requires multiple repairs (in both the spoken English and the signed English forms), clarifications, and making explicit those concepts expressed through implicature.

spoken Vietnamese sociolinguistic conventions, whereby speakers establish, maintain, and end interactions according to age and status hierarchies.

The first time I observed the privileging of spoken Vietnamese in otherwise sign language-based settings was during my first visit to the EP. I had just completed an HCMSL lesson and returned to the EP office with one of my HCMSL teachers, Mỹ Uyên. As we conversed in HCMSL and nonstandard gestures (as I had just started studying HCMSL), one of the EP codirectors and Mĩ (EP staff and interpreter) entered the room, speaking Vietnamese. I waved. They glanced at me, nodded, and continued talking in Vietnamese as they sat down at their desks. At that moment I realized that I had expected them to switch to HCMSL. I also wondered what Mỹ Uyên expected them to do and, more important, what she wanted them to do.

As Mỹ Uyên and I continued signing with one another, I scanned her face for a reaction. If she did react, I was not able to perceive it then. I tried to imagine not being able to hear the codirector and the assistant and visually searched for other kinds of cues as to the nature of the exchange: Both were turned with their backs to each other and with their eye gaze directed at their respective tasks while they continued to speak. Thus, their lip movements and facial expressions were largely unavailable from their profiles. Because I was unfamiliar with Vietnamese at this point, I had no access to the discussion; I must have been staring because Mỹ Uyên tapped me on the shoulder to get my attention and signed NEVER MIND [THEM/THAT] . . . WE WILL CONTINUE SIGNING TOGETHER. Two weeks later Mỹ Uyên, who a year later became a focal research participant and partner, made a remark that clarified her position on HEARING people's communication practices:

> I don't like it when hearing people who know how to sign talk in front of me. Deaf people don't like it. I wish they would sign, but it's what hearing people do. I must focus on finishing school so I can graduate and teach Deaf children. That way they will have a teacher who always uses sign language.

This instance of speaking Vietnamese in front of Deaf students at the EP revealed an assumption I had made about the EP as a sign-based educational program: that program personnel would use HCMSL—if not all of the time, then at least when in the presence of EP students. Moreover, Mỹ Uyên's comment underscores an important fact that might go underappreciated: Despite substantial obstacles, some non-Deaf special school teachers in Việt Nam are learning sign language from Deaf people and are using it in instructional contexts. However, they are not doing so as part of either a democratizing or modernizing project per se, but because they recognize that Deaf students communicate meaningfully among themselves using sign language and that speech does not promote such communication.

These examples and commentaries make it clear that language policy and planning play a role in the differing forms of institutional, programmatic, and interpersonal negotiations of language use. These diverse forms have not, until recently, involved Deaf people. The leaders of the HDC and other Deaf social organizations are now changing the Deaf education and language policy terrain by, among other actions, participating in INGO projects, community-based and social media campaigns, and collaborative partnerships (e.g., Global Action Week on Education and Disability 2014); training with international Deaf organizations (e.g., national associations, World Federation of the Deaf); taking part in large-scale multilateral activities, such as the first ever disability rights street march, hosted by the Asia Pacific Development Center on Disability in Hà Nội on November 29, 2014. The march included an estimated 500 people, approximately eighty of whom were Deaf people (representatives from ten Deaf associations), along with interpreters and families with Deaf children. In addition, these leaders and organizations are continuing to conduct HCMSL classes in the community for families, interested community members, and aspiring HCMSL-Vietnamese interpreters.

This terrain is markedly different from the social opportunities available to Deaf people even five years ago, and their social action initiatives. Next I describe both the circumstances that characterized state-led efforts on behalf of people with disabilities in HCMC and Deaf people's commentaries on those circumstances.

National Charitable Aid, International Disability-Related Development, and Deaf Social Aims: Equity Not Charity

As already mentioned in this chapter and earlier in the book, Việt Nam now has thousands of smaller and larger community-based organizations, officially or informally recognized *câu lạc bộ* [clubs], national and international nongovernmental organizations, and, over the last two decades, an increasing number of organizations established and run by and for people with disabilities (DPOs). Given my discussion of the methodological and analytic issues associated with USAID's (2013) *Disability Projects Review Assessment and Analysis Report,* I cautiously draw the following reported figure from that source but do so because it is consistent with observations by others, including the Vietnamese state's own NCCD (2010): "According to Action to the Community Development Center (ACDC), a civil society organization established in 2011, there are 20 DPOs with legal status" (Lynch & Phạm, 2013, p. viii). In addition to such officially recognized DPOs more than 20 unofficial Deaf clubs or associations are operating throughout the country. Most of these are self-supporting through membership dues, and a few receive funding from community, business, and INGO partners.

In order to understand the circumstances of the rapidly changing disability-related development sector, we need to grasp the nature of disability-related journalism in Việt Nam. In 2008 and 2009 I conducted a series of interviews with "Thịnh," who, as a reporter for *Báo Lao Dộng-Xã Hội* [Labor and Society Newspaper], was assigned to cover disability-related topics. In the process, Thịnh became politicized when he saw the conditions facing persons with disabilities in Việt Nam. Thịnh described the institutions of both *hội bảo trợ* [lit., National Assembly–sponsored programs] and *tự phát, tự nguyện* (local people's voluntary assistance), which provide food and minor cash assistance to people with disabilities. He evaluated these institutions in the following way:

> *Ở Việt Nam chúng tôi, ngay từ Trung ương đến địa phương cũng đều có những tổ chức để hỗ trợ cho người khuyết tật. Nhưng sự hỗ trợ này chỉ mang tính từ thiện hơn là mang tính hỗ trợ. Bởi vì là người làm báo nên tôi biết được nguyện vọng của người khuyết tật.*

Người khuyết tật không phải là mong vào sự từ thiện, họ không mong chờ để nhận từng phần quà. Và tôi thấy rằng nếu những tổ chức từ thiện của Nhà nước chỉ lo làm những việc như làm từ thiện, những thành quả như thế này là không có giá trị!

In Việt Nam we have, from the national level to the local level, organizations to help people with disabilities. But this type of support is only charity, not basic support. As a journalist I have come to know the hope of people with disabilities. Disabled people are not looking for charity, they are not looking forward to each small handout. And I think that if these state organizations only do this kind of charity work, the fruit of this charity has no value!

Thịnh went on to describe the situation of Deaf people living in cities such as Sài Gòn and Hà Nội as "much better" than that of those living in the country because the former had access to at least some programs and schools. *Tuy nhiên* [Nevertheless], he continued:

những người khuyết tật mà cụ thể là những người Điếc, khi tôi có dịp trao đổi thì họ nói rằng cái mà họ cần là được hòa nhập [trong xã hội] với những người bình thường khác, chứ không phải họ cần những phần quà. Họ muốn việc làm . . . Mong muốn của tôi bây giờ là tôi muốn không chỉ người câm Điếc được học ngôn ngữ kí hiệu mà cả người bình thường cũng được học ngôn ngữ kỲ hiệu trong các trường phổ thông. . . . Có một điều đáng buồn là hầu như Nhà nước, Chính phủ Việt Nam hầu như không quan tâm đến ngôn ngữ kỲ hiệu. Hiện nay ở TP.HCM có hai trường đào tạo sinh viên để làm người hỗ trợ, người trợ giúp, làm giáo viên dạy cho người khuyết tật. Chẳng hạn như Đại học sư phạm thì đào tạo giáo viên dạy cho người khuyết tật; còn trường Lao động xã hội thì đào tạo người hỗ trợ người tàn tật, có nghĩa là trợ giúp cho người tàn tật, và cả hai nơi này đều không dạy ngôn ngữ kỲ hiệu.

people with disabilities and in particular those who are Deaf, when I had a chance to communicate with them, said that what they need is to be integrated [into society] with normal people, not a handout. They want jobs. My wish is that it is not only Deaf people who should learn sign language but normal people should learn sign language in school, too. . . . Sadly, the Vietnamese state, the government has little interest in sign language. Currently, in Hồ Chí Minh City there are two programs that teach about people with disabilities. For example, the HCMC Pedagogic University, which trains teachers to teach people disabilities, and the Department of Labor and Social Affairs, which trains assistants for people with handicaps, to help people with handicaps, and neither of these programs uses sign language.

When I asked him how he thought the situation could be changed, Thịnh answered, with a mischievous expression on his face:

Hai mươi năm nữa. Vời tôi thì phần lỗi thuộc về chính phủ. Tôi nghĩ rằng để đạt được mục tiêu đó thì cần phải đi một đoạn đường rất xa, và ngay bây giờ điều đầu tiên cần phải làm là thay đổi [người ta] nhận thức. Chẳng hạn như bây giờ có một sinh viên có được tư tưởng đó thì chúng ta phải chờ đến khi sinh viên này lên làm thủ tướng thì đến lúc đó xã hội mới thay đổi? Có thể sau hai mươi năm nữa chính phủ và sinh viên sẽ thay đổi. Một vấn đề nữa, có thể trong thời buổi hiện nay thì đồng tiền có giá trị nên người ta quan tâm đến đồng tiền nhiều hơn, ngôn ngữ ký hiệu không quan trọng! . . .Chúng tôi đặt vấn đề là chính phủ cần quan tâm hơn đến vấn đề hỗ trợ cho người khuyết tật bằng những công việc thiết thực chẳng hạn như mở lớp học ngôn ngữ ký hiệu, nhưng chẳng ai quan tâm đến . . . hoàn toàn là sự im lặng.

In 20 years [it will change]. For me, I blame the government because, to achieve this goal, we have a long way to go, and right now the first thing we need to do is to change [people's] perception. For example, there are students who have that idea, but then we have to wait until these students can become prime minister, and only at that time will society change. Maybe in 20 years the government and the students will change. . . . Another problem is that, in the current society, so many people think about money more than other things. Sign language is not important. . . . Last year I wrote a piece in which I said that right now the government does not care about people with disabilities, and the government should open a class to teach sign language. No one contacted me about this story . . . there was complete silence.

Like Thịnh, Deaf research participants also described the Vietnamese state's approach to citizens who are Deaf and those that have disabilities as *từ thiện* [charity]. In 11 interviews (10 individual interviews with EP students and one group interview

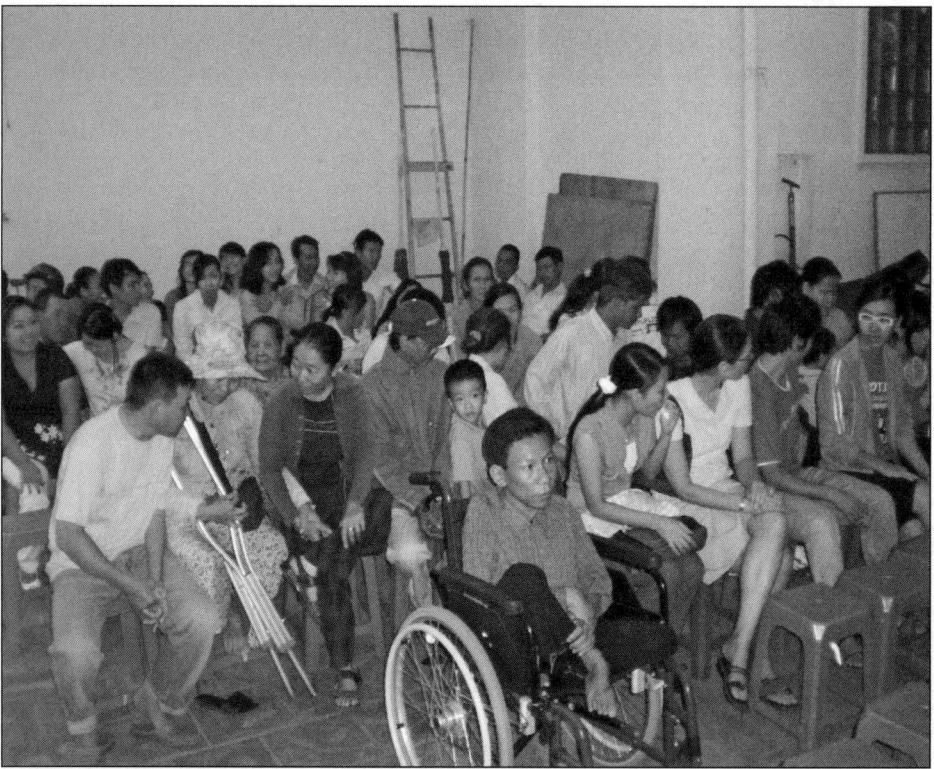

Figure 5.4. Audience at the eighth annual festival to celebrate the Lunar New Year, HCMC (the author is seated in the front row, third person from the left).

Deaf Marginalization, Deaf-Led Social Change and Disability-Oriented Development 167

Figure 5.5. Charity bags arranged on the stage: eighth annual Lunar New Year assembly festival, HCMC.

with five Deaf residents of HCMC), the interviewees commonly referenced the government's practice of holding charity ceremonies, such as those held at the Vietnamese Lunar New Year (Tết). At these ceremonies, the Hội Bảo Trợ (Government Patronage Association) dispenses small sums of cash in the range of $3 to $5 US ($60.000 to $100.000 VNĐ) and bags of practical gifts, such as snacks, toiletries, clothing, and other small items (figures 5.7 and 5.8).[12]

Broadcast on television as media events, these ceremonies were overwhelmingly described by the research participants as UNFAIR [không công bằng]. They explained that the government expects them to attend, but, for many attendees, the small cash allowance often does not even cover the cost of transportation to and from the ceremony. All 15 of the research participants remarked that, after the ceremony, as one female of approximately 45 years of age said, "Our life—the life of Deaf people—is the same. Nothing changes."[13]

---

12. The Assembly Festival is celebrated every year during the Tết holidays. As 2009 was the year of the Water Buffalo, the charity festival was officially titled Lễ Hội Cây mùa nhân ái, xuân kỷ sửu thứ VIII (Eighth Annual Assembly Festival, Season of Giving, Year of the Water Buffalo). In figure 5.7, I am seated in the audience, middle of the front row.

13. Similarly, Thịnh described an article he wrote on a Deaf family with seven Deaf members, who live in Cần Thơ province (south of Hồ Chí Minh City). Known to the community as being terribly poor, he reported that community members try to give the family money and food, but they refuse. Thịnh said, "Họ chỉ cần muốn việc làm" [They only want jobs].

One EP student described acts of *từ thiện* as an expression of the QUAN ĐIỂM [fingerspelled "perspective" or "point of view"] of government agents and other HEARING [PEOPLE]:

> When they [the government] *từ thiện* they also *an ủi* [lit., give consolation, comfort; negative affect accompanying the sign suggests pity]. They think they are consoling us for our problem. But being Deaf is not a problem. Not allowing us to use sign language in school is a problem. Not allowing us to contribute to Việt Nam by working is a problem.

In interviews with five research participants following our attendance at the Eighth Annual Assembly Festival, I pursued this notion of an ủi, asking interviewees whether they would describe the festival as a form of từ thiện, which implied an ủi: All agreed. Recalling discussions at the HCMC Deaf Club involving ways of encouraging the government to "bảo vệ Deaf people" [lit., protect, defend], I asked these interviewees whether they would also describe từ thiện as the government's way of providing sự bảo vệ [lit., protection, defense]. All five interviewees vigorously rejected the notion of government charity as a form of protection. One interviewee said, "Protection means that you respect the experience and the perspective of the person, their culture, their language, and you do something to support their independence. Protection is about fairness."

Illustrating this notion of fairness, two interviewees stated that, were the charity ceremonies "fair . . . if the government did *bảo vệ*," it would provide HCMSL-Vietnamese interpreters:

> Usually we [Deaf people] go to the [từ thiện] ceremony, and we sit there. We do not know what the presenters are saying. So we stand when they tell us to stand and take a bag when they hand us a bag. But we cannot participate. They could be saying anything, and we have no idea.

The notion of fairness not only connects to a national discursive field by describing state-sponsored charity events but also more broadly to the whole egalitarian socialist project. Here, lack of government fairness results in both Deaf people's marginalization and dependence, calling into question the Vietnamese national motto: Độc lập—Tự Do—Hạnh Phúc (Independence—Freedom—Happiness).

Following the interviews just described, I conducted a group interview with twelve EP students who were then attending their first year of college in preparing to become primary-level Deaf education teachers. During the interview I asked whether education provided by the special schools was an example of an ủi or bảo vệ; the group responded unanimously that the special schools regarded *them* from the perspective of an ủi. One interviewee then said the following:

> They think they have to take care of us; they don't think we can think for ourselves. And they don't know what we think because they do not use sign language. We [students] want teachers to sign with us. But they think signing is wrong.

Echoing this adult learner's comments, in an interview that followed an HCMSL-Vietnamese interpreting workshop hosted by the HDC and the EP which was attended by special school principals and teachers (see chapter 6), one of the EP codirectors made the following remarks:

> One thing I do regret not asking [the workshop participants] is—you remember they said they wanted to "help" the Deaf students?—I would like to see how they answer the question: Are the Deaf students going to help you in any way? You know, 'cuz I'm afraid they're going to say, "We need to help the Deaf students, but we don't need any help from the Deaf students." Or they may say "they are helping us learn sign language," but I don't know if any of them would ever say, "Oh, some Deaf people are really smart, and they tell me things I don't know." I don't know if they would ever come up with something like that.

From the data discussed in this and the preceding section, it is clear that EP students and HDC leaders' description of Deaf education special school personnel's language use is consistent with the latter's own descriptions. Special school personnel tend to speak Vietnamese, sometimes accompanied by signing in Vietnamese word order. Sometimes they use a number of signs and/or gestures (*cử chỉ diệu bộ*), although the students do not always understand these. My data also show that—whether couched in an imaginary of "helping," "rehabilitation," or some other framework—special school principals and teachers have little to no linguistic understanding of HCMSL and are also unfamiliar with sign language pedagogy, best practices, or even what other teachers are doing in their special school classrooms. Accordingly, though they may believe that their students are intelligent, teachers have difficulty developing their students' intelligence through linguistically rich interaction and content area instruction. Such circumstances reinforce the reproduction of comments about Deaf students as, if not STUPID, CRAZY, LAZY (see chapter 3), then, at the very least, underperforming.

Nevertheless, much like the "fence-breaking" model of political change (chapter 3), "Individuals, groups, and social forces outside official channels can also affect the political system" (Kerkvliet, quoted in Gray, 2003, p. 122). In the examples examined earlier (and throughout this book), Deaf education special school students, former students, principals, and teachers respond to their circumstances as quasi-official groups that influence the educational system from outside official channels from within or while connected to official institutions. For instance, in the Deaf education special schools they are working to obtain permission for nonnormative sociolinguistic practices to inhabit a place within the national education system (and, by extension, Vietnamese society, to whatever degree). They are also striving to enable the practice of analysis of and responses to inequality in education and other social domain in Deaf social organizing circles.

Without the persistence of Deaf students (both young and adult learners alike) asserting their preferences for the sociolinguistic practices most meaningful to them, it is unlikely that Deaf education special schools would employ any form of signing. Without the actions of Deaf education special school personnel, it is also unlikely that adults would be using any form of signing in the special schools. In addition, school principals and teachers often stay in touch with former graduates and invite them to participate in school events. For example, during Tết, former students typically visit the special schools they attended in order to thank the principals and teachers for their contributions toward their development, during which they often interact with current students.

Although special school administrators and teachers seem to mostly agree that it is preferable for Deaf students to learn to speak, they also seem to agree that the current state of special school education is inadequate. Their remarks and programmatic practices nevertheless reflect an ambivalence toward the status of sign language and wariness about incorporating HCMSL into school pedagogy. Moreover, as my interview data attest, educational leaders and school personnel overwhelmingly ascribe to a view of Deaf people as *khiếm thính* [having a hearing impairment] and persist in using this descriptor even when Deaf people ask them to desist.

In the context of new disability-related INGO opportunities, new market-socialist prospects, and the increasing availability of individually owned smartphones and social media tools, Deaf social organizers' responses to prevailing notions of Deaf people as somehow different—and indeed, not Điếc at all but *khiếm thính* [having a hearing impairment]—are now circulating via social messaging. These responses make claims about Deaf people's knowledge, capacities, social contributions, and desires.

Conclusion

The commentaries of Deaf social leaders who attended Deaf education special schools and completed high school as full-time students in their adult years (through the one INGO-funded program that offer such an opportunity) illuminates not only the circumstances of contemporary Deaf education but also certain, if incremental, transformations in the educational administration of that system. Thịnh's response to my question—*how might the situation change?*—was quite prescient as it did take nearly 20 years for things to change.

> *Hai mươi năm nữa. . . . đạt được mục tiêu đó thì cần phải đi một đoạn đường rất xa, và ngay bây giờ điều đầu tiên cần phải làm là thay đổi [người ta] nhận thức.*
>
> In 20 years [it will change]. . . . [we] have a long way to go, and right now the first thing we need to do is to change [people's] perception.

The EP was established in 2000, and, since students began their studies with lớp 6 (grade 6), the first ones graduated in 2007. In 2008–2009 that first cohort of students then began college courses through the EP's partnership with the teaching college (now university), with which it has maintained a cooperative arrangement. In 2012 and 2014, respectively, two cohorts of students earned their college degrees in primary Deaf education from that university. In 2012, credentialed Deaf teachers then began to enter the Deaf education school system, working in Hà Nội, HCMC, Đà Lạt, and Tiền Giang. At the time of this writing, however, only six of seventeen credentialed teachers from two cohorts have been hired in the field for which they were trained. So, to be clear, the EP is the only educational setting of its kind. The sociolinguistic practices and programmatic opportunities offered there have not been instituted in the national system of Deaf education special schools. As graduates of the EP's college and university tracks begin entering the Deaf education school system as teachers, Deaf education in Việt Nam will change. For this to happen, the Vietnamese state's continued and increased leadership in promoting the hiring of Deaf professionals and support for their advancement into positions of teaching, administration, curricular design, and other roles in the educational sector is crucial. Also crucial is the state's promotion of Deaf, DeafBlind, and Hard of Hearing people's use of VSLs in all social sectors and activities.

In the next chapter I discuss the market sector and focus specifically on an examination of what I term the *disability marketplace*. The chapter shows how the disability marketplace enlists the participation of Deaf people and the use of HCMSL in market activities. It also explains how such forces affect Deaf social organizing efforts, especially with respect to promoting the use and recognition of HCMSL (including Deaf leaders' efforts to encourage the use of VSLs in national and international forums), the recognition of national Deaf clubs and associations, and the growth of a professional VSL(s)-Vietnamese interpretation field.

6

HCMSL-Based Citizenship and Market-Socialist Futures

Interactions in the Disability Marketplace

AFTER THE PREVIOUS description of some of the ways that state-institutionalized ideologies about VSLs condition educational and social opportunity for Vietnamese Deaf people, this chapter centers on opportunities and tensions emerging at the juncture of new forms of Hồ Chí Minh Sign Language–based social organizing and the category of disability as both a recent economic and a sociopolitical formation. According to my analysis, structural organization of Deaf education special schools during the political reform period is conditioned on notions that circumscribe Vietnamese Deaf persons as exceptional subjects—having a disability, not normal, and backward (Cooper 2011). Such formations facilitated social policies and international partnerships that shaped national language policy and programming, which, I argue, further contribute to the ideological reproduction of Vietnamese Deaf people as educational and economic exceptions. Corresponding to national economic reform efforts, their exceptional status is framed largely in economic terms—as *economic burdens,* rather than economic actors aspiring to contribute to the national economy. Activities undertaken by Deaf *persons* reflect and respond to such ideological materials by advancing claims to productive labor and claims to language-centered social participation, contribution, and self-determination. Moreover, unlike *deaf subjects* described in other world locations (North Atlantic countries in particular),[1] the southern Vietnamese Deaf social organizers described in this book advance a vision of social change that involves *both deaf and hearing people,* as well as an expectation that both should dedicate themselves to national development goals by advocating access to, use of, and protection of VSLs.

Throughout this book I discuss the effects of state differentiation of "disabled" and "normal" students (people, citizens), including the disciplining and regulating of language use and embodiment practices deemed to deviate from normative sociolinguistic hearing/speaking practices. So, recalling earlier examples, within the Deaf education special schools, speech-only instruction sought to repair or cure something that officials in

---

1. See Brueggemann (2009), Emery (2006, 2009), and Ladd (2003) for theorizing on Deaf subjects in North Atlantic contexts. See Okombo (2008) for discussion of Deaf linguistic minority marginalization (i.e., subject status), written from the view of African democratic and democratic-seeking states. Also see Mbewe's (2015) *Deaf Women in Africa* for a description of Deaf women's economic and sociopolitical mobilizations, and Lord and Stein (2015) for a continent-wide survey on *Deaf Identity and Rights in Africa: Advancing Equality through the Convention on the Rights of Persons with Disabilities.*

the Ministry of Education and Training and the Ministry of Labor, Invalids, and Social Affairs (Bộ Lao Động—Thương binh và Xã Hội) perceived to be defective. During the first decades of market-socialist reform, state agents promoted speech training as one mode of national (re)production. In this imaginary, knowledge, productive skill sets, and, indeed, national citizenship are understood as outcomes of certain intellectual and linguistic capacity—or, as the examples explored in previous chapters show, often simply *the appearance of* capacity—all of which are premised on normative hearing and speaking embodiment. In turn, access to education, employment, and other national citizenship rights (drivers' licenses, marriage certificates, and so forth) have also been conditioned on the demonstration of such capacities.

From 2005 to 2015—as development and modernization efforts generated new political-economic, legal, and global aid and trade formations, and as the country ascended to lower middle-income status—new market niches proliferated throughout the country, linking together and leveraging this array of formations. Whereas prior to 2010 Deaf education special schools prohibited the use of VSLs as a matter of government policy, prohibitions on the use of VSLs in educational settings officially ended with the passage of the 2010 Law on Persons with Disabilities. Nevertheless, linguistic isolation and lack of access to educational content prevail in many settings of inclusive education and Deaf education special schools. Among the reasons for this is that MOET has not established protocols for training teachers in the use of VSLs, assessing their proficiency, monitoring the quality of instruction in these languages, and establishing the mechanisms to prioritize employment of credentialed Deaf teachers in Deaf education special schools—or other locations where their talents would be put to great advantage. Moreover, a vast global medical establishment continues to generate scientifically erroneous accounts of Deaf "children with insufficient access to sound [as being] at considerable risk for speech, language, and academic delays" (Nelson et al., 2014, p. 66), and as possessing signed languages whose grammatical structures are disordered. Such expert viewpoints are prominent in Vietnamese educational scholarship as well (ibid.; Nguyện Đ. T. & Nguyên T. P., 2012; Nguyễn & Võ, 2010).

These circumstances contribute to a situation in which VSLs and VSL users continue to be marginalized within educational and other domains where the state maintains a central role in directly structuring, monitoring, and evaluating programming. In the market domain, however, there is considerable flexibility for businesses and corporations—and, indeed, national and international NGOs—to set the terms of engagement with employees and partnering groups. Thus, whereas in the special schools, Deaf students confront significant pressure to conform to mandates to perform spoken Vietnamese, outside the schools, sign language is achieving positive social visibility—as my discussion of Trang's appearances on television indicates in the introduction to the book—and increasing in number and type of reporting over the past 6 years. Much as other areas of social and political-economic interest were once controlled solely by the state but are now undergoing "socialization" (or "privatization," as capitalist economies prefer), this chapter focuses on the ways that HCMSL is invoked by the media and private businesses, both visually and textually, for the purposes of generating profits. Such media and profit-oriented deployment of HCMSL are significant forces that influence Deaf social organizers' HCMSL-centered initiatives.

The Disability Marketplace in Việt Nam

In 2008, market-socialist reformers passed a set of laws offering tax shelters and subsidies to businesses employing and/or providing services to people with disabilities. These included the prime minister's April 2008 Decision no. 51/2008/QD-TTg, which implemented, according to its title, a "support policy of the State for business and production establishment for the disabled," which exempted businesses from paying business property taxes. In July 2008, Guidance no. 1680/NHCS-TD followed, implementing new instructions to the Việt Nam Bank for Social Policies (Ngân hàng Chính sách Xã hội Việt Nam) regarding capital lending to disability-related business ventures. In accordance with that new lending protocol, prospective business owners were required to demonstrate that their businesses promoted "stabilizing jobs for the disabled and attracting more laborers who are disabled" in order to receive capital funding (Section 2, Project Preparation). However, as this book explores in varying ways, the Vietnamese state's interest in the social welfare of its citizens is not new.

Since the first national constitution of the Democratic Republic of Việt Nam (1945, Part 3, Article 32), the Vietnamese state has officially recognized *các tàn tật* [the crippled, handicapped], which, during the anticolonial and early postreunification periods, focused on provision for war-related disability. In the past decade, the emergence of the sociopolitical identity *người khuyết tật* [disabled person] has challenged the state's charitable and medicalized approaches to handicapped citizens (see the introduction to this book). Since the passage of the 2010 disability law, the state has increasingly used the term *người khuyết tật* in official rhetoric and programming and decreased its use of *tàn tật*, which is widely viewed as a pejorative term by disability advocates and community members with disabilities. The state has also expanded its collaboration with the latter groups, among them Deaf clubs and associations throughout the country—this, despite its prevailing lack of official recognition of the latter. Nevertheless, changes in official rhetoric and active collaboration with constituent groups are major indications of changes in the state's official stances toward disability (figure 6.1).

At present, disability is a hot commodity—not simply because of activist and scholarly efforts over the past thirty years that brought attention to the extreme poverty and social marginalization that "persons with disabilities" everywhere tend to face. This is the consensus of the leading sources of data on worldwide disability and poverty (e.g., WHO, ILO, World Bank). However, it is especially the case for Việt Nam, which is in the tragic position of planning for long-term Agent Orange decontamination and learning about the differing life experiences of persons affected by the neurotoxic poison. Although many countries now face devastating forms of environmental destruction, only a few, such as Việt Nam (Kimmons, 2014; Martin, 2009) must cope with the legacies of dioxin poisoning. It is in this context that the Vietnamese state's leadership in broadening the scope of legally protected rights to and the provision of universal education, health care, and employment must be applauded.

However, what is permitted in the market domain exceeds, and often directly conflicts with, state policy and institutional programming. As business law and social policies promote the opening of economic opportunity to persons with disabilities, Deaf individuals and groups continue to encounter discrimination in the world of work— whether they are employed or not.

Figure 6.1. Disability aid donation collection boxes. Figure 6.1a is a Vietnamese Red Cross donation box at a roadside tourist center. Figure 6.1b is a donation box at the Hà Nội Noi airport with the label Hòm Từ Thiên, Trẻ Em Đặc Biệt Khó Khăn (Donation Box, Special Children [with] Difficulties). (Courtesy of the author, January 2013).

176 Chapter 6

Figure 6.2. Hướng Dẫn Du Lịch Cho Người Khiếm Thính (Tour guides for people with hearing impairment). Thái Bình for *Tuổi Trẻ* (newspaper), September 20, 2008.

One of the first disability-related employment opportunities that entrepreneurs created following the 2008 passage of Decision no. 51/2008/QD-TTg and Guidance no. 1680/NHCS-TD (hereafter, Decision 51 and Guidance 1680) was the creation of jobs producing and selling goods for the tourism trade (Nguyễn, Rahtz, & Schultz, 2014). Also in this period, "new tourist niches" began to appear (Suntikul, Butler, & Aiery, 2008, p. 68). One of the first of these was "hearing impaired tourism," as it was termed by hearing entrepreneurs who sought to attract "hearing impaired" travelers from the United States and Europe (figure 6.2).

In a chapter for *It's a Small World: International Deaf Spaces and Encounters* (Friedner & Kusters, 2015), I address the circumstances of Deaf social leaders' responses to ASL-based tourism in Việt Nam, which centered on the sovereignty of VSLs broadly and the encroachment of ASL in the tourism domain, particularly by those who are not citizens of Việt Nam or culturally Vietnamese Deaf persons. In that chapter I describe interviews and ongoing discussions with five Deaf social leaders in December 2013 and July 2014—one from Hà Nội and four from HCMC—that led to the following observation:

> In their responses, tourism emerged as a central concern with extended commentaries addressing hearing-run ASL-based tourism activities in northern and southern Việt Nam, one person's experience with an ASL-based "Deaf Tour" to Cambodia, and upcoming ASL-based tours to Việt Nam organized by Deaf tour operators from the United States. These topics resulted in emotionally charged group-level discussions regarding two issues that interviewees agreed demanded some form

of action: (1) how to prevent foreign tour operators from conducting ASL-based tours in Việt Nam, and (2) how to prevent domestic tour operators from using ASL. In these discussions, themes of language displacement overlapped with themes of economic development. (Cooper, 2015, p. 104)

The argument I develop there also applies here:

[T]he disability marketplace in Việt Nam largely benefits hearing conationals and Deaf foreigners rather than the communities and languages upon whose existence that part of the marketplace depends. Deaf community leaders' interests in protecting Vietnamese Deaf cultural and linguistic resources should be, therefore, of great interest to the Vietnamese government, the UNWTO [United Nations World Tourism Organization], as well as to domestic and international tourism partners alike. (ibid., p. 108)

The sections that follow in this chapter illuminate and extend these conclusions (ibid.).

Of the disability-related business owners I met in southern Việt Nam (approximately six individuals) in the 2008 to 2012 period, none self-identified as a person with a disability, and only one was Deaf. The Deaf individual was a woman who had set up a small outdoor stand in Hồ Chí Minh City selling hats and accessories. By 2012 she had acquired her own storefront and was doing quite well (and, as this book goes to press, her business has expanded, and she has even been able to purchase her own home). The other five businesses were owned by HEARING people who marketed textiles and crafts to shops locally and abroad or ran tourism companies specializing in Deaf travelers. Deaf people work in some of these companies. One company—Công ty Cổ Phần Khiếm Thính Bảo Chung (hereafter, Bảo Chung)—leverages the handicraft skills long-taught mainly to Deaf girls in the special schools. It hires them to make and sell their wares in local markets in HCMC (an example of another such business is given in the next section). In 2008 the owner of Bảo Chung told me that she exports crafts to shops in the United States, primarily California. Several Deaf people also work in the Bảo Chung business office, where they do computer data entry. The owner also participated in the HDC's International Women's Day event (March 2009), which was recorded for later news broadcast. At this event she invited HDC members to apply for jobs with her company; while no HDC members obtained employment with Bảo Chung after this event, television and print media journalism presented a glowing image of a model business that advances Deaf employment opportunity.

Another company, Smile Tours International, based in HCMC, markets guided-tour packages to Deaf travelers from other countries and employs Vietnamese Deaf people to conduct these trips. The owner of Smile Tours decided to market these services to predominantly North American and European-based audiences, and to Deaf travelers who used American Sign Language.[2] Focusing on Deaf people as both her labor pool and her market niche, the owner of Smile Tours made decisions about her choice of

---

2. Articles written about Smile Tours include, among others, *Hướng dẫn du lịch cho người khiếm thính* [Travel guides for the hearing impaired] (*Tuổi Trẻ* newspaper, September 20, 2008), and "When hands speak louder than words" (*Thanh Niên* newspaper, November 19, 2008).

sign language and the marketing of sign language. Next I discuss the implications of these choices and their effects on HCMSL users. See also Cooper (2015) for an extended discussion of the circumstances of "hearing impaired" tourism and the Deaf community's responses to the encroachment of ASL in Việt Nam.

To establish her business, the owner of Smile Tours sought out persons who could train her tour guides in the use of ASL. As she and I were both attending an HCMSL class at the Development Center, and the HCMSL teacher told her I was from the United States, the Smile Tours business owner tried to enlist me to teach ASL to her tour guides. One of the EP's codirectors later told me that she had also approached both him and one of the EP's visiting scholars from the United States. The EP codirector described how he and the American scholar met with the owner of Smile Tours and encouraged her to market her tourism services in HCMSL: Describing similar models established in other countries, they pointed out the ways in which the use of the local sign language attracts Deaf travelers as a kind of cultural exchange. Ultimately the owner hired two Deaf people from Australia to teach ASL to her tour guides.[3]

I describe the circumstances of the emergence of disability-related businesses, which are subsidized by the Vietnamese state, to make two points. First, although disability has been an ongoing postwar concern in Việt Nam, the abilities of Deaf people have also long been obscured by the ideologies of "helping," "need," and "dependence." New legal frameworks facilitating the participation of people with disabilities in business activities implicitly challenge these notions. At the same time, as the example of Smile Tours indicates, Deaf people who use VSLs are at risk of being subjected to a new set of mandates, which are now conforming to hearing people's market-centered interests. To be clear, learning a new sign language such as ASL is not, in and of itself, problematic. However, such opportunities that are supported in the market sector are hard to reconcile with state programming that limits Deaf and hard of hearing people's access to education and employment generally, and harder still to reconcile with programming that limits use of VSLs specifically. As Deaf community responses to these circumstances indicate (Cooper, 2015 and 2014; Cooper and Nguyễn 2015), issues of linguistic and cultural sovereignty are of the utmost concern to Vietnamese Deaf people, along with their interest in both leading and participating in decision-making about their (multiple) languages.

Reinvigorating Traditionalism: Deaf Employees as Manual Laborers

In 2008 and 2009 I had the extreme good fortune—as a person and as a researcher—to make the acquaintance of Thịnh, the photojournalist assigned to cover disability-related events (see chapter 5). Together we participated in Deaf community meetings, HCMSL classes, formal interviews with third parties, and conversations over coffee. In addition, Thịnh invited Mĩ (HCMSL-Vietnamese interpreter formerly associated with the EP) and me to join him on a motorcycle trip to neighboring Long An province to

---

3. ASL and Australian Sign Language, or Auslan, are two distinct languages with two distinct fingerspelling systems (e.g., ASL has a one-handed fingerspelling system while Auslan has a two-handed system). For a linguistic description of Auslan's features, see Johnston and Schembri (2007).

visit a business that purportedly employed and provided educational services to Deaf women. This section focuses on that visit to Long An, which took place on August 22, 2008. Thịnh also figures largely in an event I examine in the next section (see Café Lang), in which we were both participants (along with Mī and other of Thịnh's friends and colleagues) but which we each perceived quite differently.

Located in a fairly isolated part of rural Long An province (in the Mekong Delta region, approximately 55 kilometers southwest of HCMC), the woman who owned the business in question established it after the Vietnamese state passed the set of laws described earlier, which offered tax shelters and subsidies to businesses employing or providing services to people with disabilities. Whereas a number of INGOs previously dominated disability-oriented development in Việt Nam, Decision 51 and Guidance 1680 facilitated the emergence of numerous disability-related business ventures, the establishment of which Thịnh had been following with both interest and skepticism.

After he was assigned to cover disability topics, Thịnh had an opportunity to meet Deaf people and later searched for and found HCMSL classes taught by EP students on the weekends at the Development Center; however, his emerging proficiency in HCMSL did not allow him to interact with Deaf employees or families involved in his news reportage as he would have liked. Thịnh took Mī and me to see this particular business, which he was aware netted a good profit from the embroidered tapestries the employees produced. His motivation was to interact directly with the Deaf employees, and to seek our impressions of the legitimacy of the business enterprise, especially its employment and treatment of people with disabilities.

Arriving before 10 AM, we stayed for several hours. We initially conversed with the business owner in her office, which was located at the front of a set of small buildings near her home. While we talked in the open-air office, occasionally one of the (approximately) ten Deaf women she employed came in to ask a question. When that happened, we introduced ourselves and invited the employee to join our conversation (with Mī alternating between interpreting and conversing, after which she would provide a consecutive interpretation). We talked with two Deaf employees at length (30–45 minutes), asking them questions about their families, their education, how they had met the business owner and learned their trade, and so forth. Both reported learning embroidery at special schools, which they had each attended only briefly, and through their current employer in Long An.

After an hour or so, the owner took us on a tour of the operation, which included the main embroidery work area—also an open-air space at the front, with exit doors at one side and at the back. In the rear portion of the main embroidery work area, there was a collective sleeping area where the employees slept, a bathroom, and place to bathe (figures 6.3).

After we looked around the work and living areas, we then spent about an hour looking at the exquisitely embroidered tapestries, which the business owner ("disability service provider") proudly reported, were "sold in the United States for a high price." She stated that she earned such a good price ($100–200 dollars per tapestry, depending on design and size) for these tapestries that she did not often sell them in Việt Nam. The price collected for these goods is certainly worth at least the transaction rate, given both the time and physical intensity demanded by the craft, as well as the artistic

(a)

(b)

Figure 6.3. Tax-sheltered business in Long An Province employing Deaf women embroiderers Figure 6.3a shows a woman blocking an embroidery pattern with chalk. Figure 6.3b. An embroidery hoop (khung thêu) surrounds partially completed lotus flower embroidered design (đồ thêu).

Figure 6.4. Deaf embroiderers demonstrating their craft and materials. Figure 6.4a shows two Deaf embroiderers demonstrating embroidery techniques (the author is in the center). Figure 6.4b is a cabinet with embroidery thread (chỉ thêu).

talent necessary to satisfy the design and precision requirements, not to mention the consistency of quality.

As my own attempt to learn how to embroider clearly demonstrated to everyone present that day, artisanal embroidery is a highly developed skill, at which I failed miserably. It is also painstaking work that demands long hours of repetitive motion to create a single small work of art and puts strain on the eyes, fingers, hands, and whole body.

After our tour of the workshop floor, Thịnh, Mĩ, and I returned with the business owner to her office and sat together for about another hour. During this time, Thịnh began to pursue a line of questioning about the purported educational training provided to the embroiderers. During this discussion the business owner decried the difficulty she encountered in locating materials with which to teach her employees and also her own lack of access to sign language classes. When she pulled her educational "curriculum" down off of a nearby shelf, Thịnh, Mĩ, and I were dismayed that this was actually a vocabulary-list type of booklet—this one produced in 2002 in cooperative arrangement between the National Institute of Educational Science, USAID, and Pearl S. Buck International (figure 6.5).

This vocabulary list, a math book in English, and a children's "first book of signs" in ASL and English were the extent of her "curricular materials." This is when we began to understand that her business was simply that: a business that exploited and profited from her employees' substantial skill.

182   Chapter 6

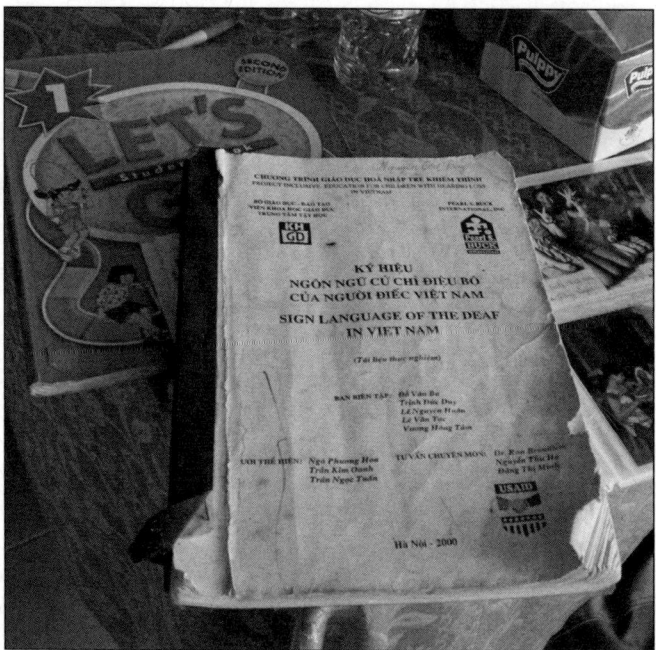

Figure 6.5. Ký Hiệu Ngôn Ngữ Cử Chỉ Điệu Bộ Của Người Điếc Việt Nam (symbols of sign language gestures of deaf people in Việt Nam).

Café Marketing and Censorship: Media-Controlled Portrayal of Deaf Employees and Patrons at Café Lặng

Café Lặng[4] was a small café whose ma The circumstances facilitating the classification in room consisted of—in 2008 and 2010—a raised platform holding approximately ten small tables with shortened legs to accommodate floor seating on cushions. The room comfortably seated about 25 people (figure 6.6).

On the evening on which this instance of censorship occurred, Thịnh, (photojournalist first introduced in chapter 5 and on p. 189) invited Mĩ and me to meet him at Café Lặng because one of his television colleagues had told him that HTV9, a state-owned and HCMC-based television broadcasting company, had arranged to do a public-interest story on the Deaf employees, and he wanted to support his colleagues with a good patron turnout.[5] Cases in which entrepreneurs leveraged signed languages as a competitive draw because of their own perception of signed languages as unusual and thereby appealing to potential café clientele resemble those described by Friedner (2013) for Indian brewmasters and Hoffman-Dilloway (2011) for advertisements featuring d/

---

4. In 2008 and 2009, the sign over the entrance to Café Lặng used fingerspelled L as the first letter in "Lặng," marking sign language as a unique feature of the business. In 2010 new owners purchased Café Lang and subsequently changed the sign over the door and discontinued the use of Deaf employees.

5. HTV9 filmed this human-interest story at Café Lặng on Wednesday, February 11, 2009, and aired it later the same week.

Figure 6.6. Café Lặng, HCMC.

Deaf waiters associated with a Nepalese bakery chain (cf. Haualand, Solvang, & Breivik, 2015 and Kohrman, 2005).

Thịnh had invited 5–6 other friends, and we all sat in a circle, ordered tea, and talked as we waited for the television crew to arrive. Initially there was a Deaf host and a Deaf server, so when they came to our table, Mī and I chatted with them. Thịnh also signed with them, asking their names and inquiring how they were doing, using the polite interrogative greeting CÓ KHOẺ KHONG? [ARE YOU WELL?]. One of Thịnh's friends asked what had brought me to Việt Nam. I replied that I wanted to study HCMSL and that I had started to do research with *người Điếc của Việt Nam* [Vietnamese Deaf people]. To this Thịnh responded strongly: "The correct term is *khiếm thính*!" I answered warmly—thinking he was joking that I should refer to them as *hearing impaired*—replying that my HCMSL teachers and many people that I had interviewed told me they preferred *người Điếc*. Becoming serious Thịnh replied: "No, no, Audrey, you are wrong. This is an idea you have in America. The Deaf people in VN are not educated, so they do not know the difference. They don't know that they should use *khiếm thính*." On previous occasions and during our formal interview, Thịnh had used the term *người Điếc* himself. But at this meeting, he was adamant. One of his friends interjected: "[Thịnh] knows that if you use the word *Điếc*, people will think you are uneducated. If you use the words *khiếm thính*, people will think you are an educated person." I clarified: "You mean, hearing people judge other hearing people if that person says *Điếc*?" "Yes," the friend answered, "so you should use *khiếm thính* (Thịnh nodded as his friend spoke).

The director of the Development Center's Hearing Impaired Unit had made a similar charge of American influence in an interview she gave to an HCMC-based journal, which published a special social report through Nhà xuất bản Công An Nhân Dân (People's Public Security Publishing House). In that article, titled *Lạc vào thế giới không âm thanh* [Lost in a world without sound], the HIU director alleged that the EP taught its students *ngôn ngữ ký hiệu Mỹ* (American Sign Language; Hồ Xuân Dung, 2008, p. 74). Having published stories about the Development Center, Thịnh was well acquainted with the HIU director's view of Deaf people, the EP-trained HCMSL instructors (who had been his teachers at the Development Center), and the circumstances of the HIU director's falling out with the latter (see chapter 1). With this exchange, discussion of preferential terms of reference provoked reported[6] authority over *metasociolinguistic* claims (Jaffe, 2009), epistemic and affective stances toward propositional content (ibid.), politics of language usage (Duranti, 1994), and implications for situational and social agency (Ahearn, 2001a, b; Duranti, 2007).

During the interaction at Café Lặng it became apparent that Thịnh—who had never visited the EP and rarely joined HDC meetings but was spending increasing amounts of time with the HIU director and engaged in HIU activities—seemed to have adopted the HIU director's perspective on Vietnamese Deaf people. That perspective presumes that Deaf people are not like "normal people" [người bình thường] and that they lack the intellectual and linguistic capacity of normal people. This presumption forecloses the possibility of Deaf people's insight into their language usage, sociolinguistic circumstances, and their ability to fulfill the sociolinguistic conditions of social propriety. It also limits Deaf people's ability to act on their own behalf as autonomous, self-determining agents. Thịnh might also have believed—as the HIU director told me—that the language policy of the EP program should not have used HCMSL in its programming. Such usage, according to the HIU director—and now Thịnh—evidenced "poor grammar" because HCMSL did not correspond to the Vietnamese language.

Moreover, both Thịnh and the HIU director stated that they believed HCMSL to be ASL, which they both believed the EP was teaching to Deaf adult learners. Rather than seeing the use of HCMSL in the EP's programming as an opportunity for Deaf adult learners to share their ideas in an ongoing way while they acquired content area knowledge not available to them through prior schooling. Because of these circumstances, EP students would coin new words—symbolic representations of the concepts they encountered through their studies and discussed on a routine basis, Thịnh and the HIU director apparently viewed the EP suspiciously. In their eyes, the EP was an American-run organization that was supplanting Vietnamese perspectives with American ones. This interpretation of events is easily understandable given

---

6. I note the "reported" nature of metasociolinguistic claims here to indicate that this was a heated exchange between HEARING people (those who do not sign and are unfamiliar with Deaf peoples and cultures) and signing non-Deaf people with close ties to Deaf individuals and groups.

the structural differences between the EP and the Vietnamese education system: As I described earlier, the former allows for interactive teacher-student exchanges and peer-to-peer instruction, while the latter is overwhelmingly teacher centered (despite MOET officials' statements and NIES's reform efforts for the country's system of teacher-training colleges).

Thịnh and the HIU director have both have witnessed the spread of the English language throughout Vietnamese society, especially through business, education, and international development circles. Thịnh's perspective on ASL as a photojournalist and the HIU director's perspective on ASL in a peer-based organization run for and by people with disabilities, suggests their concerns that ASL will encroach on Việt Nam as English has. However, it is their presumption of Deaf people's supposed inability to understand and act on these circumstances that is most striking here: Their comments suggest Vietnamese Deaf people are recipients of, and indeed vulnerable to, the ideas they encounter at the EP and elsewhere. Such perspectives do not include the possibility of Vietnamese Deaf reflection, critique, or creative reconfiguring of the ideas they encounter as a likely, or even potential, force influencing the course of contemporary circumstances.

At about this point in my reverie and our group's conversation, the reporter and the cameraman from HTV9 arrived at Café Lang. Mī and I turned to talk with some of the café employees. The reporter saw us signing and asked Mī to invite me for an interview. I agreed. The event that followed mirrored the exchange I had just had with Thịnh:

Reporter: *Café Lang như thế nào?* [What do you think of the cafe?]
Cooper: *Café Lang là rất đẹp, rất vui."* [Café Lang is very beautiful, very fun.]

Reporter: *Tại sao hị chọn quan cafe này?* [Why did you select this café?]
Cooper: *Tôi thích người Điếc. Tôi thích nói chuyện với người Điếc bằng ngôn ngữ ký hiệu.* [I like Deaf people. I like talking with Deaf people using sign language.]

Reporter: [turns to cameraman and asks him to stop filming, then turns to Mī, and they speak rapidly in Vietnamese]
Mī: She says that you used the words *người Điếc* and that you have to use the words *khiếm thính*. She says she will ask you the questions again, and this time you will say *khiếm thính*. [Mī continues interpreting.]
Cooper: I'm sorry, but I cannot do that. I do not use the words *khiếm thính*.

Reporter: [with Mī interpreting] If you say *người Điếc*, my editors will not let me use this part of the interview. Because we are on television, many people will watch this program. It's not nice to use the word *Điếc* there because the viewers might think we don't respect Deaf people. The word *Điếc* is not nice. We will do the interview again, and you will say *khiếm thính*, okay?
Cooper: I'm sorry, but my sign language teachers and friends tell me they don't like to be called *khiếm thính*, so I use *người Điếc* out of respect for them.

Reporter: But I won't be able to show you on television.
Cooper: Okay, that's fine. Thank you.

Ultimately, they did *show me* on television, as several Hồ Chí Minh Deaf Club members reported seeing me on the broadcast; however, the only segment HTV9 aired was one of Mĩ and me as we were signing in the background with some of the Café Lặng employees.

After the interview, when Mĩ and I rejoined Thịnh and his friends at the table, a woman who had not spoken before leaned forward and said quietly:

> Tôi không cho rằng từ "Điếc" là một từ mang tính tiêu cực. Điều này phụ thuộc vào giọng nói. Chúng ta có thể nói từ "Điếc" thể hiện sự không tôn trọng, hoặc chúng ta có thể nói "Điếc" thể hiện sự tôn trọng.
>
> I do not think the word *Điếc* is bad. It depends on the speaker's voice. We can say *Điếc* in a disrespectful way, or we can say *Điếc* in a respectful way.

With this statement, Thịnh nearly jumped across the table and then said angrily: *Em sai rồi! Em không biết gì hết!* [You are wrong! You don't know anything!]. Although Thịnh's apparent change in perspective (from those he demonstrated in interactions several months prior) is intriguing, this not the most compelling feature of these interactions at Café Lặng. What *is* compelling is the way in which a seemingly innocuous, if not celebratory, gathering activated polarized social viewpoints and that—despite some differing viewpoints expressed by the hearing-speaking people present, the authority invoked by the media personnel present—Thịnh in print journalism and HTV9 in television journalism—succeeded in either suppressing or explicitly censoring minority viewpoints. Possibly the most salient feature of this contestation over identity and language through competing classifications is that the Deaf people present were not consulted, even though they sat at adjacent tables and served our tea.

The circumstances facilitating the classification of Vietnamese Deaf subjects and the disciplining of (reported) Deaf preferential terms of reference are effects of power (i.e., language ideological notions that shape institutional mechanisms) and of the significant forces that shape contemporary Vietnamese Deaf self-determination. If Deaf people cannot represent their own interest via social spaces and the media—and indeed seem to only achieve access to such spaces only under the condition of submission to prescriptive guidelines—then their opportunities for self-determination are severely constrained. In the context of economic liberalization, the owners of Café Lặng benefit from portrayal of the café as a space of new experience and openness while HCMSL and Deaf perspectives are nonetheless marginalized.

ĐIẾC or KHIẾM THÍNH: Preferential Terms and Institutionalized Rhetoric

In chapter 1, I described my first encounters with Deaf and non-Deaf people's ways of referring to each another as kinds of persons or subject-groups. Interactions with EP students evidenced early and consistent signer self-references as ĐIẾC [DEAF, as well as their references to nonsigning people as HEARING, whose sociolinguistic practices they described as distinct from ĐIẾC and VĂN HOÁ NGƯỜI ĐIẾC [DEAF CULTURE]. These were expectable forms of reference based on my previous interactions with Deaf persons inside and outside the United States. They were also expectable given that the EP's curriculum on HCMSL instruction includes coursework on world Deaf cultures and history. Vietnamese signers' references to ĐIẾC and VĂN HOÁ NGƯỜI ĐIẾC [DEAF CULTURE] were thus unremarkable to me during the early phase of the study, which informs the content of this book (2007–2008). However, when I began attending HCMSL classes and meetings at the Development Center in HCMC, I was surprised to encounter the HIU director's references to Deaf people as K-H-I-Ế-M T-H-Í-N-H [HEARING IMPAIRED],[7] particularly since she herself self-identified as hard of hearing, or to encounter HEARING people's widespread use of *khiếm thính* in Deaf education special schools and training centers. I found this particularly surprising since these sites had the most direct contact with Deaf students and adults, as well as with televised and print media sources.

A chance occurrence at the HCM Deaf Club that took place after the Café Lặng incident illuminates the sociolinguistic circumstances of KHIẾM THÍNH [HEARING IMPAIRED] for southern Vietnamese Deaf members of the HDC. That meeting in February 2009 was attended by a number of people from HCMC and other cities south of HCMC.[8] During the course of the usual meeting events, one of the HDC leaders mentioned the televised broadcast of the public interest story on Café Lặng, which was not only located near the HDC but also frequented by HDC members, several of whom were also employed there. Since Mĩ and I had been present at Café Lặng during the taping of the segment and were both present at the meeting of the HDC that morning, the HDC leaders, to whom we had related the full story, asked us to tell the membership what had happened and how the actual events differed from what ultimately aired in the broadcast. When we got to the part of the story where we described my decision to decline the reporter's request to tape the interview segment again in order to substitute the words *khiếm thính* [hearing impaired] for *Điếc* [Deaf], the HDC leaders noticed confused looks on members' faces. The leaders responded by asking the approximately 110 persons in attendance that day whether they understood the meaning of K-H-I-Ế-M T-H-Í-N-H and how this term differed from ĐIẾC. Approximately 25 persons raised their hands to indicate that they understood the distinction between these two words; several people made comments such as THAT IS WHAT HEARING PEOPLE CALL DEAF PEOPLE BUT I DON'T KNOW WHY and DEAF PEOPLE USE ĐIẾC BECAUSE WE SIGN, HEARING IMPAIRED PEOPLE DON'T SIGN. This suggests that, for the people in attendance that day, K-H-I-Ế-M T-H-Í-N-H was either unfamiliar or not meaningful to more than 75% of those present. Several of them indicated a certain level of familiarity with the term, as this comment shows: I SAW THAT WORD ON THE SIGNS FOR THE SPECIAL SCHOOLS BUT I DON'T KNOW WHAT IT MEANS. The club leaders then asked the club members how they described themselves. The membership signed unanimously and without hesitation: ĐIẾC.

Interviews with EP students showed consensus regarding preference for the term ĐIẾC [DEAF]; 17 out of 19 individually interviewed research participants rejected the descriptor *khiếm thính*, while two said they preferred *Điếc* but were uncertain about how *khiếm thính* and *Điếc* differed. Of the 17 interviewees who provided details about the circumstances of *khiếm thính*, the latter was characterized as a term popularized by

---

7. Dashes between each letter denotes fingerspelled terms.
8. A number of HCMC Deaf Club members travel from outside HCMC to attend the meetings. Some members also hail from other provinces in the south central region north of HCMC, the southeastern region (e.g., Cần Thơ), or farther south (e.g., Vũng tàu).

HEARING [NON-SIGNING] members of society generally and the CHÍNH PHỦ [GOVERNMENT] and special school personnel specifically. Interviews with EP students also approached consensus on the recent appearance and/or the EP adult learners' recent appreciation of the term *khiếm thính*. In an interview, EP student Minh Hai (30 years of age in 2009) told me they could not recall when this term came into common usage but that it was a term whose frequency they expected to gradually diminish: "When hearing people in Việt Nam become educated about sign language and Vietnamese Deaf culture, they will stop using *khiếm thính*."

Interviews with special school principals and teachers, those presumably most familiar with Vietnamese sign languages and Deaf sociolinguistic practice, evidenced a preference for the term *khiếm thính*. Special school personnel also used the term *Điếc*; however, such usage was frequently collocated with a description of negatively construed circumstances, such as when describing two of the most frequent complaints about *sinh viên điếc:* Deaf students are not able to write Vietnamese, and their signing shows "backward" grammar. When asked about the two terms, special school principals referred to the use of *Điếc* as a *rất thô* [rough] way to refer to Deaf people. Most special school teachers with whom I spoke (not signed), and, indeed, most EP teachers as well, said that the two terms had the "same meaning" but that *khiếm thính* was "nicer." "*Khiếm thính*," they explained, "is more polite" and also implied, according to the principal of Hope B special school, that the person had the potential to *vượt qua khó khăn của bị điếc* [overcome the difficulty of being Deaf].

At the time of this writing I have not seen evidence of a conventionalized way in which HCMSL signers symbolize the concept of *khiếm thính* [hearing impaired]. While conducting research and while working as a consultant and trainer for World Concern Development Organization, I also did not observe Deaf people in southern or northern Việt Nam spontaneously fingerspell *khiếm thính* or initiate discussion of *khiếm thính*; however, most

Figure 6.7. Initial position K of the nonce sign K-T [Khiếm Thịnh (hearing impaired)].

non-Deaf research participants used the term *khiếm thính* frequently, regardless of whether they were signers or nonsigners. By contrast, it was only when I asked direct questions about this concept that Deaf research participants and colleagues used the term, and even then they fingerspelled it or used an abbreviation or a nonce sign such as: KT.

Nonce signs are forms established between interactants simply for the purpose of the immediate exchange (i.e., it is not conventionalized). Where concepts are meaningful, signers, like speakers, tend to create and conventionalize signs (words). Among the southern Vietnamese Deaf research paeticipants in this study, there is no conventionalized way to index *khiếm thính* suggesting that it is not meaningful on the level of everyday communication or in more formal situations (e.g., HDC meetings, meetings with potential employers and INGO partners). However, some signers produce the nonce sign KT in formal settings, as one southern signer did when interviewed by VT9 for a public-interest story on one Deaf club's activities in December 2010 (Cooper & Nguyễn, 2015). Figure 6.7 shows a signer establishing the nonce sign KT with the letter K in the initial position:

Deaf students associated with the EP told me that, in the early years of the EP, periodicals began publishing stories about them on a regular basis. Prior to such interviews, the EP students told me, they routinely explained to journalists the distinctions between Vietnamese and HCMSL and also requested that that journalists refer to them as *người Điếc* [Deaf person/people] in their final published essays, *not* as *khiếm thính* [hearing impaired]. Once the essays went to press, however, these final versions rarely contained descriptions of HCMSL or referred to the interviewees as *người Điếc*. In 2012 and 2013 a subset of HDC members hosted a series of *giao lưu* [cultural exchanges] with local college students, NGO workers, and the Communist Youth League of HCMC (Cộng đoàn Thanh niên Tp. HCM). Invited to present at one of these *giao lưu* in July 2012, I was intrigued to see that an early section of the HDC members' presentations directly addressed their collective experiences of the metasociolinguistic differences between ĐIẾC and KHIẾM THÍNH, as introduced by the slide below which HDC members prepared for the *giao lưu* (see figure 6.8).

Very similar to the way in which I describe (see discussion in chapter 3) the differences between Sign-Supported Vietnamese and *signing fluently in the manner of Vietnamese Deaf people*, these presenters described the social identity of K-H-I-Ế-M T-H-Í-N-H as aligning with HEARING sociolinguistic practices and values and that of ĐIẾC as aligning with and celebrating the fluent use of VSLs, including the use of nonmanual grammatical markers (i.e., facial and body movement). Next I discuss the ways in which Deaf social organizers use claims about VSLs and HCMSL, Deaf identity, and collective self-determination to effect social change in southern Việt Nam.

Deaf Social Organizing and Self-Determination in the Disability Marketplace

In this section I focus on activities undertaken by the HCMC Deaf Club to address social inequalities that sometimes facilitate Vietnamese Deaf people's entry into a highly constrained set of market sectors and positions relative to notions of disability. At other times, however, they bar their entry altogether, relative to negative ideologies

Figure 6.8. Power Point presentation: Sự Khác Nhâu Giữa KHIẾM THÍNH| và ĐIẾC (The difference between having a hearing impairment and being deaf).

that surround signed language usage. Such activities prominently include promoting and participating in the training of HCMSL-Vietnamese interpreters; advocacy efforts to gain official state recognition of the HDC and other Deaf clubs and associations throughout the country; and advocacy efforts to obtain official state recognition of HCMSL and other VSLs.

HCMSL-Vietnamese Interpretation

With the reunification of northern and southern Việt Nam, the use of interpreters in Việt Nam was limited largely to spoken and written language translation for governmental and diplomatic purposes. Since Việt Nam's initiation of their open-door policy, spoken language interpreters and translators have also been appearing in business, trade industry, and other venues. Signed-spoken language interpretation is an even newer phenomenon, initially appearing in southern Việt Nam in July 2008, approximately six months prior to Trang's invitation to participate in "310 Years of Đồng Nai" (see introductory chapter). Prior to that broadcast, research participants associated with the EP who hailed from southern Việt Nam reported having seen only a single other instance of a signing Deaf person in a televised event working with an

HCMSL-Vietnamese interpreter.⁹ This first instance had occurred six months prior to "310 Years of Đồng Nai," with the annual *Hội Thi Kể Chuyện Về Tấm Gương Đạo Đức Hồ Chí Minh* (Narrative Contest on the Moral Example of Hồ Chí Minh). The *Narrative Contest* was hosted in Đồng Nai province, while related events took place throughout the country, all involving invited participants whose task it was to recite passages written by or about Hồ Chì Minh, Việt Nam's most famous anticolonial revolutionary leader and the first president of the Democratic Republic of Việt Nam. Following each recitation, participants were tasked with commenting on the influence of Hồ Chí Minh's example on the course of their life actions.

At the Đồng Nai event, which I attended, solemn piano music accompanied each person's performance; each recitation prompt and corresponding commentary also concentrated on those of Hồ Chí Minh's activities that had been directed at children, poor people, elderly persons, and people with disadvantages. Two students from the EP were invited to perform at the program.¹⁰ Trang (who later appeared on "310 Years of Đồng Nai") presented a story from Hồ Chí Minh's life, which was accompanied by a reader—not an interpreter, but someone who recited the story as Trang signed. Later in the program one of Trang's junior classmates—whom I am calling Tân (see chapter 3)—signed in tandem with a recording of Thuận Yến's 1979 classic song "Bác Hồ một tình yêu bao" la [Uncle Ho, an Immense Love] (figure 6.9).

The audience comprised military personnel, a group of 10–15 Buddhist nuns, professional colleagues of the contestants (mostly academics), and EP students and staff. As Tân signed, I turned to scan the room. Audience members who had been slumped in their chairs were now leaning forward in their seats, craning to see Tân, some of them in tears.

Throughout the program, two HCMSL-Vietnamese interpreters from the EP also took turns simultaneously interpreting from the stage. According to the HCMSL-Vietnamese interpreters (one of them, an EP codirector), the presence of Deaf signers and interpreters was apparently so surprising to both in-house and home-viewing audiences that Đồng Nai Television invited the interpreters to interpret a show it was producing, *Gặp Gỡ Những Anh Hùng Thầm Lặng* [Meeting Silent Heroes], which aired on July 26, 2008, within a week of the first show. The focus of this program was elder society members, who told stories of their war time activities that had not been told before or socially recognized. During the airing of that program, hearing viewers called in to the television studio, saying, as one man reportedly did, "What am I seeing? I don't know what it is, but I like it!" (pers. comm. with interpreter). This viewer's response ("I don't know what it is, but I like it!") must be evaluated against the backdrop of the viewer's

---

9. None of the research participants who grew up in the south remembered seeing Deaf people or HCMSL-Vietnamese interpreters on television before 2008. By contrast, Deaf persons living in Hà Nội attested to the occasional HNSL-Vietnamese interpreter on television beginning in the early 2000s and also to the sporadic televised news story about activities conducted by the Hà Nội Association of the Deaf (Chi Hội Người Điếc Hà Nội).

10. Trang and Tân were not asked to join the competition but rather to perform as part of the evening's entertainment. Several groups of performers were featured: men in military dress who sang patriotic songs, and women who danced in *áo dài* [tunics and long, flowing pants deemed risqué during the revolutionary period of the 1920s and 1930s but now regarded as traditional feminine dress].

Figure 6.9. HCMSL performance of a popular song, "Bác Hồ một tình yêu bao la" [Uncle Ho, an Immense Love].

own experience with national modernization mandates and the television program's themes of colonial and U.S. occupation, national sacrifice, leadership, and ongoing market-socialist development. His positive response to "it" (i.e., HCMSL) suggests the material potency of embodied practices contextualized, in this case, to the contemporary promise of socialist incorporation by the homeland, as well as to the promise of recuperation through things such as technology (television) and new forms of expertise (interpretation) (figures 6.10).

These circumstances resemble those of the Nepalese case reported by Hoffman-Dilloway, in which deafness is widely attributed to karmic debt and whereby a new entrepreneurial positioning of d/Deaf people and signed language "helps constitute the hearing participant as modern and *bikashi* (developed)" (2011, p. 374). They also resemble the circumstances of the Chinese state's national recuperation of disability after Deng Pufeng (Deng Xiao Peng's son) survived, in an apparent suicide attempt, a fall from his dormitory room and went on to mobilize a disability movement within China and the establishment of a corresponding bio-bureaucracy (Kohrman, 2005).

In the instances of the Narrative Contest on the Moral Example of Hồ Chí Minh and the television program *Meeting Silent Heroes*, Deaf people's participation in these events and HCMSL-Vietnamese interpretation are both mobilized by the event organizers and television producers to establish Việt Nam's social and political leaders as people with new perspectives. Here, the nation is indexed as—much like Hoffman-Dilloway's example—*hiện đại* [modern], as well as *cởi mở* [open minded], as such programming literally includes the persons and the stories that prevsiouly had been excluded from mass social circulation.

Following Hoffman-Dilloway's analysis, HEARING audience members' interest in Deaf and non-Deaf persons' use of HCMSL heavily "relies on the semiotic associations with deafness," which has multiple and differential effects in the market-socialist moment for Deaf and non-Deaf persons (ibid.). Such effects are facilitated by the circumstances in which non-Deaf people's multilingualism is a highly valued skill in the context of the new service-oriented market, wherein the most highly sought employees are those who can accommodate Việt Nam's extensive tourism business in the language of individual travelers, who now also include Deaf tourists. It is in this context that multilingualism has also become a trope in Việt Nam for global knowledge, class mobility, and the possibility of foreign travel, study, or relocation. Nevertheless, whereas I often observed non-Deaf people positively evaluating each other's multilingualism—and was attributed with such evaluations myself—I did not observe non-Deaf people indexing Deaf people's multilingualism with positive commentary. For example, earlier I described how I joined HCMSL classes offered by the Development Center and the EP. In both locations, non-Deaf students often remarked to me about my signing ability and would even direct questions about the structure of HCMSL to me *rather than to their teacher*, who was present in the room. In these instances I attempted to redirect my fellow HCMSL classmates to our instructor; nevertheless, following their observation of my conversations with the HCMSL instructors, classmates often commented on my language skills rather than on their Deaf instructor's language ability and communication skills in conversing *with me*, a nonnative HCMSL user. That is, they ascribed to me a remarkable or unusual skill but did not seem to appreciate the fact that I was only able to communicate effectively because of our instructor's prodigious ability to facilitate linguistic production during our exchanges.

Ideological elevation of non-Deaf people's bilingualism in HCMSL-Vietnamese also contributes to this group's prevailing control over emergent government-subsidized HCMSL-Vietnamese interpretation employment, most conspicuously that of sign language–interpreted news programming, which has aired daily in both North and South Việt Nam since 2010. Deaf social leaders' concerns about interpretation quality—full and rich linguistic access to programming content—are evidenced in the HDC's requests for meetings with HTV9 programmers and their 2010 submission of a petition to the broadcast management to hire interpreters who use HCMSL. Their complaint centered on the fact that HTV9 had hired Deaf education special school teachers who used Sign-Supported Vietnamese and were not proficient in HCMSL. As this book goes to press, these same interpreters are still working for HTV9, with the effect that southern Deaf people widely report that they do not watch the "interpreted" news programming because they cannot understand it.

Despite growing interest in HCMSL beyond state institutions of education and training, presently there are no training programs offering ongoing instruction in HCMSL (or other VSLs) or signed/spoken-language interpretation. Although slated to be one of the EP's three core programmatic components, the HCMSL-Vietnamese interpreter-training track did not materialize until late 2012, and then only for in-house staff members. In the summer of 2015, the EP opened their

Figure 6.10. The HCMSL-interpreted television program, *Gặp Gỡ Những Anh Hùng Thầm Lặng* (*Meeting* Silent Heroes). Figure 6.10a. The television program with HCMSL-Vietnamese interpreter at lower right corner of screen. Figure 6.10b. Two HCMSL-Vietnamese interpreters watching the program.

in-house training courses to a small number of interpreters who had already received training through the World Concern Development Organization. A 2009 interview with one of the EP codirectors revealed that the interpreting track was not established earlier due to a number of factors, including lack of proficient signers ready for advanced training; lack of interpreter training faculty; and lack of state institutional infrastructure to pay for interpreter services. These circumstances began to change in 2012 with state support for INGO projects such as the *Intergenerational Deaf Education Outreach Project* that introduced methods for working with families, their Deaf children, and special school teachers to promote school readiness in VSLs and in written Vietnamese—and that featured a project component centered on VSLs-Vietnamese interpretation.

In the 2009 to 2016 period, VSLs-Vietnamese interpreting began to be recognized as a specialized discipline.[11] Remuneration has shifted dramatically in that interpreters are now being paid for their labor, as VTV9's contracts with local interpreters indicate. In 2009 one of the EP codirectors stated that Việt Nam possessed approximately 4–5 people working as interpreters in the North, while in the South approximately 10 people worked as interpreters; however, at that time, the EP codirector evaluated the professional preparation of interpreters in this way:

> Most of the interpreters in VN—we are called interpreters—but we ourselves know that we are not really interpreters yet because we don't have training. We don't have certification. We just do it because we know sign language, and we think we can help hearing and Deaf people communicate together. (Nguyễn in Cooper, 2009, p. 19)

It was in this context that the HDC teamed up with the director of an HCMC-based center for the research and education of children with disabilities, the EP codirectors, and me to host a signed/spoken-language interpreter-training workshop in February 2009. The next section describes the circumstances and outcomes of this workshop.

Hội Thảo: Thông Dịch Viên Ngôn Ngữ Ký Hiệu Tp.HCM
[HCMSL Interpreting Workshop]

In August 2008, HDC leaders discussed hosting an interpreting workshop. They approached me and asked whether I would teach it. My response was to suggest that they teach it themselves since they had long been involved in teaching Vietnamese HEARING people how to sign and, by the way they conducted everyday exchanges involving HCMSL and Vietnamese, also how to interpret. I agreed to join them in their preparations and to present content in the areas they deemed useful. Over the course of two months of preparation we met two to three times each week for

---

11. In September 2015 Hà Nội Sign Language–Vietnamese interpreters teamed up with members of the Hà Nội Association of the Deaf to establish the Hà Nội Team of Sign Language Interpreters (HTSLI). In addition to educating the public about Vietnamese Sign Language–Vietnamese interpreting, the team also offers a range of services, including HNSL-Vietnamese interpretation and Deaf and non-Deaf interpreters working in teams to advocate and provide communication services in family, medical, legal, and judicial situations (see https://www.youtube.com/watch?v=4ksIDTZoLPw). Unlike the HTSLI, HCMSL-Vietnamese interpreters in southern Việt Nam have not established public services or begun to professionalize.

approximately three hours each time. We discussed issues such as the content areas they wanted to cover, whom they might invite and how they wanted to approach prospective participants, and, given that we were sending out an invitation by email, how they wanted to screen prospective participants with whom they were unfamiliar.

Held the first weekend after the Tết holidays, the workshop was a two-day event attended by approximately forty people.[12] Next I describe details of the workshop announcement and participant selection. It is not my intention to belabor the description of the logistical arrangements. Nonetheless, these activities contain insights for ensuring the quality of workshop participation with respect to language proficiency and attitude toward the workshop topic and structure. They also secured the participation of credentialed Deaf HCMSL instructors and other Deaf people trained in the structure and analysis of HCMSL as the appropriate individuals to assess language proficiency. Finally, they guaranteed the participation of credentialed Deaf HCMSL instructors (as the most appropriate people for conducting training related to their language and sociocultural materials, as well as interpretation into Vietnamese). Whereas by 2009, the latter were well established in the EP, such ideas (social formations) were unfamiliar to most people outside the EP and had not been ratified by Deaf education special school administrators. In this context, these logistical details take on significance for Việt Nam and possibly other contexts that demand working through social-hearchical and/or bureaucratic channels in particular ways. Next I first discuss the logistics of screening prospective workshop attendees and then describe the workshop itself.

To announce the workshop, one EP codirector and I set up an email account from which to send out workshop-related correspondence, after which we drafted the training announcement. During that meeting, the EP codirector decided that it would be best to hold the workshop on an "invitation only" basis to ensure that those who attended were not simply curious onlookers but knew HCMSL to some degree and were also directly involved with Deaf people. The announcement included the requirement that participants contact the EP codirector to assess their appropriateness for participation.

One week after we sent out the workshop announcement we had received no responses. The following week I had a meeting scheduled with the principal of Hope A. During that meeting I inquired whether she had received the announcement. She said she had but that she did not reply because "we [Hope A personnel] do not know sign language very well, so it is not right for us." I explained that the HDC and the EP were aware that each special school used different signs. She appeared surprised and acknowledged that this was indeed the case. I said that the workshop was meant to start bringing the schools together so that they could share their knowledge and ideas. They might also learn some of the theories and techniques related to signed/spoken interpretation, which they might already be using but not be aware that they were doing so. She said she would like to attend and suggested two of her teachers as potential participants.

---

12. In my dissertation (2011) I reported that the workshop had 23 attendees. This number did not include the EP graduates, who played various roles in the workshop (e.g., presenting, facilitating rapport-building activities, documenting the event on film and in photos, and making logistical arrangements), the interpreters, or the director of the center hosting the workshop.

Given that I was neither a native HCMSL user nor trained in signed language teaching or linguistics, I arranged with the principal of Hope A to return the next week for a follow-up meeting so that a (Vietnamese Deaf) HCMSL instructor could assess the signing proficiency of prospective participants and confirm their registration. Another significant reason for collaborating with HCMSL instructors was so that local Deaf leaders—themselves HCMSL experts—controlled the process of determining workshop participation, also establishing their authority and legitimacy prior to the actual workshop event.

Conjecturing that the principals of the other schools might be responding to the workshop announcement with concerns similar to those of the principal of Hope A, I discussed the situation with HDC leaders and Mĩ. (Since January 2009 Mĩ had held a voluntary position as one of two HDC interpreters and also worked with me on a regular basis as a Vietnamese-English interpreter.) We all agreed that we wanted to approach the remaining four schools in a manner that communicated a warm welcome to join the workshop even if they were not confident in their own HCMSL proficiency. We also wanted to assure them that they would have access to the workshop activities. At the same time, we wanted them to understand that Deaf people would lead or co-lead all of the activities, which meant that the participants would need to come prepared to engage in the activities by signing.

Whereas we had structured the workshop activities to be conducted primarily in HCMSL, with approximately 75% of the activities interpreted into Vietnamese, it was essential that attendees have, at minimum, conversational skills in both receptive and productive modes (HCMSL comprehension and expression). Without such language knowledge, attendees would not have access to the workshop materials. Possibly most important of all, they would not have access to the HDC leaders' reflections on their experiences as former special school students, particularly their sense of sociolinguistic marginalization, though not necessarily *affective* marginalization. Many of the HDC leaders, in fact, expressed feelings of mutually shared affection with their former teachers (a number of whom ultimately attended the workshop).

To fulfill our planning objectives, we decided to make appointments with the principals of the remaining schools—Hope B, Hope C, DC1, and DC2—and asked them to invite teachers and/or staff that they thought possessed the best sign language skills. We did this through phone calls, as the principals seemed reluctant to discuss the workshop by email, having not answered our prior emails about the workshop.

We then decided to conduct the screening appointments as a team. The team members included an HCMSL instructor (who would explain the agenda for the workshop and observe the potential participants' conversational proficiency), Mĩ (who would interpret between HCMSL and Vietnamese, and between English and Vietnamese when necessary), and me (I would explain both the rationale for the workshop and the expectations for participants' experiential/learning outcomes). Two of the five principals and their school personnel used Sign-Supported Vietnamese (see chapter 3); two principals did not use any signs; and one principal (Hope C) declined both the appointment to discuss the workshop and participation in it (for herself and her school personnel). Altogether, our three-member team conducted four screening appointments. These concluded with the HCMSL instructor interviewing each prospective candidate by asking a few questions about the candidate's background, training, interest in the workshop, and commitment to attending the entire workshop (a whole weekend). For each school appointment we found that all of the principals and teachers were interested in the workshop, even though many of them did not meet selection criteria because of their lack of signing ability. Despite their lack of signing ability, the HCMSL instructors and Mĩ expressed surprise that school personnel were quite willing to have a HCMSL instructor assess their signing ability with the hope that they have a chance to attend. Ultimately, four schools decided to participate, with over forty participants in attendance. The participants were principals and assistant principals (whom we invited whether they knew how to sign or not): twenty-three special school teachers and principals (all were able to use signs to some degree, typically SSV); fifteen EP graduates, all of whom were active in various workshop roles; two language researchers, a linguist and I; two interpreters (one who worked in HCMSL-Vietnamese and the other, in Vietnamese-English); and the director of the center for research on and the education of children with disabilities, who hosted the event in her facility.

Once information got out about the upcoming workshop, non-Deaf people began approaching the HDC to request participation. These individuals included special school personnel whom we had not met in the screening appointments, children and friends of Deaf adults, and those who were simply interested in the topic. Because of this show of interest, we held an open assessment and registration during one of the HDC's weekly meetings: Only two people showed up, however, and they did not possess the requisite proficiency in sign language. From this we surmised that, aside from the usual schedule conflicts, a number of people were simply curious about the emergent area of HCMSL-Vietnamese interpretation; nonetheless, such curiosity required more than an occasional workshop.

The workshop consisted of two days of activities, beginning with the HCMC Deaf Club's invitation to workshop participants to attend its regular Saturday morning meeting from 9 to 11 AM. After lunch, the workshop opened with welcoming remarks from the HDC chair and the director of the program allowing the HCMC Deaf Club and the EP to use her space. Day one consisted of four presentations and one activity: First, an introduction, given by two senior EP students in HCMSL, and a PowerPoint translation in Vietnamese described the focus of the workshop (Vietnamese Deaf people who use a VSL). These presentations were contextualized by a brief history of Deaf education in Việt Nam, including the pioneering work of hearing people who had learned a VSL and interpreted between hearing and Deaf people without pay. During the next presentation, titled the History of Interpreting Models, I focused on notions about Deaf people and sign languages (medical model, social model, linguistic model) and invited participants to identify what models they had observed or used in Việt Nam. The following presentation, titled Deaf Socialization Experiences in Việt Nam, included 8–10 narratives given by different signers, who expressed the feelings associated with being denied the use of sign language at home and at school. Then, Visual World, a socialization icebreaker, used colored gamecards that the participants exchanged for small gifts. This was followed by the main lecture of the day: With several EP senior students as copresenters, the EP director discussed the linguistics of HCMSL.

The EP director's lecture made such a strong impression on the special school principals and teachers that the EP director agreed to come back the next day to continue the description of HCMSL structure and its comparison to Vietnamese and other languages (spoken and signed). This was followed by three other workshop segments: (1) HCMSL Discourse Structure and Features, presented by two HCMSL instructors, followed by participants who identified these elements in an HCMSL presentation; (2) Cointerpreting Techniques, where I discussed, using the same video clip, discourse structuring, clarification, and other techniques employed by the signer and the interpreter; (3) in Text Analysis I and Text Analysis II, I presented two short lectures on textual analysis of HCMSL and Vietnamese, each followed by group activities. We ended the workshop by then opening the floor to comments by participants. These comments (both during and after the workshop) revealed an array of school personnel perspectives of Deaf people, sign language, and educational and social needs (as the segments included in chapter 5 suggest).

At the end of the interpreting workshop the principal of Hope A opened the comment period by saying (in Vietnamese, with Mĩ translating for me): "This weekend I learned many things during the workshop that I had not had the opportunity to learn before. But we need this workshop for our teachers. The teachers who work with Deaf students every day do not have this information." She then turned to the HDC leaders and the EP students, seated in rows to her right, and signed to them: "You taught me today. Several of you were my students [at Hope A]. I want to say I am sorry. I did not understand about HCMSL. I hope that you will come to my school and talk to my students, teach my students." Approximately six other participants spoke, thanking the presenters for the workshop and asked when the next workshop would be. They then requested, if there were a next workshop that it focus on instructional methods rather than interpretation; they said that they needed tools for the classroom immediately and that interpreter training could follow.[13] Follow-up interviews with the principals of Hope A and Hope B, as well as the HDC co-organizers, showed both overlapping and contrasting interests regarding future training needs (discussed later).

I met with the principals of Hope A and Hope B approximately one week after the interpreting workshop. At that time, both principals informed me that they had contacted each other, as well as the IE director (see chapter 5), to discuss inviting the EP director to host a teacher-training workshop. The principal of Hope A expressed her changed perspective about sign language and teacher training in this way:

> For us leaders in the schools, we don't have the opportunity to study the education of Deaf children, so we don't understand clearly. This is the first thing. And the interpreting program—this is very necessary . . .
>
> We need training. When normal people see something a Deaf person writes, just two or three phrases, we know who wrote it—Deaf or hearing. We know right away. Before we would see the difference in the way they write, but we didn't know *why* they wrote this way [emphasis in the original]. [The EP director] explained and now we know.
>
> So [before] when we ask questions in class and the students answer the wrong way, we don't know why. We [teachers] have a habit of saying *"người Điếc ngược"* or "they speak the wrong way." So, for example, when [the EP director] showed us the Japanese

---

13. Several months after the interpreting workshop the EP director and codirector held a one-day workshop just for teachers.

sentence and asked us if the Japanese person speaks the wrong way—but, of course, we don't say it's the "wrong way"—we say they speak Japanese! This is also true for sign language.

The principal of Hope B made very similar remarks regarding her own shifting perspective on sign language and the need for teacher training:

> The [EP director]'s example made the point that we would never say the Japanese language is "ungrammatical." So that means that if the grammar of the Deaf is okay—this is no problem—we have to accept it. We should not correct them. Before, we corrected them. We told them they are wrong. We should not tell them they are wrong. But the problem is that we have to know the right way to teach them how to write Vietnamese. Because we have a different grammar. We don't know how to change from the grammar of sign language to the grammar of Vietnamese. That's the problem right now.

I replied: "Yet there are still many people who believe that you should not use sign language to teach Deaf students. What would you say to them?" The principal of Hope B answered: "The way we will convince teachers is by bringing Deaf people to meet with them and talk as we are now, then ask the Deaf person if they understood what we just said. We must talk directly with teachers." I followed this by asking: "What if the teacher says that her students understand her just fine?" The principal replied: "No! They don't understand. They don't understand . . . because I look at their [the Deaf pupils'] faces! The teachers must learn, and they must accept this." The principal went on to describe how she wished that the HCMSL instructors from the EP would train her teachers how to sign and described how one of her own students—Minh Hai—had "opened my mind"; however, she added, she had not been able to invite him to teach because, since the HCMSL teachers do not hold university certificates, the state will not reimburse the school for their work.

The principals of both Hope A and Hope B agreed that teachers required training first and that HCMSL-Vietnamese interpreting should come later, after enough people had developed sufficient skill in HCMSL. The principal of Hope B described the situation in this way:

> Right now *all* of the schools don't have so much sign language. So they worry if—for example—if I don't have so much sign language, then I can't interpret. That's right. So we want so much to learn sign language. Then after that, we learn to interpret. First study sign language and when we know that more, then study interpreting. I think that's okay. In the future, for example [gets paper], suppose you want HCMC to have many interpreters for the Deaf children. In 10 years [she draws a horizontal line on the page and writes "10 years" at the right end of the line, then bisects the horizontal line with a vertical line]. So first, for five years they study sign language (she traces the horizontal line from the beginning to the midpoint—this is 5 years— after that, they are ready to [study] interpreting (she traces from the 5-year mark to the 10-year mark with her pen). It's okay.

In a group interview with nine of the HCMC Deaf Club leaders and Senior EP students who had cohosted and presented the interpreter workshop, all agreed that special school teachers in particular needed to be trained on the use of HCMSL and visual teaching methods. However, rather than postponing interpreter training until these special school teachers developed a certain level of fluency (as one of the EP directors recommended), the HCMSL instructors stated that they would prefer that special school teachers be exposed to interpreting methods earlier, regardless of proficiency, so that they might begin practicing HCMSL and interpreting skills during school assemblies and meetings with school visitors.

They also added an unusual perspective on who might make both the best HCMSL and interpreting students: *people who are unfamiliar with the special school system*. Trang stated:

> The special school teachers have a hard time learning sign language. For many years they believed signing was wrong, so it is hard for them to change now. We had the same experience in the EP. The teachers who had the most difficulty were teachers who used to teach in the special school. Even when we teach them the grammar of HCMSL, they sign and speak at the same time. It is better to find people interested in sign language and let Deaf people teach them the right way.

Whereas the special school principals believed that special schools would benefit the most from HCMSL training and that such instruction should start there, these HCMSL instructors themselves placed their hopes of expanding hearing people's knowledge and use of HCMSL outside the special school system. Moreover, they saw the possibility of training special school teachers in HCMSL and interpreting methods not as an either/or proposition but as something that could happen simultaneously, possibly in tandem with training for community-based interpreters.

According to interviews with other workshop participants (teachers, one interpreter from Hà Nội), this workshop made, on one hand, a "big impact"; on the other hand, participants said it would be necessary to require the ongoing study of sign language structure, as well as the theories and techniques of interpretation, in order to make any real change following from theoretical understanding. Three of the interviewees saw the EP director as the only resource present in Việt Nam for delivering teacher training, and two saw HCMSL instructors as resources for the language instruction of special school teachers. However, at the time of the interviews, interviewees talked about plans to appeal to the voluntary participation of the EP directors and EP graduates to conduct such activities rather than go through official channels, such as the special education training programs at HCMC Pedagogic University. Thus, in these comments, the circumstances of the gap between state educational mandates and state-subsidized training remained, for the most part, implied (as they do at the time of this writing). See also Cooper and Nguyễn (2015) for a microanalysis of one example of the ways in which HDC leaders and language researchers collaborated on the presentation of linguistic information, which resulted in facilitating shifts in language ideologies among the workshop participants.

HCMSL Teaching and State Recognition

When Deaf social organizers established the HDC in December 2008, they also began offering HCMSL classes to the community. These classes were initially geared toward HEARING community members, but when Deaf people who had little or no opportunity to attend school and/or little or no contact with other Deaf adults began attending the club meetings, the HDC decided to also offer HCMSL classes to Deaf community members.

During the research period, the weekly meetings of the HCMC Deaf Club that I attended included frequent reference to the HCMSL classes, as well as to strategies specifically for increasing HEARING people's attendance at these classes. In 2008 and 2009, a questionnaire given to 38 non-Deaf HCMSL students taking classes from EP-trained instructors illuminates these circumstances further.[14] The *Bảng Câu Hỏi Dành Cho Người Học NNKH Tp. HCM* [Questionnaire for Hồ Chí Minh City Sign Language Students] contained the following nine questions:

1. *Bạn đã học NNKH được bao lâu rồi?*
2. *Có bao nhiêu giáo viên dạy NNKH mà bạn đã được học?*
3. *Điều gì đã làm bạn quyết định tham gia vào lớp học NNKH?*
4. *Điều gì dễ học và dễ tiếp thu trong khi bạn học NNKH?*
5. *Điều gì khó học và khó tiếp thu trong khi bạn học NNKH?*
6. *Bạn đã có biết người Điếc nào không trước khi bạn học NNKH? Nếu có, bạn đã giao tiếp với người Điếc như thế nào?*
7. *Bạn không biết gì về người Điếc trước khi tham gia vào lớp học NNKH, và nay là một học sinh trong lớp học NNKH, những điều nào bạn đã học được khi tham gia vào lớp học này (những điều có liên quan đến người Điếc), điều trước đây bạn chưa được biết?*
8. *Khi tham gia vào lớp học NNKH, những người bạn của bạn hoặc gia đình của bạn đã có ý kiến gì về việc học NNKH của bạn?*
9. *Sau khi kết thúc khóa học NNKH này, bạn có quyết định tiếp tục tham gia vào khóa học kế tiếp không? Tại sao?*
   1. How long have you studied HCMSL?
   2. How many teachers have you had?
   3. What made you interested in studying HCMSL?
   4. What do you find easy about learning HCMSL?
   5. What do you find difficult about learning HCMSL?
   6. Did you know Deaf people before learning HCMSL? If yes, how did you communicate?
   7. As a student of HCMSL, what have you learned about Deaf people that you did not before?

---

14. The EP-trained HCMSL instructors and I developed the questionnaire to elicit feedback on questions directly applicable to their teaching and so that I might learn more about non-Deaf persons' motivations to learn HCMSL. Regarding the administration of the questionnaire, when I initially approached Mỹ Uyên about the questionnaire, she asked Mĩ (former EP staff member and interpreter) and me to come to her class so that students could have an opportunity to ask her questions (in Vietnamese) about HCMSL and her experience as a Deaf person and an instructor. This first survey and Mỹ Uyên's question-and-answer period dovetailed. Minh Hai then distributed the questionnaire to his class of four students in July 2008. In February 2009, Minh Hai and three other teachers collected 28 additional surveys. Mỹ Uyên's class was the only class for which I was present during the survey.

8. What do your friends or family members say about you studying HCMSL?
9. Will you continue studying HCMSL after this course is finished? Why/why not?

Student responses to Question 3 (What made you interested in studying HCMSL?) were particularly interesting to the HCMSL instructors and to me. They included thirteen different reasons for the students' interest in HCMSL. Two of these occurred more frequently than the rest. Fourteen respondents (36.8%) reported that they wanted to communicate with Deaf people, and seven respondents (18.4 %) said that, later on, they wanted to teach Deaf students as paid employment. In answer to Question 9 (Will you continue studying HCMSL after this course is finished?), all of the respondents replied in the affirmative; nine respondents (23.7%) said they could not, however, continue to study HCMSL if doing so did not help them get a job afterward.

These findings have a bearing on the interpreting workshop inasmuch as the attendees were very interested in how the workshop might help them improve the quality of instruction in their Deaf education special schools and their knowledge of HCMSL and interpreting skills. Because special schools are often the first place that the police or the court system turns to when Deaf persons are either charged with or are a victim of a crime, these reasons are plausible.[15]

State Recognition of the Hồ Chí Minh City Deaf Club and Countrywide Deaf Clubs and Associations

In early 2008, HDC leaders and membership began to request official recognition of the HDC. Contacting representatives in MOLISA, they were originally told that they must first establish chapters in each of Việt Nam's 58 provinces and 5 municipalities (Cần Thơ, Đà Nẵng, Hà Nội, Hải Phòng, and Hồ Chí Minh City). Later that year they were told by a different MOLISA representative that they must establish chapters in at least 50% of the provinces (approximately 30 sites). One of the EP codirectors told me

---

15. At all of the Deaf education special school sites and the EP, the research participants reported that the police routinely contacted them when they arrested Deaf people. The courts did the same when Deaf people appeared in court, as either defendants or plaintiffs. Mĩ explained that, the first time she interpreted for the court, she was still an employee at Hope C. At that time she knew only speech-based methods, so she expected the Deaf defendant to use spoken Vietnamese. He did not, however, and when he tried to do so, she could not understand him. Now, after having worked for the EP for 16 years, Mĩ uses HCMSL when she is asked to interpret at the police station or in court. According to one of the EP codirectors and Mĩ, in the latter part of the first decade of the twenty-first century and the early 2010s, neither the police nor the courts considered HCMSL-Vietnamese interpretation as a profession. For example, in the spring of 2009 Mĩ was asked to interpret for a court case involving a robbery. During the trial, which lasted a week, she went to the courthouse every day, worked alone, and at the end of the week the court officials did not thank her for her work; rather, a lower-echelon administrator called her into his office and gave her 50.000 Vietnamese Dong, the equivalent of about $3 dollars US, and excused her from his office. Mĩ considered this an affront and said: "It would be better if he had just said 'thank you.'" Note that, because HCMSL-Vietnamese interpreting was not a recognized profession, Mĩ could not request payment for services; yet Vietnamese norms of cultural and economic propriety would reasonably lead to financial compensation that recognized she devoted a week of her work life to the court system.

that this is a regulation of the Vietnamese National Coordinating Council on Disability, established circa 1987–1988. At that time, the EP codirector surmised that, if even 20 clubs could be established, that number would be convincing enough to achieve official status.

At the July 26, 2008, meeting of the HCMC Deaf Club, official recognition was discussed at length. Deaf Club leaders described the differential positions of Deaf organizations and blind organizations. It was their understanding, Deaf Club leaders told the membership, that there were far fewer blind than Deaf persons in Việt Nam; however, the government had conferred official recognition on organizations of blind people because they had a preponderance of members who had served in the various wars. Deaf organizations were therefore at a disadvantage, the club leaders argued, either by not having national recognition of war service or by not being able to prove the existence of war service. Deaf Club members talked about how they might locate Deaf persons who had served in a war and bring them forward for recognition. They also talked about who might be appropriate intermediaries to assist them in bringing their interest in official recognition to sympathetic government agents, such as judges. In order to represent their position, they would also need to increase the pool of interpreters on whom they could rely. With only two volunteer interpreters available to the HDC, such circumstances limited the number and frequency of advocacy meetings the HDC leaders and members could pursue.

HDC leaders hoped they could use the then upcoming January 2009 meeting of the Asia-Pacific Development Center on Disability to raise the issue of official recognition and related concerns. At that meeting of the HDC, club leaders used the first part of the meeting to do a practice run of the presentation they planned to give at the APCD in Hà Nội. In their talk, the club leaders introduced a 12-point program for national Deaf cooperation, in which they emphasized the importance of building a national system of Deaf clubs. At the club's February 21, 2009, meeting, the four representatives who had attended the APCD meeting reported on their presentation. Their comments focused on six topics covered during the APCD meetings: establishment of Deaf clubs; "OPPRESSION" of Deaf students by special school teachers; unemployment; potential membership in the World Federation of the Deaf; state recognition of VSLs; and the establishment of democratic voting procedures for selecting club leadership. Their comments also included a topic they encountered, and later addressed, at the APCD meeting: the need for training and remuneration of HCMSL-Vietnamese interpreters.

In an interview, the four Deaf club representatives who had participated in the APCD meeting recounted several issues regarding interpreters that had arisen prior to and during that meeting. The first involved APCD's expectation that the HCMC Deaf Club and the Development Center's Hearing Impaired Club would attend the meeting as one combined club representing HCMC. In chapter 3 I describe the formation of the HDC, which was prompted by the HIC leaders' refusal to allow the club members to vote and also participate in the selection of HIC leaders. A related contention was the form of language (Sign-Supported Vietnamese, speaking in Vietnamese while signing in Vietnamese word order) promoted by the HIC leaders. At issue for the HDC leaders at the APCD meeting thus was not that the HDC and the HIC were attending the meeting together; rather, it was APCD's assumption that all Deaf participants from HCMC shared a language and that they would therefore communicate by means of a single interpreter. According to the APCD's decision, this would be the same interpreter who had been appointed president of the Hearing Impaired Club and who signed in Vietnamese word order. Both the HDC chair and one of the EP codirectors attempted to explain to the APCD the differences between HCMSL and SSV, as well as the historical difficulties between the leadership of the two clubs. The APCD relented and allowed the HDC to bring its own interpreter; however, the APCD did not remunerate the interpreter for her services.[16]

Once the HDC participants arrived at the meeting, however, they were confronted by APCD organizers, who wanted the HDC and the HIC interpreters to work together, taking turns interpreting for the whole audience. The HDC representatives had to explain yet again that two different kinds of interpreting were happening in the room (i.e., HCMSL and SSV). Following this discussion, APCD facilitators agreed to allow both sets of interpreters to work simultaneously and only for their designated groups.

The APCD's demands on the Deaf social organizers is hardly unique. Deaf club leaders and members were constantly being put in a position of having to explain the legitimacy of HCMSL. Further, their requests for HCMSL-Vietnamese interpretation were a precursor to advocacy for institutional and policy change in education, employment, and government recognition of civil society membership organizations. This situation is emblematic of official responses to HDC leaders' efforts to gain recognition for HCMSL as a language and recognition for Deaf-led local and national clubs and associations. As of 2016 more than 24 Deaf clubs were functioning throughout the country. In 2013 and 2014, the President of the World Federation of the Deaf (WFD), Colin Allen, visited Việt Nam on two occasions, and provided leadership training to national Deaf leaders, as well as met with various ministry officials and INGO partners. In 2016, WFD Vice-President Joseph Murray also visited Việt Nam, attending meetings of local Deaf Clubs and Associations throughout the country. The Hội Người Khuyết Tật Tp. Hà Nội [Hà Nội Association of People with Disabilities, or HNAPWD] was officially established on May 15, 2009, by the Hà Nội People's Committee Decision no. 2270 QĐ-UBND. Since that time, the HNAPWD has convened meetings to discuss signed language training and official recognition for the nation's Deaf clubs (see the introduction to chapter 2). However, Deaf people are not always present at these meetings. An additional force that constrains the leadership potential of Vietnamese Deaf

---

16. APCD's track record in providing access to Deaf participants has been disappointing. In 1996, Eiichi Takada, then director of the World Federation of the Deaf's regional secretariat for the Asia and Pacific region, reported that when he attended Campaign '95, an APCD conference held in Jakarta, Indonesia, to prepare for the Asia-Pacific Decade of Disabled Persons, the APCD failed to provide interpreters for local attendees. Takada had brought his own interpreters. He halted the meeting and requested that Japanese Sign Language interpreters interpret from the podium. "This request was granted," reported Takada to the World Federation of the Deaf News, and, with this, "the participants became aware of the Deaf presence at the conference" (Takada, 1996, p. 28). More than 12 years later, the January 2009 meeting of APCD in Hà Nội demonstrated no improvement in the APCD's accountability for interpreting services.

people is control exerted by non-Deaf and non-signing people with disabilities over disability related activities.

Engaging the Vietnamese State through Active Deaf Citizenship

From late to January to March 2009, Deaf club leaders addressed the topic of obtaining official membership at nearly every meeting. Club leaders from Hà Nội were invited to attend one of these meetings and to join the discussion about creating a shared agenda for the building of national clubs. At another meeting, HDC leaders invited club members who had relocated to HCMC from other cities to talk about Deaf organizing in their home cities. In the latter meeting, two women took the platform and talked about their Deaf club in Đà Nẵng, which they described as small and poor. After they spoke, the club chair (Su) thanked the two women and applauded the existence of the Đà Nẵng Deaf club. Su then turned to the membership and encouraged everyone to stay in contact with Deaf people back home and to help them organize:

> When you go back to Đà Nẵng, or Đà Lạt, or wherever your family home is (quê hương), it does not matter if you have only 15 or 20 people. Get together, talk, share ideas, stay in contact. Your Deaf clubs will grow. And it is important that we each do that because it helps all of us develop. Like Japan [where the chair had participated in Deaf leadership training]. They started with just one club and now they have 47 . . . 47![17]

Adding to Su's comments, Trang[18] (who was then an HDC leader and who had also attended the APCD meeting), stated that, even in bigger cities like Hải Phòng, Deaf clubs have few members and little or no sign language interpreting. She then emphasized that national affiliation would allow all of the Deaf clubs to share funds and other resources as needed.

The issues the four HDC representatives raised at the APCD meeting reflected discussions held with the club membership over the preceding months. For example, at the July 19, 2008, meeting of the HDC, a question from a member regarding the practice of taking weekly attendance occasioned a discussion about the overall purpose of the club. The HDC leaders explained their interests in organizing as a club as one of social integration, in which Deaf people must first: (1) help Deaf members who need to learn sign language; (2) foster national Deaf equality; (3) organize the public education of hearing people;[19] and (4) respond to Deaf detractors.

During a discussion of Deaf equality, for example, one HDC leader implored, "If you meet a Deaf person who does not know sign language, do you walk away? No! Tell them

---

17. As of July 2010 the Development Center's HIC and the HCMC Deaf Cultural Club were both unofficial groups.

18. Each reference to Trang refers to the same individual—a former EP student and graduate who also appeared in "310 Years of Đồng Nai" and the "Narrative Contest."

19. During discussion of the public education of hearing people another club leader said, When you meet hearing people and they ask about Deaf people or sign language, it is important that you give them the right information. Some Deaf people do not know what to say. These are things we talk about here.

about the club!" During a discussion of Deaf detractors, HDC leaders referenced the split between the Development Center's HIC and the HDC, and one leader counseled: "If you meet Deaf people who have never attended the HDC but say it is not good, you decide what is right. If they do not give you clear reasons why the HDC is not good, do not follow them. Also, invite them to the HDC so they may decide for themselves." This discussion, lasting approximately 20 minutes, was followed by one on the social changes necessary to allow Deaf people living in HCMC and throughout the country to contribute to Vietnamese society more fully: (1) closed-captioning of television programming; (2) training and provision of VSLs-Vietnamese interpreters in schools, hospitals, and workplaces; (3) Deaf teachers and hearing teachers proficient in sign language in the special schools, and (4) Deaf people learning and using their own languages in school.

In the HDC's organizing activities described earlier, a connection is discernible between certain structural changes (e.g., the use and study of sign language in school, Deaf teachers, telecommunications access, employment) and the promotion of VSLs broadly with the aim of encouraging their use of VSLs by both HEARING and Deaf citizens. With respect to the promotion of VSLs among Deaf populations, HDC discussions focused on access to education and the establishment of Deaf clubs using local VSLs. Discussion of the promotion of VSLs among hearing populations focused on signed language instruction for families and teachers working with Deaf students and, increasingly over the research period, the training of VSL-Vietnamese interpreters. Next I describe the emphasis of each of these discussions.

With respect to encouraging the use of VSLs among Deaf populations, having confronted the Development Center's HIC leadership for barring Deaf people from leadership positions and their refusal to use HCMSL, HDC organizers sought to establish an organization run by Deaf and hard of hearing people who agreed to use HCMSL, as well as other VSLs (for instance, when people visited the club from other provinces and cities). Unlike in Japan, where D-Pro leaders are breaking away from the Japanese Federation of the Deaf in order to establish a "separatist Deaf identity" based on the "American cultural Deaf model" and the promotion of "pure" sign language (Nakamura, 2006, pp. 1–2), HDC leaders aimed for maximum inclusion of those who were either already using or wanted to learn how to use a VSL. The use of văn hóa [lit., culture] in the HDC's (actual) name thus follows a practice begun under late socialism. This practice marks group-associative gatherings according to their status as Vietnamese cultural affiliations and shared traditions; therefore, văn hóa modifies "Vietnamese" as much as it modifies "Deaf."

By instantiating the descriptor văn hóa, Deaf club leaders connected the activities of marginalized Deaf populations to both a socialist discourse and a discourse of heritage or tradition. This identifies the HDC as distinctly Vietnamese and as a distinct entity of the national socialist project. Thus, the model of sociolinguistic organizing and identity strongly in evidence throughout this study was not separatist but complexly participatory and oriented toward citizenship in a national community and, according to HDC leaders, a *Vietnamese* language.[20]

---

20. See Burch (2000) for a discussion of similar findings in her examination of Deaf linguistic identity in Russia.

One indication of the HDC's national citizenship interests is its prioritizing of club activities. For instance, official recognition of the HDC was prioritized because, without that approval, the group could be disbanded. Moreover, and primarily, without such validation, the HDC would not be "REAL [TÍNH CHÍNH]" to the Vietnamese state. The HDC leaders prioritized state recognition of VSLs, and HCMSL specifically, because VSLs were what they as Vietnamese Deaf people actually use to communicate with one another and also the medium through which they had improved their lives. They wanted similar benefits for other Deaf people as well, beginning with Deaf children, the majority of whom, they were aware, were not attending school. By contrast, although HDC leaders and members engaged in certain self-identificatory practices among themselves—claiming differing identities such as DIÉC and half hearing/half Deaf—disputing identificatory labels attributed to them by others was not a priority for them.

Thus, even though individual and group interviews with EP students and HDC leaders revealed a preference for *người Điếc* [Deaf person] and a rejection of *khiếm thính* [having a hearing impairment]—for instance, by instructing HCMSL students to refer to them as *người Điếc*—I did not observe them ever correcting anyone's use of *khiếm thính* or other classificatory labels. Rather, during interviews the latter research participants emphasized what the use of *khiếm thính* suggested to them about special school teachers' and policymakers' understanding of Vietnamese sign languages. To them, HEARING people's use of *người Điếc* and *khiếm thính* served as a measure of the effectiveness of their own activities on a Deaf self-determining form of social inclusion (e.g., teaching HCMSL classes, giving newspaper interviews), specifically, citizenship according to Vietnamese sign languages. For these research participants, the conditions of living were at issue, not forms of labels. To address the conditions of living, HDC leaders aimed to increase the participation of Deaf people in the club and in advocacy activities related to the various VSLs as legitimate Vietnamese linguistic and cultural expression.

One of the ways in which the HDC leaders encourage participation in club activities is by attending to issues of language variability. In southern Việt Nam, the multiple sign language varieties correspond to the various special schools—as classroom ecolects, not necessarily instructional modalities (see also LeMaster, 2003; Nakamura, 2006; and Reilly & Reilly, 2005).[21] This presented HDC leaders with the challenge of creating an inclusive setting in which language variety could be negotiated. Aware that Deaf people continue to be linguistically isolated from one another, from 2008 to 2010, HDC leaders rarely referred to the form of sign language used in the club as "HCMSL." Instead, in seeming acknowledgment of the actual or imagined local sign language varieties in circulation, they typically used the broadly conventionalized term [fluent] signing (see discussion in chapter 3 and figure 3.4). Moreover, if individual club members used Sign-Supported Vietnamese or signing in Vietnamese word order, HDC leaders did not decry such practices; rather, they maintained the use of HCMSL in their activities and routinely checked with the audience regarding their comprehension of their own and other signers' comments.

---

21. LeMaster (2003), Nakamura (2006), and Reilly and Reilly (2005) document the development of sign language varieties in Ireland, Japan, and Thailand, respectively, which have emerged in the context of peer and cohort use (i.e., not via direct instruction or the use as the language of instruction).

The HDC leaders' rationale for using the more general term [FLUENT] SIGNING rather than HCMSL is reflected in comments made by the club chair, Su, during an individual interview:

> We are Vietnamese. And we are Deaf. Now that Deaf people have a chance to meet, we talk together easily. But we want to contribute to Vietnamese society. So we need to find a way to break down the barriers so that Deaf people can participate in society. The way to do that is through forming more clubs so that the government will recognize us and through teaching hearing people how to sign.

The chair's remarks connect an emergent Deaf linguistic identity with ongoing national development, particularly the growth of Vietnamese "society" (*xã hội*). They do not, however, invoke a national agenda pursued by a separate-leaning Deaf nation, nor do they stress deafness at all. Rather, they mirror the comments of EP-trained HCMSL instructors, four of whom were also HDC leaders (between 2008 and 2010) and one of whom was HDC president in 2016. These people were also core research participants, and I talked with them at length during the approximately 20 hours of working sessions to prepare for the interpreting workshop. Through Công, these research participants told me the following:

> In the workshop activities we don't want to focus on differences between Deaf and hearing people. We want to focus on what Deaf and hearing people share. We are all Vietnamese. And we can all contribute to Vietnamese society. If we show them [workshop participants] how we are connected, they may understand how we feel and why it is important to use sign language.

The first way in which the HDC leaders sought to help connect hearing people and Deaf people was to offer classes in HCMSL. Around 5–6 HCMSL instructors taught HCMSL classes on Saturdays following the club meeting and on Sundays, in both the morning and afternoon. During the weekly club meetings, the leaders encouraged the membership to invite hearing friends, family members, and other associates to the classes so they could develop their signing skills. Although these classes maintained a relatively stable census, HCMSL instructors complained, during individual and group interviews, that none of the students who completed the Level 1 HCMSL courses went on to Level 2. Thus, even though the classes remained full, they always contained new students. This put the instructors in the position of always teaching Level 1, never allowing them to get experience teaching advanced coursework or to prepare advanced students for the study of interpretation. As previous discussion of my survey of HCMSL students indicates, survey responses indicated that the reality of earning a living conflicted with the reality that learning and using a VSL had, at that time (2008) little professional presence or monetary value in Việt Nam. In 2016, this situation had improved somewhat, and interpreters were able to find contractual and even full-time employment for particular INGO projects. However, given that no VSL-Vietnamese training programs are publicly available and no mechanism exists for assessing interpreter quality, signed/spoken language interpretation is an area that warrants a great deal of attention and funding. This holds for professional practice development, professional assessment and credentialing, processes for ethical practice violations, and related research.

All of these descriptions of HCMC Deaf Club activities and objectives, including teaching HCMSL, training interpreters, pursuing official recognition, and using peer training to teach presentation skills to club members (see also chapter 5), coalesce around the expansion of Vietnamese Deaf social interest beyond the borders of Deaf community activity. Indeed, in order to carry out Deaf club objectives, club leaders instantiate "languages of stateness" both to advocate Deaf participation in the state (e.g., official recognition) and to critique the lack of opportunity thereof (e.g., access to education in VSL) (Hansen & Stepputat, 2001, p. 8; see also chapter 2).

During the research period, HDC initiatives also increasingly aimed at both drawing in various Deaf and hard of hearing constituencies in HCMC and aligning with Deaf groups from cities and rural villages throughout the country toward a project of national recognition. Seeking such recognition according to a Vietnamese language (i.e., HCMSL) entails negotiating a system of hierarchies through forms the state already recognizes. It is to assert a place within that system that, implicitly, reinforces the legitimacy of those hierarchies. At the same time, to claim HCMSL as a Vietnamese language implicitly challenges the linguistic and embodied foundation of those hierarchies and the modern socialist project.

In 2003, Woodward's research on Vietnamese sign linguistic and social identity found that HCMSL users had a distinct Deaf identity but not a national Deaf identity (2003, p. 295). The data discussed here suggest that such conditions are now undergoing transformation. Currently, HDC initiatives aim at deepening organizational ties to Deaf clubs throughout the country, promoting the establishment of a Vietnamese National Association of the Deaf, and invoking Deaf people as a Vietnamese cultural group. These actions form a strong response to government policies and practices that presently undermine the use of VSLs and Deaf social participation.

In contrast to the form of signing that Deaf students routinely encounter in national special schools (e.g., spoken Vietnamese with or without signing in Vietnamese word order), the HDC also aims to promote social understanding of VSLs as natural forms of language. If it is citizenship "which names the new status of life as the origin and ground of sovereignty," it is such differently configured notions of citizenship that the state may perceive as a threat to sovereignty (Agamben, 1998, p. 129). Regulation and disciplining of sign language use and Deaf self-determination within and outside the special school system preempt Deaf claims to citizenship, transforming *Deaf people as Vietnamese citizens using different Vietnamese languages* into *defective persons with a diminished citizenship capacity*. The activities of the HCMC Deaf Club thereby aim to recuperate Deaf people as Vietnamese nationals and VSLs as Vietnamese languages, instantiating signing citizenship as a historically deep variety of Vietnameseness.

Conclusion

The market-socialist futures examined in this chapter are clearly already under way. New legal frameworks have created substantial opportunities for Deaf people to engage in social organizing and employment activities. At the same time, these legal frameworks have facilitated new forms of control over Deaf people's labor, languages, and citizenship contributions. Among the forms of state-society control of Vietnamese Deaf and signing people examined in this chapter is the role of censorship by proxy, wherein agents of the state (such as broadcast production crews) limit the use, and thereby the circulation, of HCMSL. My search of the Ministry of Information and Communication (Bộ Thông Tin và Truyền Thông) and other relevant websites failed to locate directives or decisions regarding officially mandated forms of reference to Deaf people in Việt Nam (i.e., mandated use of *khiếm thính,* as the reporter at Café Lặng invoked); nevertheless, the fact that media personnel are making determinations about HCMSL usage suggests that they and similar outlets hold significant positions as extensions of the Vietnamese state.

Live televised events would seem to offer Deaf citizens a platform not available through news periodicals. To the extent that HCMSL-Vietnamese interpreters communicate signers' interests accurately, their comments would be available for audience consumption. My description of Trang's appearance on "310 Years of Đồng Nai" in the introduction to this book is a good example of just such an opportunity. Also produced during a televised public-interest program (on VT2 in 2010) were an HCMSL narrative and its rendering into spoken Vietnamese. As the subject of a comparative microanalysis, the HCMSL-Vietnamese interpreters' linguistic accuracy and alignment with the signer's sociolinguistic values and perspectives were found to contribute to an interpretation that was true to the original text. It thus did not interfere with the claims made by the signer and related social-change goals (Cooper & Nguyễn, 2015).

In other instances, the intervention of media workers as agents of the state places strong constraints on Deaf people's self-determinative expression. In this chapter I described the circumstances of the public-interest story videotaped at Café Lặng, which later prompted a discussion of the terms ĐIẾC and K-H-I-Ế-M T-H-Í-N-H [HEARING IMPAIRED] during a meeting of the HDC. That dialog then went on to explore the HDC members' perceptions of these terms. Taken together, these examples demonstrate that: (1) notions connected to Deaf citizen-subjects and HCMSL take on significance in social locations and venues beyond centers of Deaf education and social organizing, and (2) Deaf citizen-subjects may face disciplining for their use of VSLs in everyday sites of interaction *beyond institutions of the state.* In fact, such confrontations involve not only Vietnamese HEARING people but, as the data in chapter 4 demonstrate, transnational interactions with non-Vietnamese Deaf persons as well.

7 Conclusion

We are never as steeped in history as when we pretend not to be, but if we stop pretending we may gain in understanding what we lose in false innocence. Naiveté is often an excuse for those who exercise power. For those upon whom that power is exercised, naiveté is always a mistake. (Trouillot, 1995, p. xix)

BY EXAMINING RELATIONSHIPS between language practices, ideologies, policies, and programming, this book takes interactions that occur in Deaf education and Deaf community organizing as primary sites of sociopolitical inquiry. Contending that educational structuring reflects language ideological notions of sign language (*ngôn ngữ ký hiệu*) and Deaf people as a subject group that is marked by ambivalently regarded sociolinguistic practices and statuses, the book focuses on ethnographic instances of inclusion and exclusion which I observed and which Deaf research participants described to me. Deaf people's responses to educational structuring and other social and political economic forces demonstrate the ways that HCMSL-centered social action contributes to sociopolitical formation among and between Deaf and non-Deaf people, as well as the ways in which signed language–based social action furthers broader sociopolitical transformation.

The ethnographic data and other materials examined throughout this book demonstrate the ways in which Deaf and non-Deaf people's notions about language and Deaf people's social capacities reflect and respond to concerns about the changing demands and limits of citizenship under contemporary market socialism, particularly those connected to the development-oriented state. Initiating this research project just as the most recent wave of worldwide economic crises began in 2008, by the midpoint of the study (2012), Việt Nam had achieved lower-middle-income status and improvement in its human rights record; thus, even in a time of crisis, Việt Nam's economic and social indicators equaled or surpassed those of other so-called developed and developing countries.

The gains that Việt Nam demonstrated during this period are described in detail in the Vietnamese state's various governmental reporting instruments, and in international reporting mechanisms such as the *Millennium Development Goal Full Report* (Ministry of Planning and Investment, 2013; hereafter, 2013 MDG-VN). According to the United Nations, the Millennium Development Goals (MDGs) are "the world's time-bound and quantified targets for addressing extreme poverty in its many dimensions—income, poverty, hunger, disease, lack of adequate shelter, and exclusion—while promoting gender equality, education and environmental sustainability" (UN Millennium Project/UN Development Programme, 2006). In the 2013 MDG-VN, Việt Nam reports substantial improvements in the eight MDG target areas.[1] However, if we look more closely at circumstances ignored by MDG monitoring and evaluation (e.g., lesser-known language groups such as Deaf signed language communities, people with disabilities, gender and sexually marginalized persons), then MDG outcomes are revealed to be inaccurate, for some groups more than others.[2]

For instance, the 2013 MDG-VN 2013 reports a net primary education enrollment rate of 97% in 2008–2009 and a 97.67% enrollment rate achieved in 2012–2013. These figures would be markedly lower if they included enrollment data from Deaf education special schools. A 97% enrollment rate cannot be reconciled with the National Coordinating Council on Disability's 2010 report, which states that people with disabilities "illustrated an alarming situation of themselves and for their lives" (p. 8). The latter report also measures the education enrollment of people with disabilities (in the aggregate), showing that only 9.1% of persons with a disability complete high school, and only 1.7% complete a vocational training program. Therefore, given that both of the two most recent national census instruments describe large populations of people with disabilities (GSO, 2006, 2009),[3] it is unlikely that the government is counting Deaf students (and others categorized as having a disability) in their general educational surveying protocols. This recalls my discussion of the bracketing of regular and special education (chapter 3). The circumstances of such bracketing have major implications for national and international development planning for a wide array of areas, including distribution of national resources to the ministries and institutions responsible for education and training; educational programming and coordination; language policy and planning; school-to-work transition; sustainable employment; and other domains.

Analysis of the 2013 MDG-VN reveals two additional insights: Unlike the 2006 and 2009 GSO census surveys and the 2010 NCCD report, the 2013 MDG-VN's health section does not report data on people with disabilities. Second, the various sections of the

---

1. MDG targets for the 2000–2010 period aimed to: (1) eradicate extreme hunger and poverty; (2) achieve universal primary education; (3) gender equality and empower women; (4) reduce child mortality; (5) improve maternal health; (6) combat HIV/AIDS, malaria, and other diseases; (7) ensure environmental sustainability; and (8) develop a global partnership for development. For the 2016–2030 period, the UN's Sustainable Development Goals established 17 areas with 5 of the goals (Goals 4, 8, 10, 11, and 17), addressing inclusive and equitable social conditions for people with disabilities; see https://www.un.org/development/desa/disabilities/about-us/sustainable-development-goals-sdgs-and-disability.html).

2. For more information on lack of disability inclusive development associated with the MDGs and the United Nation Development Programme-led effort to understand these circumstances, see the UNDP's extremely detailed accounting of barriers to disability-inclusion within its own organizational operations (2016) *Evaluation of Disability Inclusive Development at UNDP*.

3. The GSO (2006) report describes 15.3% of the total country population above the age of 5 as having one or more disabilities (with 3.2%, or approximately 2.5 million persons considered to have a "hearing disability"). The GSO (2009) report describes 7.8% of the total country population above the age of 5 as having one or more disabilities (with 1%, or approximately 1 million persons considered to have a "hearing disability").

2013 MDG-VN report that address ethnic minority groups do not mention Deaf people or signed languages (see the sections on MDGs 3 and 7). In fact, despite the overrepresentation of Deaf people confronting poverty (in Việt Nam and worldwide), and their meager access to education and health care (also in Việt Nam and worldwide), Deaf people, special schools, and signed languages are not mentioned in the 2013 MDG-VN at all.

In the introduction to this book I note that, between the time of Trang's appearance in "310 Years of Đồng Nai" (2008) and the time of this writing, attention to Deaf people's signed language–based social participation has expanded considerably. This remains true despite whatever critiques this book might make regarding national reporting mechanisms, such as the 2013 MDG-VN. Deaf people who use signed languages in Việt Nam are today active participants on the national stage. Deaf associations and clubs now number more than twenty-four around the country, and coordination between Deaf associations strengthens membership activities and social campaigns carried out at the local level. As a result, Deaf associations are poised for official recognition as a single national-level association (which will also allow them to pursue membership in the World Federation of the Deaf). Several highly regarded INGO projects have also offered training that advanced Deaf people's interests in pursuing higher education and trade-specific training. Deaf people with undergraduate degrees in primary-level Deaf education now work in several special schools in various parts of the country. Signed language linguistic and linguistic anthropological projects are also a small but consistent mainstay of the work being done by and with Deaf constituencies.

From one perspective, it is intriguing that, in 2008, a signing Deaf person would be asked to appear on a show commemorating the historic accomplishments of Đồng Nai province. Đồng Nai province was and is subject to the same mass education mandates as other provinces. Moreover, in recent decades it has—also as in other provinces—opened schools for children with disabilities, and in most of these locations, the education of Deaf children is carried out primarily in spoken and written Vietnamese. Therefore, inviting a signing Deaf person to appear on "310 Years of Đồng Nai" gives the appearance of historical depth to the use of *ngôn ngữ ký hiệu* [NNKH; sign language]; it also gives the appearance that NNKH is authorized by both the Vietnamese state and the Communist Party. In such circumstances a signing Deaf person may lend credibility to the socialist state and the Communist Party as both protectors of tradition and a relevant and benevolent modernizing force. Yet, because these situations obscure Deaf people's histories and present realities in Việt Nam, we might also regard them as instances of national appropriation (rather than national recognition). State-managed media (mis)representation of Deaf people facilitates both positive exposure to and ambivalence toward HCMSL (and VSLs generally). Such circumstances warrant further social scientific inquiry into the roles that Deaf people have and are playing in social, political, and economic change in contemporary Vietnamese society. They also warrant commitment to supporting Deaf (and non-Deaf) people's efforts to contribute to multilingual and ethnocultural Vietnamese prosperity, which draws on and is immanent in sign language-related social organizing.

From another perspective, the presence of signing Deaf people on television and other state and social media is an outgrowth of many decades of socialist work to transform the nation, as well as everyday circumstances, for all of Việt Nam's citizens. Deaf people communicating their own ideas and perspectives in conjunction with an

HCMSL-Vietnamese interpreter is one marker of the efficacy of the socialist model and the achievement of socialist progress. Signing Deaf people's success in school and at work is another indicator of the modern socialist project and ongoing progress (tiến độ). Whereas critique of Vietnamese mass education prevails, the Vietnamese state's ability to demonstrate educational effectiveness—especially for students that many perceived as social burdens and as unteachable—allows it to then flex its muscles as decidedly *not backward* (lạc hậu). To the extent that foreign signed languages buoyed up by recent market forces supplant VSLs, one pressing question is whether the Vietnamese state will continue to draw on Vietnamese Deaf citizens as a source of legitimacy within a generation or two. Or will it instead turn toward outside signed languages and Deaf constituencies (e.g., American Sign Language, Auslan)?

Two points that cannot be overemphasized is that the Vietnamese state agents who initiated speech-only Deaf education in the late 1980s are not the same agents who are making decisions about Deaf education today (with the exception of a few high-level MOET members). It is also incontrovertible that the contemporary Vietnamese state has made a significant shift toward greater engagement with Deaf people and toward greater commitment of resources to VSLs and Deaf education in VSLs. Notably, the state has also increased its support of national and international development projects involving Deaf people as staff members and cotrainers (not just participants). It has also created partnerships that involve the use of one or more VSLs within a given project activity or program. Since 2010 the national news has been interpreted in both Hà Nội Sign Language and HCMSL (although not without issue).[4] The Vietnamese state also formally supported the first-ever disability rights street march, held in the capital city on November 29, 2014, even though those who participated in the march could have been viewed as criticizing the Vietnamese state for having yet to "Make the Right Real."[5]

The state has also subsidized instruction in VSLs in several provinces.[6] Moreover, on February 5, 2015, it ratified the Convention on the Rights of People with Disabilities; containing articles on the right to use sign language, the CRPD is an

---

4. For local Deaf populations and government broadcast leadership, the signed language varieties used in daily news programs are a contested area. These entities dispute government control of the selection of signed language varieties used to interpret the news, selection of interpreters, and, according to research participants, broadcast station pressure to sign in Vietnamese word order. See Cooper (2011) for a discussion of this issue and ethnographic examples from southern Việt Nam.

5. Titled *Vì một thếgiới hòa nhập, không rào cản cho người khuyết tật* [lit., An Inclusive World, No Barriers for People with Disabilities], the march was hosted by the Asia Pacific Development Center on Disability as part of "Make the Right Real," a rights-implementation initiative that the center is promoting throughout Southeast Asian from 2014 to 2018. For information about "Make the Right Real" see http://www.apcdfoundation.org/?q=content/apcds-implementing-incheon-strategy-make-right-real-persons-disabilities-asia-and-pacific-20. News reports have estimated that 500 people marched, including approximately 80 Deaf representatives from ten Deaf associations, along with interpreters and families with Deaf children.

6. One example of a MOET-sponsored sign language course is one that was offered in the Thanh Xuân District of Hà Nội from October through December 2014, organized by MOET's Special Education–Educational Science Institute of Việt Nam and the Association of People with Disabilities. See http://thanhxuan.gov.vn/portal/home/print.aspx?p=1542

international convention that many countries, including the United States, have yet to ratify. Thus, although the Vietnamese state's approach to and engagement with Deaf people demonstrates many contradictory trajectories of development and ideologies of linguistic and human capacity, clusters of state agents are nevertheless working with Deaf people to transform institutional opportunities for Deaf and hearing people throughout Việt Nam.

This book has described the circumstances of special school education and both the historical experiences of and contemporary interests represented by current and former EP students. Thus Trang's comments about *vượt qua rào cản xã hội* [overcoming social barriers] connect to a collective project that converge at the juncture of insight into national social conditions and insight into Deaf subjective experience. When Deaf interviewees described retrospection (TỰ NHÌN LẠI MÌNH), their comments always contained an explicit comparison of the time before and after they had gained insight into themselves as Deaf people and HCMSL as a true language (see chapter 5). Even though many of these interviewees named the EP as the place that facilitated such retrospection and insight, the very notion of retrospection marks the presence of preexisting knowledge and epistemologies. Accordingly, Vietnamese Deaf people's experiences of themselves in the world and interactions with one another are the core of Vietnamese Deaf social meaning. At the same time, having a place in which to share their ideas facilitates both the deepening of appreciation for and the creating of concrete action plans to implement those ideas. How such embodied meaning encounters, interacts with, explains, negotiates, and/or contests non-Deaf (and other) epistemologies in contemporary Việt Nam should be a matter of significant interest not only to Vietnamese Deaf people but to their kinspeople, as well as to researchers who are interested in understanding late-modern sociopolitical formation and change.

References

Abrams, Philip. 1988. Notes on the difficulty of studying the state. *Journal of Historical Sociology*, 1(1), 58–89.

Adam, Robert. 2015. Standardization of sign languages. *Sign Language Studies*, 15(4), 432–445.

Agamben, Giorgio. 1998. *Homo sacer: Sovereign power and bare life* (Daniel Heller-Roazen, Trans.). Palo Alto, CA: Stanford University Press.

Agamben, Giorgio. 2005. *State of exception*. Chicago, IL: University of Chicago Press.

AG Bell. 2008. Position statement: American Sign Language. Alexander Graham Bell Association for the Deaf and Hard of Hearing. Retrieved from http://www.agbell.org/Document.aspx?id=387#sthash.AoJ2kJgp.dpuf

Agboola, Isaac. 2014, Spring. Andrew Foster: The man, the vision, and the thirty-year uphill climb. *Deaf Studies Digital Journal*, 4. Retrieved November 28, 2015 from http://dsdj.gallaudet.edu/index.php?issue=5&section_id=2&entry_id=177

Agha, Asif. 2003. The social life of cultural value. *Language and Communication*, 23, 231–273.

Agha, Asif. 2006. *Language and social relations (Studies in the social and cultural foundations of language)*. Cambridge, United Kingdom: Cambridge University Press.

Ahearn, Laura M. 2001a. *Invitations to love: Literacy, love letters, and social change in Nepal*. Ann Arbor: University of Michigan Press.

Ahearn, Laura M. 2001b. Language and agency. *Annual Review of Anthropology*, 30, 109–137.

Ahearn, Laura M. 2003. Writing desire in Nepali love letters. *Language & Communication*, 23, 107–122.

Ahearn, Laura M. 2011. *Living language: An introduction to linguistic anthropology*. Chichester, United Kingdom: Wiley-Blackwell.

Ahmed, Sara. 2006. *Queer phenomenology: Orientations, objects, others*. Durham, NC: Duke University Press.

Ahmed, Sara. 2007. A phenomenology of whiteness. *Feminist Thought*, 8, 149–168.

Ahmed, Sara. 2012. *On being included: Racism and diversity in institutional life*. Durham, NC: Duke University Press.

Althusser, Louis. 1971. Ideology and ideological state apparatuses (Notes towards an investigation). In *Lenin and philosophy, and other essays* (Ben Brewster, Trans.) (pp. 127–186). New York, NY: Monthly Review Press.

Americans with Disabilities Act of 1990. 1990, July 26. Public Law 101–336. 108th Congress, 2nd session.

Anderson, Benedict. 1991. *Imagined communities: Reflection on the origin and spread of nationalism*. New York, NY: Verso.

Antia, Shirin, & Stinson, Michael S. 1999. Some conclusions on the education of deaf and hard-of-hearing students in inclusive settings. *Journal of Deaf Studies and Deaf Education*, 4(3), 246–248.

Apter, Emily. 2001. On translation in a global market. *Public Culture*, 13(1), 1–12.

Aretxaga, Begona. 2003. Maddening states. *Annual Review of Anthropology*, 32, 393–410.

Aristotle. 2004. *History of animals*. Whitefish, MT: Kessinger.

Armstrong, David F., & Wilcox, Sherman E. 2007. *The gestural origin of language*. Oxford, England: Oxford University Press.

Asad, Talal. 2003. Remarks on the anthropology of the body. In Sarah Coakley (Ed.), *Religion and the body* (pp. 42–52). Cambridge, United Kingdom: Cambridge University Press.

Aslam, Abid (Ed.). 2013. *The state of the world's children: Children with disabilities*. New York, NY: UNICEF.

Bahan, Benjamin B. 2004. Memoir upon the formation of a visual variety of the human race. In H. Dirksen Bauman (Ed.), *Open your eyes: Deaf studies talking* (pp. 16–35). Minneapolis: University of Minnesota Press.

Baker, Lee D. 1998. *From savage to Negro: Anthropology and the construction of race*. Berkeley: University of California Press.

Baker, Lee D. 2010. *Anthropology and the racial politics of culture*. Durham, NC: Duke University Press.

Bakhtin, Mikhail M. 1981. *The dialogic imagination: Four essays* (Michael Holquist, Ed.; Caryl Emerson & Michael Holquist, Trans.). Austin: University of Texas Press.

Bamgbose, Ayo. 2000. *Language and exclusion*. Piscataway, NJ: Transaction.

Bamgbose, Ayo. 2011. African languages today: The challenge of and prospects for empowerment under globalization. In Eyamba G. Bokamba, Ryan K. Shosted, & Bezza Tesfaw, Ayalew (Eds.), *Selected proceedings of the 40th annual conference on African linguistics: African languages and linguistics today* (pp. 1–14). Somerville, MA: Cascadilla Proceedings Project.

Bao Anh. 2009, February 19. Homosexuals still feel the media's lash. *Thanh Niên News*. Retrieved from http://www.thanhniennews.com/2009/Pages/200921917152404623o.aspx

Bảo Minh. 2012, February 23. Ra mắt chương trình "Dạy Ngôn Ngữ Ký Hiệu" trên truyền hình [Launching the program "Teaching Sign Language" on television. Giáo Dục & Thời Đại (Education & Era)]. Retrieved June 21, 2015, from http://giaoducthoidai.vn/kinh-te-xa-hoi/ra-mat-chuong-trinh-quotday-ngon-ngu-ky-hieu-tren-truyen-hinhquot-63763-u.html

Bao Van. 2010, June 25. Vietnam still has a hard road to hoe, labor report finds. *Thanh Niên News*. Retrieved from http://www.thanhniennews.com/2010/Pages/20100626175256.aspx

Bartky, Sandra. 1995. Subjects and agents: The question for feminism. In J. K. Gardiner (Ed.), *Provoking agents: Gender and agency in theory and practice* (pp. 194–207). Champaign: University of Illinois Press.

Bauman, Richard. 2004. *A world of others' words: Cross-cultural perspectives on intertextuality*. Malden, MA: Blackwell.

BBC (Vietnamese staff photojournalist). 2012a, August 5. Anh: Diễu hành của người đồng tính ở VN [Photo: parade of gay people in Vietnam]. Retrieved November 29,

2015, from http://www.bbc.com/vietnamese/pictures/2012/08/120805_viet_pride_photos.shtml

BBC (Việt Nam staff reporter). 2012b, August 5. Cần luật bảo vệ quyền của người đồng tính [Need laws protecting the rights of homosexuals]. Retrieved from http://www.bbc.com/vietnamese/multimedia/2012/08/120805_viet_pride_parade

Beasley, Chris, & Bacchi, Carol. 2000. Citizen bodies: Embodying citizens—a feminist analysis. *International Feminist Journal of Politics, 2*(3), 337–358.

Bell, David, & Binnie, Jon. 2000. *The sexual citizen: Queer politics and beyond.* Cambridge, United Kingdom: Polity.

Beresford, Melanie. 2003. Economic transition, uneven development and the impact of reform on regional inequality. In Hy V. Luong (Ed.), *Postwar Vietnam: Dynamics of a transforming society* (pp. 55–80). Lanham, MD: Rowman & Littlefield.

Beresford, Melanie. 2008. *Doi Moi* in review: The challenges of building market socialism in Vietnam. *Journal of Contemporary Asia, 38*(2), 221–243.

Berliner, Tom, Tành, Đỗ Kim, & McCarty, Adam. 2013. *Inequality, poverty reduction, and the middle-income trap in Vietnam.* Commissioned and funded by the EU Delegation to Vietnam.

Bernal, Victoria. 2004. Eritrea goes global: Reflections on nationalism in a transnational era. *Cultural Anthropology, 19*(1), 3–25.

Bernal, Victoria. 2006. Diaspora, cyberspace and political imagination: The Eritrean diaspora online. *Global Networks, 6*(2), 161–179.

Bich, Thanh. 2009, February 8. Education for the disabled needs more attention. *Thanh Niên News.*

Biwako Millennium Framework for Action. 2002. Biwako millennium framework for action towards an inclusive, barrier-free, and rights-based society for people with disabilities in Asia and the Pacific. UNESCAP. Retrieved February 15, 2017, from http://www.unescap.org/resources/biwako-millennium-framework-action-towards-inclusive-barrier-free-and-rights-based-society

Black, George. 2016, May 20. The Vietnam War is still killing people. *New Yorker.* Retrieved from http://www.newyorker.com/news/news-desk/the-vietnam-war-is-still-killing-people

Blanc, Marie-Eve. 2004. An emerging civil society? Local associations working on HIV/AIDS. In Duncan McCargo (Ed.), *Rethinking Southeast Asia, rethinking Vietnam* (pp. 153–164). London, England: Routledge.

Blommaert, Jan. 2005. Situating language rights: English and Swahili in Tanzania revisited. *Journal of Sociolinguistics, 9*(3), 390–417.

Blommaert, Jan. 2013. *Ethnography, superdiversity, and linguistic landscapes: Chronicles of complexity.* Bristol, United Kingdom: Multilingual Matters.

Blommaert, Jan, Collins, James, & Slembrouck, Stef. 2005. Spaces of multilingualism. *Language and Communication, 25,* 197–216.

Bộ Giáo Dục Đào Tạo [Ministry of Education and Training]. 2008. Sách giáo khoa Lớ p 9, Môn Lịch sử (Tái bản lần thứ 4). TP. Hồ Chí Minh, Việt Nam Bán quyền thu ộc Nhà xuât bản Giáo Dục-Bộ Giáo Dục Đào Tạo in Tại Công Ty cô phân in Sách Giáo khoa.

Boudreau, John. 2015, October 8. The biggest winner from TPP trade deal may be Vietnam. *Bloomberg.*

Bourdieu, Pierre. 1984. *Distinction: A social critique of the judgement of taste.* Cambridge, MA: Harvard University Press.

Bourdieu, Pierre. 1991. *Language and symbolic power.* Cambridge, United Kingdom: Polity.

Bourdieu, Pierre. 1998. *The state nobility: Elite schools in the field of power.* Palo Alto, CA: Stanford University Press.

Bradsher, Keith. 2015, July 8. Trans-Pacific partnership's potential impact weighed in Asia and the U.S. *New York Times.*

Branson, Jan, & Miller, Don. 2002. *Damned for their difference: The cultural construction of deaf people as disabled.* Washington, DC: Gallaudet University Press.

Branson, Jan, & Miller, Don. 2007. Beyond "language": Linguistic imperialism, sign languages, and linguistic anthropology. In Sinfree Makoni & Alastair Pennycook (Eds.), *Disinventing and reconstituting languages* (pp. 116–134). Clevedon, United Kingdom: Multilingual Matters.

Branson, Jan, & Miller, Don. 2008. National sign languages and language policy. In Nancy H. Hornberger (Ed.), *The encyclopedia of language and education: Vol. 1. Language policy and political issues in education* (pp. 151–165). New York, NY: Springer.

Branson, Jan, Miller, Don, & Gede Marsaja, I. 1996. Everyone here speaks sign language, too: A deaf village in Bali, Indonesia. In Ceil Lucas (Ed.), *Multicultural aspects of sociolinguistics in deaf communities* (pp. 39–57). Washington, DC: Gallaudet University Press.

Bremmer, Ian. 2010. *The end of the free market: Who wins the war between states and corporations?* London, England: Portfolio.

Brisset, Annie. 2003. Alterity in translation: An overview of theories and practices. In Susan Petrilli (Ed.), *Translation translation* (pp. 101–132). Amsterdam, Netherlands: Rodopi Press.

Brook, Timothy, & Luong, Hy V. 1997. *Culture and economy: The shaping of capitalism in Eastern Asia.* Ann Arbor: University of Michigan Press.

Brown, Peter. 1988[2008]. *The body and society.* New York, NY: Columbia University Press.

Brown, Wendy. 1995. *States of inquiry: Power and freedom in late modernity.* Princeton, NJ: Princeton University Press.

Brubaker, Rogers, Loveman, Mara, & Stamatov, Peter. 2004. Ethnicity as cognition. *Theory and Society, 33*(1), 31–64.

Brueggemann, Brenda Jo. 2009. *Deaf subjects: Between identities and places.* New York: NYU Press.

Buckup, Sebastian. 2009. *The price of exclusion: The economic consequences of excluding people with disabilities from the world of work.* Geneva, Switzerland: International Labour Organization.

Bui Tat Thang. 2000, Spring. After the war: 25 years of economic development in Vietnam. *National Institute of Research Advancement Review,* 21–25.

Bulwer, John. 1648. *Philocophus, or the deafe and dumbe man's friend in London.* British Deaf History Society: ISBN 1-902427-24-6; also, Ann Arbor: University of Michigan, Digital Library Production Service.

Burch, Susan. 2002. Transcending revolutions: The tsars, the Soviets, and deaf history. *Journal of Social History, 34*, 393–402.

Burton, Orisanmi. 2015, June 29. Black lives matter: A critique of anthropology. *Cultural Anthropology*. Retrieved November 22, 2015, from http://culanth.org/fieldsights/691-black-lives-matter-a-critique-of-anthropology

Calhoun, Craig. 2007. Nationalism and cultures of democracy. *Public Culture, 19*(1), 151–173.

Cao, Sy Kiem. 2007. East Asian economic integration: Problems for late entry countries. In Indermitt Gill, Yukon Huang, & Homi Kharas (Eds.), *East Asian visions: Perspectives on economic development* (pp. 128–141). Washington, DC: World Bank.

Cao Thị Xuân Mỹ. 2013. Quá trình hình thành và phát triển ngôn ngữ kí hiệu. *Tạp chí Khoa học ĐHSP Tp. HCM, 46*, 181–185.

Cao Thị Xuân Mỹ, & Đỗ Thị Hiền. 2007. Xây dựng CD "Bé vui học vần hỗ trợ việc học vần cho học sinh khiếm thính. *Tạp chí Khoa học ĐHSP Tp. HCM, 12*, 152–162.

Carozzi, Maria Julia. 2005. Talking minds: The scholastic construction of incorporeal discourse. *Body and Society, 11*(25), 25–39.

Cf. Carruthers, 2002

Chalfin, Brenda. 2006. Global customs regimes and the traffic in sovereignty. *Current Anthropology, 47*(2), 243–276.

Chen Pichler, Deborah. 2009. Sign production by first-time hearing signers: A closer look at handshape accuracy. *Cadernas de Saude, 2*, 37–50.

Coates, Jennifer, & Sutton-Spence, Rachel. 2001. Turn-taking patterns in deaf conversation. *Journal of Sociolinguistics, 5*(4), 507–529.

Collier, Stephen J., & Lakoff, Andrew. 2004. On regimes of living. In Aiwha Ong & Stephen J. Collier (Eds.), *Global assemblages: Technology, politics, and ethics as anthropological problems* (pp. 22–39). Hoboken, NJ: Wiley-Blackwell.

Comaroff, Jean. 2005. The end of history, again? Pursuing the past in the postcolony. In Ania Loomba, Suvir Kaul, Matti Bunzl, Antoinette Burton, & Jed Esty (Eds.), *Postcolonial studies and beyond* (pp. 125–144). Durham, NC: Duke University Press.

Comaroff, Jean, & Comaroff, John L. 2000. Millenial capitalism: First thoughts on a second coming. *Public Culture, 12*(2), 291–343.

Cooper, Audrey C. 2009. Sign language interpreting in Vietnam: An interview with Nguyen Thi Hoa and Bui Bich Phuong. *VIEWS: Publication of the Registry of Interpreters for the Deaf, 26*(2), 17–20.

Cooper, Audrey C. 2011. *Overcoming the "backward body": How state institutions, language, and embodiment shape deaf education in contemporary Southern Việt Nam* (Unpublished doctoral dissertation). American University, Washington, DC.

Cooper, Audrey C. 2014. Signed languages and sociopolitical formation: The case of Hồ Chí Minh City Sign Language. *Language in Society, 43*(3), 311–332.

Cooper, Audrey C. 2015. Signed language sovereignty in Việt Nam: Deaf community responses to ASL-based tourism. In Michele Friedner & Annelies Kusters (Eds.), *It's a small world: International deaf spaces and encounters* (pp. 95–111). Washington, DC: Gallaudet University Press.

Cooper, Audrey C., & Nguyễn, Trần Thủy Tiên. 2015. Signed language community-researcher collaboration in Việt Nam: Challenging language ideologies, creating social change. *Journal of Linguistic Anthropology, 25*(2), 105–128.

Cooper, Audrey C. and Nguyễn, Trần Thủy Tiên. 2017. Composing with signed and written languages: Our process. *Composition Studies*, 45, 13–18.

Cooper, Audrey C., & Rashid, Khadijat K. (Eds.) 2015. *Citizenship, politics, difference: Perspectives from Sub-Saharan Signed Language Communities*. Washington, DC: Gallaudet University Press.

Cordall, Simon Speakman. 2012, September 18. Landmines still exacting a heavy toll on Vietnamese civilians. *The Guardian*. Retrieved from https://www.theguardian.com/world/2012/sep/18/vietnam-unexploded-landmines-bombs

Crawhall, Nigel. 1995, December. Sign of the times: Deaf rights in South Africa. *Bua! 10*(1), 4–7. Salt River, South Africa: National Language Project.

Crystal, David. 2014[2000]. *Language death*. Cambridge, United Kingdom: Cambridge University Press.

Csordas, Thomas. 1990. Embodiment as a paradigm for anthropology. *Ethos, 18*(1), 5–47.

Csordas, Thomas. 2008. Intersubjectivity and intercorporeality. *Subjectivity, 22*, 110–121.

Curran, Enda. 2015, March 22. Asia's about to spawn a new tiger economy: Good morning, Vietnam. *Bloomberg Business*. Retrieved February 15, 2017, from http://www.bloomberg.com/news/articles/2015-03-22/asia-s-about-to-spawn-a-new-tiger-economy-good-morning-vietnam

Damasio, Antonio. 2005[1994]. *Descartes' error: Emotion, reason, and the human brain*. New York, NY: Penguin.

Dancygier, Barbara, & Sweetser, Eve. 2015. *Viewpoint in language: A multimodal perspective*. Cambridge, United Kingdom: Cambridge University Press.

Đặng, Ngiêm Vạn. 2001. *Ethnological and religious problems in Việt Nam*. Hà Nội, Việt Nam: Social Sciences Publishing House.

Dang Phong, & Beresford, Melanie. 1998. *Authority relations and economic decision-making in Vietnam: An historical perspective*. Copenhagen, Denmark: Nordic Institute of Asian Studies.

Đặng, Thị Mỹ Phương. 2010. Một số biện pháp tổ chức hoạt động dạy học nhằm đảm bảo cho trẻ khiếm thính học hoà nhập thành công trong trường tiểu học. *Ý Kiến Trao Đổi*, 19, 89–96.

Davis, Lennard. 1995. *Enforcing normalcy: Disability, deafness, and the body*. New York, NY: Verso.

Dean, Mitchell. 2001. "Demonic societies": Liberalism, biopolitics, sovereignty. In Thomas Blom Hansen & Finn Stepputat (Eds.), *States of imagination: Ethnographic explorations of the postcolonial state* (pp. 41–64). Durham, NC: Duke University Press.

DeCaro, Peter A. 2003. *Rhetoric of revolt: Ho Chi Minh's discourse for revolution*. Westport, CT: Praeger.

Decena, Carlos Ulises. 2008. Tacit subjects. *Gay and Lesbian Quarterly, 14*(2–3), 339–359.

De Clerck, Goedele. 1988. *Selected philosophical writings*. Cambridge, United Kingdom: Cambridge University Press.

De Clerck, Goedele. 2005. MEET MEET, VISIT VISIT: *Nomadic deaf identities, deaf dream worlds, and the imagination leading to translocal deaf activism*. Ghent, Belgium: Ghent University.

De Clerck, Goedele. 2011. Fostering deaf people's empowerment: The Cameroonian deaf community and epistemological equity. *Third World Quarterly*, 32(8), 1419–1435.

DeFrancis, John Francis. 1977. *Colonialism and language policy in Viet Nam*. Paris, France: Mouton.

Descartes, Rene. 2004[1644]. *The principles of philosophy*. Whitefish, MT: Kessinger.

De Vos, Connie. 2012. *Sign-spatiality in Kata Kolok: How a village sign language of Bali inscribes its signing space* (Unpublished doctoral dissertation). Radboud University, Nijmegen, Netherlands.

Doan, Hue Dung. 2004. Centralism: The dilemma of educational reform in Vietnam. In Duncan McCargo (Ed.), *Rethinking Southeast Asia, rethinking Vietnam* (pp. 143–152). London, England: Routledge.

Doan, Truc. 2004, October 29. Digital hope 2004: US $40,000 for Signal [sic] Dictionary Project. *Vietnam Net Bridge Online*. Retrieved from http://english.vietnamnet.vn/tech/2004/10/340490/

Du Bois, John W. 2007. The stance triangle. In Robert Englebretson (Ed.), *Stancetaking in discourse: Subjectivity, evaluation, interaction* (pp. 139–182). Amsterdam, Netherlands: John Benjamins.

Dudis, Paul G. 2004. Body partitioning. *Cognitive Linguistics*, 15(2), 223–238.

Dudis, Paul G. 2011. The body in scene depictions. In Cynthia B. Roy (Ed.), *Discourse in sign languages* (pp. 3–45). Washington, DC: Gallaudet University Press.

Duggan, Stephen. 2001. Educational reform in Viet Nam: A process of change or continuity? *Comparative Education*, 37(2), 193–212.

Dung, Hồ Xuân. 2008. Lạc Vào Thế Giới Không Âm Thanh. In *Phong sử Xã Hội: Giấc mơ triệu Phú* (pp. 67–75). Nhà xuất bản Công An Nhân Dân.

Dương Quốc Trọng. 2013. Báo Cáo Tổng Quan Về Mất Cân Bằng Giới Tính Khi Sinh ở Việt Nam. Hà Nội, Việt Nam: Bộ Y tế. [Report on Gender Imbalance in Birth in Việt Nam. Ministry of Health.]

Duranti, Alessandro. 1992. Language and bodies in social space: Samoan ceremonial greetings. *American Anthropologist*, 94(3), 657–691.

Duranti, Alessandro. 1994. *From grammar to politics: Linguistic anthropology in a Western Samoan village*. Berkeley: University of California Press.

Duranti, Alessandro. 2007. Agency in language. In Alessandro Duranti (Ed.), *A companion to linguistic anthropology* (pp. 449–473). Malden, MA: Blackwell.

Edelman, Elijah Adiv. 2011. This area has been declared a prostitution-free zone: Discursive formations of space, the state, and trans "sex worker" bodies. *Journal of Homosexuality*, 68(6–7), 848–864.

Edelman, Elijah Adiv. 2013. "Walking while transgender": Necropolitical regulations of trans feminine bodies of color in the US nation's capital. In Jin Haritaworn, Adi Kuntsman, & Sylvia Posocco (Eds.), *Queer Necropolitics* (pp. 172–190). London, England: Routledge.

Edelman, Marc. 2001. Social movements: Changing paradigms and forms of politics. *Annual Review of Anthropology*, 30, 285–317.

Edwards, Terra. 2012. Sensing the rhythms of everyday life: Temporal integration and tactile translation in the Seattle deaf-blind community. *Language in Society, 41*(1), 29–71.

Eichmann, Hanna. (2009). Planning sign languages: Promoting hearing hegemony? Conceptualizing sign language standardization. *Current Issues in Language Planning, 10*(3), 293–307.

Emery, Steven D. 2006. *Citizenship and the deaf community.* Nijmegen, Netherlands: Ishara.

Emery, Steven D. 2009. In space no one can see you waving your hands: Making citizenship meaningful to deaf worlds. *Citizenship Studies, 13*(1), 31–44.

Emery, Steven D., & O'Brien, Dai. 2014. The role of the intellectual in minority group studies: Reflections on deaf studies in social and political contexts. *Qualitative Inquiry, 20*(1), 27–36.

Emmorey, Karen, & Falgier, Brenda. 1999. Talking about space with space: Describing environments in ASL. In Elizabeth A. Winston (Ed.), *Storytelling and conversation: Discourse in deaf communities* (pp. 3–26). Washington, DC: Gallaudet University Press.

Enfield, Nick J. 2003. Producing and editing diagrams using co-speech gesture: Spatializing nonspatial relations in explanations of kinship in Laos. *Journal of Linguistic Anthropology, 13*(1), 7–50.

Enfield, Nick J. 2005. The body as a cognitive artifact in kinship representations: Hand gesture diagrams by speakers of Lao. *Current Anthropology, 46*(1), 51–81.

Enfield, Nick J. 2009. *The anatomy of meaning: Speech, gesture, and composite utterances.* Cambridge, UK Cambridge University Press.

Engels, Friedrich. 1972[1884]. *The origin of the family, private property, and the state, in the light of the researches of Lewis H. Morgan.* Introduction by Eleanor Leacock. New York, NY: International Publishers.

Erickson, Frederick. 2004. *Talk and social theory: Ecologies of speaking and listening in everyday life.* Malden, MA: Polity.

Escobar, Arturo. 2001. Culture sits in places: Reflections on globalism and subaltern strategies of localization. *Political Geography, 20,* 139–174.

Evans, Mark, & Bui, Duc Hai. 2005. Embedding neoliberalism through statecraft: The case of market reform in Vietnam. In Susanne Soederberg, Georg Menz, & Philip G. Cerny (Eds.), *Internalizing globalization: The rise of neoliberalism and the decline of national varieties of capitalism* (pp. 219–237). Hampshire, United Kingdom: Palgrave.

Evans, Peter B., Rueschemeyer, Dietrich, & Skocpol, Theda. 1985. On the road to a more adequate understanding of the state. In Peter B. Evans, Dietrich Rueschemeyer, & Theda Skocpol (Eds.), *Bringing the state back in* (pp. 347–366). Cambridge, United Kingdom: Cambridge University Press.

Evans, Vyvyan, & Green, Melanie. 2006. *Cognitive linguistics: An introduction.* London, England: Routledge.

Facundo Element. 2012. *Hearing privilege, part I.* Retrieved from http://www.youtube.com/watch?v=1bvmf_eRsXl.

Fairclough, Norman. 1989. *Language and power.* Essex, United Kingdom: Longman.

Fairclough, Norman. 2002. Language in new capitalism. *Discourse and Society, 13*(2), 163–166.

Farber, Paul Lawrence. 2011. *Mixing races: From scientific racism to evolutionary ideas.* Baltimore, MD: Johns Hopkins University Press.

Farnell, Brenda. 1995. *Do you see what I mean? Plains Indian Sign Talk and the embodiment of action.* Austin: University of Texas Press.

Farnell, Brenda. 1999. Moving bodies, acting selves. *Annual Review of Anthropology, 28,* 341–373.

Faulks, Keith. 2006. Education for citizenship in England's secondary schools: A critique of current principle and practice. *Journal of Education Policy, 21*(1), 59–74.

Fausto-Sterling, Anne. 1995. Gender, race, and nation: The comparative anatomy of "Hottentot" women in Europe, 1815–1817. In Jennifer Terry & Jacqueline Urla (Eds.), *Deviant bodies: Critical perspectives on difference in science and popular culture* (pp. 19–48). Bloomington: Indiana University Press.

Ferguson, James. 1994. *The anti-politics machine: Development, depoliticization, and bureaucratic power in Lesotho.* Minneapolis: University of Minnesota Press.

Ferguson, James, & Gupta, Akhil. 2002. Spatializing states: Toward an ethnography of neoliberal governmentality. *American Ethnologist, 29*(4), 981–1002.

Fernandes, Jane K., & Myers, Shirley Schultz. 2010. Inclusive Deaf Studies: Barriers and pathways. *Journal of Deaf Education and Deaf Studies, 15*(1), 17–29.

Fforde, Adam. 2011. Contemporary Vietnam: Political opportunities, conservative formal politics, and patterns of radical change. *Asian Politics & Policy, 3*(2), 165–184.

Fishman, Joshua. 1971. *Language in sociocultural change.* Stanford, CA: Stanford University Press.

Fishman, Joshua. 1991. *Reversing language shift: Theoretical and empirical foundations of assistance to threatened languages.* Multilingual Matters 76, Derrick Sharp (Series Ed.). Clevedon, UK: Multilingual Matters.

Foucault, Michel. 1979. *Discipline and punish: The birth of the prison.* New York: Vintage.

Foucault, Michel. 1988. *Technologies of the self.* Amherst: University of Massachusetts Press.

Foucault, Michel. 1990. *The history of sexuality* (Vol. 1). New York: Vintage.

Foucault, Michel. 1991. *The Foucault effect: Studies in governmentality.* Graham Burchell, Colin Gordon, & Peter Miller (Eds.). Chicago, IL: University of Chicago Press.

Foucault, Michel. 2003. Right of death and power over life. In Nancy Scheper-Hughes & Phillipe I. Bourgois (Eds.), *Violence in war and peace: An anthology* (pp. 79–82). Hoboken, NJ: Wiley-Blackwell.

Foucault, Michel. 2009. *Security, territory, population: Lectures at the College de France 1977–1978.* London, UK: Picador.

Frank, Andre Gunder. 1981. *Crisis in the third world.* New York: Holmes and Meier.

Friedner, Michele. 2013. Producing "silent brewmasters": Deaf workers and added value in India's coffee cafés. *Anthropology of Work Review, 34*(1), 39–50.

Friedner, Michele. 2015. *Valuing deaf worlds in urban India.* New Brunswick, NJ: Rutgers University Press.

Friedner, Michele, & Kusters, Annelies (Eds.). 2015. *It's a small world: International deaf spaces and encounters.* Washington, DC: Gallaudet University Press.

Gallagher, Shaun. 2005. *How the body shapes the mind.* Oxford, United Kingdom: Oxford University Press.

Gammeltoft, Tine M. 2007. Prenatal diagnosis in postwar Vietnam: Power, subjectivity, and citizenship. *American Anthropologist, 109*(1), 153–163.

Gammeltoft, Tine M. 2008. Figures of transversality: State power and prenatal screening in contemporary Vietnam. *American Ethnologist, 35*(4), 570–587.

Gammeltoft, Tine M. 2014. *Haunting images: A cultural account of selective reproduction in Vietnam.* Berkeley: University of California Press.

Gee, James Paul. 2010. *An introduction to discourse analysis: Theory and method.* New York: Routledge.

Gellner, Ernest. 1983. *Nations and nationalism.* Ithaca, NY: Cornell University Press.

Giáp Văn Dương. 2010, March 5. Bản chất xã hội hóa giáo dục [The nature of educational socialization]. *Tia Sáng: Bộ Khoa Và Công Nghệ* [Morning Rays: Journal of the Ministry of Science and Technology], *5*, 14–15.

Glewwe, Paul, & Patrinos, Harry Anthony. 1999. The role of the private sector in education in Vietnam: From the Vietnam Living Standards Survey. *World Development, 27*(5), 887–902.

Global Foundation for Children with Hearing Loss. 2015. Organization Promotional Video, September 26. Retrieved April 30, 2017, from https://www.youtube.com/watch?v=wLa_Jw4Sn48

Goodwin, Charles, & Goodwin, Marjorie Harness. 1992. Context, activity, and participation. In Peter Auer & Aldo di Luzio (Eds.), *The contextualization of language* (pp. 77–99). Amsterdam, Netherlands: Benjamins.

Goodwin, Charles, & Goodwin, Marjorie Harness. 2004. Participation. In Alessandro Duranti (Ed.), *Companion to linguistic anthropology* (pp. 222–244). Oxford, United Kingdom: Blackwell.

Gould, Stephen Jay. 1981. *The Mismeasure of man.* New York, NY: Norton.

Gray, Michael. 2003. NGOs and highland development: A case study in crafting new roles. In Benedict J. Tria Kerkvliet, Russell H. K. Heng, & David W. H. Koh (Eds.), *Getting organized in Vietnam: Moving in and around the socialist state* (pp. 110–125). Singapore: Institute of Southeast Asian Studies.

Groch, Sharon. 2001. Free spaces: Creating oppositional consciousness in the disability rights movement. In Jane J. Mansbridge & Aldon Morris (Eds.), *Oppositional consciousness: The subjective roots of social protest* (pp. 65–98). Chicago, IL: University of Chicago Press.

GSO. 2006. *Vietnamese Household Living Standards Survey.* Hà Nội, Việt Nam: General Statistics Office.

GSO. 2009. *Population and Housing Survey.* Hà Nội, Việt Nam: General Statistics Office.

Gupta, Akhil, & Sharma, Aradhana. 2006. Globalization and postcolonial states. *Cultural Anthropology, 47*(2), 277–307.

Hall, Stuart. 1985, June. Signification, representation, ideology: Althusser and the post-structuralist debates. *Critical Studies in Mass Communication, 2*(2), 91–114.

Hanks, William F. 1995. *Language and communicative practices (Critical Essays in Anthropology).* Boulder, CO: Westview.

Hanks, William F. 2005. Explorations in the deictic field. *Current Anthropology, 46*(2), 191–220.

Hanks, William F. 2010. *Converting words: Maya in the age of the cross.* Berkeley: University of California Press.

Hann, Chris M. 2003. *Postsocialism: Ideals, ideologies, and practices in Eurasia.* London: Routledge.

Hannah, Joseph. 2007. *Local non-governmental organization in Vietnam: Development, civil society, and state-society relations* (Unpublished doctoral dissertation). University of Washington, Seattle. (UMI No. 3252862)

Hanoi Times (staff author). 2008. Deaf trained on traffic rules, July 11. Retrieved from http://hanoitimes.com.vn/social-affair/2008/07/81e01c14/deaf-trained-on-traffic-rules/

Hansen, Thomas Blom, & Stepputat, Finn. 2001. Introduction. In Thomas Blom Hansen & Finn Stepputat (Eds.), *States of imagination: Ethnographic explorations of the postcolonial state* (pp. 1–38). Durham, NC: Duke University Press.

Hansen, Thomas Blom, & Stepputat, Finn (Eds.). 2006. *Sovereign bodies: Citizens, migrants and states in the postcolonial world.* Princeton, NJ: Princeton University Press.

Harrelson, Erin. 2015. SAME-SAME but different: Tourism and the deaf global circuit in Cambodia. In Annelies Kusters & Michele Friedner (Eds.) *It's a small world: International deaf spaces and encounters* (pp. 199–211). Washington, DC: Gallaudet University Press.

Harris, Raychelle, Holmes, Heidi M., & Mertens, Donna M. 2009. Research ethics in sign language communities. *Sign Language Studies, 9*(2), 104–131.

Haualand, Hilde, & Allen, Colin. 2009. *Deaf people and human rights.* World Federation of the Deaf and Swedish National Association of the Deaf. Retrieved February 15, 2017, from https://pdfs.semanticscholar.org/62b9/61dc6ebffdae761dbc80c3b56cc14dbc2a33.pdf

Haualand, Hilde, Solvang, Per Koren, & Breivik, Jan-Kåre. 2015. Deaf transnational gatherings at the turn of the twenty-first century and some afterthoughts. In Annelies Kusters & Michele Friedner (Eds.), *It's a small world: International deaf spaces and encounters* (pp. 47–56). Washington, DC: Gallaudet University Press.

Haugen, E. 1959. Planning for a standard language in modern Norway. *Anthropological Linguistics, 1*(3), 8–21.

Hayes, Anne, Swift, Emma, Shettle, Andrea, & Waghorn, Donna. 2015. *Inclusion of Disability in USAID Solicitations for Funding.* White Paper on USAID Study.

Hayles, N. Katherine. 1999. *How we became posthuman: Virtual bodies in cybernetics, literature, and informatics.* Chicago, IL: University of Chicago Press.

Hayslip, Le Ly, with Wurts, Jay. 1993. *When heaven and earth changed places.* New York, NY: Plume.

Hinton, Leanne, & Hale, Ken. 2001. *The green book of language revitalization in practice.* New York, NY: Academic Press.

Hobbes, Thomas. 1904[1651]. *Leviathan: Or the matter, forme, and power of a commonwealth, ecclesiasticall, and civill.* A. R. Waller (Ed.). Cambridge, United Kingdom: Cambridge University Press.

Hobbes, Thomas. 1981[1655]. Thomas Hobbes. *Stanford encyclopedia of philosophy.* Retrieved February 15, 2017 from http://plato.stanford.edu/entries/hobbes/

Hobsbawm, Eric. 1992. *Nations and nationalism since 1780: Programme, myth, reality* (2nd ed.). Cambridge, United Kingdom: Cambridge University Press.

Hochgesang, Julie A. 2015. Ethics of researching signed languages: The case of Kenyan Sign Language (KSL). In Audrey C. Cooper & Khadijat K. Rashid (Eds.), *Signed languages in Sub-Saharan Africa: Politics, citizenship and shared experiences of difference* (pp. 11–30). Washington, DC: Gallaudet University Press.

Hoffman-Dilloway, Erika. 2011. Ordering burgers, reordering relations: Gestural interactions between hearing and d/Deaf Nepalis. *Pragmatics, 21*(3), 373–391.

Holquist, Michael. 1981. Introduction. In Michael Holquist (Ed.) *Mikhail M. Bakhtin The dialogic imagination: Four essays* (pp. xv–2). Austin: University of Texas Press.

Horvat, Erin McNamara, & Baugh, David E. 2015. Not all parents make the grade in today's schools. *Kappan, 96*(7), 8–13.

Howell, Joude. 2007. Gender and civil society: Time for cross-border dialogue. *Social Politics: International Studies in Gender, State, and Society, 14*, 415–436.

Human Rights Watch. 2006, November 12. "Children of the dust": Abuse of Hanoi street children in detention. Retrieved February 21, 2016, from https://www.hrw.org/report/2006/11/12/children-dust/abuse-hanoi-street-children-detention

Husserl, Edmund. 1931. *Ideas: General introduction to pure phenomenology*. W. R. Boyce Gibson (Trans.). New York: Collier.

Hymes, Dell. 1964. Introduction: Toward ethnographies of communication. *American Anthropologist, 66*(6), 1–34.

Ilabor, E. 2009. *Dr. Andrew Jackson Foster: The father of deaf education in Africa*. Ibadan, Nigeria: Optimistic Press.

International Labour Organization. 2008. *Mapping report of vocational training and employment for people with disabilities in Vietnam*. Hà Nội, Việt Nam: ILO Country Office.

International Labour Organization/Irish Aid. 2013. Inclusion of people with disabilities in Viet Nam. Fact sheet. Hà Nội, Việt Nam: ILO/Irish Aid Partnership Program.

Irvine, Judith T., & Gal, Susan. 2000. Language ideology and linguistic differentiation. In Paul V. Kroskrity (Ed.), *Regimes of language: Ideologies, polities, and identities* (pp. 35–83). Santa Fe, NM: School of American Research Press.

Jackson, Jeffrey. 2007. *The globalizers: Development workers in action*. Baltimore, MD: Johns Hopkins University Press.

Jacobson, Rodolfo. 2006. Language planning: Modernization. In Ulrich Ammon, Norbert Dittmar, & Klaus J. Mattheier (Eds.), *Sociolinguistics: International handbook of the science of language and society* (Vol. 3, pp. 2421–2430). Berlin, Germany: Mouton de Gruyter.

Jaffe, Alexandra M. 1999. *Ideologies in action: Language politics on Corsica*. Berlin, Germany: Mouton de Gruyter.

Jaffe, Alexandra M. 2009. Stance in a Corsican school: Institutional and ideological orders. In Alexandra Jaffe (Ed.), *Stance: Sociolinguistic perspectives* (pp. 119–145). Oxford, United Kingdom: Oxford University Press.

Jankowski, Katherine A. 1997. *Deaf empowerment: Emergence, struggle, and rhetoric*. Washington, DC: Gallaudet University Press.

Janzen, Terry. 2015. Two ways of conceptualizing space: Motivating the use of static and rotated vantage point space in ASL discourse. In Barbara Dancygier & Eve Sweetser (Eds.), *Viewpoint in language: A multimodal perspective* (pp. 156–175). Cambridge, United Kingdom: Cambridge University Press.

Johnson, Mark. 2007. *The meaning of the body: Aesthetics of human understanding.* Chicago, IL: University of Chicago Press.

Johnson, Robert E. 1991. Sign language, culture, and community in a Yucatec-Mayan village. *Sign Language Studies, 73,* 461–474.

Johnson, Robert E. 2006. Cultural constructs that impede discussions about variability in speech-based educational models for deaf children with cochlear implants. *Perspectiva, 24* [Special issue], 29–80.

Johnson, Robert E., Liddell, Scott, & Erting, Carol. 1989. Unlocking the curriculum: Principles for achieving access in deaf education. Gallaudet Research Institute Working Paper 89-3. Washington, DC: Gallaudet University.

Jonker, R. J., & Raijmakers, Mark. 2002. *Progress toward millennium development goals 2015.* Press release. Dutch Coalition on Disability and Development.

Kannapell, Barbara. 1985. *Language choice reflects identity choice: A sociolinguistic study of deaf college students* (Unpublished doctoral dissertation). Georgetown University, Washington, DC. *Dissertation Abstracts International: The Humanities and Social Sciences 47*(1), 165-A.

Katznelson, Ira. 1985. Working-class formation and the state: Nineteenth-century England in American perspective. In Peter B. Evans, Dietrich Rueschemeyer, & Theda Skocpol (Eds.), *Bringing the state back in* (pp. 257–284). Cambridge, United Kingdom: Cambridge University Press.

Kearns, Ade. 1995. Active citizenship and local governance: Political and geographical dimensions. *Political Geography, 14*(2), 155–175.

Kermit, Patrick. 2009. Deaf or deaf? Questioning alleged antimonies in the bioethical discourses on cochlear implantation and suggesting an alternative approach to d/Deafness. *Scandinavian Journal of Disability Research, 11*(2), 159–174.

Kevles, Daniel. 1998. *In the name of eugenics: Genetics and the uses of human heredity.* Cambridge, MA: Harvard University Press.

Khâm Văn Trần 2014. *Exploring the experience of children with disabilities at school settings in Vietnam context.* Springerplus, 3: open access. Retrieved from https://springerplus.springeropen.com/articles/10.1186/2193-1801-3-103

Kim, Thoa. 2014, December 9. Hỗ Trợ Người Khiếm Thính Hoà Nhập Cộng Đồng [Supporting hearing impaired people's community integration]. *Giáo Dục & Thời Đại* [Education & Era].

Kimmons, Sean. 2014, July 4. Agent Orange legacy scourges Vietnam. *The Diplomat.*

Kiyaga, B. Nassozi, & Moores, Donald F. 2003. Deafness in Sub-Saharan Africa. *American Annals of the Deaf, 148,* 18–24.

Kleinman, Arthur. 1988. The personal and social meanings of illness. In *The illness narratives: Suffering, healing, and the human condition* (pp. 31–55). New York: Basic Books.

Koh, David. 2001. Negotiating the socialist state in Vietnam through local administrators: The case of karaoke shops. *SOJOURN: Journal of Social Issues in Southeast Asia, 16,* 277–303.

Kohrman, Matthew. 2005. *Bodies of difference: Experiences of disability and institutional advocacy in the making of modern China*. Berkeley: University of California Press.

Kolko, Gabriel. 1997. *Vietnam: Anatomy of a peace*. New York, NY: Routledge.

Kovecses, Zoltan. 2010. *Metaphor: A practical introduction* (2nd ed.). Oxford, United Kingdom: Oxford University Press.

Kovecses, Zoltan. 2015. *Where metaphors come from: Considering context in metaphor*. Oxford, United Kingdom: Oxford University Press.

Krausneker, Verena. 2009. On the legal status of sign languages: A commented compilation of resources. *Current Issues in Language Planning*, 10(3), 351–354.

Krohn-Hansen, Christian, & Nustad, Knut G. 2005. *State formation: Anthropological perspectives*. London: Pluto.

Kroskrity, Paul V. 2000. *Regimes of language: Ideologies, polities, and identities*. Oxford, United Kingdom: School of American Research Press.

Kusters, Annelies. 2012. Being a deaf white anthropologist in Adamorobe: Some ethical and methodological issues. In Ulrike Zeshan & Connie De Vos (Eds.), *Sign languages in village communities: Anthropological and linguistic insights* (pp. 27–52). Berlin, Germany: De Gruyter Mouton.

Kusters, Annelies. 2014. Language ideologies in the shared signing community of Adamorobe. *Language in Society*, 43, 139–158.

Kusters, Annelies. 2015a. *Deaf space in Adamorobe*. Washington, DC: Gallaudet University Press.

Kusters, Annelies. 2015b. To the farm, again and again, once and for all? Education, charitable aid, and development projects aimed at deaf people in Adamorobe, Ghana. In Audrey C. Cooper & Khadijat K. Rashid (Eds.), *Citizenship, politics, difference: Perspectives from Sub-Saharan signed languages* (pp. 162–184). Washington, DC: Gallaudet University Press.

Kusters, Annelies, De Meulder, Maartje, & O'Brien, Dai. 2017. *Innovations in deaf studies: The role of deaf studies scholars*. Oxford, UK: Oxford University Press.

Kwon, Heonik. 2006. *After the massacre: Commemoration and consolation in Hà My and My Lai*. Berkeley: University of California Press.

Kymlicka, Will, & Norman, Wayne. 1994. Return of the citizen: A survey of recent work on citizenship theory. *Ethics*, 104, 352–381.

Ladd, Paddy. 2003. *Understanding deaf culture: In search of deafhood*. Clevendon, United Kingdom: Multilingual Matters.

Laitlin, David D. 1985. Hegemony and religious conflict: Imperial control and political cleavage in Yorubaland. In Peter B. Evans, Dietrich Rueschemeyer, & Theda Skocpol (Eds.), *Bringing the state back in* (pp. 285–316). Cambridge, United Kingdom: Cambridge University Press.

Lakoff, George, & Johnson, Mark. 1980. *Metaphors we live by*. Chicago, IL: University of Chicago Press.

Lakoff, George, & Johnson, Mark. 1999. *Philosophy in the flesh: The embodied mind and its challenge to Western thought*. New York,: Basic Books.

Lane, Harlan. 1984. *When the mind hears: A history of the deaf*. New York: Vintage.

Lane, Harlan. 1989. *When the mind hears: A history of the deaf*. New York: Vintage.

Lane, Harlan. 1992. *The mask of benevolence: Disabling the deaf community.* New York: Knopf.
Lane, Harlan, Bahan, Ben, & Hoffmeister, Robert. 1996. *A journey into the Deaf-World.* San Diego: Dawn Sign Press.
Lane, Nikki C. 2011. Black women queering the mic: Missy Elliott disturbing the boundaries of racialized sexuality and gender. *Journal of Homosexuality, 58,* 775–792.
Lane, Nikki C. 2015. *In the life, on the scene: The spatial and discursive production of black queer women's scene space in Washington, DC* (Unpublished doctoral dissertation). American University, Washington, DC.
Langacker, Ronald. 2000. *Grammar and conceptualization.* Berlin, Germany: Mouton de Gruyter.
Langacker, Ronald. 2009. *Investigations in cognitive grammar.* Berlin, Germany: Mouton de Gruyter.
Lao Động (staff author). 2009, September 8. 4,5% đồng tính nam từng bị tấn công. lao động.com.
Leap, William. 2008. Finding the centre: Claiming gay space in Cape Town. In Melissa Steyn (Ed.), *Performing queer: Shaping sexualities 1994–2004* (Vol. 1, pp. 235–264). South Africa: Kwela.
Leap, William. 2011. Homophobia as moral geography. *Gender and Language, 4*(2), 187–219.
Leder, Drew. 1990. *The absent body.* Chicago, IL: University of Chicago Press.
Leder, Drew (Ed.). 1992. *The body in medical thought and practice.* New York, NY: Springer.
Le Kha Ke. 1968. L'elaboration d'une terminologie en langue Vietnamien. In *Le Vietnamien et l'enseignement superieur en Vietnamien dans la R.D.V.N.* (pp. 121–47).
LeMaster, Barbara. 2003. School language and shifts in Irish deaf identity. In Leila Monaghan, Constance Schmaling, Karen Nakamura, & Graham H. Turner (Eds.), *Many ways to be deaf: International variation in deaf communities* (pp. 153–172). Washington, DC: Gallaudet University Press.
Lê, Minh Hằng. 2013. *Opening the gates for children with disabilities: An introduction to inclusive education in Vietnam.* Washington, DC: Aspen Institute.
Lemke, Thomas. 2007. An indigestible meal? Foucault, governmentality, and state theory. *Distinktion: Scandinavian Journal of Social Theory, 15,* 43–64.
Lê, Văn Tạc. 2000. *Inclusive education: A new phase in education in Vietnam.* Paper presented at the 2000 International Special Education Conference: Including the Excluded. ISEC: Manchester, United Kingdom.
Levinson, Stephen C. 1988. Putting linguistics on a proper footing: Explorations in Goffman's concept of participation. In Erving Goffman (Ed.), *Exploring the interaction order* (pp. 161–227). Boston, MA: Northeastern University Press.
Lewis, Oscar. 1959. *Five families: Mexican case studies in the culture of poverty.* New York, NY: Basic Books.
Liddell, Scott. 2003. *Gesture in American Sign Language.* Cambridge, United Kingdom: Cambridge University Press.
Li, Tana. 1998. *Nguyễn Cochinchina: Southern Vietnam in the seventeenth and eighteenth centuries.* Ithaca, NY: Cornell University Press.

Lo Bianco, Joseph. 2001. Viet Nam: Quoc Ngu, colonialism and language policy. In Ping Chen & Nanette Gottlieb (Eds.), *Language planning and language policy: East Asian perspectives* (pp. 159–206). Richmond, United Kingdom: Curzon.

Lock, Margaret. 1993a. Cultivating the body: Anthropology and epistemologies of bodily practice and knowledge. *Annual Review of Anthropology, 22*, 133–155.

Lock, Margaret. 1993b. *Encounters with aging: Mythologies of menopause in Japan and North America.* Berkeley: University of California Press.

London, Jonathan D. 2003, Summer. Vietnam's mass education and health systems: A regimes perspective. *American Asia Review, 21*(2), 125–170.

London, Jonathan D. 2008. Reasserting the state in Viet Nam health care and the logics of market-Leninism. *Policy and Society, 27*, 115–128.

London, Jonathan D. 2009. Viet Nam and the making of market-Leninism. *The Pacific Review, 22*(3), 375–399.

London, Jonathan D. 2011. *Education in Vietnam.* Singapore: Institute of Southeast Asian Studies.

Lord, Janet E., & Stein, Michael A. 2015. Deaf identity and rights in Africa: Advancing equality through the Convention on the Rights of Persons with Disabilities. In Audrey C. Cooper & Khadijat K. Rashid (Eds.), *Citizenship, politics, difference: Perspectives from Sub-Saharan signed language communities* (pp. 198–218). Washington, DC: Gallaudet University Press.

Lucius, Casey. 2009. *Vietnam's political process: How education shapes political decision-making.* Abingdon, United Kingdom: Routledge Southeast Asia Series.

Luke, Allan. 2002. Beyond science and ideology critique: Developments in critical discourse analysis. *Annual Review of Applied Linguistics, 22*, 96–110.

Luke, Allan. 2003. Literacy and the other: A sociological agenda for literacy policy and research. *Reading Research Quarterly, 38*(1), 132–141.

Luke, Allan. 2007. Underneath hypercapitalism. *International Multilingual Research Journal, 1*(2), 101–104.

Luke, Allan. 2008. On the situated and ambiguous effects of literacy. *International Journal of Bilingual Education and Bilingualism, 11*(2), 146–149.

Luong, Hy Van. 1987, Spring. Plural markers and personal pronouns in Vietnamese person reference: An analysis of pragmatic ambiguity and native models. *Anthropological Linguistics, 29*(1), 49–70.

Luong, Hy Van. 1988. Discursive practices and power structure: Person-referring forms and sociopolitical struggles in colonial Vietnam. *American Ethnologist, 15*(2), 239–253.

Luong, Hy Van. 1989. Vietnamese kinship: Structural change and the socialist transformation in twentieth-century Vietnam. *Journal of Asian Studies, 48*, 741–756.

Luong, Hy Van. 2003a. Gender relations: Ideologies, kinship practices, and political economy. In Hy Van Luong & Melanie Bresford (Eds.), *Postwar Vietnam: Dynamics of transforming society* (pp. 201–224). Lanham, MD: Rowman & Littlefield.

Luong, Hy Van. 2003b. *Postwar Vietnam: Dynamics of a transforming society.* Lanham, MD: Rowman & Littlefield.

Luong, Hy Van. 2010. *Tradition, revolution, and market economy in a North Vietnamese village, 1925–2006*. Honolulu: University of Hawaii Press.

Lutalo-Kiingi, Sam, & De Clerck, Goedele. 2015. Deaf citizenship and sign language diversity in Sub-Saharan Africa: Promoting partnership between sign language communities, academia, and NGOs in development in Uganda and Cameroon. In Audrey C. Cooper & Khadijat K. Rashid (Eds.), *Citizenship, politics, difference: Perspectives from Sub-Saharan signed languages* (pp. 29–63). Washington, DC: Gallaudet University Press.

Lutalo-Kiingi, Sam, & De Clerck, Goedele. (2016). Research on sign languages and deaf/sign communities in sub-Saharan Africa: Challenges of sign language diversity, documentation, and revitalization, sign language planning and capacity building. In Gratien G. Atindogbé & Evelyn Fogwe Chibaka (Eds.), *Proceedings of the Seventh World Congress of African Linguistics (WOCAL-7)* (pp. 354–375). Cologne, Germany: Rüdiger Köppe.

Lynch, Ellen, & Phạm Huy Tuấn Kiệt. 2013. *Disability projects review assessment and analysis report*. USAID.

Lý Thị Trần, & Marginson, Simon. 2014. Education for flexibility, practicality and mobility. In Lý Trần, Simon Marginson, Hoàng Đỗ, Quyên Đỗ, Trúc Lê, Nhài Nguyễn, Thảo Vũ, Thạch Phạm, & Hường Nguyễn (Eds.), *Higher education in Vietnam: Flexibility, mobility and practicality in the global knowledge economy* (pp. 1–28). New York, NY: Palgrave.

Makoni, Sinfree, & Pennycook, Alastair (Eds.). 2006. *Disinventing and reconstituting languages*. Clevedon, United Kingdom: Multilingual Matters.

Makovicky, Nicolette (Ed.) 2014. *Neoliberalism, personhood, and postsocialism: Enterprising selves in changing economies*. Surrey, United Kingdom: Ashgate.

Malarney, Shaun. 2003. *Culture, ritual and revolution in Vietnam*. New York, NY: Routledge.

Malarney, Shaun. 2011. *Literacy for the masses: The conduct and consequences of the literacy campaign in revolutionary Vietnam*. Literacy for Dialogue in Multilingual Societies. Proceedings of Linguapax Asia Symposium 2011.

Marazzi, Christian. 2008. *Capital and language: From the new economy to the war economy*. Los Angeles, CA: Semiotext(e).

Margetts, Helen. 2012. Modernization dreams and public policy reform. In Helen Margetts, Perri 6, & Christopher Hood (Eds.), *Paradoxes of modernization: Unintended consequences of public policy reform* (pp. 17–43). Oxford, United Kingdom: Oxford University Press.

Marr, David. 1971. *Vietnamese anticolonialism, 1885–1925*. Berkeley: University of California Press.

Marr, David. 1981. *Vietnamese tradition on trial, 1920–1945*. San Diego: University of California Press.

Marr, David. 1988. Tertiary education, research, and information sciences in Vietnam. In David G. Marr & Christine Pelzer White (Eds.), *Postwar Vietnam: Dilemmas in socialist development* (pp. 15–44). Ithaca, NY: Southeast Asia Program Publications.

Marsaja, I. Gede. 2008. *Desa Kolok: A deaf village and its sign language in Bali, Indonesia*. Nijmegen, Netherlands: Ishara.

Marshall, Thomas H. 2009[1950]. Citizenship and social class. In Jeff Manza & Michael Sauder (Eds.), *Inequality and society* (pp. 148–154). New York: Norton.

Martin, Michael F. 2009. *Vietnamese victims of Agent Orange and U.S.-Vietnam relations.* Washington, DC: Congressional Research Service.

Marx, Karl. 1973[1857]. *Grundrisse* (M. Nicholaus, Trans.). London: Penguin.

Mather, Susan A. 1987. Eye gaze and communication in a deaf classroom. *Sign Language Studies,* 54(1), 11–30.

Mather, Susan A. 1989. In Ceil Lucas (Ed.), *The sociolinguistics of the deaf community* (pp. 165–187). Washington, DC: Gallaudet University Press.

May, Stephen. 2008. Language education, pluralism, and citizenship. In Stephen May & Nancy Hornberger (Eds.), *Language policy and political issues in education* (pp. 15–29). New York: Springer.

Mbembe, Achille. 2001. *On the postcolony.* Berkeley: University of California Press.

Mbembe, Achille. 2003. Necropolitics (Libby Meintjes, Trans.). *Public Culture,* 15(1), 11–40.

Mbewe, Euphrasia. 2015. Deaf women in Africa. In Audrey C. Cooper & Khadijat K. Rashid (Eds.), *Citizenship, politics, difference: Perspectives from Sub-Saharan signed languages* (pp. 103–117). Washington, DC: Gallaudet University Press.

McGuinn, Patrick. 2015. Complicated politics to the core: The bumpy implementation of the common core and its assessments has a knot of political alliances and adversaries. *Kappan Magazine,* 97(1), 14–19.

McIntire M. L., & Reilly, J. S. 1988. Nonmanual behaviors in L1 and L2 learners of American Sign Language. *Sign Language Studies,* 61, 351–375.

Meir, Irit, Sandler, Wendy, Padden, Carol, & Aronoff, Mark. 2010. Emerging sign languages. In *Oxford handbook of deaf studies, language, and education* (Vol. 2, pp. 267–280). Oxford, United Kingdom: Oxford University Press.

Merleau-Ponty, Maurice. 1962. *The phenomenology of perception* (Colin Smith, Trans.) (Rev. Forrest Williams). London: Routledge.

Metzger, Melanie. 1995. Constructed dialogue and constructed action in American Sign Language. In Ceil Lucas (Ed.) *Sociolinguistics in deaf communities* (pp. 255–271). Washington, DC: Gallaudet University Press.

M. I. 2013, December 12. Education in Vietnam: Very good on paper. *The Economist, Banyan Asia.*

Milwertz, Cecilia Nathanse. 1997. *Accepting population control: Urban Chinese women and the one-child family policy.* Richmond, VA: Curzon Press.

Minh, Hồ Chí. 1977. *Hồ Chí Minh: Selected writings (1920–1969).* Hà Nội, Việt Nam: Foreign Languages Publishing House.

Ministry of Planning and Investment. 2013. *Millennium development goal full report: Achievements and challenges of reaching millennium development goals of Vietnam.* Hà Nội, Việt Nam: Ministry of Planning and Investment.

Miraftab, Faranak, & Wills, Shana. 2005. Insurgency and spaces of active citizenship: The story of Western-Cape anti-eviction campaign in South Africa. *Journal of Planning Education and Research,* 25, 200–217.

Mirzoeff, Nicholas. 1995. Framed: The deaf in the harem. In Jennifer Terry & Jacqueline Urla (Eds.), *Deviant bodies: Critical perspectives on difference in science and popular culture* (pp. 49–77). Bloomington: Indiana University Press.

Mitchell, Timothy. 1991. The limits of the state: Beyond statist approaches and their critics. *American Political Science Review, 85,* 77–96.

Mitchell, Timothy. 1999. State, economy, and the state effect. In George Steinmetz (Ed.), *State/culture: State formation after the cultural turn* (pp. 76–97). Ithaca, NY: Cornell University Press.

Mitchell, Timothy. 2002. *Rule of experts: Egypt, techno-politics, modernity.* Berkeley: University of California Press.

Mittelman, James H. 1996. *Globalization: Critical reflections.* Boulder, CO: Rienner.

Moges, Rezener Tsegay. 2015. Resistance is *not* futile: Language planning and demissionization of Eritrean sign languages. In Audrey C. Cooper & Khadijat K. Rashid (Eds.), *Citizenship, politics, difference: Perspectives from Sub-Saharan signed languages* (pp. 64–80). Washington, DC: Gallaudet University Press.

Mori, Soya. 2011. Pluralization: An alternative to the existing hegemony in JSL. In Gaurav Mathur & Donna Jo Napoli (Eds.), *Deaf around the world: The impact of language* (pp. 333–338). Oxford, United Kingdom: Oxford University Press.

Mufwene, Salikoko S. 2004. Language birth and death. *Annual Review of Anthropology, 33,* 201–222.

Mugane, J. M. 2006. Necrolinguistics: The linguistically stranded. In *African languages and linguistics in broad perspective.* Cambridge: Cascadilla.

Mühlhäusler, Peter. 2002. *Linguistic ecology: Language change and linguistic imperialism in the Pacific region.* London: Routledge.

Muñoz, José Estaban. 1999. *Disidentifications: Queers of color and the performance of politics.* Minneapolis: University of Minnesota Press.

Murray, Joseph. 2007. *"One touch of nature makes the whole world kin": The transnational lives of deaf Americans, 1870–1924* (Unpublished doctoral dissertation). University of Iowa, Iowa City, Iowa.

Murray, Joseph J. (Ed.). 2015. Language planning and sign language rights [Special issue]. *Sign Language Studies* 15(4).

Mỹ, Anh. 2015, May 24. Cần nhân rộng mô hình dạy ngôn ngữ ký hiệu tại Trung tâm Giáo dục Thường xuyên (Need for replication of sign language teaching at centers for continuing education). *Báo Điện tử Đảng Cộng Sản Việt Nam* (online newspaper of the Communist Party of Vietnam). Retrieved June 13, 2015, from http://dangcongsan.vn/cpv/Modules/News/NewsDetail.aspx?co_id=28340669&cn_id=703079

Nam Son. 2008, October 15. Ministry issues height requirements for drivers' licenses. Thanh Niên NewsOnline. http://www.thanhniennews.com/2008/Pages/20081015113716042882.aspx

NCCD. 2010. *2010 Annual report on status of people with disabilities.* Hà Nội, Việt Nam: National Coordinating Council for Disabilities.

Nelson, Lauri, Trịnh Thị Kim Ngọc, Nguyễn Thị Chung, & Callow-Heusser, Catherine. 2014. The impact of specialized training for teachers of the deaf to facilitate listening and spoken language skills of children who are deaf or hard of hearing in underdeveloped countries. *International Journal of Educational Research and Development, 3*(4), 66–75.

Nettl, J. P. 1968, July. The state as a conceptual variable. *World Politics, 20*(4), 559–592.

Neustupný, J. V. 2006. Sociolinguistic aspects of social modernization. In Ulrich Ammon (Ed.), *Sociolinguistics/soziolinguistik: An international handbook of the science of language and society* (pp.2421–2423). Berlin: Mouton de Gruyter.

Nga, Thu. 2010, January 9. Trong thế giới vô thanh: Học hỏi từ trò (In a world without sound: Teachers learn from students). Người Lao Động Online.

Nguyễn Bình. 2015, November 19. TPP sẽ chính thức ký vào năm 2016 (TPP will be officially signed in 2016). Tuổi Trẻ Online: http://tuoitre.vn/tin/kinh-te/20151119/tpp-se-chinh-thuc-ky-vao-nam-2016/1005892.html

Nguyen, Dinh-Hoa. 1979. Standardisation and purification: A look at language planning in Vietnam. In Nguyen Dang Liem (Ed.), *South-East Asian linguistic studies* (Vol. 4) (pp. 179–204). Pacific Linguistics, Australian National University.

Nguyện, Đức Tồn, & Nguyễn, Thị Phương. 2012. Mấy Vấn Đề Về Cú Pháp Của Ngôn Ngữ Kí Hiệu ở Việt Nam (Syntactic issues of Vietnamese Sign Language). *Kỷ Yếu Hội Thảo: Những Vấn Đề Về Ngôn Ngữ Và Văn Hoá* (Workshop proceedings of issues of language and culture), 55–66.

Nguyễn, Kim Hà. 2001. *Lessons learned from a decade of experience: A strategic analysis of INGO methods and activities in Vietnam 1990–1999*. Hà Nội, Việt Nam: VUFO-NGO Resource Centre.

Nguyễn Quang Kinh. 1994. The eradication of illiteracy (EOI) and universalization of primary education (UPE) in Vietnam. In Phạm Minh Hạc (Ed.), *Education in Vietnam 1945–1991*. Hà Nội, Việt Nam: Ministry of Education and Training.

Nguyện, Quang Lập. 2008, October 31. Vú To Mới Được Ra Đường. *Viet Info Online*: http://vietinfo.eu/tu-lieu/vu-to-moi-duoc-ra-duong-.html

Nguyễn, Thị Kim Anh, & Võ Thị Mỹ Dung. 2010. Đánh Gía Kết Quả Học Tập Của Học Sinh Khiếm Thính Tại Một Số Trường Tiểu Học Hoà Nhập, Thành Phố Hồ Chí Minh. (Evaluating the outcomes of student learning in inclusive education schools in Hồ Chí Minh City). *Tạp Chí Khoa Học ĐHSP Tp. HCM*, 19, 65–75.

Nguyễn Thị Oanh. 2012. *Lối Ra Cho Các Vấn Đề Xã Hội* (Exit from social problems). Hồ Chí Minh, Việt Nam: Nhà Xuất Bản Thanh Niên.

Nguyễn T. T. M., Rahtz, D. R., & Schultz II, C. J. 2014. Tourism as a catalyst for quality of life in transitioning subsistence marketplaces: Perspectives from Hà Lông, Vietnam. *Journal of Macromarketing*, 34(1), 28–44.

Nguyên Tùng. 2009, April 18. Giới hạn là bầu trời (The sky's the limit). *Dân Trí* (newspaper). www.dantri.com/vn

Nguyễn-Marshall, Van, Welch Drummond, Lisa B., & Bélanger, Danièle (Eds.). 2015. *The reinvention of distinction: Modernity and the middle class in urban Vietnam*. London: Springer.

Nguyễn-võ, Thu-hương. 2008. *The ironies of freedom: Sex, culture, and neoliberal governance in Vietnam*. Seattle: University of Washington Press.

Nonaka, Angela M. 2004. The forgotten endangered languages: Lessons on the importance of remembering from Thailand's Ban Khor Sign Language. *Language in Society*, 33, 737–767.

Norlund, Irene. 2007. *Filling the gap: The emerging civil society in Viet Nam*. Hà Nội, Việt Nam: UN Development Programme.

N. V. (staff author). 2009, March 29. "Thế giới thứ ba" trong phim Việt. *Thanh Niên News*. http://www.thanhnien.com.vn/News/Pages/201014/20100329225421.aspx

Nyst, Victoria A. S. 2007. *A descriptive analysis of Adamorobe Sign Language (Ghana)*. Unpublished doctoral dissertation, Netherlands National Graduate School of Linguistics, Utrecht, the Netherlands.

Okombo, Okoth. 2008. Sign language, democracy and deafness in Africa. *Language matters: Studies in the languages of Africa*, 30(1), 15–25.

Ong, Aiwha. 1996. Cultural citizenship as subject-making: Immigrants negotiate racial and cultural boundaries in the United States. *Current Anthropology*, 37(5), 737–762.

Organization for Economic Co-Operation and Development. 2012. *PISA 2012 Results*. Programme of International Student Assessment.

Padden, Carol, & Humphries, Tom. 1990. *Deaf in America: Voices from a culture*. Cambridge, MA: Harvard University Press.

Parsons, Frances M., with Donna L. Chitwood. 1988. *I didn't hear the dragon roar*. Washington, DC: Gallaudet University Press.

Parsons, Talcott (Ed.). 1975. *Social systems and the evolution of action theory*. New York: Free Press.

Paulat, Lizabeth. 2015, December 6. Vietnam passes transgender rights law, but is it good enough? *Care 2*. Retrieved February 16, 2017, from http://www.care2.com/causes/vietnam-passes-transgender-rights-law-but-is-it-good-enough.html

Pêcheux, Michel. 1982. *Language, semantics and ideology*. New York: St. Martin's.

Pelley, Patricia M. 2002. *Postcolonial Vietnam: New histories of the national past*. Durham, NC: Duke University Press.

Pels, Peter. 1997. The anthropology of colonialism: Culture, history, and the emergence of western governmentality. *Annual Review of Anthropology*, 26, 163–183.

Pennycook, Alastair. 2008. Critical applied linguistics and language education. In Stephen May & Nancy Hornberger (Eds.), *Language Policy and Political Issues in Education* (pp. 169–181). New York: Springer.

Phạm, Anh Tuấn. 2010, March 23. Giáo ục lạc hậu chỉ cách giáo dục hiện đại một bước chân (Addressing educational backwardness is only one step in educational modernization). Tuanvietnam.net. http://www.tuanvietnam.net/2010-03-22-giao-duc-lac-hau-chi-cach-giao-duc-hien-dai-mot-buoc-chan

Phạm, Hong-Luu, Kizuki, Masashi, Takano, Takehito, Seino, Kaoruko, & Watanabe, Masafumi. 2013. Out-of-pocket costs of disabilities and their association with household socioeconomic status among school-aged children in Vietnam. *Japanese Association of Rural Medicine*, 8(2), 212–221.

Phạm, Kim. 1984. *Vấn Đề Phục Hồi Chức Năng Cho Người Điếc* (Rehabilitation issues for the deaf). Hà Nội, Việt Nam: Nhà xuất bản Y học (Medical Publishing House).

Phạm, Minh Hạc. 1994. Educational reforms. In *Education in Vietnam 1945–1991*. Hà Nội, Việt Nam: Ministry of Education and Training.

Phạm, Minh Hạc. 2007. Twenty years of the renewal of education and training: Achievements and challenges. In Lý Quảng Mai (Ed.), *Việt Nam: Twenty Years of Renewal* (pp. 277–290). Hà Nội, Việt Nam: Thế Giới.

Pitrois, Yvonne. 1914, October. From the old world. *The Silent Worker*, 27(1), 12–13.

Pitrois, Yvonne. 1916, July. From the old world. *The Silent Worker*, 28(10), 196–198.

Plummer, Ken. 1995. *Telling sexual stories: Power, change and social worlds*. London: Routledge.

Portelli, Alesandro. 1991. *The death of Luigi Trastulli and other stories: Form and meaning in oral narrative*. Albany: State University of New York Press.

Rabinow, Paul. 2003. *Anthropos today: Reflections on modern equipment*. Princeton, NJ: Princeton University Press.

Radcliffe-Brown, A. R. 1955[1940]. Preface. In Myers Fortes & E. E. Evans-Pritchard (Eds.), *African Political Systems* (pp. xii-xxiii). Oxford: Oxford University Press.

Ramsey, Claire. 1997. *Deaf children in public schools: Placement, context, and consequences*. Washington, DC: Gallaudet University Press.

Reagan, Timothy G. 2007. Multilingualism and exclusion: American Sign Language and South African Sign Language. In Theodorius du Plessis, Pol Cuvelier, Michael Weeuwis, & Lut Teck (Eds.), *Multilingualism and exclusion: Policy, practice, and prospects* (pp. 162–173). Hatfield, Pretoria: Van Schaik.

Reagan, Timothy G. 2010. *Language policy and planning for sign languages*. Washington, DC: Gallaudet University Press.

Reilly, Charles B., & Nguyễn, Khanh Cong. 2004. *Inclusive education for hearing-impaired and deaf children in Vietnam: Final evaluation report*. USAID and Pearl S. Buck International/Vietnam. Retrieved February 17, 2017, from http://pdf.usaid.gov/pdf_docs/Pdact192.pdf

Reilly, Charles B., & Reilly, Nipapon. 2005. *The rising of lotus flowers: Self-education by deaf children in Thai boarding schools*. Washington, DC: Gallaudet University Press.

Reis, Nadine. 2013. Civil society and political culture in Vietnam. In Gabi Weibel & Judith Ehlert (Eds.), *Southeast Asia and the civil society gaze: Scoping a contested concept in Cambodia and Vietnam* (pp. 77–92). London: Routledge.

Rosen, Russell S. 2004. Beginning L2 production errors in ASL lexical phonology: A cognitive phonology model. *Sign Language & Linguistics*, 7(1), 31–61.

Rostow, Walt Whitman. 1960. *The stages of economic growth: A non-Communist manifesto*. Cambridge: Cambridge University Press.

Rousseau, Jean-Jacques. 1968[1792]. *The social contract*. New York: Penguin Classics.

Rueschemeyer, Dietrich, & Evans, Peter B. 1985. The state and economic transformation: Toward an analysis of the conditions underlying effective intervention. In Peter B. Evans, Dietrich Rueschemeyer, & Theda Skocpol (Eds.), *Bringing the state back in* (pp. 44–77). Cambridge: Cambridge University Press.

Sagolj, Damir. 2015, April 22. The legacy of Agent Orange in Vietnam. *Reuters: The Wider Image*. Retrieved from https://widerimage.reuters.com/story/legacy-of-agent-orange.

Sassen, Saskia. 2006. *Territory, authority, rights: From medieval to global assemblages*. Princeton, NJ: Princeton University Press.

Schafft, Gretchen Engle. 2007. *From racism to genocide: Anthropology in the Third Reich*. Champaign: University of Illinois Press.

Schafft, Gretchen Engle, & Zeidler, Gerhard. 2011. *Commemorating hell: The public memory of Mittelbau-Dora*. Chicago: University of Illinois Press.

Scheper-Hughes, Nancy. 1993. *Death without weeping: The violence of everyday life in Brazil*. Berkeley: University of California Press.

Schmaling, Constanze. 2001. ASL in northern Nigeria: Will Hausa Sign Language survive? In Valerie Dively, Melanie Metzger, Sarah Taub, and Anne Marie Baer (Eds.) *Signed languages: Discoveries from international research* (pp. 180–196). Washington, DC. Gallaudet University Press.

Schmitt, Carl. 2005[1922]. *Political theology: Four chapters on the concept of sovereignty*. Chicago: University of Chicago Press.

Schwenkel, Christina. 2006. Recombinant history: Transnational practices of memory and knowledge production in contemporary Vietnam. *Cultural Anthropology, 21*(1), 3–30.

Scott, James C. 1990. *Domination and the art of resistance: Hidden transcripts*. New Haven, CT: Yale University Press.

Searcy, Chuck. 2017. Project Renew: Ridding Vietnam of Unexploded Ordnance. Vietnam Veteran Online, January/February: http://vvaveteran.org/37-1/37-1_projectrenew.html

Seider, Rachel. 2001. Rethinking citizenship: Reforming the law in postwar Guatemala. In Thomas Blom Hansen & Finn Stepputat (Eds.), *States of imagination: Ethnographic explorations of the postcolonial state* (pp. 203–220). Durham, NC: Duke University Press.

Senghas, Anne. 2003. Intergenerational influence and ontogenetic development in the emergence of spatial grammar in Nicaraguan Sign Language. *Cognitive Development, 18*, 511–531.

Senghas, Anne. 2005. Language emergence: Clues from a new Bedouin sign language. *Current Biology, 15*(12), 463–465.

Senghas, R. J., Senghas, A., & Pyers, J. E. 2005. The emergence of Nicaraguan Sign Language: Questions of development, acquisition, and evolution (pp. 287–306). In S. T. Parker, J. Langer, & C. Milbrath (Eds.), *Biology and knowledge revisited: From neurogenesis to psychogenesis*. London: Erlbaum.

Senghas, Richard, & Monaghan, Leila. 2002. Signs of their times: Deaf communities and the culture of language. *Annual Review of Anthropology, 31,* 69–97.

Sharma, Aradhana, & Gupta, Akhil (Eds.). 2006. *The anthropology of the state: A reader*. Malden, MA: Blackwell.

Sidel, Mark. 2010, May. Maintaining firm control: Recent developments in nonprofit law and regulation in Vietnam. *International Journal of Not-for-Profit Law, 12*(3), 52–67.

Silverstein, Michael. 1998. Contemporary transformations of local linguistic communities. *Annual Review of Anthropology, 27*, 401–426.

Silverstein, Michael. 2000. Whorfianism and the linguistic imagination of nationality. In Paul V. Kroskrity (Ed.), *Regimes of language: Ideologies, polities, and identities*, pp. 85–138. Santa Fe, NM: School of American Research Press.

Simpson, Andrew, & Ho, Hao Tam. 2008. The comparative syntax of passive structures in Chinese and Vietnamese. In Marjorie K. M. Chan & Hana Kang (Eds.), *Proceedings of the 20th North American Conference on Chinese Linguistics (NACCL-20)* (Vol. 2) (pp. 825–841). Columbus: Ohio State University.

Singleton, Jenny L., Jones, Gabrielle, & Hanumantha, Shilpa. 2014. Toward ethical research practice with deaf participants. *Journal of Empirical Research on Human Research Ethics, 9,* 59–66.

Singleton, Jenny L., & Morgan, Dianne D. 2005. Natural signed language acquisition within the social context of the classroom. In Brenda Schick, Marc Marshark, and Patricia Elizabeth Spencer (Eds.), *Advances in the sign language development of deaf children (Perspectives on deafness)* (pp. 344–375). Oxford: Oxford University Press.

Skocpol, Theda. 1985. Bringing the state back in: Strategies of analysis in current research. In Peter B. Evans, Dietrich Rueschemeyer, & Theda Skocpol (Eds.), *Bringing the state back in* (pp. 3–37). Cambridge: Cambridge University Press.

Skutnabb-Kangas, Tove. 2000. *Linguistic genocide in education—or worldwide diversity and human rights?* Mahwah, NJ: Erlbaum.

Smith, David Harry, & Ramsey, Claire L. 2004. Classroom discourse practices of a deaf teacher using American Sign Language. *Sign Language Studies, 5*(1), 39–62.

Socialist Republic of Việt Nam. 2003. National Education for Action Plan 2003–2015. Government document, Hà Nội, Việt Nam.

Spitulnik, Debra. 1998. Mediating unity and diversity: The production of language ideologies in Zambian broadcasting. In Bambi Schieffelin, Kathryn Woolard, & Paul Kroskrity (Eds.), *Language ideologies, practice and theory* (pp. 103–123). New York: Oxford University Press.

Stern, Alexandra Minna. 2005[2016]. *Eugenic nation: Faults and frontiers of better breeding in modern America.* Berkeley: University of California Press.

Stokoe, William C., Jr. 1960. Sign language structure: An outline of the visual communication systems of the American deaf. Studies in Linguistics: Occasional Papers 8. Buffalo, NY: Department of Anthropology and Linguistics, University of Buffalo.

Strathern, Marilyn. 2000. Cutting the network. *The Journal of the Royal Anthropological Institute, 2*(3), 517–535.

Suntikul, W., Butler, R., & Aiery, D. 2008. A periodization of the development of Vietnam's tourism accommodation since the Open Door Policy. *Asia Pacific Journal of Tourism Research, 13*(1), 67–80.

Tagore, Saranindranath. 2006. The Possibility of Translation. *Theory, Culture, & Society, 23,* 79–81.

Tai, Hue-Tam Ho. 1992. *Radicalism and the origins of the Vietnamese revolution.* Cambridge, MA: Harvard University Press.

Tai, Hue-Tam Ho. 2001. *In the country of memory: Remaking the past in late-socialist Vietnam.* Berkeley: University of California Press.

Takada, Eiichi. 1996, April. Asia-Pacific decade of disabled persons. *World Federation of the Deaf News, 28.*

Takada, Eiichi. 2001, December. Solidarity and movements of the deaf and hard of hearing in Asia. *Asia & Pacific Journal on Disability, 4*(2), 6–19.

Taub, Sarah. 2001. *Language from the body: Iconicity and metaphor in American Sign Language.* New York: Cambridge University Press.

Taylor, Charles. 1992. *Multiculturalism and the politics of recognition.* Princeton, NJ: Princeton University Press.

Terry, Jennifer, & Urla, Jacqueline L. 1995. *Deviant bodies: Critical perspectives on difference in science and popular culture.* Bloomington: Indiana University Press.

Thayer, Carlyle A. 1992. Political reform in Vietnam: Đổi Mới and the emergence of civil society. In Robert F. Miller (Ed.), *The developments of civil society in Communist systems* (pp.110–129). Sydney, Australia: Allen & Unwin.

Thayer, Carlyle A. 2008. *One-party rule and the challenge of civil society in Vietnam.* Presentation to Remaking the Vietnamese State: Implications for Vietnam and the Region, Vietnam Workshop, City University of Hong Kong. Retrieved from http://citeseerx.ist.psu.edu/viewdoc/download?doi=10.1.1.518.4056&rep=rep1&type=pdf

Thayer, Carlyle A. 2009, April. Vietnam and the challenge of political civil society. *Contemporary Southeast Asia: A Journal of International and Strategic Affairs, 31*(1), 1–27.

Thompson, Geoff, & Hunston, Susan. 2000. Evaluation: An introduction. In Susan Hunston & Geoff Thompson (Eds.), *Valuation in text* (pp. 1–27). Oxford: Oxford University Press.

Thuan An Center (Lái Thiêu School for the Mute-Deaf). http://www.thuongvevietnam.org/webseiten/thuanan/html/thuanan_02_en.html

Tilly, Charles. 1985. War making and state making as organized crime. In Peter B. Evans, Dietrich Rueschemeyer, & Theda Skocpol (Eds.), *Bringing the state back in* (pp. 169–191). Cambridge: Cambridge University Press.

Tollefson, James W. 1991. *Planning language, planning inequality: Language policy in the community.* Language in Social Life Series. New York: Longman.

Tollefson, James W. 2008. Language planning in education. In Nancy H. Hornberger & Stephen May (Eds.), *The encyclopedia of language and education: Language policy and political issues in education* (Vol. 1) (pp. 3–14). New York: Springer.

Tran Thi Phuong Hoa. 2009. *Franco-Vietnamese schools and the transition from Confucian to a new kind of intellectuals in the colonial context of Tonkin.* Harvard-Yenching Institute Working Paper Series. Cambridge, MA: Harvard-Yenching Institute. http://hyi.scribo.harvard.edu/2009/05/06/hyi-working-paper-series-tran-thi-phuong-hoa/

Trouillot, Michel-Rolfe. 2001, February. The anthropology of the state in the age of globalization. *Current Anthropology, 42*(1), 125–138.

Trung Tân. 2009, April 4. Giảng đường không tiếng nói! (Lecture hall without a spoken word!). *Tuổi Trẻ* (newspaper).

Trương, Buu Lam. 2000. *Colonialism experienced: Vietnamese writings on colonialism 1900–1931.* Ann Arbor: University of Michigan Press.

Turner, Karen Gottschang, & Phan Thanh Hoa. 1998. *Even the women must fight: Memories of war from North Vietnam.* New York: Wiley.

Turner, Terence. 1995. Social body and embodied subject: Bodiliness, subjectivity, and sociality among the Kayapo. *Cultural Anthropology, 10*(2), 143–170.

Tylor, Edward. 1892. On the limits of savage religion. *The Journal of the Anthropological Institute of Great Britain and Ireland, 21*, 283–301.

UNDP. 2016. *Evaluation of disability-inclusive development at UNDP.* New York, NY: Authorent Programme.

UNESCO. 1994. The Salamanca statement and framework for action on special needs education. New York: United Nations Educational, Cultural, and Scientific Organization.

UNESCO. 2004. Case study and manual on guidelines for action to include children and youth with disabilities in school systems and the EFA monitoring process. Draft of Vietnam country report. New York: United Nations Educational, Cultural, and Scientific Organization.

UN Millennium Project/UN Development Programme. 2006. Retrieved May 29, 2016, from http://www.unmillenniumproject.org/goals/

Urciuoli, Bonnie. 2010. Entextualizing diversity: Semiotic incoherence in institutional discourse. *Language & Communication, 30*, 48–57.

Urla, Jaqueline, & Terry, Jennifer. 1995. Mapping embodied difference. In Jennifer Terry & Jacqueline Urla (Eds.), *Deviant bodies: Critical perspectives on difference in science and popular culture* (pp. 1–18). Bloomington: Indiana University Press.

USAID. 2013. *Disability projects review assessment and analysis report*. Washington, DC: USAID.

USAID Press Release. 2015. United States to broaden support for persons with disabilities in Vietnam. October 27: Last retrieved April 9, 2017 from https://www.usaid.gov/vietnam/press-releases/united-states-broaden-support-persons-disabilities-vietnam

Van Cleve, John Vickrey, & Crouch, Barry A. 1989. *A place of their own: Creating the deaf community in America*. Washington, DC: Gallaudet University Press.

Van-Lien Chau. 2008, August 7. Vietnam issues sex change ruling. Thanh Niên News. http://www.thanhniennews.com/2008/Pages/200887113052040983.aspx

Vasavakul, Thaveeporn. 1997. VIETNAM: The third wave of state building. *Southeast Asian Affairs*, 337–363.

Vasavakul, Thaveeporn. 2003. Language policy and ethnic relations in Vietnam. In Michael E. Brown & Sumit Ganguly (Eds.), *Fighting words: Language policy and ethnic relations in Asia*. Cambridge, MA: MIT Press.

Veniez, Daniel D. 2013, March 13. Vietnam becomes an Asian tiger. *Huffington Post*. Retrieved from http://www.huffingtonpost.ca/daniel-d-veniez/vietnam-economic-growth_b_2867804.html

Venn, Couze. 2006. Translation: Politics and ethics. *Theory, Culture, Society, 23*(2–3), 82–84.

Venuti, Lawrence. 1998. *The scandals of translation: Toward an ethics of difference*. London: Routledge.

Venuti, Lawrence. 2000. Translation, community, utopia. In Lawrence Venuti (Ed.), *The translation studies reader*. (pp. 468-488). London: Routledge.

Verdery, Katherine. 1998, May. Transnationalism, nationalism, citizenship, and property: Eastern Europe since 1989. *American Ethnologist, 25*(2), 291–306.

Việt Báo (newspaper; anonymous author). 2006, July 7. Đồng tính luyến ái: Khiếm khuyết về thể chất hay tâm lý? http://vietbao.vn/Suc-khoe/Dong-tinh-luyen-ai-Khiem-khuyet-ve-the-chat-hay-tam-ly/45210808/248/

Vietnamese Household Living Standards Survey. 2006. *Results of the Survey on Household Living Standards 2006*. Hà Nội, Việt Nam: General Statistics Office.

Vietnamese Ministry of Justice. 2000. Decision no. 147/2000/QD-TTg—Vietnam Population Strategy for 2000-2010, Section 2(Part A).

Villa, Richard A., Tac, Le Van, Muc, Pham Minh, Ryan, Susan, Nguyen Thi Minh Thuy, Weill, Cindy, & Thousand, Jacquelyn S. 2003, Spring. Inclusion in Việt Nam: More than a decade of implementation. *Research and Practice for Persons with Severe Disabilities, 28*(1), 23–32.

VIR (VietNamNet Bridge Investigative Reporter). 2015, November 18. TPP heralds new financial restructuring. *VietNamNet Bridge.* Retrieved November 29, 2015, from http://english.vietnamnet.vn/fms/business/146353/tpp-heralds-new-financial-structuring.html

VN Express News (staff author). 2016. Gender imbalance threatens Vietnam's social stability: experts. December 15: Last retrieved on April 10, 2017: http://e.vnexpress.net/news/news/gender-imbalance-threatens-vietnam-s-social-stability-experts-3513922.html

Vu, Tuong. 2010. *Paths to development in Asia: South Korea, Vietnam, China, and Indonesia.* New York: Cambridge University Press.

Weber, Max. 1921[1968]. Bureaucracy. In Guenther Roth & Claus Wittich (Eds.) and Ephraim Fischoff (Trans.), *Economy and society: An outline of interpretive sociology* (pp. 956–1005). New York: Bedminster.

Weber, Max. 1958. *The religion of India: The sociology of Hinduism and Buddhism.* New York: Free Press.

Weber, Max. 1964. *The religion of China: Confucianism and Taoism.* New York: Scribner.

Weber, Max. 1991[1918]. Politics as vocation. In Max Weber, Hans Heinrich Gerth, & Charles Wright Mills (Eds.), *From Max Weber: Essays in sociology* (pp. 77–128). New York: Routledge.

Weber, Jean-Jacques. 2014. *Flexible multilingual education: Putting children's needs first.* Bristol, UK: Multilingual Matters.

Weiss, G. 1999. *Body images: Embodiment as intercorporeality.* New York: Routledge.

Werner, Jayne. 2009. *Gender, household, and state in post-revolutionary Vietnam.* New York: Routledge.

Wilcox, Sherman, & Shaffer, Barbara. 2005. Towards a cognitive model of interpreting. In Terry Janzen (Ed.), *Topics in sign language interpreting: Theory and practice.* Philadelphia: Benjamins.

Willard, Tom. 2007, October 12. Big D seems big-headed to me. Tom's Deaf Advocacy. http://tomwillard.wordpress.com/2007/10/12/big-d-deaf-seems-big-headed-to-me/

Wilson, Fiona. 2001. In the name of the state? Schools and teachers in an Andean province. In Thomas Blom Hansen & Finn Stepputat (Eds.), *States of imagination: Ethnographic explorations of the postcolonial state* (pp. 313–344). Durham, NC: Duke University Press.

Winston, Elizabeth. 1995. Spatial mapping in comparative discourse frames. In Karen Emmorey & Judy Reilly (Eds.), *Language, gesture, and space* (pp. 87–114). Hillsdale, NJ: Erlbaum.

Wischermann, Jörg. 2011. Governance and civil society action in Vietnam: Changing the rules from within—potentials and limits. *Asia Politics & Policy, 3*(3), 383–411.

Woll, Bencie, & Ladd, Paddy. 2011. Deaf communities. In Marc Marschark, Patricia Elizabeth Spencer, & Peter E. Nathan (Eds.), *The Oxford handbook of deaf studies, language, and education* (Vol. 1) (2nd ed.) (pp. 153–187). Oxford: Oxford University Press.

Woodside, Alexander. 1971. *Vietnam and the Chinese model: A comparative study of Vietnamese and Chinese government in the first half of the nineteenth century*. Cambridge, MA: Harvard University Asia Center.

Woodside, Alexander. 1983a. The historical background. In *The Tale of Kiêu* (Huỳnh Sanh Thông, trans.). New Haven, CT: Yale University Press.

Woodside, Alexander. 1983b, Autumn. The triumphs and failures of mass education in Vietnam. *Pacific Affairs, 56*(3), 401–427.

Woodward, James C. 2003. Sign languages and deaf identities in Thailand and Viet Nam. In Leila Monaghan, Constanze Schmaling, Karen Nakamura, & Graham H. Turner (Eds.), *Many ways to be deaf: International variation in deaf communities* (pp. 283–301). Washington, DC: Gallaudet University Press.

Woodward, James C., & Nguyen Thi Hoa. 2012. Where *Sign Language Studies* has led us in forty years: Opening high school and university education for deaf people in Viet Nam through sign language analysis, teaching, and interpretation. *Sign Language Studies, 13*(1), 19–36.

Woodward, James C., Nguyen Thi Hoa, & Nguyen Thi Thuy Tien. 2004. Providing higher educational opportunities to deaf adults in Viet Nam through Vietnamese Sign Languages, 2000–2003. *Deaf Worlds, 20*(3), 232–263.

Woodward, James C., & Nguyễn Thị Hòa, with Nguyễn Đình Mộng Giang, Lê Thị Thu Hương, Nguyễn Hoàng Lâm, Đỗ Thanh Sơn, Nguyễn Trần Thủy Tiên, Lưu Ngọc Tú, & Hồ Thu Vân. 2007. Ngôn Ngữ Kí Hiệu Tp. Hồ Chí Minh, Sách Học Viên 2, Trình Độ 1. Biên Hòa, Đông Nai: Công ty Nghiên cứu Ngôn Ngữ ký hiệu.

World Bank. 2009. IDA at work: Vietnam: Laying the foundation for sustainable, inclusive growth. World Bank. Retrieved from http://documents.worldbank.org/curated/en/756951468132584821/Vietnam-Laying-the-foundation-for-sustainable-inclusive-growth

World Bank (staff author). 2015. *Helping deaf children in Vietnam communicate and access education through sign language*. August 10. Retrieved April 10, 2017: http://www.worldbank.org/en/news/press-release/2015/08/10/helping-deaf-children-in-vietnam-communicate-and-access-education-through-sign-language

Wrigley, Owen. 1999. *The politics of deafness*. Washington, DC: Gallaudet University Press.

Yoder, Julie. 2004. Training and employment of people with disabilities: Vietnam 2002. Ability Asia Country Studies Series. Bangkok: International Labour Office.

Young, Iris Marion. 1990. *Justice and the politics of difference*. Princeton, NJ: Princeton University Press.

Index

Figures and tables are denoted by "f" and "t" following page numbers.

Abrams, Philip, "Notes on the Difficulty of Studying the State," 59
Action to the Community Development Center (ACDC), 164
active citizenship, xxvii–xxviii, 120–22
   deaf clubs and, 190–91, 206–10. *See also* Deaf social organizing
Adam, Robert, 43n12
adult learners. *See* Education Project
Agamben, Giorgio, 61–62, 62n26, 115, 116
Ahmed, Sara, 64
Allen, Colin, 205
Althusser, Louis, 56–58, 60, 137–38
American Sign Language (ASL)
   in African mission schools, 42
   alphabet chart in book, 30
   conventional communication methodology and, 162
   encroachment by, xxxvii, xliv, 176–78
   idealized perceptions of, 122
   language literacy and, 41n10
   tourism and, xxix, 73n5, 122, 176–78, 178n3
   in Vietnamese book, 155–57, 157f
Americans with Disabilities Act (1990), 146, 146n2
American-Vietnamese War, 1, 2, 10, 21–22
anticolonial citizenship education, xxviii
APCD. *See* Asia-Pacific Development Center on Disability
Apter, Emily, xliv
Aretxaga, Begona, 57
Aristotle, 39, 53
ASEAN (Association of Southeast Asian Nations), 15, 74, 151
Asia-Pacific Development Center on Disability (APCD), 105, 137n13, 164, 204–6, 205n16
   "Make the Right Real," 215n5
ASL. *See* American Sign Language
"Assisting Vietnamese People with Disabilities between 2006 and 2010," xviiin3

attested signs, 154
Australian Disability Discrimination Act (1992), 146n2
Australian Sign Language (Auslan), 5n7, 178n3
Azemar, Father (missionary), 18–19

Bacchi, Carol, 62
Bahan, Benjamin B., 139
Bakhtin, Mikhail M., 59–60, 59n25
Bảng Câu Hỏi Dành Cho Người Học NNKH Tp. HCM (questionnaire for HCMSL students), 202–3, 202n14
Bảo Chung (business), 177
Báo Lao Động-Xã Hội [Labor and Society Newspaper], 164
Beasley, Chris, 62
Bell, Alexander Graham, 53, 153
Beresford, Melanie, 68–69, 74
Berliner, Tom, 123
Biển Đong (Eastern Sea), 74, 152, 152n9
Biên Hoà, 3
bilingualism, xxx, 148
   in open-setting conversations, 162–63, 162n11
Biwako Millennium Framework for Action (UN), 146n3
Blommaert, Jan, xxiii, 43–44, 48, 79–80, 121
Bourdieu, Pierre, 46, 66
Bringing the State Back In (Evans, Rueschemeyer, & Skocpol), 55–56
British Sign Language, 5n7
Brook, Timothy, 63
Brown, Wendy, 56
Buckup, Sebastian, *The price of exclusion*, 77, 78
Bùi Huy, 132–33
Bulwer, John, *Philocophus*, 39n7
Burton, Orisanmi, *Black Lives Matter*, 58

Calhoun, Craig, xxiii
censorship, 183–87
Central Deaf Services, 137n13
charity [từt hiện], 164–68

Chen Pichler, Deborah, 139, 158
Chinese colonialism, 2, 18
Chữ nôm (ideographic script), 18, 18n20
citizenship, xxvii–xxviii, 56, 62, 62n26
   sovereignty and, 52, 60, 61
cochlear implantation (CI), 46–48
Collier, Stephen J., 66
colonialism
   anticolonial and early socialist modernization, 18–23
   anticolonial citizenship education, xxviii
   Chinese, 2, 18
   French, 1, 2, 14, 17–22
Common Core State Standards (U.S.), 41n10
common signs [*ký hiệu chung*], 154
communication strategies
   bilingualism in open-setting conversations, 162–63, 162n11
   in peer interactions, 123–26, 128
   school personnel conversation methods, 161–63
   sign-supported speech and, 12
   teacher-student interactions, 81, 87, 87n20, 92–93, 102–3
      misinterpretation of student sign practices, 137–38
      in special school on citizenship education (vignette), 123–26
      teacher frustrations, 159–60
Comprehensive Poverty Reduction and Growth Strategy (2002), 26–27
Confucian education, 17, 18, 18n19
Confucius, xviin2, xxvii
Công (Deaf student/instructor), 110–11, 118–20, 122
Convention on the Rights of Persons with Disabilities (CPRD), xxi–xxii, xxiin9, 3n5, 8, 37, 38, 151, 215–216
Cooper, Audrey C., 43, 46, 122, 148, 176–77, 201, 215n4
   in public debate over "Deaf" vs. "hearing impaired," 184–86
coordinated action, 120, 125

Dang Phong, 68–69, 74
Davis, Lennard, xxvii, 51, 145
DC1 and DC2. *See* Disability Centers
Deaf children, treatment and rehabilitation of, 27, 29–30
Deaf clubs. *See also* HCMC Deaf Club
   growth in, xxvi, 108n34, 214
   national clubs organization as goal, 206, 210
   sign-language teaching at, 87
   state recognition and, 203–6

Deaf [*Điếc*] vs. hearing impairment [*khiếm thính*]
   in café interview (vignette), 183*f*, 183–87
   MOET use of *khiếm thính*, xxix
   preferential terms, debate over, 46, 170, 188*f*, 187–90, 208
   recognition of *người Điếc* [Deaf people], 37
Deaf education
   adult learners. *See* Education Project
   as "dilemma," 153
   in *đổi mới* reform policy, xxiv, 25–30, 74
   Education Project, 95–104. *See also* Education Project
   emergent sociolinguistic identities and sociopolitics, 109–15
   ethnographic sites, 3–6
   HCMSL in, xxi. *See also* HCMSL
   higher education, 32, 95
   history of
      in Việt Nam, xviii, xxiv–xxv, 1
      worldwide, 39–40, 39n7
   inclusive education, 8–10. *See also* inclusive education
   language modernization and, 17–23
   mainstreaming in, 147
   MOET and sign language, 11–12, 33
   multilingualism in, 127, 137–41
   natural language interaction as active citizenship, 120–22
   peer-initiated instruction and, 101–2
   school attendance statistics, 73
   secondary education, limited access to, xviii, xviiin5, 93, 95, 117, 141
   sign-based education aspiration (vignette), 118–20
   social action and, 77, 169–70
   special school outcomes vs. regular education, 6–7
   special schools, 83–95. *See also* special schools
   speech-based education, 27, 30–33, 40–41. *See also* speech-based education
   students as state subjects, 36
   suppression of sign language in, 30–31, 145
   teachers/administrators as state agents, 36–37
   transformations in, 170
   VSLs standardization, 154–61
      reference books and variations among, 154–58, 155–57*f*
      schools' input on, 154
      teacher training and methodology, 158–61

Deaf mutism, 27
Deafness
  as disability [khuyết tật], 27–29, 74
  medical view of, xix, 51, 147
  stigmatization of, 41, 41n11
Deaf people [người Điếc]
  "backward" association, 31, 42, 188
  on charity vs. aid, 164–68
  communication methodology in presence of, 161–63
  driver's licenses for, 76, 76n10
  families of, 32, 34, 41–42, 142
    sign language and, xxv, 38, 81, 117, 133, 149, 164
  as figures of dependency/disability, xxviii, 75, 172–73
  foreign encroachment and, 2
  hearing people and, 45, 45n15
  media coverage of, xvii–xxi, xviiin3, 38, 38n4, 211, 214
  misperceptions of, 13–14
  "overcoming difficulty" and, xx–xxi, xxn7, 7, 188
  population of in Việt Nam, 1, 1n1
  preferential terms for and debate over, 183–90
  social inequalities and, 46, 78
  as state subjects, xix, 36–37
  as Việt Nam's "55th cultural group," 2, 2n4, 34n37
Deaf self-determination, 161, 186–87, 210, 212
Deaf social organizing, xxii, 214
  activist movements, 77, 163–64
  Deaf club activism, 190–206. See also HCMC Deaf Club
  economic status and social inequality, 123
  education and, 169–70
  HCMSL-centered citizenship, 172–73. See also HCMSL
  organizers as state subjects, 36–37
  reframing of VSLs, 2, 46
  retrospective narratization and, 122
  signed language inclusion and exclusion, 2
Deaf Travel Vietnam (Hà Nội), 73n5
Dean, Mitchell, 60
Decision no. 23/2006/QD-BGD-DT, 9
Decision no. 51/2008/QD-TTg, 174, 176
Decision no. 147/2000/QD-TTg, 75
Decision no. 4385/QD-BGDDT, 23
De Clerck, Goedele, 43, 130
Decree no. 01/2006/CT-TTg, 38–39
Decree no. 25/2001/ND-CP, 26
Decree on Associations (2010), 105

Decree on the Organization and Operation of Cooperative Groups (2007), 104
Democratic Republic of Việt Nam (DRV), 20–21, 68, 174
Denison, James, 51n20
Department of Labor and Social Affairs, 165
Department of Social Evils Prevention, 26n29
Development Center (DC) (pseud.), 109–15, 111f, 178, 179, 184, 194, 207
Điếc Tủy [Deaf to the marrow], 122, 124
Điều ước Thứ [Saturday Wishes] (TV program), 38n4
dioxin contamination, 2, 10, 24, 75, 174
Directive 33/CT-TW, 25n28
Directive 64/CT-TW, 25n28
Disability Centers (pseud.). See also special schools
  class sizes at, 87
  as research sites, 83
  DC1
    communication and instructional languages at, 88–89, 90t
    sign-language teacher training at, 161
  DC2
    communication and instructional languages at, 89, 89n22, 90t
    sign-language teacher training at, 85, 161
disability [khuyết tật]
  deafness portrayal as, xix, 27–29, 74
  economic development and, 75
  education enrollment and, 213, 213n3
  gendered disparities and, 135–36
  inclusive education and, 8–10
  international development aid and, 164
  national living standards survey and, 73
  pathologizing of, 29
  street march on disability rights, 164, 215, 215n5
  USAID report on, 147–50
disability law, 8–9, 9n9, 146–47, 146n2
disability marketplace, 174–78, 175–76f
  ASL encroachment in, xxxvii, xliv, 176–78
  censorship in café interview (vignette), 183f, 183–87
  Deaf employees and manual labor, 178–81, 180–81f
  Deaf social organizing and self-determination in, 190–206, 192f, 194f
  HCMSL and, 172–73
Disability Projects Review Assessment and Analysis Report (USAID; 2013), 1 47–50, 164
disability-related development industry, 151–53, 164–70

Disabled Persons' Organizations (DPOs), 12–13, 147, 164
Doan, Hue Dung, 71
đổi mới (economic reform policy). *See also* market-socialist reform
   characteristics of period, 69
   Deaf education and, xxiv, 25–30, 74
   education and training priorities under, 24–25
   education quality and, 71, 73
   history of, 15
   state formation and, 68–69
Đồng Nai People's Committee, 96
Đồng Nai Province, xvii–xxi, 3
DPOs (Disabled Persons' Organizations), 12–13, 147, 164
DRV. *See* Democratic Republic of Việt Nam
Dutch Coalition on Disability and Development, 153

education. *See also* Deaf education; inclusive education
   decline in quality of, 69–71
   đổi mới reform policy and, xxiv, 24–25, 71, 73, 74
   educational system in Việt Nam, 71–74, 72f, 141
   Millennium Goals report on, 213–14
   national curriculum, 22–23, 23f. *See also* national curriculum
   national goal of, 71
   socialization of, 32
Education and Human Resources Sector Analysis, Synthesis Report (UNESCO/UN report; 1992), 71
Education in Vietnam: Situation, Issues, Policies (MOET report; 1994), 71
Education in Vietnam 1945–1991 (MOET report; 1994), 71
Education Project (EP) (pseud.), xvii–xxi, 95–104. *See also* HCMC Deaf Club
   adult learners at, 4, 101, 102
   author's interactions with, xxx–xxxiv, xxxvi–xl, 5–6
   characteristics of, 3–4
   communication methods by teachers/staff at, 161–63
   funding for, 96, 96n23
   graduates as Deaf education teachers, 38, 38n5, 170
   HCMSL
      in classroom instruction, 88, 98–103, 127–28
      instructional materials on, 159
   interpreter training, 97, 99, 103, 149, 194–96, 198–201
   teaching and training of, xxvi, 4, 4n6, 32, 85, 97–99, 131, 202n14
   on "hearing impaired" vs. "Deaf" terms, 188, 189, 208
   higher education and, 32–33, 32n33, 95
   history lesson (vignette), 126–29
   history of, 95–97
   instructional levels at, 84t
   instructional methods at, 100–101
   misperceptions of, 184–85
   optional tracks at, 97–99
   outcomes and national exams, 98–99, 98n26
   peer-initiated instruction at, 101–2
   police/court assistance and, 203, 203n15
   sign-based education aspiration (vignette), 118–20
   sign-based instruction at, 95, 97, 141
   on sign language standardization, 154
   special schools vs., 98, 100, 102–3, 142
   student census, 84t, 141n15
   survey of students at (about special schools), 89–92, 91t, 95
   teachers, 142
      HCMSL and, 97–99, 97n24, 169
      retention and replacement, 99–100
      teacher census, 85t
employment
   communication limits and, 133
   English language and, 121n6
   job creation incentives, 174
      embroidery shop, 178–81, 180–81f
      "hearing impaired tourism," xxix, 176–78, 176f
   job growth and generation, 77
   manual labor and deaf workers, 93, 94f, 178–81, 180–81f
   report on disabilities and, 95
   vocational training for, 93–95
English language instruction, xxxiv, xxxivn21, 5, 121n6
EP. *See* Education Project
ethics of location, xlv
ethnographic research, 36
   research sites, 3–6. *See also* Education Project; HCMC Deaf Club; special schools
eugenics, 53, 54, 153
evaluation, 121
Evans, Peter B., 55–56
eye gaze
   in Deaf club meeting, 132
   in native vs. nonnative signers, 139–40

in peer interactions, 120, 123
in teacher interactions, 102, 127, 139–40

Fairclough, Norman, 78
fairness/unfairness, 167, 168
Family Mentorship training, 149
FEIGNING COMPREHENSION (HCMSL sign for), 124, 124f
"fence-breaking" model, 69, 169
fingerspelling
    ASL and, 178n3
    in Vietnamese book, 155–57, 157f
    perceptions of, 30
    in teaching English, xxxiv, 5, 5n7
foreign language schools, xliv, xlivn27, xlvf
Foster, Andrew J., 42, 43
Foucault, Michel, 57–58, 58n24
French colonialism, 1, 2, 14
    deaf education and, 17–22
Friedner, Michele, 176

Gal, Susan, 52
Gallaudet University, xxxi
Gammeltoft, Tine M., 45, 75, 120
gay issues. *See* homosexuality
Gellner, Ernest, 62
gender assignment surgery, 76, 76n11
gender disparities, 135–36, 135n11, 136n12
General Statistics Office (GSO), 6, 213, 213n3
gestures and gestural language, 27, 28, 39n7, 102, 139. *See also* eye gaze
Giáo Dục và Thợi Đại [Education & Era] (newspaper), 37
giao lưu [cultural exchange events], xxi, 6, 87, 190f, 190
Global Foundation for Children with Hearing Loss, 30n32, 33
governmentality theory, 57–58, 58n24
government-founded schools [*công lập*], 22
Great Britain, 51n20
GSO (General Statistics Office), 6, 213, 213n3
Guatemalan Disability Discrimination Ordinance (1997), 146n2
Guidance no. 1680/NHCS-TD, 174, 176
Gupta, Akhil, xxiii

Hải Phòng Deaf Club, 104
Hải Phòng Sign Language, 1n2, 12n12
Hall, Stuart, 57, 58, 60
handicrafts production, 93, 95, 96f, 179–81, 180–81f
Hà Nội Association of People with Disabilities, 33, 37, 205

Hà Nội Association of the Deaf, 104, 118, 191n9
Hà Nội Sign Language (HNSL), 1n2, 12n12
    at special school, xxvin12, 32n33
    television and, 33, 191n9
    tourism company and, 73n5
    WAKE UP [*nhận thức*] sign, 130–31, 130f
Hà Nội Team of Sign Language Interpreters (HTSLI), 195n11
Hansen, Thomas Blom, 44, 59–60, 62, 66–67
HCMC. *See* Hồ Chí Minh City
HCMC Deaf Club (HDC), 103–9, 190–206
    active national citizenship and, 206–10
    Education Project and, 104
    finances of, 106
    goals of, 106
    HCMSL use and, 108, 136, 137
    weekly classes, 209
    HCMSL-Vietnamese interpretation, 191–95, 194f
    workshop on, 168–69, 195–201
    on "hearing impaired" vs. "Deaf" terms, 190f, 190, 208
    history and characteristics of, 4–5, 104–5, 109–10
    INGOs and, 137, 137n13
    leadership structure of, 105, 106f
    meeting structure, 107–8, 132
    sign language classes by, 85–87, 201–3
    as site of inclusive inclusion, 142–43
    social inclusion and, 108
    social networking and, 106, 106n33, 108, 108n34
    social organizing by, 190–91
    state recognition of, 106, 203–6
    targeting social change (vignette), 132–37
    văn hóa [culture] descriptor and, 207
HCMSL (Hồ Chí Minh Sign Language), xviii, xxviii–xlvi, 1n2. *See also* HCMC Deaf Club
    body appearance as social provocation, 80–83
    books on, 12n12
    Deaf clubs and, 109–15, 111f
    Education Project and, xxvi, 4, 4n6, 32, 127–28. *See also* Education Project
    FEIGNING COMPREHENSION sign, 124, 124f
    fluent HCMSL vs. Vietnamese word order, 88, 89f, 208–9
    grammar of, xxviii–xxix, 12–13, 13nn13–14, 159, 185, 201
    hearing people and, 193–94, 202–3, 202n14
    interpretation as growing phenomenon, 191–95, 195n11. *See also* sign language interpreting

Deaf club's interpreting workshop, 168–69, 195–201
Không đủ điều kiện [children ineligible to attend school] sign, 46, 47f
linguistic understanding of, 169
RETROSPECTION [*Tự nhìn lại mình*] sign, 128–29, 128f, 216
SOCIAL INCLUSION [*hòi nhập xã hội*] sign, 108f
in special schools, 85–89, 90t
state-level significance of, 44
use of in various settings, 12–13
wake up [*nhận thức*] sign, 129–31, 129f
HDC. *See* HCMC Deaf Club
hearing aids, 29, 30n32, 145, 149
hearing embodiment, 137, 140
Hearing Impaired Club (HIC), 109–15, 114n39, 204–5, 207
Hearing Impaired Unit (HIU), 109–14, 114n38
director's views on Deaf people, 184–85
hearing impairment [*khiếm thính*], xix
Điếc [deaf] vs., xxix, 37, 46, 170, 187–90
hearing people [*người nghe*], 34
Deaf community and, 45, 45n15
Deaf [*Điếc*] vs. hearing impairment [*khiếm thính*] and, 208
HCMSL classes and questionnaire for, 202–3, 202n14
HNSL. *See* Hà Nội Sign Language
Hobbes, Thomas: *Leviathan*, 49–50
Hochgesang, Julie A., 43
Hồ Chí Minh, 20–21
Hồ Chí Minh City (HCMC), xvii
ethnographic sites in, 3–4
history of Deaf education in, 1
population of, 1n1, 3
Hồ Chí Minh City Pedagogic University, 30n31, 33, 83, 152, 165, 201
Hồ Chí Minh Sign Language. *See* HCMSL
Hoffman-Dilloway, Erika, 193–94
Holquist, Michael, 59n25
homosexuality, 76–77, 76n12, 82–83
hope schools (Hồ Chí Minh City). *See also* special schools
class sizes at, 87
communication and instructional languages at, 88–89, 90t
computer training at, 95
Deaf teachers at, 87
overview, 83
teacher census, 85t
teacher training at, 161
Hope A, 31

at HCMSL interpreting workshop, 196–97, 199
principal on signing frustrations, 159–60
sign language standardization and, 154
Hope B, 31
Hope C, 32, 92–93
Human Rights Watch, 25n28
Husserl, Edmund, 63, 65

ICED. *See* International Congress on Education of the Deaf
IDEO. *See* Intergenerational Deaf Education Outreach Project
IE. *See* inclusive education
ILO (International Labour Organization), 77, 95
Inclusion of Disability in USAID Solicitations for Funding (2015), 150–51
inclusive education [*hoà nhập*] (IE)
Deaf students and, 92–93
development of in Việt Nam, xviii, 8–10, 41
secondary education and, 117
sign language and, 33
language standardization, 154
teacher communication frustrations, 160
USAID assistance for, 146
inclusive-exclusion paradigm, xxiv, 61–62, 62n26, 115, 116, 141, 142
infrapolitics, 115
INGO. *See* International Nongovernmental Organizations
interactant, xxx, xxxn17
Intergenerational Deaf Education Outreach Project (IDEO), xxxi–xxxii, 105, 119, 149, 195
International Congress on Education of the Deaf (ICED), 30, 40, 51, 51n20
International Labour Organization (ILO), 77, 95
International Nongovernmental Organizations (INGO), 38, 122, 135, 137, 137n13, 147, 164, 214
international relations
trade agreements, 69, 74
transnational development assistance, 144–51, 153, 154
International Sign Language, 156
interpreting. *See* sign language interpreting
invented signs, 154
Irvine, Judith T., 52
It's a Small World: International Deaf Spaces and Encounters (Friedner & Kusters, Eds.), 176–77

Japanese Federation of the Deaf, 207
jobs. *See* employment
Johnson, Mark, 65–66
Johnson, Robert E., 138, 140–41

Kannapell, Barbara, 141
Khăm Văn Trân, 10
Không đủ điều kiện [children ineligible to attend school] (HCMSL sign for), 46, 47f
Komitee Twee, 30, 30n32, 43, 43n13, 144–45
Kroskrity, Paul V., 11n11
Kusters, Annelies, 43, 176
Ký Hiệu Của Người Điếc Việt Nam, Sác 1–3 [Signs of Deaf People in Việt Nam, Books 1–3], 154–56, 155f, 159, 181, 182f

Lái Thiêu School for the Mute-Deaf (Trường Câm Điếc Lái Thiêu), xviii, xxiv
  history of, 18–20, 22
  manual work at, 93, 94f
  name change for, 30, 31f
  as sign language-based school, 40
  speech-based methods at, 30, 30n32
  teacher training and, 30n31, 144–45
Lakoff, Andrew, 66
Lan (EP student), 81
Lane, Nikki C., 113, 141
Ms. Lang (school administrator), 10–13
language ideologies, xxii, xxvii. *See also* Vietnamese language and literacy policy
  features of, 11n11
  governments' use of, 52
  special education structuring and, 10–11, 145, 159–60, 211
  spoken languages vs. signed languages, 122
  Vietnamese linguistic structure and, 13
language management, 16–18, 16n17, 137
language planning, 137, 141
languages of stateness, 44, 60, 210
Law on Child Protection, Care, and Education (2004), 3n5
Law on Disabled Persons (1998), 3n5
Law on Education (2005), 3n5
Law on Persons with Disability (2010), xxi, xxiv, xxivn10, 3n5, 33, 37, 38, 151, 173
Law on the Protection, Care, and Education of Children (1991), 146
Lê (Deaf club leader), 133, 135
Lê, Minh Hàng, 9, 10
Leap, William, 64, 82
Leder, Drew, 65
l'Épée, Charles-Michel de, 39n7
Lê Văn Tạc, 9, 37–38, 150

Lewis, Oscar, 54
linguistic ideologies. *See* language ideologies
linguistic inaccessibility, 81, 125, 173
literacy. *See* Vietnamese language and literacy policy
"Living with Hearing Loss" (conference, 2008), xxxi, 110
Lo Bianco, Joseph, 17
London, Jonathan D., 67, 68, 73
Lord, Janet E., 146n2
Luong, Hy V., 63
Lutalo-Kiingi, Sam, 43
Lưu Ngọc Tủ, 45–46
Lynch, Ellen, 149

Maas, Betty, 43n13
mainstreaming, 147
Makoni, Sinfree, 44
Malarney, Shaun, xxn7
Malteser International, 105, 137n13
Marazzi, Christian, 78–79
marginalization, xxiii. *See also* Deaf people
  conversation methodology and, 161–63
  of Deaf women, 136
  government charity and, 166–69
  during postunification transition, 144–51
market-socialist reform. *See also đổi mới*
  disability marketplace and, 174
  education reform and, 22–23, 36
  history of, 2
  modernization and educational stratification, 23–34
  postunification problems and transnational encounters, 144–51
  speech-based instruction and, 173
Marxist theory, xxvii, 54–57
Mather, Susan A., 140
Mây (Deaf club member), 135
Mbembe, Achille, 50, 63
media
  Deaf people coverage in, xvii–xxi, xviiin3, 38, 38n4
  as state agents, 211
  VSLs and national news, 215, 215n4
Mẹ ơi, con không nghe! Hãy giúp con! [*Mother, I cannot hear! Please help me!*] (book), 29–30, 29f
Merleau-Ponty, Maurice, 63, 66
methodology
  ethical concerns and, xliv–xlv
  ethnographic research sites, xxx–xxxiv, xxxiiin20, 3–6, 83–109. *See also* Education Project; HCMC Deaf Club; special schools

HCMSL acquisition and socialization, xl–xlii
"hearing" or "deaf" status, xxxviii–xl, xxxviiin22
interactions during fieldwork, 5–6
pseudonyms and research subjects, xviin1, xxxviiin24
researcher access and privilege, xlii–xliv
surveys, xxxvi–xxxvii
translation issues, xliv
Mĩ (EP staff and interpreter), xxxiv–xxxv, 93, 103, 103n30, 142, 163, 178–81, 183–86, 202n14, 203n15
Milan Congress. See Second International Congress on Education for the Deaf
Millennium Development Goals, 153, 213n1
Millennium Development Goals-Việt Nam, 212–14
Minh Hai (Deaf adult student), xxxviii–xl, 188, 202n14
Ministry of Education and Training (MOET)
  Deaf education access and, 117, 173
  educational improvement directives, 23
  Education Project and, 32–33, 32n33, 100
  HCMSL instruction, 159
  sister project to, xxviin12
  "hearing impairment" as preferential term, xxix
  inclusive education and, 8
  Komitee Twee and, 30
  reports on education deficits, 71
  on sign language standardization, 154, 159
    reference books, 11–12, 12n12, 154–58, 155–57f
  sign-language training and, xxvn11, 131, 158, 160, 173, 215n6
  on special education teacher salary incentive, 159, 159n10
  special schools' jurisdiction, 83
  shortfalls in, 160–61, 173
  teacher training and, 33
Ministry of Health, 76, 83
Ministry of Labor, Invalids, and Social Affairs (MOLISA), 26n29, 83, 154, 160, 172–73, 203
Mirzoeff, Nicholas, 51
Mitchell, Timothy, 57
modernization
  anticolonial and early socialist modernization, 18–23
  characteristics of, 16
  history of, 15–16
  language management and literacy, 17–18
  market-socialist modernization and educational stratification, 23–34
MOET. See Ministry of Education and Training
MOLISA. See Ministry of Labor, Invalids, and Social Affairs
Mori, Soya, 42–43, 43n12
Moriarty Harrelson, Erin, 43
multilingualism, 127, 137–41, 194
Muñoz, José Estaban, 57
Murray, Joseph, 205
Mỹ Uyên (Deaf club member/instructor), 111, 112, 135, 163, 202n14

Nam (Deaf club member), 113–14
Narrative Contest on the Moral Example of Hồ Chí Minh, 191–93
National College for Education [Trường Cao đẳng Sư phạm Trung Ương] (Hà Nội), xxvin12, 32n33, 95
National Coordinating Council on Disability (NCCD), 105, 164, 204, 213
National curriculum, 22–23, 23f, 71, 84, 87, 116
  Education Project and, 5, 32, 32n33, 98, 126
National Institute of Educational Science (NIES), 9, 33, 87, 105, 150, 156, 158
national language, xxvii–xxviii, 16, 16n17, 34, 121
natural signed languages, 14, 43
Nettl, J. P., 52
Neustupný, J. V., 15, 16n17
Next Generation Science Standards (U.S.), 41n10
Nga (sign language instructor), xxxvi
Nghe Bằng Mắt [Listening by eye] (video), 2n4, 34n37
ngôn ngữ ký hiệ [sign language], 35, 214
Ngôn Ngữ Ký Hiệu Dành Cho Các Cấp Học Phổ Thông, Quyển 1 [Secondary-level sign language, Book 1], 156–58, 157f
NGOs (nongovernmental organizations), 2, 147, 164
Nguyễn, Khanh Cong, 9, 10, 67
Nguyễn, Trần Thuy Tiên, 43, 201
Nguyễn Tấn Dũng, 38
Nguyễn Thiện Nhân, 100, 100n28
Nguyễn Thi Hoàng Yế, Giáo Dục Đặc Biệt Và Nhung Thuật Ngữ Có Bán [Special Education and Terminology], 8
Nguyễn Văn Tần, 135n11
Nguyễn Văn Trương, 19–20, 19f, 19n22
Nguyễn-võ, Thu-hu'o'ng, 25, 71, 141

Nhân Chính Private School for Deaf
    Children–Hà Nội, 118, 118n3, 122
NIES. *See* National Institute of Educational
    Science
Nigerian Disability Decree (1993), 146n2
Nippon Foundation, xxxii, 137n13
nonce signs, 188f, 188–89
nongovernmental organizations (NGOs),
    2, 147, 164
North Atlantic Deaf studies, 44–45

oralism vs. manualism debates. *See* speech vs.
    sign debate
oral production charts, 85, 86f

Parker, Joakim, 150
Parsons, Frances M., 42, 43
Paul (Deaf student), 138
Pearl S. Buck International, 12n12, 154
Pêcheux, Michel, 57
Pennycook, Alastair, 44
people-founded schools [*dân lập*], 22
Phạm, Kim, *Vấn Đề Phục Hồi Chức Năng Cho
    Người Điếc* [*Rehabilitation Issues for the
    Deaf*] (book), 27–32, 28f
Phạm Huy Tuấn Kiệt, 149
Phạm Minh Hạc, 24
Pitrois, Yvonne, 19nn21–22
Population and Housing Census (2009), 78
Portelli, Allesandro, 82
prostitution, 71

quốc ngữ (writing system), 18, 20–21, 34

Rabinow, Paul, xix–xx
Radcliffe-Brown, A. R., 53–54
Ramsey, Claire, 138
rationalist project, 49
reception errors, 138–40
Regional Comprehensive Economic
    Partnership (RCEP), 74
Reilly, Charles B., 9, 10, 67
Reis, Nadine, xxvii, 120, 121
RETROSPECTION [*Tự nhìn lại mìn*] (HCMSL sign
    for), 128–29, 128f, 216
retrospective narratization, 81–82, 120, 122
Rhodes, Alexander de, 18
Rồng, 102–3, 119, 120
Rousseau, Jean-Jacques, 49–51
Rueschemeyer, Dietrich, 55–56

Salamanca Statement on Special Needs
    Education (1994), 8, 146–47, 146n3
Sassen, Saskia, 62–63

Scheper-Hughes, Nancy, *Death without
    Weeping*, 64
scientific racism, 51–52
Second International Congress on Education
    for the Deaf (Milan, Italy; 1880),
    xxviin14, 39–40, 39n7, 51, 51n20, 53, 153
second-modality acquisition, 138–39, 158
Seider, Rachel, 60
semiotic economies, 52, 77
shared decision making, 120
Sharma, Aradhana, xxiii
signed languages. *See also* American Sign
    Language (ASL); HCMSL; Sign-
    Supported Vietnamese; Vietnamese
    signed languages
  the Deaf body and, 51–53
  handshape in second-language
    learners, 139
  history of, 39–40, 39n7
  misconceptions about, 152–53
  native vs. nonnative signers, 138–40
  social formation and, xxiii–xxiv
  standardization of, 42–43, 43n12, 154–61
  world ban on in Deaf education, xxviin14,
    39–40, 39n7, 51, 51n20, 53, 153
sign language interpreting
  author's experiences with, xxx–xxxii
  HCMSL-Vietnamese interpretation, 4n6
  EP and, 97, 99
  growth in, 148–49, 191–95, 195n11
  as profession, 203n15
  television and, 191–93
  interpreting workshop by Deaf club,
    168–69, 195–201
Sign-Supported Vietnamese (SSV), 12, 88,
    120, 131, 142, 208
Simultaneous Communication (SimCom),
    41n10, 88, 162
Skocpol, Theda, 55–56
Smile Tours International, 177–78
SOCIAL INCLUSION [*hội nhập xã hội*] (HCMSL
    sign for), 108f
social media
  American Sign Language and, 122
  ASL use on, 122
  HCMC Deaf Club and, 106, 106n33, 108,
    108n34
  sign language use and, 89
social problems, 25–27, 25n28, 26f, 71
sociolinguistic practices, xlvi
  in classroom interactions, 138
  "deaf" and "hearing" identities and, 161
  Deaf clubs and self-determined social
    participation, 109–15

Education Project and, 170
at HDC meetings, 136–37
language rights, 43–44
nonnormative practices in schools, 169
peer interactions and, 123–26
spoken language and, 137, 138, 140, 142, 162
the state as actor in language control, 79–80
sociopolitical analysis. *See also* state formation
importance of language and bodies to, 55–67
state as actor, 36, 55–57, 79–80
state as effect, 36, 57–58
state as embodiment, 36, 63–67
state as imagination, 36, 59–63
South China Sea, 152n9
sovereignty, 49–50, 53, 62
citizenship and, 52, 60, 61
spatializing relational terms, 127, 127n10
Special Education Teacher Training Program, 158–59
special schools, 83–95
age range of students in, 93
author's interactions with former personnel of, 6
characteristics of, 3–4, 84
citizenship education (vignette), 123–26
class size at, 87
computer training at, 95
corporal punishment and, 92
EP vs., 98, 100, 102–3, 142
HCMSL interpreting workshop and, 196–201
on "hearing impaired" vs. "Deaf" terms, 188
instructional languages at, 88–89, 90t
instructional levels at, 84t
MOET jurisdiction of, 83, 160–61
naming of, 83
outcomes, 92–95
inclusive education option, 92–93
manual labor and vocational training, 93, 94f
police/court assistance and, 203, 203n15
school attendance statistics, 73
speech-based education at, 30–32, 85, 87–92, 98
student census, 84t
survey of former students on experiences at, 89–92, 91t, 95
teachers
characteristics of, 84–85
Deaf teachers, 85, 87–88

signing frustrations and, 159–60
sign language training of, 85–87, 131
teacher census, 85t
teacher-centered learning, 87, 87n20
speech-based education
Dutch NGO training and, 43, 144–45, 145n1
goals and benefits of, 145
history of, xviii, xxiv, 27, 40–41
market-socialist reform and, 173
oral production charts used in, 85, 86f
at special schools, 30–32, 85, 87–92, 98
teacher training, 33
speech vs. sign debate, xxvii, 12–14, 39–48, 52
Spencer, Herbert, 20
Sri Lanka Protection of the Rights of Persons with Disability (1996), 146n2
SSV. *See* Sign-Supported Vietnamese
stancetaking, 121, 122
state formation, xxiii, 36–67. *See also* Việt Nam
signed language use and the state, xxiv, 37–39
social science theories on, 53–55
sociopolitical analysis, 55–67
state as actor, 36, 55–57, 79–80
state as effect, 36, 57–58
state as embodiment, 36, 63–67
state as imagination, 36, 59–63
speech vs. sign debate and, 39–48
state agents and subjects, 36–37
Western liberalism and, 48–52
States of Imagination (Hansen & Stepputat, eds.), 59–60
Stein, Michael A., 146n2
Stepputat, Finn, 44, 59–60, 62, 66–67
street march on disability rights (2014), 164, 215, 215n5
Su (Deaf club leader), 133–35, 206, 209

Tai, Hue-Tam Ho, 18, 20
Takada, Eiichi, 205n16
Tấn (EP student), 81–82, 192f, 193
teachers. *See also* Education Project; special schools
communication methods by. *See* communication strategies
sign-language production and reception errors, 138–40
sign-language training
CD-ROM as tool, 158–59
lack of, xxiv–xxv, xxvn11, 131
at Lái Thiêu School, 144–45
at special schools, 85–87

VSLs standardization and, 158–61
special education salary incentive, 159, 159n10
speech-based education and, 30, 33
"Teaching Sign Language" (TV show), 33
Temple of Literature (Văn Miếu Trấn Biên), xvii, xviin2, xixf
Tết (Lunar New Year) Assembly Festival, 166–68, 166–67f, 167n12
Thái Nguyên Deaf Club, 104
Thanh Niên News, 77
theory of language, 59–60, 59n25
Thịnh (newspaper reporter), 164–66, 178–81, 183–86
"310 Years of Đồng Nai Province" (TV show; 2008), xvii–xxi, xxf, 113, 191, 214
Thuận (Deaf club member), 132–33
Thuận An Center, 30, 30nn31–32, 31f, 33. See also Lái Thiêu School for the Mute-Deaf
Total Communication (TC), 42
tourism (for hearing impaired), 71, 73n5, 122, 176–78, 176f
Trang (EP high school graduate), xvii–xxiii, xx, xxi, xxv, 136, 191–93, 201, 206, 211
Trần Hữu Tước, 27, 30
Trans-Pacific Partnership, 74
Trouillot, Michel-Rolfe, 57
Trường (Deaf student), 126–27
Từ Điển Truyền Thông Đa Ngôn Ngữ với Ngôn Ngữ Ký Hiệu Mỹ [Dictionary of multilingual communication with American Sign Language], 155–56, 156f
Tuổi Trẻ (newspaper), 135n11, 136n12
Tylor, E.B., 54

UNICEF, 137n13
United Nations, 146–47, 146n3. See also Convention on the Rights of Persons with Disabilities; Millennium Development Goals
United States
  Deaf education in, 147
  development aid in Việt Nam, 147–51
  disability law in, 9n9
  Milan Congress vote and, 51n20
  military's dioxin and unexploded ordnance in Việt Nam, 2, 10, 24, 24n25
U.S. Agency for International Development (USAID), 12n12, 145–51, 154

Vấn Đề Phục Hồi Chức Năng Cho Người Điếc [Rehabilitation issues of the deaf], 153
Văn Hoá Người Điếc [Deaf culture], 187. See also Deaf people [người Điếc]

VCP (Vietnamese Communist Party), 24, 68–69, 214
Venuti, Lawrence, xliv–xlv
VHLSS. See Vietnamese Household Living Standards Survey
Việt Nam. See also Vietnamese economy; Vietnamese language and literacy policy
  active deaf citizenship in engagement of, 206–10, 214–16
  body-oriented interventions by, 75–77, 76n11
  charity vs. protection, 168
  citizens and state control over, 120–21
  colonialism and, 1, 2, 14
  disability marketplace and, 174–78, 175f
  disability-related development industry and, 151–53, 164–70
  disabled persons, new stance on, 174, 175f
  education system, 71–74, 72f. See also Deaf education
  market-socialist reform in, 2. See also market-socialist reform
  recognition of deaf clubs by, 203–6
  social evils campaign, 25–27, 25n28, 26f
  state alignment of special statuses, 74–80
  on health care, 74–75
  on stabilization and quality of population, 75
  state formation, 68–69, 70f
Việt Nam Bank for Social Policies, 174
Vietnamese Communist Party (VCP), 24, 68–69, 214
Vietnamese economy. See also đổi mới
  GDP growth, 69, 69n1, 71
  language in "new economy," 78
  middle-income status, 69, 122–23
  modernization and, 15–16
  world market system and, 74
Vietnamese Household Living Standards Survey (VHLSS) (2006), xviiin5, 73, 77, 78
Vietnamese language and literacy policy, xxviii–xxix, 1–35. See also Deaf education
  anticolonial and early socialist modernization, 18–23
  in contemporary Deaf education, 6–14
  historical overview, 1–3
  language management and literacy, 17–18
  market-socialist modernization and educational stratification, 23–34
  minority-language users and, 78
  modernization discourses and language modernization, 15–17
Vietnamese National Association of the Deaf, 106, 210

Vietnamese national constitution (1992), 8
Vietnamese Red Cross, 175f
Vietnamese signed languages (VSLs), xvii, xxii. *See also* Deaf education; Deaf social organizing; HCMSL
    ASL and, 122
    in economic development goals, 77
    emerging openness toward, 151
    grammar and, 155, 159, 200
    growing support for, 1–2
    hearing people and, 202–3, 207
    marginalization of, 73
    MOET and books on, 11–12, 12n12, 154–58, 155–57f
    name signs, xxxviiin24
    in schools, 88. *See also* special schools
    speech vs. sign debate, xxvii, 39–48
    standardization and, 154–61
    state attention on "unified sign language," 37–39
    state recognition and, 208
    suppression of, 145
    teacher training and, xxiv–xxv, xxvn11, 158. *See also* teachers
    television and, 191, 191n9
    use of in homes, 149, 150
    varieties of, 1n2
    Vietnamese word order and, xxv, xxviii–xxix, 7, 12, 13nn13–14, 88, 89f, 169
Vietnam Veterans of America, 24n25
Volunteer Service Overseas, 114n39
VSLs. *See* Vietnamese signed languages

WAKE UP
    HCMSL sign for [nhận thức], 129–31, 129f
    HNSL sign for [nhận thức], 130–31, 130f
Weber, Max, 54
Wilson, Fiona, 61–62
Wischermann, Jörg, xxviii
women
    Deaf club and women's leadership, 106
    vignette, 132–37, 134f
    in media, xvii
Woodside, Alexander, 21–22
Woodward, James C., 1n2, 44, 145, 210
World Bank, 69n1
World Concern Development Organization (WCDO), xxxi–xxxii, xli, 105, 119, 137n13, 149, 194–95
World Federation of the Deaf, 204, 205, 205n16
Wright, Barry, 43n13

Xã Đàn School, 118, 118n2
Xhosa language, 52

Yen Fu, 20
Yogyakarta Principles, 76n11